The Sibling Bond

THE
SIBLING BOND

STEPHEN P. BANK
MICHAEL D. KAHN

Basic Books, Inc., Publishers

NEW YORK

The authors gratefully acknowledge permission to quote from the following sources:

"Twice Times," from *Now We Are Six*, by A. A. Milne. Copyright 1927 by E. P. Dutton & Co., Inc. Copyright renewal © 1955 by A. A. Milne. Reprinted by permission of the publisher, E. P. Dutton.

Selections from *The Price*, by Arthur Miller. Copyright © 1968 by Arthur Miller and Ingeborg M. Miller, trustee. Reprinted by permission of Viking Penguin, Inc.

"My Sister's Papers," from *Kon in Springtime* (Oxford University Press, 1968), by Tony Connor. Reprinted by permission of the author.

From Ovid's *Metamorphoses* (Bloomington: Indiana University Press, 1958), translated by Rolfe Humphries. By permission of Indiana University Press.

A portion of "Soliloquy," from *Carousel* (1953), by Rodgers and Hammerstein. By permission of The Welk Music Group.

From *Rilke on Love and other Difficulties: Translations and Considerations of Rainer Maria Rilke*, by John J. L. Mood. By permission of W. W. Norton & Company, Inc. Copyright © 1975 by W. W. Norton & Company, Inc.

Stephen P. Bank and Michael D. Kahn. From "Freudian Siblings," *Psychoanalytic Review* (1980–81) 67: 497ff–503. By permission of Human Sciences Press.

Library of Congress Cataloging in Publication Data

Bank, Stephen P., 1941–
  The sibling bond.

  Bibliography: p. 337
  Includes index.
  1. Brothers and sisters. 2. Developmental psychology.
I. Kahn, Michael D., 1936-   II. Title. [DNLM:
1. Sibling relations. WS 105.5.F2 B218s]
BF723.S43B36   155.9'24   81-68401
  ISBN 0-465-07818-4 (cloth) AACR2
  ISBN 0-465-07819-2 (paper)

10 9 8 7 6 5 4 3

To

Josh, Danny, and Penny · Kim Lee, Tammy, and Ben

—who inspired us

CONTENTS

CONTENTS

ACKNOWLEDGMENTS

THIS BOOK is the result of eight years of endeavor whose conceptualizing, interviewing, writing, and rewriting we fully shared—a partnership reflected in the alphabetical arrangement of our names. Chapter 1 and the epilogue were written by us both. Primary responsibility for chapters 2, 3, 4, 6, 7, and 11 belongs to Michael Kahn, while that for chapters 5, 8, 9, and 10 belongs to Stephen Bank. Writing and conducting research are arduous and lonely jobs: we frequently turned to one another for ideas, insights, and encouragement. Should the reader wish to discover the joys (as well as the complexities) of a sibling relationship, we heartily recommend the experience of co-authorship.

In our work we were nourished and helped by many people. Stephen Bank's interest in psychology and in helping others was kindled by my father, Stanley Bank, who, as my first mentor, showed me at the bedside of his patients the crucial importance of understanding the whole human being. My mother rekindled that interest: Dorothy Deane Bank brought life and energy into a local mental health association when the public seemed unconcerned about the welfare of mentally troubled individuals. Later, as an undergraduate in Dartmouth College's Department of Psychology, I was stimulated in the classrooms of committed and imaginative teachers; it was there that Rogers Elliott showed me the important and necessary links between behavioral research and the work of the psychotherapist. Still later, I had the opportunity to study psychotherapy with Irving Frank. Most recently, Daniel R. Miller, of Wesleyan, has broadened and deepened my understanding of the interplay between motivation, relationships, and identity. I have valued his scholarly and practical insights. I have also grown from the many informal and caring conversations I have had over the years with Bertie Feist and Bill Roberts. Donald J. Hiebel and Nancy D. Johnson, my colleagues, have wonderfully supported me and competently served our patients during my absence while writing the book. Elaine Feist Bank, my wife, put protective boundaries around me and my work when I needed them most, and she gave our children hope that *The Sibling Bond* would some day be finished. She has been my best friend, my most honest critic.

Michael D. Kahn would like to thank the many people who have helped influence and guide him in the long odyssey from Haifa to Hartford. Particularly important are those to whom I owe a special debt: my grandmother, the late Hedwig Baum; my parents, Helen and Lester Kahn; and my friends and fellow psychologists, Stanley Rustin and Jacob Lomrantz. Mary Henle, of the New School for Social Research, gave me an appreciation of the phenomenological approach to human experience; while Martin Lakin, of Duke University, showed how to bridge the world of group process and that of the self. It was Douglas Schoeninger, at the University of North Carolina at Chapel Hill, who first showed me the fascinating vistas of the family system. Woody English, Director of the Rockland County Mental Health Clinic, gave me my first opportunity, back in 1965, to be a psychotherapist.

Recently the Department of Psychology of the University of Hartford provided a sabbatical leave and made available resources that allowed this effort to continue: special thanks go to James Vinson, Dean of the College of Arts and Sciences, and particularly to Harry Leonhardt, Chairman of the Department of Psychology. Throughout our long association, my colleague John Schloss could always be counted upon for support. Stuart Sugarman and Roger Meyer, of the Department of Psychiatry at the University of Connecticut School of Medicine, encouraged my work, as did the members of the Family Study Center of Connecticut. More than anyone else, my wife, Ruth Jacobson Kahn, has been the most important intellectual influence and spiritual force in my professional career. She set an example of the importance of inquiry, of the satisfactions inherent in helping others, and of the dedication and effort needed to bring any endeavor to the level of excellence. She helped me immeasurably in the early stages of the writing. Ruth has always been my loving and encouraging companion.

Other people helped both of us at various points in the project. James Bozzuto, Albert Dreyer, Cecily Dreyer, Don Hiebel, Nancy Johnson, Bland Maloney, Augustus Napier, Robert Steele, and Edward Swain read drafts of the manuscript and provided helpful advice. Doreen Pratt and Claire Silverstein prepared (seemingly) endless drafts of the manuscript, all with patience, competence, and a sense of humor. Over the years, others have provided able technical assistance, including Tom Monta and Robert White (video) and Shirley Siegel (secretarial). Good students have helped at many stages of the project: Kathryn H. Adams, Leora Freedman, Tim Hoffman, Richard Jenkins, Kim Lee Kahn, Tammy Kahn, Hei-

ACKNOWLEDGMENTS

di Kreuger, Monica Mayer, Beth Jean Masterman, Betsy Nathanson, and Amy Stieglitz.

We benefited immensely from the guidance and encouragement of Jane Isay, co-publisher at Basic Books. She not only believed in this project from the start but gave us direction and helped discern the eventual shape of the book. She also selected a most talented person, Phoebe Hoss, in whose sensitive hands the manuscript became truly communicative.

Finally, we are grateful to all of the people who allowed us to enter their worlds, and whose experiences are recorded in these pages. Speaking with them was moving; it has been a privilege to have shared in their lives.

The Sibling Bond

CHAPTER 1

Unraveling the Sibling Bond

Eighty-two-year-old Lillian, in a pink-flowered robe, was dressed up for the occasion. As the nurses wheeled her into her younger sister's room, she started to complain, "Becky, your room is so dark and stuffy. Why don't we go up to *my* room where it's sunny and there's a better view?"

Rebecca, after more than seventy years of counteracting her bossy older sister's power, smilingly ignored her and greeted the psychologist who had come to the nursing home to interview them about "sibling relationships." The two women were each other's last surviving connection with a large family that had once included their parents and four brothers, all of whom had died.

"Did having a sister make any difference?" the psychologist asked Rebecca.

She straightened a trace. Spreading her parchment hands palms up and shrugging quickly, she flashed a glance of irritation to let the interviewer know that he had missed the obvious.

"Of course it makes a difference! I *know* I have a sister! She's my flesh and blood. And I don't even have to see her all the time. To have a brother, to have a sister—" She paused, groping for the right words for her deep feelings. "To know they're just—*around*—that's all I need to know."

"What would it have been like without brothers and sisters?" asked the psychologist.

"I would have been lonesome—very, very lonesome. We were always close. We always had a wonderful relationship. We always shared. There were always ties. Our mother taught us to always share. When I got married, Lillian and her husband moved in with me, and we all lived together for thirteen years."

And Lillian, listening, smiled and punctuated her sister's narrative with nods of approval.

As Rebecca and Lillian extolled their relationship, the psychologist wondered whether these old women were denying lives of hardship with nostalgic reminiscences. Had there been no grudges, no rifts, no rivalries, no hurt feelings? The psychologist pondered a mystery. If their lives to-gether had indeed been so wonderful, why did they insist on living on separate floors of the nursing home when they could be roommates. Why was it that—as the nurses reported—these now-talkative sisters barely ac-knowledged each other's existence? How to account for the reports of other family members that bitter quarrels had often erupted between them? And why, at the end of their long lives, were these dear old ladies still together—reminiscing, yet, in crucial ways, remote from one another?

The psychologist left the nursing home asking a central question: What is the bond that has linked these sisters—and all brothers and sisters—from birth? What causes this bond to grow stronger or to wither? These and many other puzzling questions motivated the psychologist and his colleague to spend eight years in an effort to research the sibling bond, to understand it, to unravel its separate strands, and to discover what makes it one of life's most enduring and influential relationships.

Those eight years of research have culminated in this book, which ex-amines the emotional connections between siblings, their irrational rival-ries and touching loyalties, their primal bonds in earliest childhood and their ties in old age, their painful disappointments, their secret passions, their guilt. This is a book about how people grow together and grow apart, about how very different they become and how much they remain the same, about their reactions to each other's living and to each other's dying. And this is also a book about how parents influence, for better or worse, their children's sibling relationships.

As psychotherapists and teachers who are by training and experience experts in family relationships, we were surprised, when we first began our research, and a bit relieved, to admit to one another how little each of us knew about siblings. We were usually able to respond intelligently to our patients, in individual and family psychotherapy, when they discussed the bonds between parents and children or those between husbands and wives. But we found ourselves poorly prepared to understand and connect with what our patients, as *siblings*, were saying when they spoke of their feelings about brothers and sisters whose emotional presence still cast a shadow over their lives. The sexual, economic, and affectionate ties that bind married couples, and the biological ties that bind children and their parents, appeared to have a different texture from those that bind siblings.

In our Western culture, the rituals of infant baptism, circumcision, con-firmation, bar mitzvah, even graduation mark important changes between parents and children. The bonds between husband and wife are celebrat-

4

ed by engagements and weddings, legalized by marriage and divorce, and invigorated or attenuated by the recent development of marriage and divorce therapy. But there are no rituals of church or synagogue that celebrate sibling bonds (Roberts 1982), nor legal means to make or break them. Thus, when we tried to exercise our skills as psychologists in the emotional, and largely irrational, realm of sibling relations, we felt as if we were in a foreign country without a map.

Previous Research on Siblings

Our confusion was not unusual for psychologists and psychotherapists of our generation, for we had been taught that siblings are, at best, minor actors on the stage of human development, that their influence is supposed to be fleeting, and that it is the parents who principally determine one's identity. We had also been taught that, after one leaves home, the main influences upon an adult's life and sense of self are spouse, children, and job. The prevailing theories of human development seemed strangely silent about siblings and provided few conceptual principles or useful information to help us understand the emotionally charged, real-life dramas that were being enacted each day in our consulting rooms. Before we embarked on the development of a new theory about siblings, we spent more than a year trying to fit the disparate findings from existing areas of research on siblings—psychoanalysis, twin research, family systems, birth order, and sociology—to the actuality of our patients' lives.

PSYCHOANALYSIS AND TWIN RESEARCH

When psychotherapists have written about siblings, they have tended to focus on rivalry for the love of a parent during early childhood. This point of view appears to be a legacy from psychoanalysis,° where a heavy emphasis on rivalry has dominated the literature about siblings (Oberndorf 1929; Levy 1937). The psychoanalysts have had little to say about the larger family context which affects the way brothers and sisters conduct their relationship. Other psychoanalysts have made cogent observations about the psychology of twins, who in strange ways appeared to remain emotionally entangled with each other (Benjamin 1957; Arlow 1960). But

---

° Alfred Adler (1959) is the only major neo-Freudian to discuss sibling influences at any length.

the twin literature has often consisted of collections of unusual and droll anecdotes which few writers have related to the lives of nontwin siblings.

FAMILY SYSTEMS

Family experts, with their sensitivity to group dynamics and reciprocal social influences in the family, acknowledge that siblings are a subsystem, but seem to ignore this subsystem's special rules and effects.

When it comes to sibling interaction, family-systems writers—particularly those influenced by general systems theories—apply cybernetic concepts such as "feedback loops" (Jackson 1970), cross-joining, deviation amplification (Hoffman 1970), and homeostasis or social structural ideas such as "triangles" (Bowen 1970). Such family-systems theorists avoid speaking about the self or about the feelings inside people, and have little to say about the intrinsic experience of being a brother or a sister. In their view, there is no individual person in the process of becoming, no rich description of what brothers and sisters mean to, or think about, each other, no words to capture what dictates some of their important and even irrational behavior. In repudiating the self as an active agent, these theorists usually view every child as part of a general subgroup—"the children"—who are seen as being in compliance with, or in defiance of, another subgroup—"the parents." While developing a valuable perspective about the family as a dynamic unit, family-systems theorists have given little attention to the emotions and feelings within the sibling subgroup itself.*

BIRTH-ORDER RESEARCH

Birth-order researchers present a different viewpoint. Some have made enthusiastic claims, based on clinical observations (A. Adler 1928; Toman 1971), that one's order of birth largely dictated how personality would unfold. Other researchers in academic settings have compared *groups* of siblings who have in common whether they are first born, second born, or later born, and then correlated these factors to information about separate traits such as intelligence, personality, educational achievement, or occupational success. Birth-order researchers have, over the last thirty years, compiled a mountain of data, much of it inconsistent. They look for statistically significant differences—for example, between the personalities of

---

*Such therapists as Donald Bloch (1973), Augustus Napier and Carl Whitaker (1978), and Norman Paul and Betty B. Paul (1975) do emphasize the importance of feelings while also considering how the family system functions.

eldest and youngest children—and then speculate about the causes of each difference. Thus far, this approach has produced, at best, marginal scientific advances. One writer has thoughtfully noted:

> Questions framed in terms of group averages, implying that the effects of certain family positions can be separated from all surrounding circumstances, do not necessarily represent the best scientific strategy. In actual life, pairs of siblings cannot be isolated from their surroundings. . . . The way in which they affect one another's development is always subordinate to the total pattern of influences prevailing in the family. (White 1976, pp 87–88).

Birth-order researchers have not studied sibling relationships in particular life circumstances; and the controversy over whether birth-order effects are meaningful has raged for many years. (The interested reader can find critical summaries by S. Schachter 1963; Altus 1966; Sutton-Smith and Rosenberg 1970; Schooler 1972; and Conley 1981).

SOCIOLOGY

Sociologists of the family, like the birth-order researchers, have studied general aspects of the sibling phenomenon and have found, for example, that there are gender differences in the way sisters and brothers structure their relationships, or that "sociability" and "solidarity" characterize siblings at certain stages of life (Adams 1968; Cumming and Schneider 1961). Although knowledge of such broad trends is useful to a degree as "background," they say little about the life-and-death issues in people's lives. Like the birth-order researchers, sociologists often rely on the questionnaire or interview method with large groups of individuals. By obtaining answers about relationships in nonstressful circumstances, from people who have no vested interest in revealing the painful, conflicted areas of their lives, sociologists often fail to portray the rich details of people's lives.

While in the many months we spent investigating the literature in these five areas, we did find clues to understanding separate aspects of sibling relationships, nowhere did we find a description of a relationship in its totality. The findings in each of the five islands of research are stated in a language that is incompatible with the other four. Family-systems experts do not acknowledge narcissism as an important aspect of sibling relationships, and the birth-order researchers appear uninterested in the riptide of circular influences that make siblings a special social system. Some people have explored siblings at age four and declared them "conflicted and rivalrous," while others have studied them at forty-four and declared them "helpful."

As we emerged from this tangled thicket, we realized that different people had been describing different parts of the same elephant called "siblings." We realized that the answers to the clinical questions our patients were raising could not come from existing research and theory for three major reasons. First, few studies have ever focused on sibling relationships and the parent relationship *simultaneously*. Second, no one has ever attained *intimate familiarity* with siblings over an *extended time*. American psychologists often take quick snapshots of relationships and do not wait long enough to obtain a film that reveals the dynamics of any one relationship, or how it has changed (Lofland 1976). Third, few studies have ever been conducted of siblings in *crisis* situations; it is during these times that the deep structures and meanings of a sibling relationship can be brought to the surface, and the ritual masks and self-presentations can be cast aside.

A CLINICAL VIEWPOINT

During our research we made copious notes whenever an individual patient or a family member expressed distress about a relationship with a sibling. Among them were:

- A brother and a sister, ages eleven and thirteen, respectively, are given up for adoption by their parents after the Department of Protective Services for Children removed them from a multiproblem family where they were badly abused. There has been some incestuous contact between this brother and sister, and they seem to care about one another. Shall they be placed together or separately? What are the risks and advantages of separation or togetherness?

- Three sisters keep postponing the decision about placing their failing mother in a nursing home. The eldest and the youngest sister expect the middle sister, who was always favored by the mother, to make the choice *and* to pay for nursing care (despite the fact that both the eldest and the youngest sisters have much more money than the favored middle sister). Meanwhile, as her daughters hesitate, the mother's health deteriorates.

- A ten-year-old boy whose younger brother was killed by an automobile begins speaking of suicide. Six weeks after his brother's death he has a serious bicycle accident, landing him in the same hospital where his brother died.

- A man begins to neglect his marriage and his job, as he overinvolves himself with his emotionally disturbed brother who, for the second time in five years, has required in-patient psychiatric care.

- A thirteen-year-old boy is beaten brutally by his delinquent older brother, yet does not complain to his parents. When asked by a therapist why he doesn't fight back or tell his parents, he states that the older brother is his idol, his hero.

- A divorced woman with three children reaches out to her well-to-do physician brother who lives a continent away in California. She believes that they once cared about each other, but now her entreaties are rebuffed, as he grudgingly accepts her telephone calls and gives her a cold shoulder.

- Two children, age three and five, prefer one another to the almost total exclusion of any other children. Inseparable, they cling to one another and, as a result, refuse contact with others. The parents barely notice this situation, but it is clear to outsiders that the children are not developing normal social skills.

Responding intelligently to dilemmas such as these seemed a tall order indeed. Possessing the "healing intent" did not in itself lead us to competent interventions in these peoples' lives, nor did it help us to make sense of the largely *irrational* elements of sibling relationships.

Our patients' reactions to being asked about their brothers and sisters were astonishing. In response to the right questions, many people suddenly developed insights into sources of their self-defeating patterns and came away feeling more able to cope with problems. Others did not change, but seemed puzzled and wanted to find out more about this little-investigated area of family life. Yet others became so defensive—their reactions being charged with emotion—that we (and they) knew a sensitive area had been hit and needed deeper exploration. There were still *other* people who, when asked about their siblings, appeared neither defensive nor conflicted nor curious. Rather, they were emotionally "flat" about brothers and sisters and did not respond, smile, or scowl when we asked questions. For this group of people, other family members—parents, grandparents, spouses—seemed to be much more important influences on their development.

Sibling Access

We realized that the emotional bond between brothers and sisters depends on something that we came to call "access." Clearly there are numerous pairs of siblings who go through life *not* resonating to one another. Such siblings appear to have little emotional impact upon one another. These are what we call "low access" siblings, and have some of the following characteristics: They are often separated by more than eight or ten years, acting almost like members of different generations. They have shared little time, space, or personal history, partaking of different schools, friends, and parents (since people are different parents at different ages) in very different ways. They lack the sense of a shared history. They have not needed one another, nor have their parents needed for them to need each other.

Similarity in age and sex promotes access to common life events. Difference in age and sex diminishes access. The most extreme case of high access would therefore be identical twins. This is not to say it is impossible for there to be a bond between a brother and sister aged thirty and fifteen—circumstances may have so arranged it. Nor is it necessarily true that two children aged ten and nine must feel a bond, especially if they have been reared by separate parents or have seen little of each other. But high accessibility during the developmentally formative years is the almost routine accompaniment of an influential sibling relationship. Siblings who are high in access have often: attended the same schools, played with the same friends, dated in the same crowd, been given a common bedroom, (even the same bed), worn each other's clothes, and so on. The earlier access begins, and the more prolonged it is, the more intense will be the relationship between siblings when it is stressed by the issues of separation, death, and social comparison in later life. Many of the people described in this book are high-access brothers or sisters.°

TRENDS TOWARD GREATER FREEDOM AND SEPARATENESS

On the one hand, siblings in today's families appear freer than ever to go their own separate ways, to have little formal access to each other. Primogeniture—the custom that decreed that first-born males would inherit property and titles and therefore were entitled to power within the sibling group—has all but died out; the women's movement has (somewhat) equalized the respective rights and privileges of sisters and brothers; and parents' power to keep adolescents tied to the family and to one another has certainly declined. In addition, the formal obligations toward extended kin, so far as they live together under the same roof, seem to have weakened as grandparents and other relatives are encouraged to live in separate dwellings. Furthermore, people are freer than ever to marry

° Controlled investigations, such as that conducted by V. Cicerelli (1975) and Helen Koch (1960), support the idea that closeness of age and gender likeness intensify siblings' influence on one another in childhood.

whom they wish, and to settle where they wish, as communication can be made by phone, letter, or a quick trip home.

The loosening of obligatory ties in families during the twentieth century has been noted repeatedly by sociological writers (Goode 1970); and sibling relationships appear also to share in the trend toward greater freedom of choice. The greater freedom of family members gives parents few external criteria by which to guide their children's emotional relationships to one another. Lacking a way of setting their children's emotional gyroscopes into a "standard" sibling relationship, parents appear to impose ambiguous and paradoxical rules for their children's relationships:

- Be close, but distant enough to be separate and distinct individuals.
- Be loving, but don't become intensely or sexually involved.
- Be cooperative, but don't become dependent on each other.
- Be loyal, but not in preference to caring about your parents.
- Be admiring, but don't let your sibling take advantage of you.
- Be competitive, but don't dominate.
- Be aggressive, but not ruthless.
- Be tolerant, but defend your own point of view.

In today's America, siblings are free to be involved or not to be involved. They are unlike immigrant siblings who swarmed to America in the great migratory waves, who had to cling together for cultural continuity and survival as they faced hostility and uncertainty in a strange land. Brothers and sisters of that era had little choice but to depend on one another.

But the prevailing norms of "sibship" are ambiguous; thus the *rules* for conducting a sibling relationship have become equivocal and open to negotiation, and hence to ambivalent and intense feeling. Each person, except as it may suit the wishes and expectations of the parents, is free to conduct the matter of being a sibling as he or she sees fit. How to be a sibling becomes for many people a matter of choice (Aldous 1978). But, as we shall see throughout this book, that freedom of choice may be curtailed by traumatic losses and family hardships.

TRENDS TOWARD GREATER INTERDEPENDENCE

Though sibling relations are generally "a matter of choice," high-access siblings have often had intense involvement with one another and, as we kept hearing in the clinical context, have played an important role in the formation of many of our patients' personalities and vitally influenced their feelings and problems. By examining other indicators of social change, we realized that many other forces may be propelling siblings into greater contact and emotional interdependence than ever before. Certain changes in our modern world seem to be simultaneously placing brothers and sisters in a position of greater accessibility to each other. Among the cultural transformations that have accelerated within the last hundred years or so, the following may be giving the sibling relationship greater rather than lesser relevance: *shrinking family size, longer life spans, divorce and remarriage, geographic mobility, maternal employment and alternative sources of child care, competitive pressures, and stress and various forms of parental insufficiency.*

Family Size. Family size has shrunk considerably since the turn of the century. Although the idea of having a family is, as Mary Jo Bane (1976) put it, very much here to stay, today the average child has one sibling in the typical two-child family (David and Baldwin 1979; Lieberman 1970). In 1900 it was not uncommon to have four or five brothers or sisters. Having only one brother or sister creates the potential for interdependence and intensification of the relationship; it gives one sibling an enormous power to have exclusive influence over another sibling. When a sibling dies, departs for college, becomes enormously successful, he or she is the only reference point for the other brother or sister. Lacking a variety of other brothers and sisters with whom to share joy or misery, or with whom one can identify, today's siblings can be "locked in" to relationships which are intense and limiting.

Today's children are born somewhat closer together than children of yesteryear. If the mother has aspirations for her own success in the world of work outside the home, she may want to have fewer children and to finish with childbearing so that she can quickly re-enter the professional mainstream in her own run for success. Couples usually plan to have children within a short time span, within three or four years, and usually space their two children about two years apart; whereas a sibling of eighty years ago was one of a group of children whose ages could cover a considerable range, and whose births were not planned. Narrow age spacing can force children into contact, dependence, and competition and heightens opportunities for mutual influence.

Longer Life Spans. While family size may be dwindling, one consequence of improved nutrition and medical care is the lengthening of life. Where Americans in 1900 lived to an average of forty-seven years, by 1979, they were living to a ripe old age of about seventy-four, and women were living into their eighties.° By 1980 the four-generation family had become a reality. Siblings now spend a much longer period of their lives together than ever before. While one might spend forty to fifty years with one's parents, life with a sibling can last sixty to eighty years! Siblings like Lillian and Rebecca, at the end of the twentieth century, will undoubtedly be more likely to share apartments (and nursing homes), ending their lives together rather than apart. Few parents in conceiving, and setting age differences for, their children project what the latter's lives will be like in sixty years. There is growing evidence that siblings provide a highly supportive social network in old age when spouses die, and children have gone their separate ways (Cicerelli 1977; Townsend 1957). Thus the decision made by a twentieth-century parent to have only one child can have consequences for life in the twenty-first century: the loneliest person in the world may well be the aged, unmarried only child who has no children and no siblings to love or be loved by (Lynch 1979). The diminution of family size makes one potentially more vulnerable at the end of life; when one's only sibling dies, one can lose one's main human connection between past and present.

Geographic Mobility. Ours is a highly mobile society: When a family moves, disruption occurs. Parents change jobs, friendships and social networks are disrupted, schools and teachers change, environments are strange and different (Packard 1972). It is not uncommon for children to go through two or three school systems, neighborhoods, and friendship groups before graduating from high school. One constant person to turn to, for better or for worse, during such dislocation, is a brother or a sister.

Divorce and Remarriage. In 1975 more than one million marriages in the United States ended in divorce. Since 1900 the rate of divorce has increased sevenfold, and it has doubled in the decade from 1964 to 1974. There are currently more than five million single-parent households, and it is estimated that 40 percent of all children born in the 1970s will, before they turn eighteen, live for a period of time in a single-parent household (Keniston 1977). Few divorced parents would argue that it is initially easier to bring up children single-handedly (see Wallerstein and Kelly 1980; Blechman 1982). The shock of divorce itself is often followed by the shock of remarriage, since the majority of divorced individuals remarry within several years, bringing children into new family units. Although each child experiences his or her parents' divorce and remarriage differently, siblings today confront *together* the trauma of parental breakup

° These figures were supplied by the United States Public Health Service.

13

and dislocation. The combined family, with its complicated network of relatives and divided loyalties, presents siblings, half-siblings, and step-siblings with a mélange of potentially distressing experiences.° It is not clear whether these bring them closer, make them more neutral, or produce conflicts; but the sibling relationship is inevitably activated by the dislocations of the larger family (Ransom et al. 1979; Duberman 1973; Reeves 1982).

Maternal Employment and Child Care. Divorced or married, more mothers are working. Whether pressured by the economic hardship created by divorce, or by a desire to strengthen a two-parent family's income or to participate more creatively and vitally in today's society, women today are heading toward equal participation in the world of work outside the home. The percentage of women who work, at least part time, doubled from 26 percent to 54 percent in the nearly thirty years from 1948 to 1976. In that same period, the percentage of working mothers of preschoolers—the developmental period in childhood most seriously affected by disruption and confusion of nurturing care—tripled from 13 percent to 37 percent. Thus, many children live in a vacuum of parental care and depend upon parental surrogates such as babysitters or day-care workers. While there is considerable debate (see Etaugh 1980) about the negative impact of these other forms of caretaking, it appears that young siblings today have large amounts of time when their relationship is not monitored by a personally committed adult. Required to babysit for one another, children are spending more and more time together unsupervised.

Competitive Pressures. The pressures on parents to work are paralleled by pressures on children to compete with one another. There is a growing body of evidence that young girls are beginning to feel the positive effects of the women's liberation movement and are feeling better about themselves in competitive situations. The likelihood of a sister competing successfully with a brother and with her sisters in the world of school and sports may be greater than ever before. And because our culture becomes more exacting and competitive as it becomes more technological, the competitive pressures between children in the same family for success in the outside world (who goes to the best college?) are likely to increase, forcing siblings to use one another as yardsticks for comparison.

Stress and Parental Insufficiency. Sibling relationships may be activated because many parents today are experiencing severe stress and become, in the process, temporarily unavailable. The bad effects, upon the

° We are deliberately not discussing stepsibling and half-sibling relationships; the topic is so complex that it requires entirely separate treatment.

individual child, of alcoholism, of various emotional disorders, of child abuse, and of deprivation of parental care have been the subject of numerous clinical studies; but rarely have these traumas' effects on the sibling relationship been noticed.

In sum, while changes in the family over the last century are not necessarily "bad"—since social change always has bad and good effects, depending upon one's point of view (Bronfenbrenner 1970 versus Bane 1976)—children today are growing up in a vastly more complex world than did their grandparents—a world where opportunities for *contact*, *constancy*, and *permanency* are rare. Children are biologically propelled by these vital needs—what some psychologists call "object constancy"—to turn for satisfaction to any accessible person. In worried, mobile, small family, high-stress, fast-paced, parent-absent America, that person can be a brother or a sister.

The Sibling Bond

DEFINING THE BOND

In a sense it is presumptuous to attempt to call this book "the" sibling bond, because siblings form many different kinds of bond with one another. There is no simple, time-honored, socially approved, all-pervasive sibling relationship; rather, there are a multiplicity of bonds that arrange themselves into a finite number of predictable patterns. A "bond" can be many things:

- A tie that unites.
- An obligation or an agreement.
- A connection or a system of connections.

And "bondage" is the state of being bound, or enslaved. All of these characterizations can describe the emotional transactions of siblings.

We propose that the sibling bond is a connection between the selves, at both the intimate and the public levels, of two siblings; it is a "fitting" together of two peoples' identities. The bond is sometimes warm and positive, but it may also be negative. Thus, for example, rivalrous siblings who hate each other can be considered to be "bound" if their identities have any influence on one another. Through the sibling relationship, one gets the sense both of being a distinct individual and of constancy through knowing a sibling as a predictable person. Even when the relationship is uncomfortable, brothers and sisters derive a sense of a familiar presence, however upsetting. To understand many of the satisfactions in the relationship, we must understand how one sibling's behavior and self-image fit, on an unconscious level, the identity of another. Thus, for example, one sibling may let another dominate because he or she likes feeling taken care of, while the one who dominates may enjoy the continuing sense of omnipotence which comes from making that brother or sister a submissive victim. Only an investigator who has become intimately acquainted with these siblings over a long period of time, can become aware of the pattern of rewards each sibling receives from these repeatedly enacted life scripts.

Waxing and waning, the relationship between siblings peaks during times of stress and change. Except in the case of identical twins who never marry, the sibling relationship has periods of quiescence and periods of intense activity, depending upon where individuals are in the life cycle. Sibling relationships come most sharply into focus during childhood and adolescence; then, as each sibling forms a new family and has children of his or her own, they appear to grow dormant. Once each sibling's children have grown up and leave home, the sibling identity process is reactivated, as elderly parents require extensive health care.

STUDYING THE SIBLING BOND

We have studied sibling relationships at first hand, discovering the innermost feelings of brothers and sisters in their *own* terms, and within particular family and cultural contexts. John Lofland's eminently sensible definition guided our approach:

> To be intimately familiar with a sector of social life is to have easy, detailed, dense acquaintanceship with it, based on free-flowing and prolonged immersion. This immersion, first and initially, may take the form of direct, bodily presence in the physical scenes of the social life under scrutiny. (1976, p. 8)

This kind of participant observation, we believe, was long overdue in sibling research. Thus, we have tried to enter the lives of siblings, not only to look at them but, as therapists, to join their struggles as directly as possible.

In order to study the connections between identities, one must simultaneously consider siblings from four perspectives:

- How do parents arrange or fail to arrange their children's relationships?
- How do siblings themselves, as a semi-autonomous group who have feelings

about each other, affect one another, separate from the influence of parents?

- How do biological changes (adolescence or illness of a sibling, for example) and social changes (marriage of a sibling, economic hardship) affect the connection between siblings?
- How do larger contexts (ethnic, social class, religious, economic) affect siblings' experience of each other?

Our participant observation of the sibling bond over the last eight years benefited from our being individual and family psychotherapists and allowed us to address those very factors that other researchers have ignored. Because people, as a condition for psychotherapy, are willing temporarily to lower their private shields in order to improve their lives, they are more willing to give access to someone who sympathetically joins them in discussing the emotional aspects of their sibling relationships. In addition, many patients, both children and adults, have been willing to ask their siblings to meet with us in order to be helped. Siblings, called upon to help a brother or a sister in a crisis, have often traveled enormous geographical distances. Thus, we were able to interview all the members in the relationship at one time, an opportunity not permitted to most researchers.

We began by keeping detailed notes whenever any patient described a "sibling issue." Our patients were of all ages, ranging from toddlers and infants through aged people in their late seventies; we interviewed siblings of different social classes, ethnic origins, and life experiences. We accumulated approximately 250 "high interest" sibling situations for careful study; most of these were gleaned from our own patients, but some also came from other psychotherapists and colleagues who requested consultation for their own patients. We followed leads wherever we could find them, sometimes inviting for interviews people who were *not* patients, but whose sibling relationships appeared unusual or interesting.° We obtained volunteers from a variety of settings: college campuses, social service agencies, and professional organizations. We also solicited diaries and letters as additional evidence of the important transactions between brothers and sisters. Of the 250 "high interest" cases, we audiotaped or videotaped sessions with nearly 100, so that verbatim transcripts could be made for detailed analysis. Approximately one fifth of these interviews were conducted at peoples' homes, so that we could have a closer encounter with the world in which siblings' real lives were orga-

---

° In the transcripts that are quoted in this book, we use the term *therapist* whenever the discussion took place as part of psychotherapy, and the term *interviewer* when the information was gathered from people who were not in treatment.

nized. Our information base was a potpourri of situations, of human types, of different problems, ages, sexes, and social classes. We had the distinct advantage of being able to delve into the most innocent and developmentally normal situations as well as into situations whose uniqueness and psychological repercussions extended through three successive generations in a single family. In many instances, family members were seen together for a few hours, with the focus then changing to individual psychotherapy.

To do justice to the study of siblings, we had to adopt not one approach but many and, in so doing, became an amalgam of field investigators, psychodynamically oriented therapists, family-systems researchers, historians, and, at times, investigative reporters.

When our information was insufficient, we interviewed people repeatedly, getting to know more than one third of them for periods longer than a year; while with others, two or three hour-long interviews over six weeks gave us the relevant information. When facts were unclear, we invited parents and other siblings to share their experiences and their memories with us. The goal of these interviews was to have conversations that encouraged what one researcher called "the unhurried, free-flowing kind of talk which brings out a wide range and many levels of topics" (John Lofland 1976). We followed principles of focused and open-ended interviewing (Kahn and Cannell 1957; Sullivan 1954). As the reader will discover, the interviewees usually responded with an unusual degree of candor. Many appeared eager to help us, having been told that we were attempting to understand their experiences in order eventually to help other therapists and ourselves increase our effectiveness with siblings. We have preserved the anonymity of all who participated in our study: we have changed names, locations, dates, occupations, and certain contextual information that would be identifying, and have done so, we believe, without committing any serious injustice to the data or its interpretation.

Why the Sibling Bond Develops

We discovered three recurring, predictable conditions that allow strong sibling bonds to develop:

- High access between siblings.
- The need for meaningful personal identity.
- Insufficient parental influence.

18

Unraveling the Sibling Bond

Sibling bonds will become intense and exert a formative influence upon personality when, as children or adolescents, the siblings have had plentiful access and contact *and* have been deprived of reliable parental care. In this situation, siblings will use one another as major influences, or touchstones, in a search for personal identity. When other relationships—with parents, children, or spouses—are emotionally fulfilling, the sibling bond will be weaker and less important. Thus, when other relationships cannot be relied upon, intense sibling relationships are activated. The results of this intensification can be helpful or harmful, depending upon the circumstances of each family, the personalities of the children, and the actions and attitudes of parents.

This, the major theme of this book, will be demonstrated in every chapter. Chapters 2, 3, and 4 constitute a developmental overview of how sibling bonds develop in early childhood, middle childhood, and adolescence. We demonstrate, in chapter 2, that early sibling influences on personality, when parental care is deficient, can produce the intense negativity that is so often said to characterize some later sibling relationships or the closeness and caring of others; and, in chapter 3, that siblings change so rapidly that they bewilder their parents, who are not changing. In chapter 4, we consider the issue of identification—the "glue" of sibling relationships. There are at least eight major patterns of sibling identification, and understanding them is crucial in helping to account for how siblings will deal with one another during times of stress and crisis.

Chapters 5 through 10 cover the major relationship problems and crises that brothers and sisters experience during their lifetimes; here we reemphasize the part that parents play in nurturing or disturbing those relationships. These problems and crises include extremes of loyalty and overburdening commitment, rivalry and aggression, sexual influence and involvement, disturbances of identity resulting from the emotional turmoil of one's siblings, and the unresolved grief reactions to the death of a brother or a sister. Chapter 11 explores the question of whether and how sibling relationships can be changed, and shows what psychotherapists, parents, and other helpers can and cannot do to help siblings become, on the one hand, more separate and distinct and, on the other hand, more cooperative and caring.

CHAPTER 2

Attachment and Separation in Early Childhood

Debbie, the dream that evolved from the pain and yet the void filling four-year-old Monica's soul.

The dream became reality and then a wonder, emitting warmth, love, and joy, never ceasing nor disappointing.

I loved you so, and your acceptance and return of it assuaged the despair raging inside.

The wonder became a miracle. For as we grew up, sisters became friends.

I love you without bounds. Your beauty dazzles.

Monica

IN THIS CHAPTER we shall try to understand why and how young siblings form long-lasting feelings that are not only deep and intense but ambivalent. Some siblings have the sense that a brother or a sister was a presence as constant as their mother or father, and that they "know" their sibling in the most intimate way. Other siblings feel that they must remain forever at odds with one another; yet they seem enmeshed and deeply dependent. Still other siblings react to the absence or the death of a brother or a sister as if they have actually lost a part of themselves, and stay dominated by the wish to reunite or merge with their lost counterpart. We believe that some of the roots of these phenomena lie in early childhood relationships.

Two sets of factors determine how siblings influence one another early in life. The first are largely *outside* of a child's control: social factors, such as when one is born (and therefore the age space between sibs); one's family's economic situation; where one is born—city, suburbs, or country; gender; health; temperament; parental attitudes; and emotional factors in the parents which would determine the role and identity of each child. The second set of factors are those subtle ones operating *within* each child and *between* the children. Even though external factors have a powerful influence on siblings, as a child each person develops special feelings about one's siblings and oneself. It is these private, unspoken aspects of a sibling relationship that are so difficult to detect. They occur in the period from birth to three years of age, before language has adequately developed, and are often experienced on a visceral, "gut" level. That they are important is less obvious when siblings are young children, "innocently" playing together, sitting next to one another in front of the television set or at the dinner table. It is when they become adolescents and adults that they noticeably begin to act *compulsively* and *compellingly* with each other, carrying their irrational feelings, their ancient scripts that could only have been forged early in childhood. For some siblings, this early relationship becomes the foundation for their lifetime relationship.

The concepts in this chapter are based on the reflections of older siblings, who are displaying the mere tip of an iceberg of unconscious, primitively experienced transactions from long ago. These experiences are never clearly articulated; the psychologist must do a great deal of inferring and probing in order to get a clear picture of what "really" went on. In order to understand this period in life, we first need to describe all of the primary ways parents determine their children's early relationships, creating the context in which the siblings will carry out their lives with one another.

The Parent's Influence on Role and Identity

PREGNANCY AND BIRTH

Even before a baby's birth, each parent has begun to anticipate what the child's identity will be, and what role the child will play in the evolv-

ing family dynamic.° Confirmation that a woman is pregnant will often
unleash a torrent of parental fantasies and wishes about the prospective
baby's identity and about what its sex will be, what will happen to the
new family, and even what that child's fortunes will be later in life. If
there are other children, the nature of the sibling relationship will also be
anticipated (for example, "They'll play together as my brother and I did,"
or "Won't it be nice for our daughter to have a baby sister she can be
friends with?").

Rodgers and Hammerstein's wonderful song "Soliloquy," from *Carousel* (1953), expresses a husband's joy upon hearing that his wife is pregnant. The prospective father quickly imposes an identity ("my boy Bill")
and anticipates the role that his unborn child will play in their family
("he'll have more common sense than his puddin-head father," and so
on.)†

Pregnant women may begin to define the child they are expecting as
"troublesome" or "calm" or "active." By attributing certain characteristics to the new baby who is "giving me trouble" or "is making me tired,"
these women can react to the changes in themselves caused by the pregnancy. Unconscious resentments and satisfactions about being pregnant
are also elements in this critical period during which the identity of a
child can be imposed. Events that occur during childbirth, the relative
ease or difficulty of the delivery, the health and responses of the baby in
the immediate postnatal period, and later the quality of attachment between mother and child, all help determine how parents view the personality of their new infant. Injuries to a newborn can also mark that child's
identity for a lifetime. In a case of twins that we will describe in detail
later in the chapter, one of the infants was born with a broken hip. The
baby's hospitalization for six weeks longer than her more robust twin
quickly won her an identity as "fragile." The mother visited her infant
daughter daily at the hospital, worried about her, and continued to feel

°We are using *role* to mean the socially expected actions of a child in the family. *Identity,* on the other hand, refers to the child's personality as viewed by himself and by other
family members. For example, a child's identity might be that of an "angel," while one's
accompanying role is to be helpful, kind, and self-sacrificing. When role and identity are
congruent, everyone derives a sense of security, knowing what is "expected" of the child,
even when these expectations are negative. When role and identity are not congruent,
people become upset: either the role or the identity must change. Thus, the "family angel"
who begins acting unruly, will be pressured to change his or her actions, or a new identity
("troublemaker") must be created.

†When fantasizing what his boy will become as an adult, the father shows great flexibility: "I don't give a hang what he does, as long as he does what he likes." When he sings of
his daughter, however, he constructs her identity narrowly—typical of the 1940s—as "pink
and white as peaches and cream," and says she has "gotta be fed and sheltered and
dressed," and so on.

anxious about her health. An identity as "the fragile, sickly twin" developed, stuck until adolescence, and partially dictated this twin's role in the family and her relationship with her "stronger, healthier" twin sister.

TEMPERAMENTAL CONTRASTS IN INFANCY

Another factor contributing to the identities that children acquire stems from biological differences in temperament. Differences in temperament (Thomas, Chess, and Birch 1968; Escalona and Heider 1959) among infants of the same biological family often result in an early identity imposition and role assignment for each child by the older family members. They often do this by contrasting one child's reactions with those of another. A placid baby girl may become identified as the "calm one" or the "easy one," while a more active, stimulus-sensitive sister may become known as the "excitable one," the "lively one," or the "troublemaker." Even in the case of identical twins, assignment of roles and separate identities usually occur at birth (Allen, Pollin, and Offer 1971). Such arbitrary factors as which twin is born first, and which is heavier or lighter, help determine, for possibly a lifetime, such identity elements as intelligence, strength, and vulnerability.

For parents, the anticipated differences and, later, the actual differences in their children help create a sense that their growing family is an alive, organic, exciting, and challenging system. The ability of parents to recognize individual differences in their children is viewed by many clinicians as one of the attributes of a healthy, well-functioning family (Lewis et al. 1976; Brazelton 1974; Satir 1972).

THE NEED FOR VARIETY: MAKING EACH CHILD DIFFERENT

Some variety in the traits, personalities, skills, and talents of children, regardless of temperament, is generally considered desirable by all the members of a family. The most obvious variation that many parents typically want is to have children of both sexes; but beyond such a basic difference, it appears that in most families there is only one person who can occupy a certain psychological space in a family at any one time. One child's identity is cultivated as "gentle," "kind," "dependable," the "little one," and so on and, as such, pre-empts the possibility that any of his or her siblings can take over that role. If one child becomes the "brain," the other children will have to become something else. When parents extend and elaborate these differences over the years, such original trait assignment may even become a person's lifelong and satisfying identity. However, a negative identity, such as being the "fool" or "bad" or "the jerk," can become a yoke around a child's neck: it may begin innocently, dictating sibling and parent-child interaction; but, once set in motion, remains fixed and even grows (a "deviation amplification" [Hoffman 1971], with terrible consequences for a lifetime. This book offers many examples of sibling conflict over such rigid identities.

Each child ultimately absorbs a unique blend of what the parents hate and love about themselves. The sibling relationship, no less than any other relationship in a family, is in part determined by these projections and wishes. It seemed to us, as we interviewed brothers and sisters, that their identities, each bearing the imprint of these projections and wishes, were being fitted to one another, sometimes arbitrarily, sometimes like the pieces of a complex mosaic. This mosaic of children, with the sibling relationships helping hold it together, ultimately generates some gratification and allows every parent to feel whole and immortal. Children without siblings have no brother or sister to be "fitted to" and must instead rely upon their parents' personalities. An only child often complains ambivalently of being the prized narcissistic extension of the parents' hopes and dreams, while being the only available person in whom the parents can lodge their projections. Thus, the advantage of having siblings is that no one child has to be the sole bearer of the family projection process.

FUSING THE CHILDREN

In healthy families, children's roles and identities are not just fixed at birth or rigidly imposed early in life. They are somewhat flexible and are allowed to change. In other families, however, parents fuse their children, treating them as if they were the same, rather than assigning each young child a clear role, space, or identity: the children are lumped together in what Murray Bowen (1966) calls an "undifferentiated family ego mass." They are referred to as "the kids," not just in word but in deed. Treated as if they were each other's twin—despite differences in age, stage, sex, and temperament—the children can become fused in one another's minds because they are fused in the parents' minds.

In many of these cases, these siblings become fused early in life through parental default. When parents are overwhelmed, anxious, or absent, they have less sensitivity to the individual needs of their children and less energy to care for them. This fusing process is likely to become prolonged if the siblings are the same sex and close in age. Parents who lump their children together may refer to them only as "the girls" or "the boys" and often assume that they have identical needs and personalities. Individual differences get blurred, as the children are bathed together, sent to bed at the same time, punished and rewarded together, and given the same recreational opportunities. Usually such parents will not take the time to ascertain which child is responsible for having done something wrong, and will reprimand both; or they will rationalize their twinning attitude by claiming that they want to avoid "playing favorites."

Moisy Shopper (1974) has pointed out that such parents erroneously assume that children who are treated the same, will not be jealous of one another and will reduce their fighting and quarreling. In fact, the opposite usually occurs. Fusing the children is much more likely to create an impairment of reality testing and a blurring of what is self and what is "not-self." If not corrected, identity confusions will develop in either or both of the children.

Shopper describes five sets of high-access siblings who were pushed into twinlike relations with one another. These siblings became so entangled that they were constantly trying to imitate one another and could never tolerate separation. A common theme for all five sets of twins was the absence of adequate parental nurturance and an insensitivity to each child's emerging, individual needs.

"GIVING" A CHILD A SIBLING

No parent can satisfy all the emotional needs of a child, and very few parents are willing always to try to do so. Many gladly welcome any developmental change that signals that their youngster can be more independent and can give them some "breathing room." What better way to balance the potential overinvolvement and child-centeredness of a mother with her first child than to have at least another one? Many young parents, while realizing that, by having only one child, they can give more of themselves to that child, simultaneously lament the possibility that their first child might grow up without siblings. No matter what type of sibling relationship parents had when they were young, they tend to view sibship as more advantageous than "onlyship." The decision by parents to have at least one more child is rationalized as offsetting loneliness in the firstborn, creating opportunities for healthy competition, and providing each child with the "gift" of a ready-made playmate or companion. Once there is a second child, the first is often envisioned as a helper to Mama with the new baby, while the baby can absorb the energies of the older child and channel them in productive directions. As an example, a mother of a four-year-old girl and a six-month-old baby unabashedly said, when interviewed:

25

INTERVIEWER: Is Diane a support for you with the baby?

MOTHER: Definitely, definitely. It also gets Diane off my back. [*Laughs*] Diane's usually a nonstop talker, and I can't take that.

INTERVIEWER: So she directs the talking to the baby, and everybody gets something out of that.

MOTHER: There are times when I think I'm not going to get a playpen for this baby because that would separate them too much, and then it would require more of my attention, which I'm not willing to give. Besides, they get along so well.

But little Diane faces a complicated task. She must cheerfully accept this "gift" of a baby sister whom she never bargained for, while suppressing her angry feelings about being swept from the maternal nest (Lasko 1954; Kendrick and Dunn 1980).

Parents often fantasize that their children will magically become close, affectionate, and mutually responsive and may even remain life-long friends—a parental legacy expressed in the phrase "After we're gone, you'll always have each other." Such fantasies can be compensatory, stemming from either parent's memories of his or her own painful sibling experiences in childhood. For many parents, regardless of their histories, envisioning a close and cozy set of siblings fulfills their ideal of the "perfect" family.

AGE SPACING AND SHARED LIVES

In addition to giving their child brother(s) and sister(s), parents determine the age spacing of their children, that all-important factor which will determine their children's access to one another. The closer children are in age, the greater the opportunity for sharing developmental events in similar ways. Among the many things we have mentioned that such high-access siblings share (see pages 9–10) may be a special children's language:

The only one who I was *really* close to when I was little was my youngest brother who's a year and a half away from me. Because we always communicated together, my mother says that when he was one and a half, he was supposed to start talking, but he didn't start talking until I did and then all we did was talk to each other! So we grew up pretty close. . . . We didn't talk personally too much, but we really understand each other. He's kind of quiet and stuff, but I still think I understand what's going on with him. We're the closest, I think. My other brothers are six, eight, and nine years older. it was much harder to get close to them.

These children have parallel sibling "careers" (Aldous 1978). They share much with each other, but sharing is two-edged: the children can develop a common language about the same world, each knowing what the other is talking about. Yet by virtue of their closeness in age, they may also collide and struggle with one another more frequently. They cannot avoid one another as well as can, say, a pair of children in which the five-year-old goes off to kindergarten for half a day and has a separate peer group and different interests from his twenty-three-month-old sister who is just learning the joys of opening her mother's kitchen cabinets.

The notion that closely spaced children become emotionally involved receives some support from carefully controlled investigations, such as that conducted by Helen Koch (1955), who found that children who were zero to two years apart had much in common. They had a difficult time tolerating separation from each other, often played with the same friends, and frequently sought each other's company. By contrast, children separated by four to six years appeared less connected and far less influential with one another. When children are close in age, the opportunities for cross-joining with one another (Hoffman 1976) become extremely rich; and both conflict and affinity, the poles of sibling ambivalence, can flourish. The most dramatic instances of this connection occur, as we will see, with identical twins who, in addition to sharing genetic material, also share their environment at exactly the same time. From the moment of birth, twins participate in similar family processes.

Attachment: Early Sibling Dependence

Human beings cannot survive without a warm, predictable attachment to another person. Lacking an attachment, young children become disturbed, physically sick, or retarded; and under extreme conditions, its absence can be fatal (Spitz 1965). It is now accepted as fact that if development is to proceed normally, adequate attachment must occur some time during the first year of life. Among mammals, and especially among human beings, the hunger for affection, contact, and relatedness is so strong in early life that we are willing to settle for substitutes, on the principle that a little bit of attachment or an unhappy attachment is better than none at all.

Human infants will take whatever contact they can get—cold, luke-warm, inconsistent, abusive—so long as they have no better alternatives. It should, therefore, come as no great surprise that some siblings can, and do, attach themselves to each other, especially when there is some insufficiency in their parents. John Bowlby states:

> Many of the most intense emotions arise during the formation, the mainte-nance, the disruption, and the renewal of attachment relationships. . . . On the way in which an individual's attachment behavior becomes organized within his personality turns the pattern of affectional bonds he makes during his life. (1980, pp. 39–41)

Siblings are not mentioned in this quotation or in most of the other theo-ries that describe a child's early psychological development; and there is very little to indicate the more subtle, complicated, and ambivalent feel-ings that arise in a sibling who is asked to give affection and nurturance to a baby brother or sister.

We all recognize that baby brothers or sisters are seldom entrusted to the complete care of their older siblings. In using the term "mother fig-ure," Bowlby and other attachment theorists initially meant biological mothers (Ainsworth 1972; Bowlby 1969, 1973) and only recently expand-ed it to include other adult caregivers (Ainsworth 1979). We believe, how-ever, that sibling attachment does occur, although it is usually *incomplete*, *unsatisfactory*, and of an *anxious* nature. While we acknowledge that the parent is *potentially* the most stable figure for attachment, we believe that sibling attachments can play an important role in the early develop-ment of a child's personality. In such instances, the sibling is providing a supplementary life-giving force, filling a void left by the less available parent. Some theorists, such as Bowlby (1980), believe that these "multi-ple" attachments, however, can create psychological problems in the in-fant. If a parent has become less available, and a brother or sister is pres-ent for attachment, the infant's sense of constancy and security can begin to fragment, as the sibling and the parent respond to the baby in different ways. A sibling can cuddle, feed, clothe, play, and protect a baby brother or sister but is far less likely to have the maturity, the sensitivity, and the psychological competence that any adequate adult caregiver could provide.

Aggressive and hostile attitudes of siblings, lasting even into adulthood, can stem from the ambivalent and early position of the infant's having expected love and object constancy from an older brother or sister, who, unlike a parent, may be uncooperative, demanding, and thoroughly self-centered. It seems reasonable that the significance and the quality of sibling attachment will be strongly affected by the *characteristics* and the *age* both of the sibling who needs to turn to a substitute attachment figure, and of the sibling attachment figure to whom the distressed child turns. An older brother or sister who is chosen by the parents to be the preferred "babysitter," can be a constant object to which an infant can turn for reassurance, security, and a warm embrace. If, however, that sibling caretaker has mixed feelings about being put in such a role, the infant may become anxious and forever tentative in its responses toward its sibling who does not provide adequate nurturance.

Ruth Meyendorf (1971) has reported a striking example of an infant who suffered a serious depression due to her separation from her two older siblings, and concluded that the older siblings must have been attachment figures for the child. The nineteen-month-old girl had been placed in her aunt's home, accompanied by her five-year-old brother and three-year-old sister, because her mother had suddenly been hospitalized. There was no remarkable reaction to that separation. However, after one week the girl was moved to another relative's home, but this time *without her siblings.* Within the next week, the child had become stuporous, had lost her power of speech, refused food, was withdrawn and agitated, and resisted the affections of anyone, including the mother and father when she was reunited with them. She looked as if she were dying, and would sit listlessly, sometimes calling out her siblings' names. Only after her brother and sister were returned to her, did she seem emotionally responsive, begin to look alive, regain her speech and usual demeanor, and once more become physically active. Meyendorf stated that the siblings appeared to have been auxiliary attachment figures. Their absence was of importance to the girl and could not be assuaged merely by her thinking about them; the depressive process could be reversed only when she was reunited *both* with her siblings and with her parents.

In another study (Bowlby 1973), a group of children, ranging in age from thirteen to thirty months, were observed in a residential nursery, where they had been temporarily placed while their mothers were hospitalized (in seven cases, while the mother was having another baby). Four children, who entered the nursery accompanied by an older *or* a younger sibling, remained calmer and exhibited less agitated behavior than the other children:

> They cried less and showed fewer outbursts of marked hostility. During the early days especially, siblings sought each other's company, talked and played together. To outsiders they presented a united front, with exclamations such as "She's not your sister, she's my sister." (P. 11)

29

Even when parents are not absent, infants can prefer following and imitating their older siblings (Lamb 1978).

The availability of older siblings to an infant may hasten a child's social competence and help develop mastery. But now we must go beyond observations of play and interaction and explore the feelings of young siblings toward one another.

OBJECT RELATIONS AND THE SEARCH FOR CONSTANCY

> I know that we will always remain close. I somehow feel that we're very much the same, that my fate is linked to yours, and that wherever I go, I carry part of you inside of me.

Such intensely experienced sibling relationships are, we believe, not unusual. Siblings, early in life, can acquire meanings for one another and become locked into a complementarity in which a vital part of one sibling's core identity becomes fitted to deep parts of the other's core identity. Such notable theorists as Melanie Klein (1952), Henry Dicks (1967), and Heinz Kohut (1971) have made hypotheses to explain how one's self-concept as a young child emerges from one's earliest intimate relationships, and how as a grown person, in intimate relations such as marriage, one repeats that pattern of involvement in a healthy or a disturbed way.

The term *object relations* refers to psychological processes that all people use, early in life, to create internalized images of the self and other people. These internal patterns and images are known as "object representations." The dynamic relationship between these inner structures creates the foundation for intimate relationships throughout one's life. The development of identity, the deepening of the capacity to endure frustration and fluctuation in intimate relationships, the growth of the ability to love and empathize, to be faithful and trusting, all stem—in the object-relations view—from the quality and the durability of the people upon whom one depends, and from the way in which the child internalizes these experiences in the first years of life.

Because mothering is always imperfect, and the infant cannot be completely satisfied, he will experience rage, and the phenomenon of "splitting" will occur. In splitting, uncomfortable, "bad" feelings are sealed off in primitive, preverbal ways. Some infants blame the depriving person for the bad feelings, attributing harmfulness or malevolence to that person.

Alternatively, the infant can become depressed and internalize the feelings of badness, refusing to attach bad qualities to outsiders. When hostility and rage are locked tightly within, the child feels that he or she is a "bad-me" (Sullivan 1948).

While there is consensus among object-relations theorists about the serious consequences to the child of deprivations early in life, little has been written about the early influence of siblings and about any functions that they might serve. These theorists have assumed, as did the attachment theorists, that the parent is the most important person with whom the young child interacts. We, on the other hand, acknowledge that in today's world the parents are often much less available than they might optimally be. A young child needs a stable, reliable environment or "object constancy"; a child cannot be totally self-reliant. In our view, a brother or a sister close at hand becomes a likely candidate to be that warm and reassuring important external object. This can be a two-way process, since both the younger and the older child can be driven by hunger for a satisfying contact. The child who can fuse or merge with another person, will feel more whole, more integrated, and less vulnerable to the vagaries of an uncertain world. This blending of aspects of oneself with those of another makes any child feel that he or she is more complete. In this way, a brother or a sister becomes a valued object representation from which a child's own self-representation gathers sustenance and esteem.

SIBLINGS AS TRANSITIONAL OBJECTS

If a mother is available and competent, siblings are unlikely to become figures for symbiosis and attachment for each other. But as the months go by, a mother will usually begin to pull farther and farther away, will give less to her growing child, perhaps even much less when a new infant is born.

Siblings can use one another to make the transition away from their mothers and thereby become "transitional objects." Donald W. Winnicott (1951) observed that the infant tends to cling to inanimate objects that provide a constancy, once the infant moves beyond the timeless symbiotic boundaries of the mother's embrace. The familiar and present transitional object (T.O.) provides comfort to the child during the stage of separation and individuation (Mahler 1968, p. 53). Between eighteen and thirty-six months, the T.O. comforts the child in the face of a world that can be unsatisfying, uncertain, or frightening. It is the first "not-me" possession, usually a doll, a stuffed animal, or the much popularized and satirized blanket, the prized possession of Charlie Brown's pal, Linus. Winnicott, observing infants with their T.O.'s, noticed certain aspects of their relationship with the T.O. The infant assumes rights over the object; it is loved, cuddled, hated, and mutilated; it has to be pliable, seeming to give warmth, showing that it has a vitality of its own. Later, Winnicott (1965, 1971) recognized that a person can be a transitional object if that person is sensitive and willing to subordinate his or her needs to those of the infant. We would add: siblings can become important and meaningful objects of transition for one another, especially when circumstances lead to deficits in parenting.

This transitional relationship, while satisfying, may be intensely frustrating for both children. Behind the lovely photograph in the family album of an older sibling cuddling a baby brother or sister, a powerful drama may actually be taking place. No child can satisfy all of a sibling's demands for nurturing. Each child, facing some of the same frustrating circumstances of life, must come to resent the neediness, demandingness, and sense of entitlement that a sibling assumes. Here lie some of the origins of sibling ambivalence.

In each sibling pair, the dynamic will differ according to the particular parents and is catalyzed by the particular needs of each child. For example, older children, at age three or four, are often seen trying to teach their younger sibs to do things, to perform, to talk. Sometimes it seems as if the younger sibling is a toy or a pet. The eighteen-month-old baby boy delights his three-year-old sister when he plays patty-cake, but receives a scowl of disapproval when he refuses to cooperate. Here the three-year-old's sense of omnipotence, as well as her search for competence, can be fulfilled by teaching her baby brother. This sibling interaction provides one small rite of passage, giving the teaching sibling a chance to prove that she is autonomous. The baby, in turn, gets a chance to develop ego mastery, with stimulation and contact as a bonus (see White 1959). The children thus give a kind of testimony to each other's existence. When such testimony is given repeatedly in many situations, the children's relationship becomes important, and their feelings about one another are intensified.

But each child in a sibling twosome may experience frustration whenever a brother or a sister refuses to play, stimulate, or provide contact. Younger siblings always look to their older siblings for this nurturance and, just as likely, meet with rebuff. It is then that one sibling can use the other as an object on which to project any of his or her own bad feelings. Frustrating feelings that have been incorporated as the "bad-me" are experienced, on a visceral level, as anxiety, fright, fear, and, in extreme situations, as annihilation. Such feelings must be disowned. These feelings become the "not-me" that is projected outside the self, where these feelings can seem to disappear, or at least their existence within the self can be denied.

If the T.O. is an older sibling, then there is likely to be conflict. The younger sib's need to disown bad feelings and project them onto the T.O. (the older sibling), and the older sib's need to merge with the younger cannot be mutually satisfied. By the same token, if the older sib withdraws his attentions, the younger sib loses his T.O. and suffers intense disappointment.

There are abundant possibilities for siblings not adequately meeting each other's needs. Out of these disappointments arise the structural underpinnings of the split feelings of good/bad, me/not-me, closeness/distance that characterize so many sibling relationships in late childhood and in adulthood. Complete fusion with a sibling, which can result in totally losing one's self, or complete avoidance, which can result in being a stranger to one's sibling, are two extreme resolutions of this T.O.-attachment dilemma.

Let us now turn to the example of two adult siblings whose intense and frustrating early relationship created later misunderstanding and perpetuated underlying feelings of resentment. Like other adults who have experienced a serious disruption of early nurturance in the first years of life, one of these women feels perpetually anxious and driven and cannot understand why she and her younger sibling do not get along. In this case, we see how the parents, through their unhappy marriage and their attitudes about their children, created a context in which the siblings, conflicted and unhappy, found their dissatisfactions spilling over from early to late childhood, and then into adulthood.

Anxious Attachment and Later Conflict: Barbara and Jennie. Barbara had been involved in various forms of psychotherapy for a long time. She had attempted individual, group, and, while married, couple therapy, spending a total of seven years in treatment. But the therapy had failed to remove her chronic anxiety, feelings of isolation, periodic loneliness, and depression. Although she was a competent photographer and owned her own small studio, she couldn't shake her basic sense of being vulnerable. At twenty-eight, Barbara complained that her twenty-five-year-old sister had "all that she didn't have." Her sister Jennie was married, had a two-year-old son, and was in the seventh month of her pregnancy. When Barbara saw Jennie together with her child, bulging with another baby-to-be, and doted on by their aging parents, she was filled with envy and jealousy. In the very first family therapy session, which she coerced her family to attend, she blurted out her grievance: She wanted more time with her little nephew. Why couldn't her sister let her have him more than once a week? She would love and nurture him as *if he were hers!* But Barbara felt her mother and sister were in an alliance against her. The therapist asked:

THERAPIST: Why is it so important for you to have access to your nephew?

BARBARA: It's because they don't trust me, because my mother and sister often talk and they both say things. There's this kind of subtle feeling like they don't trust me . . . like I don't know what to do with him, what to do with a kid. . . . They say it all the time—"Well, you're not a mother yourself. You don't know unless you're a mother!"

For Barbara, taking care of her nephew was to prove her worth as a family member; but she felt that her sister didn't trust her. Jennie, on the other hand, felt that Barbara had always been different, even when they were children, and said that they seldom played together, that they had "different" personalities. Barbara was studious, Jennie was playful; Barbara was quiet and detached, Jennie was always in the thick of things. Why should she let Barbara have access to her child? By insisting that she was different from Barbara, Jennie slyly emphasized to her parents, the therapist, and to her sister that Barbara was as peculiar and needy as ever, and that she might even be capable of killing the baby:

JENNIE: I'll be honest with you—that day, when you took him to the park, I was *worried!* I was really *scared!* I don't know *why* I was scared, I knew you wouldn't really *hurt* him, physically.

BARBARA: I've gotten that feeling a lot from you—a lot.

JENNIE: But I was *scared*, I was really *worried* all the time you were gone. I just sat in my living room and I was like, I was in a cold sweat because *I felt like she couldn't—she hated me so much that I didn't know if you might* ____

BARBARA: Like I would do something to him?

JENNIE: ____ do something to hurt me, even though you might not hurt him *bodily* but I really didn't know what my fear was, like my husband said, "Well, what exactly are you worried about? She's level-headed—she's not gonna go dump him in the woods or something." I said "I *know*," but I really didn't know what my *concern* was, but I was just—I was really *upset*.

It was her older sister's intensity about her child that worried Jennie. But Barbara explained herself. She began to reveal that her nephew seemed like her soulmate in this family and would "listen" to her as she spoke to him. She would *never* want to hurt him. She knew that, unlike the others, he would respond to her. He could be like a living doll, to hold, to sing to, to identify with—as if she, too, were getting the benefits of the nurturance and caring she was heaping upon him. This was not just sibling rivalry, in which she wanted a baby as her sister had, but rather an example of Barbara's wish to be taken care of, and to receive vicariously what she gave to the baby.

Over the next few months in family therapy, Barbara finally was able to recall her longing for her own younger sister when they were young children. The girls' mother began to explain that she had been seriously depressed for long periods of time during their childhood. Barbara was only sporadically nurtured. The mother, who had grown up in a large, impoverished family, was burdened at having a new baby and was unable to resolve her own feelings of frustration and despair about her marriage. The father was a hard-working laborer who provided for his family, but he was emotionally restricted and rebuffed his wife. When angry, he would drink; and whenever his wife demanded his attention, he would stay away from her. In desperation, the mother finally attempted suicide. When Jennie was born, Barbara, in her own neediness, turned to this new baby sister. Anxiously attached to her depressed mother, Barbara wanted her sister's support. Whenever she was upset, Barbara would go to her baby sister, hoping to be soothed and comforted by her. Jennie became her transitional object. When they were somewhat older, Barbara remembered that she was often frightened, especially at night. Instead of going to her parents, she would crawl crying into her younger sister's bed. Barbara thought that her sister Jennie seemed to have the same feelings that Barbara had. To their mother, Barbara had always seemed too "serious," too "unhappy," too preoccupied with vague, undefinable concerns; and the spontaneity and gaiety of her new baby Jennie was a welcome contrast to the tedious and whiny complaints of her first child. By the time the girls were three and six, the mother was determined that Barbara would not "contaminate" Jennie. The more Barbara tried to cling to her sister, to merge with her, and use her as a substitute figure for attachment, the more the mother would intercede in an effort to ensure that at least her second child would be happy.

By the time both girls were of school age, their contrasting identities seemed set. Jennie was playful, tomboyish, popular, and outgoing, while

Barbara was a serious student, who stayed inside and read, wore a sad face, and had no friends. By now Jennie was refusing to associate with her sister. She no longer was willing to sit and talk with Barbara for long stretches, and began avoiding her. Barabara grew up with continuous feelings of anxiety, always felt "strange," and was seemingly without hope that there would be any change in her bleak and unfulfilling existence. She demanded that the new therapist "fix" her emptiness, this fatalistic feeling that she did not belong in her own family. She felt that her sister's son had become her only passport back into the family group, and worried that this new opportunity for merging and belonging was—just as had happened, first with her mother, then with her sister—going to be denied her:

> The way I feel is like I'm gradually just being excluded from the family. Like everybody's just giving up on each other—all of a sudden . . . and . . . and, we're so *separate,* so distant now even though we see each other a lot. I'm getting to know everybody less and less—they're becoming strange to me. I've always felt this way. I can't go any place until I finish this business. I have this urge to start doing things, to live my life, to move. But I can't move away. I'm so *attached,* I can't do anything. I'm stuck. I'm just sitting here waiting, and we're not going any place. We're moving farther apart.

Barbara's uncertainty is striking. She was unable to feel good by herself or comfortable with others and kept waiting, in some passive, helpless way, for her family to sustain and nourish her.

Rebuffed by their overburdened mother early in life, Barbara tried, unsuccessfully, to attach herself to the next most available person, her little sister, who, aided and abetted by their mother, also rebuffed her. Her attempts to merge with her sister, which Barbara sustained through their adult years, appeared to be a way of extracting demands for reparation of a wound, a loss that had been initially experienced with the mother. Again and again she turned to her sister and eventually to her sister's child for closeness. Again and again she was rejected, unable to ward off the bad feelings that her mother's emotional abandonment and rejection had ignited. The younger sibling, in this case, as in many others, could not fulfill the older sibling's needs for a warm relationship and, under the direction of the mother, withrew, leaving Barbara angry, anxious and hungry for affection.

Attachment and Separation in Early Childhood

The younger sibling who looks to and merges with an older sibling has a better chance of having the need for love satisfied. An older sibling can at least try and be an adequate caregiver to a needy younger sib. The older sibling can attempt to model the mother, and can feel superior or even omnipotent. But if the older sibling turns to her younger sibling for an enduring, satisfying bond, she is less likely to receive the warmth she desperately craves. Looking for deep emotional satisfaction with a person who is, to paraphrase Heinz Kohut (1971), unempathic, unpredictable, and emotionally shallow, can only lead to frustration. When this type of sibling relationship occurs early in life, it will become a Gordian knot, defying easy understanding or decisive resolution. Until a psychotherapist pointed it out, no one saw the misery-producing dynamic that determined the past and perpetuated the present.

This case illustrates several important principles we see in many other sibling relationships:

- If anxious attachment with the mother has occurred in the first year of life, a child will be left with unresolved feelings of helplessness, weakness, and pervasive neediness.
- By the third year of life, such a child may try to find, in a baby sibling, an opportunity to merge, so as to ward off the "bad feelings."
- It is unlikely that such an immature object can fulfill the older sibling's primitive needs; therefore, the older child will remain unsatisfied and anxious.
- Parents will usually respond with alarm to the older child's possessiveness toward the younger sibling. They may separate the children, thereby further frustrating the older child's object needs.
- If parents do not interfere with this process, and the children are allowed to spend a great deal of time together, the younger sibling will feel burdened. In order to differentiate, the younger sibling will have to push the needy older one farther away. The young child's identification with the older child will become strained; and as they grow older, their relationship will be fraught with conflict.
- The older sibling who feels better because his younger sibling is warm and affectionate, will often identify with the playful, primitive, aspects of the baby. The older child will be less likely to tolerate the more mature qualities the younger sibling shows as they both grow up. The older one will often play one-upmanship games, pushing the younger one back into the "junior" role.
- As they grow into adults, neither sibling will be able to understand why they are unable to "get along." Relationships of this type, established early in life, usually baffle the parents, who keep asking, "Why can't you two ever get along?"

Emotional Closeness and Interdependence

Some families are "enmeshed" (Minuchin 1974). Their members resonate to changes in one another like a can of worms in which the wiggling of one sets off a chain of reactions in all the others. Siblings in these families start out closely interlocked, with a development in one child crucially affecting the well-being of another child. When closely entwined, brothers and sisters can develop an acute sensitivity to one another, using each other as fundamental reference points.

MERGING, TWINNING, AND MIRRORING

Heinz Kohut's (1971) extrapolations about early personality development provides a useful model for further understanding sibling dynamics. He describes three essential processes that develop in stages over the first three years of life. These processes are merging, twinning, and mirroring; and if they are not adequately resolved, their effects last a lifetime.

Initially, out of a need for a safe and secure reality, the infant wishes to *merge*. This archaic merging, which dissolves the self-other distinctions, occurs during the attachment phase and helps perpetuate a symbiotic relationship. We believe young brothers or sisters, always playing together and protesting separation, may be supplying their own motive force for their togetherness, out of one child's need to merge. This child always seems to feel better when with a sib. Erik Erikson provides a description of what occurs when such merging becomes prolonged:

> It is as if our patients surrendered their own identity to that of a brother or sister in the hope of regaining a bigger or better one by some act of merging. For periods they succeed: the letdown which must follow the breakup of the artificial twinship is only the more traumatic. Rage and paralysis follow the sudden insight that there is enough identity only for one, and that the other seems to have made off with it. (1959, p. 137)

The second process that Kohut describes is an alter ego stage, or *twinship*. As the child grows older, he becomes more differentiated than during the merging stage. In the twinship stage the child begins to recognize he is different from others. Now the child can tolerate being physically separate. But if the child could speak, he might say: "You're like me and I'm like you," leading to "What I feel, you, being the same, must also feel." One can observe that a sibling who is still twinning will become enraged if a brother or a sister insists on holding a different opinion. A child's recognition that the "twinned" sibling now sees the world differently may produce anger, frustration, and then—what parents mistakenly assume to be meaningless—fights between the kids.

Kohut's third early developmental stage is that of *mirroring*. At this point the child expects the other to be an audience and to provide feedback by reacting with pleasure and delight over the child's every production. The other person exists separately, but as a pleasantly colored mirror that reflects only what satisfies the child's narcissistic desires. It requires a certain self-denial for an older child to serve as a mirror for younger siblings. When a young child wants an older sibling to watch him dance, the older must feel secure enough to sit down and patiently observe and applaud. A certain degree of parental identification must have occurred, even a wishful feeling that the baby could be the older sib's baby, a source of pride and pleasure. For example, a sister, six years older than her brother recalls:

> I remember when he was born. I remember when he came home from the hospital, holding him, taking care of him and wheeling him around in his carriage. I used to love to do it and began having fantasies of having babies too.

And:

> I remember lots of things about him as a little boy, when he was two, three, four, and five. He was a very attractive, pretty, very smart, and lively, vivacious, darling-looking person. I felt very proud of him as a kid. He always used to make us laugh, he was such a bright little button. It was always fun to be with him back then.

A child is fortunate to have a sibling feel this for him or her. By being provided with a mirroring experience, one can develop the capacity for empathy. Experiencing such positive reflections of the self allows the child to feel sufficiently secure to begin taking on the role of the other; and out of this mutual regard for each other a positive relationship unfolds. As George Mead (1934) pointed out, there is no self outside of social experience. The mirror is vital to self-knowledge.

Twins: The Special Case of Close and Intense Siblings

Although twin births are only 1 percent of all births in the United States, for many people they continue to be the most fascinating aspect of sibship

(Farber 1981). Dressed alike, looking alike, Tweedledum and Tweedle-
dee, twins have represented everyone's fantasies of having another self,
with whom to trade places. Throughout Western mythology, history, and
literature, twins have nearly always been regarded with reverence and
even awe. In many cultures, they have been viewed as leading charmed
lives.

While twin stories are fascinating, we find that the study of twins is
important because it helps clarify the identification processes that occur
between *all* high-access siblings. Many authors (Karpman 1953; Leonard
1955, 1961; Orr 1941; Slater 1953; Joseph 1959, 1961; Glenn 1966) describe twins as siblings who always have an intimate sixth sense about one
another, even to the extent that they think they magically know each
other's thoughts, feelings, wishes, and innermost secrets. Twins offer striking illustrations of what can occur when boundaries of separateness between any siblings become fuzzy, when mirroring and fusing predominate, and when self-object differentiation is blurred. From twins we can
learn much about the mirroring and twinning processes that occur with
many high-access siblings.

Dorothy Burlingham offers, in her classic monograph *Twins: A Study
of Three Pairs of Identical Twins*, a lovely description of three sets of
twins who were brought as infants to the Hampstead Nursery in England.
Without attachment to a parent, each twin rapidly formed an intense
bond with the other. They often displayed envy, blame, and jealousy of
each other; but they also showed positive attitudes through praising, protecting, helping, sharing, and giving affection. For example:

> At two years, when Jessie was going to have her rest she first went to
> Bessie's bed and kissed her and said "my Bessie," Bessie kissed her
> too.
> At two years, two months, Jessie and Bessie lay in the same bed. Jessie
> was saying "my Bessie, my Bessie" in an affectionate voice putting
> her face quite near hers. Bessie was putting bits of rusk [dry toast]
> into Jessie's mouth. Jessie repeated "my Bessie" several times until
> the rusk was eaten up. Then she crawled to her side of the bed and
> went to sleep. (1952, p. 62)

Fused by being put in the same playpen, bathed, and fed together, and
encouraged by their parents to stay and play together, twins become emotionally entwined. H. Lytton, D. Conway, and R. Sauve (1977) found that
twins have slower speech development than nontwin siblings, since their
parents rely on the children to keep each other company, and speak less

to them than they would to single children. Twins can, however, develop serious problems with ego boundaries. Cycles of intense fighting and intense affection often dominate their relationship; yet they often appear to be unable to live without each other.

George L. Engel, a distinguished professor of psychiatry, was himself a twin. He has described the narcissistic advantages of being a twin and the process of merging and mirroring which we believe can occur with any fused siblings.

> Through much of my childhood, even well into adolescence, our parents referred to us collectively as "the twins" while often misidentifying us as individuals. We were dressed alike, provided identical possessions, and from earliest infancy, certainly spent far more time interacting with each other than any other person, including mother. It seems that to be physically close to my twin was important in mitigating the trauma of separation from my parents. But at the same time this closeness accentuated the wish and advantage to be as much like my twin as possible. . . .
>
> As children we were retarded in language development and social communication. Like many twins, we enjoyed a private language, remnants of which persisted well into latency period. We never addressed each other by our proper names. . . . As early as the age of two we began to address each other as "Other Man." Over the years this became shortened to "Othie" and finally to the more curt "Oth." This shared appellation constituted an elegant compromise for it simultaneously differentiated self from the other while maintaining the dual twin identity distinct from the rest of the world.
>
> The narcissistic advantages of being a twin are a major factor that is intuitively appreciated by non-twins who typically envy twins their constant companionship, which they imagine to be totally without ambivalence . . . Such narcissism constitutes a powerful force working against achieving separateness. For us, the narcissistic gain of being twins was reinforced early in childhood, as well as by family, and, later on, by the extraordinary power we felt in our ability to deceive others (1974, p. 33).

EXCESSIVELY DEPENDENT TWINS

The Engel twins came from a family that encouraged individual abilities; but other twins are not so fortunate. If twins are excessively dependent on one another, the self-images of each can become seriously confused (see Parrish 1978). Our own clinical observations about twins underscore this point. The close identification that each twin has with the other prevents them from separating and thus convinces us that their self and object representations are often seriously distorted. Twins are the extreme examples of sibling togetherness in which impairments in reality testing can dominate.

EXCESSIVE MERGING AND MIRRORING

> Fat and Skinny went to bed,
> Fat rolled over and Skinny was dead.°

"I Want to Be Different from You Even If I Have to Die": Vickie and Marilyn. The consequences of too much and too prolonged an attachment between siblings are often profound. As the children get older, their old relationship agreements about sameness are strained by their need to go separate ways and to develop separate identities. But if the children have been twinned by parents, and continue to use each other as narcissistic mirrors, their attachment may become rigid: like Siamese twins fused at head and back, when one tries to become a separate self, the other feels pain. Early and close merging of identities between siblings carries severe risks: The children can lose themselves in each other and, by later childhood, fail to make friends or healthy contacts with the outside world. These children may struggle, compulsively or brutally, to shake free of the merging that still binds them.

A vivid instance of this process is provided by Marilyn and Vickie, identical twins. The girls displayed many of the hallmarks of twins. They had always been together—shared a crib as infants, been bathed together, fed together. As the youngest of six children, they were treated as a distinct pair within the family. When the older children grew up and left home, Marilyn and Vickie became even closer to one another. They were each other's constant companions, and, when the parents went out for an evening, were appointed each other's babysitter. Their access to one another was, had always been, total. As adolescents, they still shared a bedroom and monitored and participated in each other's activities. Their high access, merging, and mirroring had, early in their lives, been promoted by their mother's absorption with caring for her four older children, while their father was a tired, depressed, and passive man who worked two jobs and was unable to give his wife much support.

From birth, the twins did have one obvious difference: Marilyn had been born with a broken hip and hence was seen by their mother as the more vulnerable of the two. This background of having a physical fault assigned Marilyn a weak role which was played out against Vickie's relatively greater strength. The family used this single difference as the only reason to treat the girls differently; otherwise they were seen as alike and interchangeable.

By early adolescence, Marilyn decided that she had to be different,

° A children's limerick, origins unknown. Courtesy of Ben Kahn.

and, at the age of thirteen, went on a crash diet and almost stopped eating. Subsequently diagnosed as having anorexia nervosa, she had two unsuccessful hospitalizations and, in spite of being force-fed, refused to maintain a normal weight. On her initial visit to the office of the clinical psychologist, one year after the first hospitalization, she weighed in at seventy-six pounds. When the therapist saw the twins, he could hardly believe that they were twins, much less members of the same family. They only faintly resembled each other. Vickie was chubby and cherubic, with rosy cheeks and the healthy appearance of an early maturing adolescent. Marilyn was a little girl, three inches shorter, her reduced height the result of the near starvation and poor nutrition over the many months when she should have been growing. With black rings under her sunken eyes and a gray pallor to her skin, she had the skeletal look of a concentration camp survivor. Her caved-in shoulders, skinny legs, and oversized jacket made her appear a shriveled stick when she stood next to her plump, healthy-looking twin. The therapist asked Vickie's weight. "One hundred twenty-one pounds," she replied proudly. "Forty-five more than Marilyn." Marilyn and Vickie then made an astounding revelation: each had agreed to be different by maintaining a constant and conspicuous difference in body weight from her fellow twin.

Locked together in this "till death do us part" agreement, the girls insisted that they were really unlike one another; yet owing to their fusion and twinship, each was continually looking to the other as a yardstick of comparison. Unconsciously they had agreed to differentiate according to a criterion (weight) that could be fatal for Marilyn and disfiguring for both girls. When Vickie felt too heavy, she would start dieting; but only a 2-pound drop in her weight would be sufficient to start skinny Marilyn dropping close to a life-endangering level. When Marilyn became too skinny, and everyone panicked (she had once reached 65 pounds), she would be forced to eat and gain weight again. And then Vickie made herself gain, in order to remain different. Thus, if Marilyn gained to the normal weight for her age (110 pounds), Vickie would have to become grossly abnormal and weigh 155 pounds. If Vickie at 121 pounds decided to lose 5 pounds, Marilyn at 76 pounds would have to drop to 71 pounds—a crucial loss of 5 pounds which could produce more malnutrition, susceptibility to infection, and ketoacidosis, a condition that precedes coma.

Up and down went the girls, in a cross-joined ritual of striving to be different. Their fear of fusion and of becoming too separate was solved temporarily by this destructive agreement, which simply redistributed the power each had to run and ruin the other's life. The "I'm different—no,

I'm not" confusion in both of these sisters dominated their every waking moment.

Daily they weighed themselves in front of each other, ate together, cooked together, and told each other their innermost worries. Marilyn and Vickie were fascinated by food, counted calories, weighed portions, shopped for special foods. In the summer, when asked by their parents to come out of the kitchen to help with yard chores, they decided instead to start their own vegetable garden. Yet, even here they wanted to be different from one another: one planted leafy vegetables; the other, root vegetables. They fantasized that one day they would become dietitians in a hospital, as co-directors of different parts of the same service. They exercised furiously, Marilyn running five or six miles some days, with Vickie's encouragement. The following note to her therapist reflects Marilyn's "caloric vigilance" over the much-needed difference from, and simultaneous attachment to, her sister:

Hi! How are you? Sunday Vickie and I went out to dinner. For lunch I had a plain yogurt with some lettuce. I had eaten no breakfast. For dinner we went to the Farm Shop. There I had a Peach Salad Delight. That is a plate which has lettuce and 2 peach halves—2 small type scoops of cottage cheese and 2 slices tomato. Vickie on the other hand ate the Fruit Salad with cottage cheese and sherbet. That is a plate which consists of lettuce, no tomatoes, grapefruit sections, orange sections with some pineapple pieces, a small scoop cottage cheese and a scoop of any flavor sherbet. Vickie picked out lime sherbet.

If you were to compare both of these dinners which would be lower in fat? calories? Then . . . get this, we walked home . . . and then around 3:30 . . . went back to the Farm Shop 'cause we had to get out of the house. Well . . . we had a cup of plain tea, then decided we'd have an ice cream cone.

Oh! I was so hesitant about it but I had a vanilla ice-cream in a waffle cone and Vickie had a triple sherbet in a waffle cone—orange, raspberry and lemon sherbets mixed together.

You wouldn't believe what a pig I felt like after eating it. I felt like killing myself! The reason I chose ice cream was because I thought sherbet was higher in calories, right?

Does sherbet have any fat? You see after eating that it was around 4:30 and all we did was walk home and stay in our rooms and study. Now, with what I ate, and with what activity I did, I must of gained weight, right? Oh! I'm so worried 'cause I had so much to eat and a high fat intake!

I don't know why I feel the way I do! That's where I need help I think!

In family therapy, the girls and their parents finally began to work on the important issues of sameness and difference. The therapist thought it necessary for the twins to be temporarily separated, and sent Vickie off to summer camp for four weeks, where she gradually made friends and, for the first time, met a boy she liked. Skinny Marilyn panicked. She could no longer monitor her sister's weight, could no longer have an accomplice at her side with whom to defy the world, could no longer see this inflated mirror image of herself, and now had to depend more on her other siblings, parents, therapist, and herself.

After Vickie returned, and three additional months of family therapy, Marilyn's weight began gradually to increase. Vickie was more secure and no longer felt the need to be fatter in order to be different. The twins were now only 26 pounds apart, the heavier one becoming thinner and the thinner one becoming heavier. However, Marilyn was now extremely depressed at losing her skinny edge. She showed her therapist this note:

> Dear God,
> It seems as if you're the only one I can talk to right now. I need your help. I'm depressed, so depressed I want to kill myself—hurt myself in some way. I hate myself. It seems the thing which I was afraid of has happened.
> I'm now fat—the other extreme now. I've gained 15 lbs.!
> I exercise and really try to cut down my total intake but I gain. Something's wrong. I'm ugly—not ugly skinny any more, now I'm *ugly fat*. I don't think I'll ever be in between. I've seemed to have lost all bodily control.
> I'm disgusted with myself, my body. I look just like Vickie now. That's the most terrifying thing about it. That's what I didn't want. . . . I have to fulfill my goal of always weighing less than my sister.
> Please, what should I do? I guess suicide is not the answer. I guess I should confront my problem, face it, work it out somehow.
> Help! I'm desperate.

By December, Marilyn, through her messages to God, could openly express her rage at Vickie for breaking their solemn pact. Marilyn was being forced to become an individual. Her crazy confusion about being exactly the same while being different was now challenged by the therapist. Marilyn became desperate and wrote the following letter:

> Christmas, 25 December
> God,
> I really don't know how to express myself right now—maybe the simplest word is very tense, sad, mad—
> *"frustrated"*
> I wish I were dead! Just wish I could die right now!
> It seems that Vickie really has changed! She's such a showoff.
> God, she thinks she's beautiful and thinks everybody around her loves her. I think she thinks she can get every guy around, but this is besides the real thing I'm mad at.
> *Her attitude* is the definite thing about her which has changed. She says to

me that I act like the kids at school. Me? Maybe I do but at least I'm damn near pigheaded enough to admit it.

Her? Admit that? Never! Never! She's too damn *proud!* I really shouldn't be mad at her. I suppose I can't blame her for being herself.

I guess I'm mad at me! I'm so *GOD DAMN FAT.* But I don't want to sound like I'm sorry for myself. Lord! I'm not.

I swear I just don't know what I am.

I'm confused I guess about everything.

I'm depressed about me!

I want to die!

Help me overcome my depression! It's Christmas. Why aren't I happy? My Lord?

Marilyn did not kill herself. She gradually accepted that she could be different from Vickie without being skinny. Within three months of this letter, Marilyn was up to 105 pounds and Vickie was down to 112. Marilyn became her class vice-president, joined the glee club, began making friends, and even found a boyfriend of her own. Vickie did equally well, but in different ways. Both sisters now ate the same food as their parents did, at the family dinner table. Fusion was no longer an advantage; it had become a developmental encumbrance. The sisters, while still problematic and in need of more supportive psychotherapy, were well on their way to leading separate lives. Their fusion and merging no longer existed.

Excessively attached children rarely manifest such a deadly linkage, but twin phenomena and excessive attachment can occur periodically or for a lifetime in siblings who are not twins. We will return to this issue in chapter 5, where we consider how profound loyalties develop.

Conclusion

By describing the process that began so early in life, we can see part of the foundation upon which siblings build their relations in middle childhood and adolescence. Attachment, developing object-relations, self-object differentiation, and the emergence of transitional objects are major and inevitable milestones in each child's psychological development. These are the precursors of the fascinating transactions between siblings as they struggle to claim separate identities. A sibling who has been a major player in the unfolding drama of a child's development, becomes represented as a object inside that child through the following *inclusive processes:*

incorporation, merging, twinning, and mirroring. Such inclusive processes involving a brother or a sister create feelings of closeness.

On the other hand, a sibling can be rejected through the following *defensive processes:* denial, projection, and projective identification.° When defensive processes involving a brother or a sister predominate, feelings of distance and alienation about the sibling are generated. Closeness lays the groundwork for later feelings of sameness, while distance creates later feelings of difference.

Given all the countless events that can determine how and when young siblings who are close in age, spend their time with each other, some combination of these inclusive and defensive processes is likely to have taken place. This mélange of processes accounts for much of their ambivalence toward each other. Since young siblings are psychologically immature and still developing, they will struggle with the important basic issues of being close or distant, accepting or rejecting, merging or separating, and feeling the same or different. Conflicts and dissatisfactions within the sibling relationship are bound to occur.

We are convinced that these issues are crucial to understanding the needs of the older or the younger member of any sibling pair. Identification and de-identification—processes that occur later in life and are more complex, conscious, and verbally accessible—may rest largely or entirely on this foundation of experiences early in life. When an adult says he or she "likes" or "dislikes" a brother or a sister, this is often just the tip of an iceberg, whose details are submerged in unconscious or preconscious experiences that the adult feels but cannot readily articulate.

° Projective identification is seeing in the other person those characteristics that one abhors in oneself (Klein et al. 1952), and that can flourish only in an ongoing relationship (Framo 1970; Boszormenyi-Nagy 1965; Slipp 1973; Wynne 1968). Young siblings offer one another a fertile field for this process. See chapter 9 for a further discussion of projective identification.

CHAPTER 3

Childhood and Adolescence:
The Struggle for
Separate Identities

There were Two Little Bears Who lived in a Wood,
And One of them was Bad and the other was Good
Good Bear learnt his Twice Times One—
But Bad Bear left all his buttons undone.

And then quite suddenly (just like Us)
One got Better and the other got Wuss.
Good Bear muddled his Twice Times Three—
But Bad Bear coughed in his hand-ker-chee!

There may be a Moral, though some say not;
I think there's a moral, though I don't know what.
But if one gets better, as the other gets wuss,
These Two Little Bears are just like Us.*

A. A. Milne

$\mathbf{T}$HE EVOLUTION of any sibling relationship is a continuous process, seldom resting on a foundation of only two to three years. Throughout all of childhood and adolescence, a complex interplay of psychological

---

* We should like to thank Edward Swain, who used to read this poem to his younger siblings, for reminding us that the major theme of this chapter had long ago been thought of by A. A. Milne.

48

forces is steadily growing within each child and within the family and contributes to the development of a sibling bond. Above all, the question Who will I become?, the search for a meaningful personal identity, emerges as the vital ground where brothers and sisters become significant to one another.

The need for such a close tie is often difficult for siblings to describe. Even though they may share a room, friends, and adventures throughout childhood, high-access, close-in-age siblings are often at a loss to understand the ambivalent and contradictory feelings they have toward one another. A woman groped for the right words about her older sister:

> I think if I answered quickly, I'd say that she's always been a real pain in the ass. I'm sorry that we gave each other so much trouble always. There were times when I wished I were an only child or that I had other siblings. But, at the same time, there's some kind of indescribable closeness between us. It doesn't just come from her sharing things with me from childhood on. It's some kind of a bond that's there. Maybe because, in my own loneliness, with the distance I created, she was the one who was in closest proximity to me. I don't know, but there's an attachment that will always be there. No matter how many fights we had as kids, I think we'll always keep getting back to each other. So, I'd have to say I'm not sorry that she's my sister. And I'm not wishing that she'll stay on the West Coast forever either. I think of her fondly when I'm not in the same room with her. I wonder about her, and I worry about her. I guess I'm really glad that she's my sister, even though, at times, I *could wring her neck.*

As the matter of identity attains increasing importance for the growing children, they look to their intimate family members for confirmation or disconfirmation of their personal worth and sense of esteem. By the fourth and fifth years, a child's capacity to identify himself or herself as similar to, or different from, mother, father, and siblings becomes a sharp force, a growing edge. This discovery of new aspects about oneself is an ongoing process, a dialectical dance, with these close, available, significant others. The quest for a secure identity is achieved only by asking, "Who are you to me?", "Why should I be with you?", and "What do we have in common?" A brother and a sister, up close, at the same table, in the next room, or away at school, becomes an object for more conscious comparison and identification than had been possible in the first years of life.

Yet brothers and sisters do not sit around and ask each other existentially loaded questions during their childhood. They fight over toys, go to school, run separately to Mommy or Daddy if they are hurt, sit quietly next to each other watching television, play games together, and feel resentment if one gets some privilege or extra edge over the other. If children have high access to each other, the bond between them grows inexorably and surely. The quality of that relationship will be deeply affected by the parents, but it is left increasingly to each sibling to determine the final shape of the relationship—although no word may ever pass between the children about their feelings. By school age (assuming that there are other children to play with in the neighborhood), siblings begin to have a much freer choice over whether they will be with each other and over the nature of their transactions. Out of the growing desire to matter, to feel separate and unique, and yet also to feel close and similar to others, each brother and sister continually propels himself or herself in and out of the sibling relationship(s). Mothers and fathers dictate ever less whom the objects of identification for each child will be. By adolescence the child has become more in charge of the unfolding of these intricate processes that determine identity.

Sibling Twosomes

Siblings appear to organize themselves into emotionally significant pairs, which can be either negative or positive, in the service of either love or hate. Each sibling appears to obtain more pain or more pleasure from one sibling to the exclusion of other children in a family. Whether siblings have been pushed together to be friends, are born close in age, are conveniently paired in a bedroom, or have complete freedom of choice in playing together, they tend to form these dyadic bonds of love, hate, or misunderstanding, through their own actions and reactions, identification, and lack of identification. A young woman in college recalled:

> We always stayed close because we used to like to do things like sleep out in a tent, or go sledding, just horse around together. You couldn't horse around with my sister, but you certainly could with my brother.

Yet, even when there are such feelings of affinity, events may weaken, rather than strengthen, the bond. This same student told us:

Until he got to be about fourteen, we spent all our time together. Wherever he went, I went, but then he stopped being interested in spending time with his little sister, and my mother wouldn't let me tag
along because he was going places I was too young to go. She felt that
he shouldn't have the responsibility of me tagging along. I really felt
sad about that and for the next few years really didn't go many
places on my own.

When close siblings grow to maturity and leave home, they often sadly
realize that their twosome will never be so close again. A brother, older
than his sister by two years, found himself weeping suddenly and uncon-
solably at her wedding. He was about to leave his family home for the
first time, to attend an out-of-state graduate school; and, although a much
younger sibling had already left home, it was this sister's marriage that
jolted him into realizing that he and she were now, perhaps forever, going
separate ways. The sister's wedding, with its message that he and she
could never again be the "pals" they had been since childhood, inspired
his tears and brought home to him the sense of passing years.

As each child becomes an adolescent, the opportunities for identification with *one* other bonded sibling seem to increase. There is no neutrality or indifference in this sibling world; a particular sibling is the one who
really "counts." In families where there are three children, two always
seem more intensely involved with each other, leaving the third odd man
out. Four-children families often form into two pairs of dyads, and five-
children families again leave a fifth to find his or her identity, without the
aid of a meaningful sibling connection. Even when there is even age spacing and high access (for example, three children aged thirteen, fourteen,
and fifteen), and a middle child can identify and form close bonds with
both the older and the younger siblings, one sibling always seems more
important to him or her than the other does. One sibling is always more
prominent, eliciting passionate feelings of hate or love; rarely are such
feelings distributed evenly. This finding, which emphasizes the importance of sibling pairs, is consistent with the dyadic theories of attachment,
object relations, and the social psychology of love. In addition, systems
theorists who have examined coalitions and alliances between three people attest to the inherent instability of a triadic system (Framo 1972; Caplow 1968). Two people will inevitably seek closeness, even fusion, leaving
the third person to fend for himself or herself.°

° Jay Haley (1979) has observed that a child who has no coalition partner, often becomes
a helpless victim of the coalitions between other family members. A family therapist can
offset such an imbalance by joining with the isolated child.

THE SIBLING BOND

*Yardsticks and Social Comparison: The Looking-Glass Self**

What factors in personality attract siblings to one another or repel them apart? A child's identity or sense of self is certainly influenced by conspicuous characteristics such as gender, age, intelligence, physical appearance, abilities, health, or emotional strengths and weaknesses. In the struggle to develop a self-concept, one always looks to a sibling close in age and compares oneself with his fellow traveler in life's voyage. Whether he or she is tall or short, beautiful or ugly, artist or scientist, genius or clod, confident or confused, these socially appraised attributes all help to determine how siblings identify with each other. The child's self-concept becomes organized according to such basic terms as "bad boy," "good girl," "smart," "dumb," "weak," or "strong," which are enhanced by family members who praise, condemn, project, idealize, and displace onto the youngster their *image* of him or her.

Set against the backdrop of parental ideals, wishes, values, and projections, young siblings begin to "eyeball" each other for those attributes that are desirable or undesirable. Individually, each child pays close attention to the characteristics in oneself or one's sibs that the parents might find especially endearing. Silently but progressively, each child struggles with whether he or she will become like a closely connected sibling, and thus gradually solidifies personal identity.

A man, with a brother fourteen months older, described this sibling social comparison process as it occurred during their young years:

> The vivid contrast was that at one end of the table there would be my brother, and at the other end was me, and he would rebel every time that he was told he was not eating properly or his manners were terrible or that he needed his hair cut. What I would usually do is obey them, whereas he had a rebellious sort of spirit. I knew what I shouldn't do by watching my brother.

What an advantage this younger brother had, observing how his brother was testing the parental limits and, in this family, *failing* at it. By adolescence, these brothers were on different trajectories—the older, rebellious, recalcitrant, and ever defiant, headed for difficulty; the younger, studious, sensitive, "always a good boy," who knew that to be like his brother was to court parental rebuke. *Not* to be like his brother seemed to

---

* Many of the concepts of social psychology are based on the premise that the individual can only define his or her identity through comparison with other people (Cooley 1922; Mead 1956; Sullivan 1953; Festinger 1957; and S. Schacter 1951).

be then, and seems even now, thirty-five years later, the correct instinct to follow.

PHYSICAL COMPARISONS

Obvious physical characteristics in children are among the first criteria by which siblings are attracted or repelled. Beautiful children engender admiration in and imitation by their sibs, but they can also become a source of envy, jealousy, and rivalry. Two children who are equally attractive in everyone's eyes, might enjoy their sameness but will also attempt to differentiate in some area—agility, poise, brains, charm, athletics, anything to secure the sense of a separate and valued identity.

Two sisters, both stunningly attractive in their different ways, and known as avid and excellent tennis players, seemed poised and self-assured. Yet they had resented each other as children, and their supposed differences were shallow. The younger sister said that the older one had always seemed like a china doll in childhood, and that, from then on, she, the younger, had determined to be different. On the other hand, she "resented" the older's preferred style of establishing her own worth through being "bossy":

> My sister and I are still opposites. I was more of a tomboy and she was
> more of a fragile little doll. You could sit her down and two hours
> later her clothes would be just as neat as before. She also became very
> bossy and temperamental, and I was very headstrong and didn't like
> to be bossed, even by parents. When my *sister* started bossing, *that*
> was too much to take.

This sister created an arbitrary distinction out of her need to be different. But when a sibling's physical characteristics are *clearly* not desirable, as in cases of mental retardation, the differentiation can be more extreme and the feelings more conflicted between the siblings.

By late adolescence, the process of becoming different usually prevents one child from experiencing overwhelming fears of being the same as a relatively disturbed sibling. Yet having the sense of a normal identity does not always sit easily with the more advantaged child.

The following excerpt from an interview with a normal twenty-one-year-old sister of a twenty-year-old mentally retarded brother illustrates how an early fear of sameness based on physical similarity can linger in spite of many obvious differences:

INTERVIEWER: What kinds of similarities are there between you and your brother?

SISTER: I find myself using a lot of the gestures he uses, and vice versa.

INTERVIEWER: Any other qualities?

SISTER: Certain facial expressions we have . . . I talk the same way he does a lot of the time, which bugs me because he doesn't talk very well. (*forced chuckle*) It bothers me sometimes.

INTERVIEWER: So when you hear him mumbling ——

SISTER: I hear myself mumbling.

INTERVIEWER: That distresses you?

SISTER: Yeah.

INTERVIEWER: What other similarities distress you?

SISTER: Well, we look similar. I mean, same complexion. We both have fairly light hair and are short and stocky.

INTERVIEWER: So, in other words, if people looked at you, they'd never know that your brother was retarded, and if they just saw you walking along, they couldn't see any difference in terms of intellect.

SISTER: Yeah and sometimes that *really* bothers me.

This sister, although confident that she is not retarded, nonetheless still irrationally worries that she is just like her brother. While being generous and nurturant to him, her excessively mature expressions of solicitude also represent her effort to be different. As an adolescent who is easily embarrassed by the physical similarity she has to her handicapped brother, she tries to make sure that no one else thinks that she is like him.

When the fear of similarity is too great, the abhorrent physical characteristics of a sibling can prompt the other sibs to name calling, derision, or hatred. Such a child may even receive a permanent and negative label from which there seems virtually no escape. As E. F. Vogel and N. W. Bell (1960) clearly indicated in their description of scapegoating, birth defects, extreme deviations from physical norms, and prominent facial features (such as "Big Ears" or "the Hook") can all launch a young child's identity in ways that may take a lifetime to alter. A thirty-three-year-old man wept at the memory of being called "the Hulk" when he was nine years old. A large and clumsy child, he was given this degrading label by his older brothers who scorned and avoided him, his clumsiness contrasting with their physical agility. By becoming physically powerful, over-aggressive, and a school bully, he simultaneously defended against, and attempted to live up to, this perverse identity imposed on him. As an adult, he continued to provoke fights, and boasted of his ability to "toss people around." No protection or alternative identity was offered by his parents. Thus, this awkward child had become a grown man who was fearful of his angry impulses, afraid he would lapse into "total rage," and yet—for want of an appropriate alternative—still clung to a pathetic macho identity. His tendency to exaggerate his differences fulfilled his need for a separate identity. His brothers' wish to deny that they were like "the Hulk" found a ready target in this needy younger brother who had accepted their projections.

BIRTH ORDER AND COMPARISONS

The most obvious consequence of birth order is that older siblings are larger than the younger ones. Larger size begets privilege ("Oldest first!") and power ("I'll get you"). But birth-order data clearly indicate that the complexities of being an older or a younger need to be understood over a lifetime of events. Being bigger and stronger at the start of life hardly means that one will always have that advantage. The power tactics that first-born children often use to dominate their younger sibs—such as hitting, reprimanding, teasing, ignoring (Sutton-Smith and Rosenberg 1970)—are, in our view, used primarily in the service of differentiation. Such birth-order attributes have value, not necessarily because they endure over a lifetime,° but because they allow children to feel different from, and often superior to, their siblings at a point in development when this urge for a separate identity is paramount. A younger sister illustrates this point:

SISTER: I used to beat up my sister even though she was three years older. She'd run into the bathroom and yell, "You think you're hurting me! Well, you're not!" And she'd slam the door and cry. [*Laughs*]

INTERVIEWER: What did it mean to you that you were able to do this to your older sister?

SISTER: I felt like a big shot, cause I was the littlest. I figured I had one mother and one father and I didn't need another mother. It just made me feel *really big* that I could outsmart and be tougher than someone I didn't get along with 'cause she represented everything that I didn't want to be. She would spend time putting make-up on me, and she would want to do me up like a ballerina, but I'd want to be made up like Spock, who was my childhood hero.

° Such displays of power do not necessarily become central features of the adult sibling's personality. For example, domineering older brothers in childhood do not simply become "authority figures" as adults; but, if they have tasted great satisfaction in pushing around their younger sibs, they may, given the chance, try to duplicate that enjoyment with other people.

Ah! what triumph, and how it felt special to "one-up" this bigger, older sibling.

PARENTAL INFLUENCES

We have purposely overlooked parents in our picture of childhood and adolescence until now, partly for clarity, and partly because parents organize the sibling game in powerful but *indirect* ways. Mothers and fathers are like a good set of baseball managers, responsible for getting the entire team onto the field by game time, and determining who will play (how many kids there will be). But once everyone is assembled, parents apparently allow chance, birth order, sex, and size to determine who will play what position—and thus may well wind up with three very competitive first-basemen, all wondering, "Who's on first?"

Except for vague directions (such as "Don't fight," "Protect your sister," "Share your toys"), most parents do not teach their children specific strategies for conducting themselves as siblings. What prepares a child for being a sibling? At best, children are cultivated by parents to have separate personalities, but left to their own devices to figure out the sibling relationship. There are, however, several prominent ways the relationship is influenced through the parents.

All family members are affected by what Murray Bowen has called the multigenerational family influence (1966). Key, emotionally charged events of earlier times are passed down from one generation to the next, sometimes in the form of a faithfully communicated oral history; at other times, hinted at but left unspoken. This legacy shapes and alters the ways individuals become intimate with each other. The sibling legacy is no different. Most parents are siblings and marry someone who is a sibling.[*] Children grow up not only knowing their aunts and uncles but also hearing about all their sibling events of the past: the time Dad and his brother had that exciting trip together, how Mom and her sister always fought, how Dad and his sister pulled that great stunt on their parents. But children rarely compare either past or current events, involving parents and aunts and uncles, with what is going on at the moment with their own brothers and sisters. The important thing is that parents, influenced by their own past sibling transactions, either assume them to be desirable for their own children or avoid them, hoping to spare their children from similar sibling "trauma." Some common examples we have encountered are:

[*] See Walter Toman's *Family Constellation* (1976) for a theoretical description of how people relate to each other, in marriage as a result of their birth-order positions in a family.

56

- A father was always brutalized by his older brother. Now, he vows that both his sons will always be able to hold their own against each other and provides karate lessons for both.
- A mother always "got along" with her two sibs—in a home where conflict was always avoided, where "peace at any price" was the rule. Now, when her son and daughter squabble, she becomes confused and tells them to "make up, no matter what," and is helpless to arrange a satisfactory means of conflict resolution which deals with the cause of the conflict.
- A brother always had to provide care for his depressed and physically disabled older sister. He derived some satisfaction from caring for her but felt drained and stifled by his "too good" role. Now he encourages his children to engage in rough-and-tumble play, and delights in their healthy expression of their impulses.

In addition, each child receives a share of parental projections, unresolved feelings, ideals, wishes, and hopes. Certain sibling relationships, like the three first-basemen, are an outcome of too many children being chosen to be the same person or of their clashing competitively with each other for parental favor over similar traits. Or, the cultivation of a certain characteristic in one child may intrude on the possibilities of personality development that that child's siblings might otherwise enjoy. Such parents may hope that one of their children will become a virtuoso pianist, and will then expect the others to become something else. For parents to cultivate a single characteristic in one child leaves the siblings with various other aspirations: some of these may be equally desirable (for example, lawyer), but others may be invidious (for example, family clown).

If the characteristics of any one child are continually overvalued by parents, sibling resentment often develops. We will deal with this important topic extensively in our chapter on rivalry and aggression (chapter 8), but it is important to state here that parental devaluation and overvaluation is an all-important fuel of sibling interaction. One young man we interviewed recalled with a poignant note in his voice:

I also went through a thing where I can remember my mother saying when we would be alone, "I love you best." Well, it wasn't till years later that I was having a fight with my sister, and I remember saying, "Well, Mom says she loves me best." And then a few years later, my sister saying, "Well, you know, she said the same thing to me!" And my brother said she told him the same thing, but Mother doesn't remember saying it at all to any of us. [*Laughs uncomfortably*] I can still remember the shock of thinking that I was not the favorite!

When children are not locked into inflexible roles, the family becomes alive and exciting. The "I want to do this too," "I don't want to do what you want to do" dance keeps everyone on his or her toes. On the other hand, parental wishes and expectations can be oppressive to a child, binding and limiting his or her identity and having an impact on the sibling bond. For example:

> I was supposed to be demure and unassuming and do well in school. Although my nature was to be a little cynical and sarcastic, I couldn't be these things, because they were unfeminine, so I kept it all inside. Everyone thought I was really easygoing and nice, but inside of me I was about ready to burst.

It should come as no surprise that this sister became harsh, ill-tempered, and judgmental in her relationship with her two siblings. She had nowhere else to release her tension.

Donald R. Irish has said that the large family system of many children is more conducive to a multiplicity of sibling role options. Among the traits he lists as developing in this best of sibling worlds are "intimacy, frankness, informality, cohesiveness, intensity, caretaking, companionship, and conflict resolution" (1964, p. 282). What Irish has not stressed are the painful scenarios of sibship. When parents overemphasize success, rivalry is often the sibling fallout. Parental dislike of one child may alienate the siblings from that child, and they may show their resentment, in spiteful and angry ways, of a child who is favored by a parent.

That parents help orchestrate the sibling relationship is not to say that fathers and mothers have equal influence. Various investigators (for example, Clarke-Stewart 1978; R. Kahn 1981; Lytton 1979; Patterson 1980) suggest that mothers may have more direct influence, but that the presence of the father and the quality of his relationship with his wife determine in major ways how the mother deals with her children. Any direct programming of siblings seems to come mostly by way of the mother: that is, she tells the group of children what to do. Our observations are that children are directly influenced by their father's likes or dislikes of particular traits; but fathers—who are away most of the day at work and exhausted in the evening when they come home, or are physically absent because of divorce—usually leave it to their wives to conduct the cacophonous sibling orchestra.

But mothers often cannot do the job alone, and the children are driven together in the father's absence. Three siblings—two girls aged sixteen and eleven, and a boy, fourteen—illustrate how this sibling *enmeshment* can occur. Furious with their divorced father because he had remarried and only sporadically visited them, the two younger of these children reported:

BROTHER: I just can't say things to him like Margy [the older sister] can.

SISTER: I like to look at Margy when I'm talking to Dad.

THERAPIST: So you look at each other for support, strength, and ideas?

SISTER: It's like we're all thinking the same thing.

THERAPIST: Boy, your father is really scary to you. Maybe one day you'll see he's not that scary.

BROTHER: He is. Whenever we wanted to see him, he'd be busy, and when we grow up, *we'll* be busy and then he won't be able to see *us*.

Private and Public Worlds: Levels of Intimacy

Social psychologists who have attempted to understand identity (Hilgard 1944; Heider 1958; Miller 1963), have frequently stated that the interchanges between people crucially determine the answer to the question, Who am I? Two siblings, like any other intimates, reveal different aspects of themselves: some reveal their most intimate secrets, while others remain only superficially connected.

Various theorists have defined three levels of personality which we have found useful to describe the ways siblings reject or accept each other.°

THE CORE OF IDENTITY

The core of one's identity is what William James (1890) referred to as the "truest, strongest, deepest self." It is at the core that an individual experiences one's most central being, that part of the self that is essentially unchanging and that is maintained throughout life. This core self begins to develop early in life, is based on meaningful experiences with siblings and parents, and becomes a touchstone for who one is. The core of one's identity is sometimes valued, sometimes hated, but is rarely exposed to others, and then only to a very few. A sibling and, later, a spouse, a best friend, or a psychotherapist are usually the only ones ever trusted enough to be allowed a glimpse into the core of one's self. Although all parents might wish to peer deep into the inner recesses of their children's minds, children, as we know, often hide their true feelings from their parents. A brother or a sister is much more likely to know one in this most basic sense.

° We are particularly grateful to Daniel Miller for his excellent article "The Study of Social Relationships: Situation, Identity, and Social Interaction" (1963), which helped illuminate some of these important theoretical issues.

Even though by adulthood most siblings have gradually separated and gone their different ways, the knowledge of each other's core identity remains as a legacy and a reminder of one's childhood past, submerged, unverbalized, and only partially forgotten. To meet one's brother or sister, even after many years, is to recapture the bittersweet memory of one's own essential childhood self, unmoved by the passage of time. Arthur Miller put it succinctly at the conclusion of his sibling drama, *The Price* (1969). In the play, two long-separated brothers meet and attempt to decide how they should dispose of the estate of their recently deceased father. Although Miller tells nothing of their early childhood years, the brothers now appear different: one is educated, affluent, self-indulgent, a physician; the other is undereducated, poor, self-sacrificing, a policeman. The self-indulgent, professionally successful brother, Walter, says to Vic, the brother who gave up his chance for a brilliant, scientific career to take care of their father:

WALTER: You could see why I said before . . . it struck me so that we . . . we're brothers. It was only two seemingly different roads out of the same trap. It's almost as though . . . [*he smiles warmly, uncertain still*]—we're like two halves of the same guy. As though we can't quite move ahead—alone. You ever feel that way? . . . [*Vic is silent*] Vic?

Victor answers him:

VICTOR: Walter, I'll tell you—there are days when I can't remember what I've got against you. [*He laughs emptily in suffering.*] It hangs in me like a rock. . . . And you can go crazy trying to figure it out when all the reasons disappear—when you can't even hate any more. (1969, p. 91)

In a primitive, intuitive way, Walter and Vic know each other's core self. The thrust of their entire adult lives depends on their earlier experiences with one another. The sibling bond is often experienced like this— viscerally, forcefully, without conscious understanding, but with a sixth sense that this relationship is a vital key to one's own knowledge of oneself. One's core self, seen through the eyes of a sibling, or *compared* with that of a sibling, remains as one essential reference point for personal identity. Because no words can ever capture these impressions, sibling conflict at the core remains the most difficult to resolve.

Childhood and Adolescence

THE SUBIDENTITY LEVEL

At the subidentity level are those part aspects of the total self that, less central than one's core identity, are nonetheless important: for example, "I am an athlete [New Yorker, student, musician]." Developed generally in late childhood and adolescence, subidentities are not necessarily crucial to the basic sense of who one is. They can be altered, disregarded, re-engineered, and presented more publicly than can the core identity. A brother or a sister may know a sibling only at the subidentity level, particularly if there is low access, or if they develop different interests. Much of the interaction between siblings in adolescence occurs at this more obvious, subidentity level, since each child is not certain how much of his or her core self should be revealed to a sibling. The conflicts between adolescent siblings often stem from misunderstanding each other's core issues, while communicating only on subidentity levels. In a family referred to us because of sibling "conflict," the sixteen-year-old brother practiced his saxophone loudly two hours a day, secretly fancying that he might one day become a free-spirited jazz musician and in this way express his core identity. His sister screamed that he was inconsiderate, and that his practicing made it impossible for her to study for a test. Inwardly, she worried that she did not have sufficiently high intelligence to get into a good college, a reflection of her core identity of "the dumb baby." Neither sibling realized the significance of each other's actions; neither articulated why each of their activities was personally so important. They only recognized and related to the other sibling's subidentity, the conspicuous behavior.

Siblings can, of course, be compatible at subidentity levels and maintain a cordial relationship, while their core sense of who each is may seriously conflict only when a crisis affects their lives.

THE PERSONA

Persona is Jung's (1953) well-known term for the publicly presented self, the mask that one creates to hide behind. As pointed out by Erving Goffman (1973), everyone learns how to dramatize and perform in order to create impressions in the eyes of onlookers. While young siblings in early childhood seldom attempt to present a persona to one another, by late childhood and adolescence, a brother or a sister is often the first audience upon which any child will practice this dramatization of self. Siblings often see through such efforts and, if they continue, will challenge each other. Such comments as "Stop acting so stuck up," "You think you're so smart," and "Don't make out like you're Miss Goody Two

Shoes" and the general intolerance of "phoniness" which siblings display toward one another, grow out of each sibling's awareness of what the other is *really* like.

If persona is used by a child to get in the better graces of a parent, a sibling will tend to feel resentful, especially if he or she knows something unflattering about the sib's subidentity or core identity of which the parents might not be aware. By adolescence, siblings often feel peeved, annoyed, insulted, or angry if one sibling insists upon "putting on airs." The expectation among siblings seems to be "If we're going to be close, be real. If you insist on pretending, I'll have very little to do with you." It is precisely because they have a life-long awareness of each other's core identity that siblings are often wary of one another. A sibling has the power to unmask another sibling in public. If the elaboration of self to create an impression has become a dominant feature of a sibling's personality, the other sibling who knows his or her brother or sister from childhood always has leverage to use or abuse, and can let the world know, in ways that parents seldom exercise, what that sibling is truly like. When such superficial masks are worn by adult siblings, they will seldom feel intimate, trusting, and friendly with one another.

How Siblings' Personalities Fit: Complementarity

By describing levels of the self, we draw an important step closer to understanding the impact of siblings upon one another. For two siblings to develop a uniformly positive and mutual identification with one another, there needs to be, during childhood, a relatively uninterrupted, harmonious match at all three levels of personality—core, subidentity, and persona. Thus, at the core level, one child's friendliness and openness must be matched by the other's good-natured acceptance and basic gregariousness. At the level of subidentity, a brother's daily feats as a baseball player have to be matched by his sister's tolerance for his noise and excitement and her own noninterfering demands for an equal share of their parents' resources. Finally, at the level of persona, each child must find satisfactions in the other's day-to-day "style" of relating.

As children mature into adolescence, the matter of how they continue to conduct their relationship will further determine patterns of identification and their attraction and repulsion.* This behavior will be reflected in

* Zick Rubin (1980) has considered many of these same issues in his studies of children's friendships.

four areas of interpersonal experience, all of which need to be studied if one is to understand the nature of the sibling bond: their need for human contact and intimacy, their personal interaction, day-to-day activities, the complementarity of their roles, and their personal values. A positive bond with a sibling will prevail only if each child feels relatively satisfied with a brother or a sister in all four of these areas, and when each sibling strives for balance in the relationship.

When siblings do not meet each other's needs, when they only minimally interact, find conflict in their roles, and experience little harmony in values, their relationship can only be sterile and empty. They will appear disengaged, and there will be little "glue" to hold such a relationship together. At best, such siblings will sporadically and feebly "irritate" each other. Once they are given the opportunity to separate in late adolescence, they will gladly do so, seldom recontacting one another and remaining strangers for life.

A "mixed pattern" is more representative of most siblings' relationships. Here, there is some fit and match, some meeting of needs, and some complementarity of roles, values, and identities. However, there is also frustration, confusion, ambivalence, and dissatisfaction. The relationship has its ups and downs, its low and high points. It is these mixed patterns, not the pure instances of complete harmony or total avoidance, that are the most difficult to describe. The mixed patterns are the ones that we have had to struggle with the most when attempting to understand sibling relationships, and are best captured through the special investigatory tools of the clinician. The methodologies of social psychologists usually tap only the level of persona or generate socially desirable responses to questions about the sibling relationship. Only when the core and subidentity elements of individuals are studied in depth, over time, and in sharp focus, can the mixed pattern of sibling relationships be adequately described and understood. How and why core and subidentities match or do not match is often the essence of this complex relationship.

The Impact of Change and Identification between Siblings

In general, how durable or lasting are the identification patterns between siblings during the changing years of childhood and adolescence? And if one child seems to change slightly or dramatically, how might this change affect the sibling relationship? Middle childhood (ages 6–9) is generally the most uneventful period in the sibling connection of any child. Short of catastrophic change in a brother or a sister due to a physical illness or emotional upheaval, siblings in middle childhood and pre-adolescence seem to live with the illusion that their relationship will never change. Whether funfilled or unhappy, this relationship usually provides continuity, stability, and familiarity, even if other relationships in the family system are transformed. For example, many young siblings whose parents have decided to divorce, rely heavily upon one another. Afraid of taking opposite sides in a marital war, younger sibs tend to clump together in a spirit of mutual protection as contention between the parents escalates. The parents' hope during divorce that "at least the kids will have each other" seems to be borne out by the children who help create the illusion that they are close by playing and sticking together. In many other situations where the parental system cracks, siblings turn to each other for the sense that nothing has changed and that each needs the other. Fulfillment of the need for object constancy in any form, is, after all, a driving force throughout the life cycle. Furthermore, lacking a sophisticated language, children cannot get rid of unhappy feelings about their sibling relationship through convincing arguments of hate or vindictiveness. Pre-adolescent siblings exchange words about parents and peers, about property and personal rights, about the nature of school and the world, but not about what each of them really means to one another. Pre-adolescent children exchange few comments about the real nature of their relationship. They not only lack the language but have not achieved a sufficient sense of separateness to view the other siblings in a realistic way. Child siblings may insult each other but rarely sever the relationship with as sharp a tongue as older siblings are capable of doing. For all these reasons, one's sibling during childhood is likely to be seen as unchanging.

SMOOTH AND SUDDEN CHANGES: ADOLESCENCE

With the start of adolescence, the sibling relationship is much more likely to change. Adolescence is the quintessential period for change to occur as a result of both physiological development and shifting social opportunities (high school, new privileges, new responsibilities, and so on). Children usually want to modify their existing identity: they welcome becoming teen-agers, anticipating that something, somehow will feel different. If they cannot be aware of change through inner psychological transformation, as Holden Caulfield does in J. D. Salinger's novel *Catcher in the Rye* (1951), adolescents may seek acknowledgment that they are undergoing some metamorphosis by reliance on, or stimulation from, the world outside themselves. They will take risks, dress differently, travel, and possibly experiment with drugs or break the law. One teen-ager we saw had recently become a "punk-rocker." Her streaked hair, black fingernails, and somber clothes testified to how much she wanted others to know she had changed. With any marked change in a sibling, a brother or a sister tends to experience a sense of loss; if the sibling has become "different," the two of them will no longer be able to play or talk together in the same old ways. Although change is not necessarily as dramatic as in some of the cases we will describe later, one of two siblings can experience discontinuity in the relationship when the other changes sharply, wordlessly, and with a poignancy never totally assuaged by parental reassurance.

Change can occur in continuous and discontinuous ways (Watzlawick, Weakland, and Fisch 1974). Continuous change does not alter the fundamental nature of the sibling relationship: each child grows and develops so smoothly, no one in the family experiences a severe loss. Only the glimpse of a photograph or the sudden realization that each child is bigger or stronger imparts the sense that time has moved on. Discontinuous change, however, does alter the relationship and often creates a sense that a brother or a sister has become radically different. When the changes in both a child and his or her sibling relationship are continuous, the siblings can keep an even pace with each other. Parents can help make change continuous by pointing out the ripples and nuances of development to each of their children. But when change is discontinuous, one child will leap ahead and become so different that the sibling relationship will be fundamentally, and perhaps irrevocably, altered. Whatever the reason, every adolescent is bound to change. Each child can either undergo this change easily, joyously, and with the support and encouragement of brothers and sisters, or may have to change compulsively, rigidly, or even with an overdetermined sense of desperation that alarms or immobilizes all the other family members. Those adolescents who go to ingenious lengths to proclaim their need to become different often do so out of the fear that, unlike their peers, they are not maturing or changing fast enough. Such diverse problems as alcohol and drug abuse, juvenile delinquency, and suicidal behavior can sometimes be interpreted as frantic manifestations of the adolescent's demand that important family members, including siblings, acknowledge that change has occurred.

Most groups, whether they be artificial or natural, such as families, are inherently conservative in terms of accepting change in the perceived identities of their members. The greater the actual change in a child, the more likely it is that one close to that child will strongly resist acknowledging it. Not only siblings resist and resent change in a brother or sister.

Parents, too, as many family therapists know, resist the perception of change in their adolescent children, including the recognition that their child is now becoming old enough to leave home (Haley 1980).

Thus, the personality conflicts and observed changes in an adolescent require a capacity for tolerance, understanding, and mutuality on everyone's part, even though it may sometimes hurt (H. Rosenblatt 1980). Too strong an imposition of a parent's or another sibling's needs (like fat Vickie and skinny Marilyn in the previous chapter) erodes the potential of the child to be able to understand and experience his or her own needs. A rigid imposition of roles and identities, or having a family that is intensely enmeshed, makes it nearly impossible for an adolescent to change. The end result is that the child does not freely participate in the process that Gordon Allport (1955) once called "becoming."

At the middle ranges of the adolescent experience are those relatively mundane, everyday expressions of change difficult to define. When one of the children seems to act differently, the sibling who identifies with that child on a core level, must also examine whether he or she, too, has "changed." Any transformation in the perceived identity of any one child may pre-empt the possibility that these siblings can still behave together in ways that, for them, were once customary, rewarding, and familiar. Under such circumstances, one or both may have to stop and re-evaluate their relationship in order for it to continue.

When the Touchstone Changes: Sharon and Jonathan. Sharon was fifteen and a half years old, and her brother Jonathan was fourteen, at the time their family came in for therapy. As young children, Sharon and Jonathan had always played together and gotten along well. But now Jonathan changed radically: he smoked pot in the house, kept his room in total disarray, refused to do his school work, and—through "forgetting," falling asleep, refusing to speak when reprimanded, and looking perplexed—resisted the efforts of his parents to make him obey family rules. The family wondered whether this change in Jonathan was merely "adolescence" or something more serious.

The stepfather, a highly successful, extremely fair-minded banking executive, was provoked by Jonathan's cynical and hostile attitude; open warfare for control of the family's emotional thermostat prevailed. The stepfather tried to take the lead in the first family therapy session. Grinning with feigned nonchalance but pushing his glasses back and looking hard at his stepson, he drew himself up, then hunched forward in his chair and—inspired by that wonderful line of Spencer Tracy's—spat out, "You're going to listen, Jonathan, because I eat determination for breakfast.''° To this, Jonathan responded with silence and gave his usual limp and infuriatingly passive stare.

The mother, a soft-spoken survivor of a difficult childhood, identified with the "sensitivity" shown by her son Jonathan. She had divorced the children's biological father shortly after Jonathan's birth, and remarried two years later. The second marrriage seemed solid, and the parents respected each other for being sensitive and caring partners during the serious financial and emotional struggles of their first few years together. But the mother's empathy, concern, and preoccupation with her son seemed to have left her little energy for her quiet, unassuming daughter.

Jonathan's sister, Sharon, was a shy, retiring, typical "good" girl who had always listened to her parents and done well in school. She offered no assistance to her stepfather, mother, or brother in the first few family sessions and appeared "neutral," silent, and slightly uninterested. She gave no indication that she was identifying with her brother's turmoil or going through any adolescent transformation herself. On the surface she appeared calm. Now that they were both adolescents, Jonathan seldom wanted to do anything with his sister, although the parents recalled that they had seemed closer and mutually responsive as younger children. To her parents, Sharon still seemed to be the same sweet child she had always been; at least *she* had not changed. Yet seven weeks after family therapy began, the mother handed the therapist a copy of a poem Sharon had just written for her high school English class. A striking theme in this poem is the sister's sincere empathy and identification with, and concern for, her brother. Her silent identification with him as his sibling had given her a special window into his private world, beneath his "sandy cover" and "behind his doors," and had allowed her to begin expressing, through the experience of shared pain, her own newly developing identity as a maturing woman.

JONATHAN

He was older than I in mind.
Younger than I in heart.
He understood things that I would never understand.
But, could he feel for things in his heart?
He was like a Stone on a beach, one among many,
But he was different.
He shone in the sun.
People would come and admire him for his beauty.
But never touched him in his sandy cover.
I loved him.

°From the film *Guess Who's Coming to Dinner* (1969).

I often wondered if he loved me.
Behind his doors there was a small child crying.
No one could cross the wall of his guilt, pain, and sorrow.
In the dark of the night I cry for him.
I turn away from the pain in his eyes.
(His beautiful yearning eyes.)
I ask myself am I just like the rest?
One who shuts out the light of the sun?
Oh! How I want to help him!!!
I'm a woman with a heart.
And a child who can't reach the light.
One who tried and tried to reach the light.
Only a reach of the hand.
I wish I understood what goes through the tunnel that
leads to the complicated puzzle in a beautiful gold statue.

Because of the changes in her brother, and because she had so intensely identified with him, Sharon had become aware of her own adolescent transformation. Jonathan's struggles within himself and against the family had given Sharon a newly focused view of herself. Now that she was more aware of her own changes, she had extended a public invitation to therapist, brother, and parents to help her with her own struggle. She participated more actively, maturely, and verbally in therapy and began speaking to her brother at home, drawing him out of his shell to discuss with her their mutual problems. She felt close to him once more and could identify with the changes he was experiencing. For the first time in her life, she also began sharing some of her innermost concerns with her parents. She seemed infinitely more mature and more spontaneous than the good little girl who had passively accompanied her younger brother to therapy.

Perceptions of Sameness and Difference

Changes in a sibling have both objective and subjective reality. One can begin to act differently, think differently, and be acknowledged by many people for one's accomplishments—yet, for all of the reasons we have previously cited, may not be perceived by a sibling as having changed at all. Each child observes a sibling from a personal, subjective vantage point. The phenomena of merging, twinning, and mirroring of earlier days are in adolescence replaced with a much more elaborate, sophisticated process of social comparison, projection, and identification. As one's own self-image evolves, one comes to regard one's sibling as same or different, sometimes in some significant area for long periods of time, some-

Childhood and Adolescence

times ephemerally or barely noticeably. The "I'm like you" and "You're like me" attitude, if mutually conveyed in a positive way, will usually draw siblings closer together. If the sense of sameness is focused on some reviled characteristic, siblings will usually pull apart. Conversely, the "I'm not like you" can also either exert both a centripetal force, pulling sibs closer, or a centrifugal one, pushing them apart. For example, a child's recognition of difference, especially if he or she thinks a sibling has more advantages, can pull the child closer to that sibling in the hope that sameness will replace the sense of difference, that one might learn from the other sibling and become like him or her. The sense of difference can also push sibs away from one another—especially if one considers the other to be at a disadvantage—with the sense that "we have nothing in common."

Perceptions of sameness and difference are a major influence in sibling relationships, helping to draw siblings closer together or to push them farther apart at various times. Sameness creates feelings of closeness and patterns of affinity; difference creates feelings of distance and patterns of alienation. If identification is the inner glue of the sibling relationship, then issues of sameness and of change constitute the dimensions of the relationship. Identification will always be affected by perceptions of difference and sameness, while awareness of whether a sibling has changed will advance or interfere with this process. Since the most obvious form of change is developmental, one sibling's perception of a brother or a sister can be illustrated as their relationship unfolds over time. Using the previous example of Sharon and Jonathan, let us look at Sharon's changing identification with her brother (figure 3.1).

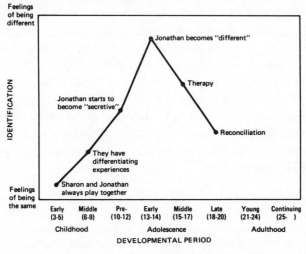

FIGURE 3.1
Sharon's Identification with Jonathan

To understand any sibling relationship, it is necessary to know how both siblings feel about one another. In the previous example, we knew how the sister felt toward her brother but very little about the brother's sibling bond. Another brother-sister pair provides a valuable reference point for understanding the type of interactive process that pairs of siblings in childhood and adolescence undergo.

Outmoded Memories and Developmental Change: Miriam and Joey. Miriam had been struggling for many years to straddle the fence of being her parents' "good" child and worrying about her brother, who still caused the family much heartache and concern. Younger than Joey by two and a half years, Miriam was left somewhat unprotected from her brother's intrusions when, as a very young child, their parents' marriage broke up. In the custody of their depressed mother, the children became attached to and, for Miriam in particular, very dependent on one another. Miriam became Joey's playmate but also bore the brunt of his teasing, baiting, ridicule, and contempt. She was an object toward whom the brother could direct his own anger and on whom he could project his feelings of helplessness. Miriam adored this brother, who could be vital, attentive, physically agile, and charming—when he was not causing her pain. As they grew older, a pattern developed in which Miriam idealized Joey, identified with him, and acted as his apologist and alter ego whenever he was in trouble. But after Miriam left home for boarding school and then college, she found herself missing Joey who had always given her a *raison d'être;* she felt guilty and worried constantly that, in leaving him, she had abandoned him to a less-than-happy fate. This fear was borne out initially by his psychiatric hospitalization, then his career problems, and finally his own marital conflicts.

At thirty-three, Miriam was successfully launched on her own career and marriage and saw Joey only on holidays and vacations. Although differentiated from him, once they were together for more than a few hours, Miriam would slowly slide into her old style of relating to her brother. She would let herself be mocked and ridiculed and would bury her resentment. She felt particularly chagrined at the realization that she and her brother were now so obviously different. During one of these reunions she wrote her therapist the following:

> I feel the loss of him and, now at least, I hate myself for harboring any fondness or tenderness for him, for bothering to feel any loss when he is so brutally uncaring. I feel like I have given so much for him and to him and like he's part of me—lodged in my heart, woven into me—and now he spits me out because he needs to, because it's convenient for him. The only way I think I could feel

Childhood and Adolescence

like somebody was to become a thing for Joey, especially not to be different from him. I got my identity by being used by Joey for his survival, but now I feel used and angry—angry at him; but even more angry at myself for allowing this to continue, allowing him to get to me the way he still can and does. Insulation. I need insulation, but what scares me is *how* to do it. I don't know how to keep him out, not to let him destroy me and make me feel so bad so easily. I no longer want to be a masochist or a knight in shining armor. But he gets to me still, and I can't keep him out. And there's this crazy feeling of not wanting to lose him, that he gave me something that I never want to lose. A simple renunciation won't do. Joey, after all, gave me my most human parts—an ability to feel for and with other people, a capacity to experience and appreciate intense feelings—joy, hatred, anger, acknowledgment of insides—that people have insides that count. And maybe even something about intimacy? No, my head tells me it can't be intimacy. Maybe caring, or company amid the terror we both experienced? I don't know. When I think about forsaking him or "betraying" him, I feel incredibly sad. And these are the words that come to mind when I think about prying myself loose from his grip.

Miriam's eloquent letter tells a great deal about the hardship that can result from a close identification with a sibling who has serious emotional difficulties. The development of Miriam's identity, once wound so tightly around the changes in her brother's life, now seems to activate an anachronistic, useless, and, even worse, self-destructive process from which she requires "insulation." Such patterns of sibling identification develop more elaborately than any that we have so far presented. The forging of separate identities is, after all, an ever-changing process for each individual; separate destinies and separate outcomes usually await each of the siblings.

Affected by continuous changes in both the entire family system and each person's life, siblings' feelings about one another can be similar or different. Each sibling interprets, in a unique way, who the other is. One may claim, "We have so much in common," while the other believes, "We have always been worlds apart." By showing how each sibling identifies with the other, we can see whether the feelings were one-sided or mutual and at what developmental stage they drew closer or grew farther apart.

Each line in figure 3.2 plots the changes in Miriam and Joey's patterns of identification with each other from early childhood to adulthood. At various points in their development, they have felt that they were similar to or different from one another. Miriam felt that she was like Joey in early childhood (almost total sameness) and gradually moved toward a permanent pattern of partial identification in which she could recognize

71

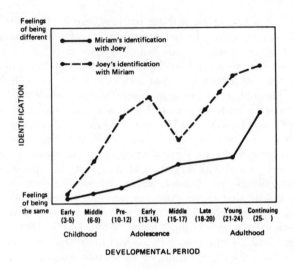

FIGURE 3.2
Feelings of Identification between Miriam and Joey

points of difference and sameness with him. Joey, on the other hand, felt that he was very different from Miriam after early childhood and, with the exception of middle adolescence, continued to feel this way as he became an adult. From the converging lines we can see that both sibs have had *similar* and *mutual* feelings toward one another *only* in their early childhood and middle adolescence. Overall, Miriam always felt more attachment, idealization, and positive patterns of identification with Joey than he felt toward her. Miriam is a typical younger sibling who has initially pursued and idealized her older sibling, while Joey has always been intolerant, evasive, and hostile toward his worshipful younger sister.

Figure 3.2 captures all three major aspects of the sibling identification process that we first illustrated for just one individual. Change and lack of change, sameness and difference, and chronological development (from early childhood to adulthood) become the ground upon which the sibling relationship is enacted. Now the patterns of affinity and reflection that mark the relationship can be more clearly seen. Feeling the same will create harmony; feeling different explains why any two siblings exhibit conflict at a particular time. Any sibling relationship, with some of its major variations over time, can, in this way, be more clearly delineated— although the possible varieties are endless.

Lack of Change

FROZEN IMAGES: LACK OF CHANGE

We have been emphasizing that change is an inevitable by-product of human development, and that a sibling relationship is bound to change. But some relationships have a "stuck" or static quality, and some seem to remain anchored in the past. No matter how much one or both siblings may attempt to change, the preceptions of one may "freeze," keeping the other sibling bound to an old identity—an indelible, irrevocable, unchanged and unchanging characterization of the self. Such a frozen image can be positive or negative, providing permanent opportunities for close or negative identification, or can serve as points for de-identification. The most extreme way a sibling's identity can become stuck is because of death. Idealization, as an example, will become frozen when an idolized sibling dies prematurely, aborting the natural tendency for this positive identification to wane gradually. In whatever way a dead sibling is remembered, whether with love or hate, the survivors seldom allow the image to melt so that it can be reshaped more realistically. (See chapter 10.)

Joseph Kennedy, the oldest son of former Ambassador Joseph P. Kennedy, was mythologized by his entire family after his death during a bombing mission in the Second World War (W. Adler 1980). The next younger Kennedy son, John, picked up the mantle of his fallen brother—a princely knight in shining armor—who became for John a standard for his own life, in which he fulfilled his father's ideal for his older brother, became President, and, in the process, came to his own tragic end. (This image of success served rather well in the case of the Kennedy brothers—not everyone can make it do so.)

On the other hand, a negative frozen image can provide survivor siblings with a smug self-certainty—that of having been powerful or charmed enough to have survived an oppressive brother or sister. By forever "pinning" the dead sibling to a perverse identity, survivor siblings can position themselves as well, can judge who they were when they were suffering the indignities of the sibling relationship of the past, and who they are now as they achieve ultimate triumph over their sibling.

The poet Tony Connor has captured the essence of a negative frozen image that a brother has maintained of his sister. In "My Sister's Papers" (1968), the poet expresses his reluctance to abandon the archaic perception of his sister who has hurt him, but yearns to escape the painful reminders of his own adolescent identity.

Her passport lies before me, open
at "that atrocious photograph."
It should be surrendered now she is dead.
But something makes me keep it; perhaps
I hope to see her face as she
saw it. To me the photograph
is a good likeness: cruel lips,
a gaze keen for fresh prey,
an arrogant smile. A good likeness
of her face at twenty, when last my sight
accepted her true image. Some
need of the heart cherishes wounds;
I would not see the changing woman
who visited home with smiles and presents.
She was still a selfish bitch, tolerated
for my mother's sake. What foolishness—
to make her pay for hurting me
by remaining the youth she hurt! Now
I study this recent photograph,
learning to hate it as she hated it.

Frozen images, positive or negative, created by death or prolonged geographical separation, are the most difficult to relinquish. Without the charged quality of vital interaction, images and identities reach a plateau, become stagnant, and blunt the possibilities for meaningful change.

FROZEN MISUNDERSTANDINGS

When we began interviewing adult brothers and sisters, we were struck by the disparity in some of their recollections of shared events. The frozen image of what the other sibling had been like in childhood was usually reinforced by memories of certain events, an understanding that was sometimes *stark, global, impressionistic,* and relatively *inarticulate.* Some siblings hang onto these remembrances of past events with a righteous insistence that "that's the way things were," no matter how much a brother or a sister insists on the opposite. These disparate recollections may well be at the root of some of the alienation certain adults feel from their sibs, and, in the consulting room, contributes to the conflicted, changing, fumbling descriptions of their backgrounds. Some of these sibs seem like two passengers on very different compartments of the same passenger liner. Two sisters told us:

OLDER SISTER: We used to play in the living room, and we had a great time. You always used to like to read to me, pretending you were my older sister. I can still remember how great those evenings were—just you and me without a worry in the world.

YOUNGER SISTER: That's odd. I can't remember that at all. The thing that stands out is how you could be so unbelievably cruel to me. Just when I thought I could depend on you and trust you, you'd turn the tables on me, complaining to Mom about something I did, or dropping me cold to go play with your friends.

Since the intellectual capacity of children is still unfolding, and since their ability to articulate their impressions is at an early stage of restricted development, these different views are not surprising. Unusual, however, are the adult siblings, with an enlarged capacity to re-evaluate past experience, who insistently hang on to these old impressions. We call these impressions "frozen misunderstandings"; and have observed that the more chaotic and unhappy siblings' homes have been, the more likely they are to maintain frozen misunderstandings and, consequently, frozen images of each other. It is as if, in a sea of uncertainty, *positive certainty* about *something* or *someone*—even about a negative person or thing—relieves tension, uncertainty, and anxiety. Finding serious deficiencies in either of the cherished and powerful parents' capacity to love, nurture, and protect is threatening to any child, whereas sizing up a sibling—one's peer and equally vulnerable—and deciding that he or she lacks positive traits, is far more manageable. To be certain in this way is a more palatable alternative; and, therefore, when we discovered such misunderstandings, they indeed seemed *frozen in place.*

Still the Same Brothers They Always Were: Billy and Russell, Delegates from the Past. Billy and Russell are two adult brothers who have maintained frozen images of each other. The surface rituals of helpfulness and brotherly concern that they exchange, have proved insufficient to sustain their being together. When in each other's company, core aspects of their identities slowly begin to dominate. The basic conflicts that riddled their relationship as children, have become frozen misunderstandings, continually coming back to life, corroding and contaminating any good feelings the brothers might otherwise enjoy.

During their childhood, these brothers had a great deal of access to one another. Children of a military family that moved frequently, theirs was an ambivalent relationship which often bordered on hostile dependence.

Once grown up, Billy and Russell had comparatively few significant encounters after leaving home. They were separated by a long distance, and their parents did not exert a warm pull to help them connect on holidays. Now, at ages thirty-two and twenty-nine, the brothers were temporarily living with one another. The older brother, Russell, had offered Billy the opportunity to move in with him after Billy's marriage had broken up. To help your brother when he is in trouble is, after all, the expected response. But the brothers soon began to clash with each other, first over petty matters and then in broader ways. Now that they were once again with each other, they found themselves drifting helplessly into the same quagmire that previously engulfed them. In spite of a mutual desire to be warm and giving and to create a new spirit, they resumed the pernicious struggle that had its origins in childhood.

By the time Billy moved in with his brother, he had come to view himself as a failure in his work, his marriage had collapsed, and he despaired of ever being accepted by his parents. Suicide was not out of the question. Billy had always been held in contempt by his perfectionistic martinet of a father. His earliest memories of rejection he attributed to having contracted spinal meningitis and having had to wear a back brace until he was twelve years old. He had also been shunned by the older Russell, who had formed a coalition with their father early in childhood and became the "favorite" son. Even after Billy recovered from his illness, was able to discard his brace, and attempted to compensate by becoming a good athlete, his brother and father scorned him. The mother was described by both of her sons as a loving, concerned, but somewhat insecure figure, living in the shadow of her husband. She was grateful to this man for having rescued her from the pervasive sadness of her family home, where she had experienced the tragic deaths of not one, but two sisters; one having died in infancy from influenza, the other in adolescence from an automobile accident. Although the mother had brothers, she did not feel particularly close to them and often felt lonely. She was easily captivated by her charming, dashing husband-to-be and later, as wife and mother, she always deferred to him. The sons came to expect that they could not rely on either of their parents. The father had to be avoided because he was much too harsh; the mother could not be depended on because she was much too soft. Even when the mother dared to express her opinions, the father overruled her and intimidated her into silence. Only when she drank could the mother ever muster her courage to confront her overbearing husband. The parents enjoyed their evening cocktails but, if they became too intoxicated, would begin to argue, then yell, and occasionally the boys thought they heard the sounds of slapping and hitting. It was at times like these that the frightened boys particularly perceived their parents as unreachable, undependable, and generally insensitive to their children. More often than not the brothers would retreat to their separate bedrooms, depressed and confused, and they spent many evenings alone and cut off from any other family member.

The mother was largely ineffective in monitoring her children's development, but she frequently pleaded for special tolerance for Billy. The father, however, set the rules for his sons and, while harsh and often arbitrary in his judgments, had a certain dash and charisma. For the boys, he was a much more powerful, however ambivalent, figure to identify with than was their weaker mother. The father detested any weakness or "softness" in himself or other family members. Billy's "defect" made him much more vulnerable to his father's projections and repressed rage. Without his brother and mother to help him, Billy could derive a sense of purpose and bitter satisfaction only from opposing and rejecting his father, showing him up, and later being contemptuous of everything he stood for. The sons—one the father's favorite, the other the father's misfortune—were identified as being so "different" from each other that they could only maintain a vigilant distance from one another. As is typical in any family in which identities are rigidly imposed, each was highly conscious of the threat that one might pose to the other at any given moment. Russell, the father's favorite son, feared that he might become weak, soft, or inadequate; while Billy, his mother's favorite, feared that he might become harsh, rigid, and unfeeling. As they grew up, Russell became a bright student, and it was only natural that he should attend the military academy; while Billy remained a flop and performed poorly in public school. In haunting ways that suggest failed dreams and bitter legacies, the family began to resemble the literary representation of Eugene O'Neill's own family, the Tyrones, in his autobiographical play *Long Day's Journey into Night* (1956).

Years later, Russell felt enormous guilt for helping to expose his younger brother to their father's rage. This residual guilt at having abandoned his "defective" brother in childhood prompted Russell to welcome Billy now that the latter was in serious trouble with no place to live. Russell had left the military and in this way was finally also beginning to fight his father's efforts to control the direction of his life. Russell now felt an affinity for his brother who had always resisted the father. But after a month of living together, the old family-dictated arrangement of childhood identities began to assert itself once again. Both brothers became burdened as they saw each other in the old, miserable ways that had always defined their identities in childhood. After three months, the younger brother, unable to tolerate these painful reminders, moved out and took an apartment of his own, still near his older brother. Needing distance but needing a connection with family, Billy could neither sever the relationship with his brother, nor bring himself to "forgive and forget" the old pain. His feelings poured forth at a therapy session with Russell's therapist:

BILLY: See, my Dad had great aspirations for all of us. He wanted Russell to be the youngest general in the army, and me, he hoped I'd fall off the edge of a cliff. [*Russell laughs*] He never appreciated me for what I was good at. You know, he thought Russell was the greatest thing because Russell was the 4.0 student in high school and went to West Point. [*Voice takes on slight sarcasm*] I was proud that my brother went to West Point and I told everybody about it. But I didn't like the idea that that was what my father wanted. On the other hand I became a good basketball player. When I graduated high school I was given a full scholarship by the university, and played on their team. I also had scholarship offers to lots of other colleges, but not a fucking word from him. Never—He never said, "that's really good." And I don't remember my father ever coming to one game. He never even said a word. Not one word, not even in the usual Christmas letter.

Even a successful subidentity didn't help Billy gain acceptance.

Later in the interview both brothers admitted their old disdain for each other:

RUSSELL: My memory of it is that we fought constantly and you were always trying to tag along with me and be with my friends. And that you were basically the "troublemaker."

BILLY: Well, I despised you because you were Dad's "right-hand man."

RUSSELL: Yeah, and I steered clear of Billy because it was guilt by association. I just steered clear of him as much as I could.

Core identity labels.

Billy carried an obsolete image of Russell, which he would not relinquish, as having been the father's favorite child, and accrued moral smugness from knowing his brother at this core level. Try as he might, Russell was still trapped in Billy's view of him as a sycophant to the powerful father:

BILLY: See that's what I didn't like and I still don't like the fact that this attitude is your schtick _____

RUSSELL: What do you mean, this is my schtick? [*Angry, defensive*] You keep talking to me like I'm Dad and I'm not Dad. I have changed.

Continued conflict at core level.

BILLY: [*Also angry, defensive*] That's exactly what this is all leading up to, that it's hard for me to not see you as Dad, because you were always Dad's pet. It wasn't, you know, "our son Billy," it was "our son, Russell." You know, "Russell is doing so good," "Russell this, and Russell that." I got so sick of it, and "Billy's a pathological liar"—that's what *I* used to hear. [*His tone calms*]

The deep schism in family-determined identities between Russell and Billy is still like a raw wound for the younger brother. Russell is his father incarnate, powerful, cruel, demanding, and unwilling to grant Billy parental largesse or the freedom to become a self-respecting person.

THERAPIST: He was the model?

Russell's persona was esteemed; Billy had none of any value.

BILLY: He was the model that I was supposed to follow, that's exactly right. In fact, I used to overhear my folks, when there was a cocktail party or something—I'd have the door open listening. "Oh, Russell, he's out at West Point while Billy's fucking around in the bathroom." [*Russell laughs*] That's exactly what it was—how would you feel if every time you turned around somebody was dropping a bomb on you?

THERAPIST: Wasn't there ever a way that Russell somehow let on that he didn't necessarily like being seen in this way? Because what I know about Russell is that he has his own bag of resentment and dissatisfaction about the family.

Keeping the core hidden.

BILLY: But I never saw that! He always kept things to himself.

THERAPIST: So where are you two guys now? Is he still projecting an image of a rigid authority figure to you?

BILLY: I do that. I project that image on him.

THERAPIST: How do you break out of that?

BILLY: I don't know. I don't know where to start. That's what we were talking about coming over here.

Now Russell's attempts to reach out to Billy are sporadic, oversolicitous, and forced. For his part, Billy refuses to budge from his own fixed perspective of himself as the identified "defective" and less-favored child. He is unwilling to accept the more emotional side of his brother. His own core identity of the "defective" gives him a moral leverage, a "one up" position of always being "one down."

RUSSELL: When I got back from this session, I was really emotional. And I went over to see him and [*speaking to Billy*] I put my arms around you and hugged you and told you I loved you. [*Starts to tear and his voice trembles*]

Billy rejects Russell's core feelings.

BILLY: That didn't bother me. It was the rest of what you were talking about and stuff that made me want to get out. [*Turns to therapist*] Just all the emotion that was coming out of him. I mean, he was standing in the office—crying and—he was telling me about this stuff and I just wanted to get out of there.

THERAPIST: Because you want to preserve a certain image of him?

BILLY: [*Pause*] I don't know. I'm not really sure. I just know that I didn't feel comfortable. I was embarrassed. I was with a guy who was crying and doing all this. I don't know.

THERAPIST: If he should change in any way that's different from the way you have conceived him to be, I'm wondering whether that would make you nervous—because it's akin to losing something. You can even hate somebody, but if they're of a known quantity, then you can position yourself against that person, and say, "Well, I know who that guy is, so then I know who I am."

Therapist probes the rigid ways identities are maintained.

BILLY: I understand.

THERAPIST: I felt that when he said that he had put his arms around you and that he loved you, he started to get emotional again. His face turned color and he looked a little bit misty-eyed to me. But then you said what you said and you closed his feeling right down again. Are you conscious of going through that cycle, Russell?

RUSSELL: Yes, I was.

The rigid identities remain fixed.

BILLY: I was conscious of it too. I knew what I was doing. I don't know why. I guess it has to do with the fact that I don't like emotion like that from somebody who I expect to be my brace, so to speak. I don't like emotion like that from Russell or anybody.

Billy had always viewed his brother as unresponsive, unemotional, and ungiving, and this identity as the father's clone cannot be easily erased. Now—only by seeing Russell as rigid and undemanding, like a hard, cold stainless steel brace—can Billy accept his brother as being supportive:

RUSSELL: I do remember Billy looking at me and being upset that I was so upset. It was disconcerting to him. He didn't ever usually see me that way. He always saw me as the hard, cold guy who razzed him about getting his chores done, who wouldn't ever let him chum around with me and my friends.

THERAPIST: Did you say that you needed him to be the prop?

RUSSELL: The brace.

BILLY: The brace, the encouragement. [*Begins to talk crisply, angrily*]

Billy clings to his misery even when Russell wants a change.

THERAPIST: The brace. That's very interesting from a guy who had enormous physical problems and wore a brace.

BILLY: I wore a back brace. [*In a bitter voice*] Up to here! [*Points to his neck*]

THERAPIST: And you wanted him to be your brace.

BILLY: Support, yeah.

RUSSELL: *Support* for what, though?

BILLY: *Me!*

RUSSELL: But isn't it supportive when I'm emotional when I show that I care about you and stuff [*breathing heavily*]

BILLY: No, that's a flaw, Russ, braces don't budge. Stainless steel, that doesn't change, it's reliable.

Billy is unwilling to grant his brother any forgiveness for what Russell did to him and what Russell still represents to him.

THERAPIST: That's an interesting metaphor—brace—because the brace must have been a reminder to you of pain. It was supportive, you needed it, and at the same time it was a constant reminder of this problem you had as a young child.

BILLY: Yeah, a brace is reliable, but cold and *never* [*pause*], asks for anything in return.

RUSSELL: Well, I guess there's nothing I can do about that [*weary resignation*].

The core identities of Russell, the father's favorite, and of Billy, the father's burden, remain entrenched. Billy has spent too many years paying the price and playing the role of persecuted victim to let any of his family easily forget what they did to him. Unable to receive anything but a stereotyped response from his parents, he searched out the one responsive link with the past, his brother, moved in with him, and then attempted to exact retribution for his childhood misery. Unless *both* Billy and Russell are willing to engage in psychotherapy, however, it is unlikely that they will easily budge the rigid roles and imposed identities they archaically, and relentlessly, continue to project on each other. Cut off from their family of origin, they struggle with each other, trapped by their unresolved conflicts, and unable to wrest nurturance and vitality from their strained relationship.

To describe Billy and Russell's relationship as an outgrowth of identification, or of lack of it, does not capture the excruciatingly powerful function each brother plays in the other's existential script. For the younger brother, his rigid, archaic image of his sibling provides him with moral leverage; it generates a sense of felt continuity from the past to the present, and helps to determine his concept of being a man and how dependent he could let himself be. For the older brother, his current role vis-à-vis the younger initially provides an outlet by which he can attempt to undo past misunderstandings and prove to himself that his core identity has changed. However, in the face of his brother's resurrected childhood perception of him as a victimizer, he becomes angry, anxious, and depressed. When he finds that there is little to be gained from his helpful stance, he retreats and once again creates the undemanding psychological distance with which both brothers are familiar.

Conclusion

These siblings are unlikely to forge a satisfactory, enduring relationship. Intelligent, educated, desperately wanting a significant sense of home, they nonetheless lack the integration and complementarity of needs, values, and roles necessary to achieve it. Frozen images of each sibling, encumbered by the bitterness of childhood, remain suspended in the mind of the other. Not only do these dominate, but they actually approach becoming, each sibling's primary core identity. Each is terrified that, in spite of the helpful attitude and yearning for acceptance that both now possess, the outmoded, primitive self of childhood that the other sibling still sees, cannot and never will be outgrown.

Many other siblings, however, as we will describe in the next chapter, seem to be able to re-evaluate the images they have of one another. As each keeps open the possibility that the other can change, the relationship can be delightful, challenging, meaningful, and a source of vital interaction. These are the siblings who become good friends as adults, who expect their spouses to understand their great fondness for a brother or a sister, who can go on vacations together, and who weather personal conflicts with one another.

Now we need to delineate the primary patterns of identification between siblings. Siblings accept or reject each other for a plethora of reasons, including most irrational ones. Their struggles do not end with the close of adolescence: they struggle with the meaning of "brother" or "sister" throughout their lives, even when parents and family no longer seem to dictate that they do.

CHAPTER 4

Patterns of Identification
and Sibling Relationships

EIGHT major identification processes accompany, on the continuum of sameness to difference, the most common sibling relationship: of these, some are transitory, and others endure for a lifetime. For convenience, we have combined them into three main groups:

- *Close identification,* in which each person feels great similarity and little difference with a sibling.
- *Partial identification,* in which each person feels some similarity and some difference with a sibling.
- *Distant identification,* in which each person feels great difference and little similarity with a sibling.

Both the close and distant types of identification tend to create rigid relationships. In such instances, one or both of these brothers or sisters has a vested interest in keeping the relationship "in place," and resists changing it. Partial identification, on the other hand, is more flexible and desirable. These siblings have emotional access to other people, without a fixed insistence that their sibling relationship—whether of love or hate— "comes before all else."

Table 4.1 (p. 85) shows how the particular process and degree of identification determine the kind of relationship that evolves between any two siblings. Any of these relationships, as they develop over time, facilitate continuing identification. The relationship is the observable bond, while identification is the feeling within each person.

84

Table 4.1

Major Patterns of Identification and Relationship between Siblings

Degree of Identification	Process of Identification	Type of Relationship	
Close	Twinning	Fused:	"We're just like each other. There is no difference."
	Merging	Blurred:	"I'm not sure who I am. Maybe I can be you."
	Idealizing	Hero worship:	"I admire you so much that I want to become like you."
Partial	Loyal acceptance	Mutually dependent:	"We're the same in many ways. We'll always need and care for each other in spite of our differences."
	Constructive dialectic	Dynamic independent:	"We're alike but different. This is challenging and creates opportunities for both of us to grow."
	Destructive dialectic	Hostile dependent:	"We're different in many ways. We don't particularly like one another, but we need each other anyhow."
Distant	Polarized rejection	Rigidly differentiated:	"You're so different from me. I don't want to depend on you, and I never want to become like you."
	De-identifying	Disowned:	"We're totally different from one another. I don't need you, I don't like you, and I don't care if I never see you again."

LACK OF SELF

VITALITY

ESTRANGEMENT

NOTE: We feel that these are the most important of the many possible types of sibling relationship, and will refer to them throughout the rest of the book. However as the dramas of loyalty, sexuality, aggression, emotional disturbance, survivorship, and psychotherapy unfold, they take their shape and substance from these identification processes, which are the psychological mortar and brick of the sibling bond.

Close Identification

There are three patterns of close identification that then create three predictable kinds of relationship:

- *Twinning*, which creates a fused relationship
- *Merging*, which creates a blurred relationship
- *Idealizing*, which determines hero worship

In all of these patterns, at least one sibling feels similar, or wants to feel greatly similar, to another. In the first example, both siblings identify strongly with each other and function as if each lacks an individual self.

TWINNING—FUSED RELATIONSHIPS
"We're just like each other. There is no difference."

When the roles and the identities of children in any family are not sharply delineated, there is great danger that their identities will be fused. Twinning, a phenomenon of early childhood we described in chapter 2, can continue through later childhood and adolescence, with each child seeing himself or herself as the other's double. If parents are not sufficiently sensitive to the separate needs and attributes of their children, two such siblings may reach an extreme by becoming undifferentiated and stuck together. Lacking adequate ego boundaries sharply marking one's identity from the other's, both children are at much higher risk for psychological difficulties. As in the twin cases we described in chapter 2, the blending of identities, and the fusing of the "me"–"not me," means that neither child can tolerate differences, developmental changes, and the ups and downs of a normal relationship. One functions as if one's sibling were an appendage, an alter ego whose constant presence one needs. Extremely fused siblings are vulnerable to what clinicians in the past called *folie à deux*, or shared madness. Continually looking to the other for self-definition, throughout childhood and into adulthood, leaves one's ego shaky and vulnerable to stress. At the extreme end of the axis of sameness is this bizarre caricature of the sibling relationship:

LONDON (AP)—Greta and Freda C., 37 and identical twins, are so alike in the way they look, think, speak, move, dress and live that scientists say they seem to share one mind. They do everything together, and they scream or sulk if parted. Most uncannily, they talk in unison when under stress—speaking the same words in identical voice patterns that create a weird echo effect. . . . A senior psychiatrist who asked not to be identified said, "Their total parallel identity, particularly their constant oneness in speaking, takes them far beyond any other sets of identical twins known to psychological medicine. This must be the nearest thing the world has ever seen to a daily unrehearsed dazzling display of telepathy." . . . Arrested for breach of the peace after jealously hounding the common object of their romantic adoration (a former neighbor), the twins appeared in court . . . each wearing one pink mitten and one brown woolen glove. . . . Officials have given some details of their life, described by their social workers as "one mind in two bodies."*

Other, poignant examples of sameness abound, testifying to the inability of some people to escape the early sibling fusion that prevents them from dealing, on their own terms, with the demands of adolescence and adulthood.

The Twin Game: Lucy and Lucinda: Everyone was once fascinated by the fairy tale in which a prince found a boy who looked like him and with whom he could trade places. The appeal of having a look-alike is that together the two can fool everyone as did the Prince and the Pauper. In the late 1960s, before we began doing family therapy, one of us received a visit at a community mental health clinic from a young Hispanic woman of twenty-five, who was dressed in bright, stylish clothes. Lucy complained that she was having dizzy spells, felt nervous, fought with her mother, and was trying to decide on either a singing career or further education, and casually mentioned that she had a twin sister with whom she sang in a local group. After completing the usual intake interview, she made another appointment.

A week later, what appeared to be the same young woman walked in, sat down, and resumed her tale of woe. But something seemed different: she was more depressed, paler, less sure of herself. She had changed her hairdo, and her clothes seemed drab. She resisted all attempts to pin down the cause of her current concern; it was just more of the same depressing problem she had explained the week before. But halfway through the interview, she stopped and slyly smiled. She hesitated, winked, and said, "We played a trick on you." She laughed nervously and paused again, savoring her position. "I was the one who wanted to come today. But I'm not Lucy. I'm Lucinda. Ha! ha! ha!" After getting over his initial shock, the therapist arranged for this twin, Lucinda, to see another therapist, and suggested that the absent Lucy should return to him. But, over the next few months, Lucy and Lucinda refused to cooperate. They claimed to trust the therapist each had been assigned to, but they constantly switched voice intonations, stories, clothes, hair styles, and therapists, in order to "confound the opposition." They laughed at their exquisite abuse of power. Neither therapist could ever be quite sure which twin he was treating.

*From the *Chicago Sun-Times*, 9 December 1980, p. 3.

The twins' undifferentiated identities and fused relationship served as an excellent cover to hide behind during their screening of the therapists. Only when each felt that she could trust her therapist on his own merits, were they willing to give up the protection of the "twin game." Each settled on one therapist and began to develop object constancy with someone other than her twin.

While twins are often at high risk to become this fused and undifferentiated, any high-access siblings can suffer the same fate, if encouraged to do so by their environment. This usually has its origins in the siblings' early years, as we described in chapters 2 and 3.

MERGING IDENTIFICATION—BLURRED RELATIONSHIPS
"I'm not sure who I am. Maybe I can be you."

If a child's identity is not sharply delineated by parents, he or she will continually search for people with whom to identify. A growing child who remains uncertain may still cling to and depend on a sibling in the search for self. What happens when both siblings lack self-confidence, but at a less intense level than the fused twosomes just described? The pursuit of sameness in such instances is generally fraught with difficulty, conflict, and ambivalence. Typically, neither sibling has the confidence to break away from the other. While these siblings do not suffer the severe consequences of twinning and fusing, they fluctuate in and out of difficulties with one another. There will be many extended and intense periods of closeness, but these siblings are often in doubt about their personal identities, and when one changes, few words pass back and forth to help the other understand what has happened. Their parents and other siblings usually do little to assuage the hurts and doubts that may mark this type of blurred relationship. One of the siblings may depend on the other, as if merging with the more self-certain sib will remove the former's pain and doubt.

Getting Away to Find Oneself: Kay and Margaret. Kay and Margaret, the two eldest of four daughters, had always seemed like a close pair when they were children. Margaret, now twenty-five, had been important to Kay, two years her junior. Always clumsy, gangly, and awkward, Kay had looked up to her seemingly self-assured, more attractive older sister. Their mother was described as being a caring, nurturant person who had grown up in a large, financially well-to-do family. She had told her daughters that as a teen-ager she had always worried that she was plain and unattractive. According to Margaret, her mother's home was "cheery"; although, to our ears, the description of that home seemed empty and strikingly devoid of details. The father was described as a kind, intelligent, and critically honest man, whom the daughters loved and respected but characterized as "being in a fog." He had been an only child and, while able to relate to each daughter individually, always deferred to his wife about his daughters' collective welfare. As a group they seemed to overwhelm him. They usually were content to bypass him, to ignore him, or to retaliate by sweetly "tolerating" him. It appeared that both parents enjoyed their children and that a good deal of mutual caring and respect existed between family members. However, the three oldest daughters—Kay, Margaret, and Jeanie—all complained of feeling insecure, chronically anxious, and uncomfortable. The mother, the more available parent, had always dealt with problems by being the eternal optimist. Whenever the daughters tried to express their concerns, the mother placated their expressed fears and used developmental psychology to explain away their problems. But she never touched the essence of any of their concerns. While intending to help, she seemed only to disarm her girls by expressing anguish that she had "failed" them as a mother. She made them feel guilty about any of their individual complaints.

During their childhood these sisters were never openly compared with one another. Specific and narrowly defined identities were never imposed on them; instead, there was a blurring of the actual distinctions between them. Each was reassured that they were like beautiful but separate "tulips," whose time to "bloom," like "bulbs" buried in the ground, would inevitably come. Kay could never accept these hollow-sounding assurances from her mother. In her impatience for her "Spring" to arrive, she kept turning to her admired older sister and tried to become like her. She saw herself as similar, went everywhere with Margaret, and was like her shadow. Maybe Kay could merge with Margaret and do what Margaret did. Eventually she began to realize the futility of clinging to her sister. Kay realized that she would never be able to match Margaret's beauty and particular style, and that she needed a field of her own in which to bloom, one that was far away, a place where she could become herself. By middle adolescence, she fantasied leaving home; and upon high school graduation, she left for a large city in a distant state to move in with a relative. There was no bitterness in this change—only a wish to become her own person. The family felt relieved. Perhaps now Kay would find herself.

During one of her visits home six years later, she agreed to participate in one of Margaret's psychotherapy sessions. Both sisters agreed that their parents had never provided sufficient clarity for their children to experience adequate self-definition:

KAY: I guess I used to feel pretty strongly that our parents were controlling. I think it's a kind of undermining one's self confidence—feeling that one is not grown-up or individual or worthy . . . that kind of thing.

MARGARET: Well . . . I feel, in spite of Mom and Dad's verbal support in a number of ways, there isn't a whole lot of validation on how one really feels about things. Mother will tell you "anything's OK, everything's OK" no matter how bad it is. It's all 'OK' [*Kay agrees*], which, while it's encouraging, at points it also sort of makes you wonder if you make things up. You know Mom has always made me out to be the most pessimistic person in the whole world, no matter what the situation is [*Kay agrees*], and I see Dad . . . sort of the message I feel I always have gotten from him is whatever it was, it was never quite good enough. There's a kind of subtle criticism which comes out all the time.

Because of the fluidity of each child's role in the family, Margaret and Kay always carried feelings of insecurity about themselves. The Pollyanna-ish climate they grew up in made each daughter desperate for validation.

In the absense of separately assigned roles and clearly defined identities, the sibling relationship became more intense. Kay's eventual realization that she would never be able to become like her older sister created a growing resentment that had been noticed by Margaret. But Margaret had said nothing about her awareness of Kay's feelings until now.

KAY: See there was a good deal when we were teenagers . . . of jealousy, jealousy of the way you looked, and your popularity, and getting 100s, and my insecurities of growing up.

MARGARET: I felt that up until the last couple of times you've been home we'd have a great time, and then something would happen, that would snap for you, and you would start to feel jealous of me again.

KAY: Uh huh.

MARGARET: And you began to hate me like when we were younger and then there was that old sort of love/hate thing.

KAY: Right, yeah.

MARGARET: I was taking you to parties, but you also hated me for it.

KAY: [*To therapist*] Right, well I can agree with that mixed feeling because it would be, one, respecting this person, and, second of all, I always wanted to be like Margaret, my big sister. I've always wanted to be like you, always.

Patterns of Identification and Sibling Relationships

Kay admitted her old desire of having wanted to become like Margaret. Her confusion and self-doubt made her look to her sister as the primary source for self-definition. She had wanted to be the same, yet she had wanted to be different. And neither the mother nor the father were able to stop Kay from mimicking her older sister:

> KAY: I only wanted to have Margaret's social ease, if only I looked like Margaret, if only I had all the boyfriends Margaret had. . . . If only I had all the friends she did . . . then everything would be fine. Then gradually, I think the dynamics started to change. Maybe, a couple of years ago, for the first time, I started to come more into my own. My mother said, "Margaret doesn't feel very self-confident, and she thinks you're much more socially adept, and you have so much nerve to go out and do the things you're doing. Look what she's done. She hasn't done so well, but you're doing quite well now."

The mother could not reassure her second daughter with her own words and, by characteristically quoting the insecure oldest daughter, unwittingly kept Kay close to Margaret. The unintended overlapping of identities was being perpetuated through the mother's continual denial and blurring of the accomplishments of the girl who had actually achieved success.

> KAY: If I had stayed here and stayed within Margaret's social circle, I might just have continued to be her shadow.
> I don't think I'm totally together now. But I think I'd be a *real* mess if I had stayed and looked up to another person and kept thinking, "If only I could be like this person."

By moving away from Margaret, Kay was more successful in finding herself. When she was close to the family, she felt doubt, uncertainty, and a centripetal pull toward Margaret which eventually became stifling and humiliating. Both daughters feel relieved that the blurring and overlapping, which had marked their childhood and adolescent interaction, no longer dominates their relationship. Now when the younger sister feels the old emotions of an adoring, envious, supplicating sibling welling up in her, she begins distancing from Margaret and returns to her new home. For such siblings, geographic distance, which permits disengagement from the family, can facilitate the establishment of a separate identity, however arduous and lonely a step that might be. While Kay appears to be the sibling with the more pronounced identity problems, Margaret is equally relieved that she no longer has to be the continual touchstone for her sister's development.

IDEALIZING—HERO WORSHIP
"I admire you so much that I want to become like you."

A child can idealize a sibling who has obvious positive characteristics, and wish to emulate these valued traits. The idealizing sib can copy and try to make his or her own what this treasured other possesses. A unilateral process, hero worship is usually directed from a younger sibling toward an older. Idealization of the other, followed by imitation of that person, provides one with the identity that one would like to experience growing and developing in oneself. A brother or a sister can become what Nevitt Sanford (1955) refers to as an "identification invoker," or one who attracts others to identify with him or her. This can even occur when an older sibling has reprehensible characteristics. Young siblings often view "bad" brothers or sisters as exciting characters to emulate, particularly if the excitement of that "badness" is a dramatic counterpoint to the drabness of the family.

In positive terms, a sibling may—by being pleasant, affectionate, loving, or lovable—serve as an ego ideal or provide a model for what one hopes to become. James H. S. Bossard and Eleanor S. Boll (1956) refer to the historian Douglas S. Freeman's description, in his biography of George Washington, of how an older brother, Lawrence, served as a powerful identification invoker for the "father" of our country. This educated and graceful brother was a model for young George who "quickly made a hero out of Lawrence and began to emulate him. . . . For the enlargement of George's mind and the polishing of his manners, Lawrence was almost an ideal older brother. . . . He was everything an admiring boy wanted to be" (1948, pp. 58, 77, 95). Idealization is usually a temporary phenomenon. Children tend to look up to their older brothers and sisters, wanting to play ball as they do, wanting to look and dress as they do, wanting the same fun, and emulating their every step. But the need to pursue one's own identity and the sober appraisal of one's sibling in more realistic terms generally modifies such hero worship by the time of late adolescence.

Idealization of a sibling can become frozen over time if circumstances, such as the death or other unavailability of a parent, compel a child to remain dependent on a brother or a sister.

Seth, a graduate student in psychology, continues to hero-worship his older sister, Mary, a psychiatric nurse. She had become his surrogate parent after the death of their mother when the boy was only five and the sister was nineteen. The father had little vitality to offer his children, for, as Seth recalled, "he would have to work long hours, get up very early, and tended not to have much energy when he would come home." Mary, on the other hand, *was* available, always gave Seth her attention, and still, to this day, although living on the West Coast, "spends hours on the phone yacking" with her little brother. Seth's choice of a helping profession is, as he put it, "directly attributable to the great job that Mary's done helping people." He proudly told us that "she would be the first person I'd call if I were in trouble," and that he would be content to live as she had. Generally, when this type of identification carries over into adulthood, one sibling tries to overlook, or avoids focusing on, the faults of the other. For Seth and Mary it is no mere coincidence that they live on opposite coasts, see each other only twice a year, and in this way preserve the positive and idealized images they keep of one another.

Partial Identification

Identification more frequently occurs—not in such total, or near total, perceptions of sameness—but at subidentity levels in which a brother or a sister feels that only some aspects of his or her personality are similar to those of a sibling who has been closely observed. This perception can occur because of obvious points of sameness that other people also recognize, such as:

- Physical similarities ("He and I look the same").
- Behavioral and attitudinal similarities ("She and I are fairly agile").
- Similarities of choice ("We both are active in politics").

Or partial identification can occur in less obvious ways, for a variety of motives, without being noticed by anyone else. A sibling may form an impression of a brother or a sister ("She's smart," "He's strong," "She's a good kid") and then ally with that sib, first through the play of childhood, and later in life by spending time and joining in activities together. To become like the other in this way helps to reduce some of the uncertainty of oneself. The "I'm like you in some ways" partially functions in the service of complementarity, filling in the voids in oneself, but usually also allows for the existence of perceptions of differences as well. Feelings of sameness, in this type of identification pattern, then eventually coexist, with the clear recognition that difference is desirable. In such identification there is some "vitality" because there is some negotiation for change. The mutual feelings of closeness and similarity provide comfort and guidance, while the mutual feelings of distance and difference give each person the freedom to determine his or her own destiny, without the encumbrance of having to remain like a sibling.

The active alliances that siblings form, and the affinities that they feel, may be outgrowths of the processes of partial identification. To help assuage a personal need for self-certainty, one may reach out to one's sibling and become his or her rescuer, friend, protector, and collaborator. The "I won't let you do that to my brother" ethic is often based on the realization that when one's sibling has been harmed, one also feels the arrows of abuse. Many siblings have lied, cheated, battled parents, or developed the same symptoms out of a special affinity for a brother or a sister who is troubled. Their sagas bear witness to the fact that brothers and sisters will willingly volunteer, even when seemingly at needless risk, to offer nurturance, alliance, or aid. This type of identification lays the groundwork for loyalty to prevail. Giving help and opposing the parents seal mutual bonds of identification and feelings of affinity between siblings; expecting the other sibling to be a reliable rescuer, because of this identification, becomes part of the expectation of who the other is. "Joining," a phenomenon we have described elsewhere (Bank and Kahn 1975), can ally siblings with a common identity as soulmates in a war against parents, serves to fill in the missing elements in each child's personality, and sometimes makes for a good fit of identities in the family system.

Allies Against the Parents: Scott & Tommy. Scott, a twelve-year-old boy had been seen by a social service agency in both individual treatment and family therapy with his parents for three years. At the time he saw the new therapist, he still ridiculed and taunted his mother and father— weak, disorganized people whose own impoverished experiences of childhood prevented them from intuitively knowing how to deal with their children. This oldest son, Scott was still a bed wetter, had been diagnosed as being "learning-disabled," and kept his room like a pigsty. His ten-year-old brother, Tommy, with no apparent difficulties, had been left out of all of the previous treatment. This younger brother did not seem nearly as fragile, had always achieved better grades, and was a true-blue boy scout to his parents, except, it seemed, when he was with Scott. We soon discovered that ten-year-old Tommy, without being intimidated by his older sib, was supplying Scott matches with which to burn school papers and books, delighted in messing up Scott's room (yet kept his own immaculate), and helped him to erect a barricade of furniture to seal off the entrance to the family room, from behind which both boys pelted their hapless parents with midget cars, wooden blocks, food snacks, and other missiles. While the boys were very different, they also could act very much the same. This younger brother had felt sufficient empathy and identification with his sibling to become an accomplice and sympathizer. Tommy could look up to his older brother, admire his bravado, identify with him, and admit to liking his form of "fun." Scott was at least spontaneous, emotionally available, and displayed a certain resoluteness that the weak parents seemed to lack. The ten-year-old told us later that he feared that he would never be brave, and had begun to hate the way his parents lived out their meager, drab existence. Tommy's partial identification with his older brother appeared to have given him what his other primary figures for identification lacked—bravado, excitement, and challenge. On the other hand, Scott's partial identification with his younger brother allowed him to emulate the good things his sibling could provide: he loved athletics as Tommy did; and when Tommy began showing interest in competitive swimming, Scott did too.

It was only when both boys were brought into treatment that the parents began to recognize that there was a surprisingly high degree of partial identification between the two brothers, a complementarity of the good and bad parts of each boy, a yin and a yang that made each feel more complete, and a range of reciprocal, mutually satisfying activities that the boys secretly had with each other. In effect, these siblings were providing certain gratifications and missing elements for each other (no matter how inappropriately expressed) which the parents were unable to fulfill.°

We have designated three patterns of partial identification which then create three predictable kinds of relationship. Because these are more complex (in social science it is often easier to describe the extremes than the middle range of any phenomenon), we have had to include some additional concepts, the notion of dependence-independence, and the idea that a relationship can be static (that is, unchanging) or dialectical (that is, dynamic). These next three types are:

° We are, of course, abbreviating our description of this case. Two additional points are worth noting: (1) the identification with the older also gave the younger an outlet for his own hostile impulses; (2) this is a simple illustration of a pattern that many family therapists commonly encounter. Symptoms in both children revealed parental conflicts and inadequacies, which could then be addressed in treatment.

- *Loyal acceptance,* which creates a mutually dependent relationship.
- A *constructive dialectic,* which creates a dynamic independent relationship.
- A *destructive dialectic,* which creates a hostile dependent relationship.

The dialectical types show an ebb and flow and a give-and-take in the relationship. In all three types, however, there is some recognition of sameness and difference, which usually permits change.

LOYAL ACCEPTANCE—MUTUALLY DEPENDENT RELATIONSHIPS
"We're the same in many ways. We'll always need and care for each other in spite of our differences."

When siblings accept each other's differences, without necessarily liking them, and still find many relevant points of sameness, they can often be generous and giving in spirit to one another. They fulfill Frances K. Grossman's (1972) criteria for a mature sibling relationship in which ambivalent feelings are likely to be experienced and acknowledged. Loyal acceptance that leads to this form of mutual respect is one of the more desirable types of sibling bond because it always tends to be pleasant in tone, fulfilling the ideal of brotherhood or sisterhood.

However, such uniformly positive perceptions by each sibling of the other often became somewhat *static.* If one sibling experiences great success, has a high status, wears a mask of confidence, and has a smooth course in life, while the other sibs have less good fortune, everyone might settle into separate and unequal niches. Once the less fortunate sibs are allowed to depend on the successful brother or sister, change is difficult since everyone derives benefit from the arrangement. The successful sib can be a beneficent "giver"; the dependent sib, the gratified "taker." These become the siblings who too readily accept each other's identities as fixed and tend not to make demands or encroach on each other in any way that creates anxiety or stress. These are relationships between two acknowledged unequals, and they remain so. The relationship stabilizes, sets, and remains loyal and respectful. This process is like an advanced, frozen stage of idealization; but in this type, *both* siblings derive gratification in keeping things the way they have always been and everyone seems to know his or her "place."

Mutual Dependency in Spite of Differences: Ralph and Philip. This set of brothers provides an example of a mutually respected relationship in which there is loyal acceptance of difference. Ralph, thirty-four, had always provided a stable model for his younger brother, Philip, age twenty-seven. Bright, successful, a plugger, who by age thirty had already become the head of the anthropology department at his university, Ralph had been the one who had persuaded Philip to consider college, had helped him select a good school, lent him money for tuition expenses, and had even arranged a research assistantship for him when the younger brother took a year off from school to do field work in anthropology. In his younger brother, Ralph saw elements of himself as a young boy who had once needed guidance. Seven years older, Ralph had gradually become a substitute father for Philip; their own father, disabled since the Second World War with a shattered leg, later developed arthritis, diabetes, and arteriosclerosis. He rarely felt physically able to do things with his boys, let alone provide them with knowledge about the ways of the world that adolescents so keenly welcome. His physical and emotional deterioration of the last fifteen years had been particularly difficult for the younger son, Philip, who turned instead to his big brother, Ralph, for guidance, reassurance, and direction:

PHILIP: I think one of the things I feared was that I would become like my father, and I still can get feelings of helplessness because sometimes he's so depressed that he just won't get out of bed. Both my brother and I seem to become depressed when we're around him very long and so by now we make our visits brief.

Having to rely on his older brother so decisively and at an early age had made Philip somewhat dependent and reluctant to challenge this brother, who was kind and lovable and could provide stability and maturity when it was needed:

PHILIP: My brother was also like my coach. He knew that I had more ability than I realized and he would provide a model and I followed that, I modeled it. He's a good internalizer—provides direction, and I became pretty good at watching it, copying it, and then making it my own. There are lots of things he started, and I don't think I'm that imaginative because he is a great originator of ideas. Maybe some of his ideas are conservative, but I'll use that as an inspiration for what I'm going to do and then go do it.

Philip's earlier idealization and unfailing respect for Ralph had a price. Philip's inability to keep up with his successful brother created a conflict between ambition and the drive for a separate identity; the younger brother eventually gave up his pursuit for similar success, in preference for an itinerant "free" life style. Ralph came to be seen in Philip's eyes as paying too heavy a price for his single-minded pursuit of achievement.

Ralph missed the opportunities for love, the freedom from responsibility, and the excitement that Philip, then in his mid-twenties, had come to enjoy. Philip regarded Ralph as the "stable one," who was, and would always be, the "good son" in the family, reserving this psychological space for himself, while Philip preferred to characterize himself as the "weird but lovable son." He had moved from a prolonged period of total idealization of this brother to one of partial identification, while maintaining the emotional dependency, love, and respect he had felt for his brother from their earlier years. With the eventual differentiation of these two brothers—one remaining the hard-working, conservative achiever, the other becoming the fun-loving, free spirit—the relationship became stable and set in place. Both brothers refused to interfere with the expression of each other's separate identities. Ralph, for his part, was troubled to see his brother take a different path, but was willing to let him live his own life.

We define a relationship such as this as mutually respectful and stable when there are long periods of developmental time in which no challenge is made to the premises of the relationship, or to the identities of the participants involved, and where a *spirit of positive feeling prevails*. At this stage in their lives, neither brother directly "interferes" with his sibling's existence.

Philip's partial identification, emotional dependence, and concern for his brother mean that he expresses disapproval only passively and in fantasy, without taking any direct action or risking antagonism:

PHILIP: I want him to be happy; that's what brothers are for. If you love someone, you want them to be happy. I know my brother is suffering from working so hard and that he's doing a dynamite job of covering it up.

INTERVIEWER: Well, what could you do about it?

PHILIP: I would love to go down and rescue my brother. I wish I could give him $100,000 to relieve that tension that comes from worrying about work, and I'd like for him to relax a little bit, loosen up, take a vacation. It feels so hopeless to me that he's so conceptually set on the idea of intellectual achievement that he views the passage of time as opportunities lost to achieve.

INTERVIEWER: Does he know you worry about him this way?

PHILIP: I guess so. But he won't change.

Relationships like Philip and Ralph's rarely take a radical and unfortunate turn. They remain fairly stable and rest on a foundation of mutual respect, some recognition of sameness, and the acknowledgment that there can be differences. They are among the least conflicted and problematic patterns of sibling relationships we have encountered. And yet because the views they have of each other are static, relationships such as these lack the punch, excitement, demand, strain, and invigorating qualities that other siblings experience throughout their lives. Both of these brothers, partly because of the tragedy of their father's life, *need* to maintain their partial and positive identification with one another, and rarely create disappointment, pain, or difficulty within their own relationship. It is as if they have said to one another, "We need each other too much—we've already had too much pain."

CONSTRUCTIVE DIALECTIC—DYNAMIC INDEPENDENT RELATIONSHIPS
"We're alike but different. This is challenging and creates opportunities for both of us to grow."

Some sibling relationships appear to be balanced on a fulcrum of equality, with brothers and sisters close in age constantly contesting and challenging each other while striving for individual uniqueness. Concepts of difference prevail but are tempered by ongoing feelings of affinity and respect. This is in many ways the most ideal of the sibling bonds, since it permits change, contact, and healthy challenge throughout life. In order for the relationship to keep its dynamic quality and not become static, these siblings must have had early and high access and maintain continual contact. In this pattern, each sib serves as an object with whom one contrasts oneself—that is, as a reference point for self-scrutiny. Estimates of sameness and difference in these dynamically independent relationships are often exquisitely juggled, with neither sibling wanting to admit that he or she is overly dependent or overly indifferent to the other. There is a feeling of electricity and balanced equality in the interaction of such a pair. Serious displays of contempt or long-lasting destructive attitudes would destroy the points of recognized similarity and feelings of affinity in such relationships. Clingingness and false mutuality would nullify the sharp edges of difference that make such a relationship an ongoing challenge to each participant. The "I'm-like-you-but-I'm-not-like-you" dialectical dance, therefore, is usually lively and ongoing, serving as a prototype for later relationships in life where it is also possible to achieve justice, balance, and equality.

While neither sibling in this type of dialectical framework wants to feel inferior, neither particularly wants to get the permanent upper hand. At the core there is too much caring and respect to permit any one-sidedness. Displays of lasting superiority by either sib can only rob the relationship of its vitality; the ongoing displays of competition must always permit an honorable channel for face saving, should there be a loser. In our opinion, the healthy, creative tone of such interaction is the prototype for the ideal in the sibling world.

Vital and Challenging: Geneen and David. This brief example of a fourteen-year-old girl and her thirteen-year-old brother shows something of the challenge of keeping up with one's sib, even though on the other's "turf," and reveals elements of generosity, competition, and equality in these siblings' core feelings. Such siblings like and respect one another and identify not out of deficiency but from their own individual strengths. Nonetheless, the older sister can feel comfortable about expressing resentment toward her competitive, charming, and thoroughly irascible little brother.

GENEEN: Sometimes when he's around I get angry at him for something because he's not nice at times. If he's nice it seems so fake it doesn't even matter. But we can get along sometimes like last night, after I came home from my rehearsal me and David played cards, had some fun together, and I *beat* him [*laughing*].

INTERVIEWER: You did?

GENEEN: Well, he, it was sort of a tie.

INTERVIEWER: Did it take any brains to beat him?

GENEEN: I don't know. He's a lot better at the card games, really likes them and is good at it, and I just learned how to play it.

INTERVIEWER: Oh, so you did equalize it then?

GENEEN: Yeah.

INTERVIEWER: One for him and one for you.

GENEEN: Well, it wasn't beating him. It's like, he had more points than I did, but I think I could catch up if I'd stayed down a little bit longer.

When Geneen and David talk to one another, there is a marvelous cadence to their voices, a rise and fall in the rhythm of their challenge to each other. Each point made by one of the participants in this process generates a bickering counterpoint. Listen:

DAVID: I thought you said you were going downtown and you went outside, then I went outside, and you and I went back in. [*Voices higher, David defensive, but not too much so*]

GENEEN: David, you shouldn't have told them I went downtown because they left without me.

DAVID: Well, sorry [*sarcastic and teasing*]. You shouldn't say you're going places when you're not going.

GENEEN: I was, but I was waiting for them to pick me up.

DAVID: You go, "I'm going downtown," you walk out the door, I hear you leave. Then about five minutes later, I go outside ——

GENEEN: I went out to play four-square. [*David's voice is angrier, Geneen's is pacifying.*]

DAVID: Yeah, but then I went out to play Frisbee, and you weren't there so I assumed you went downtown. [*David's voice loses its anger, responding to Geneen's tone.*]

GENEEN: Well, you shouldn't tell people you do stuff and don't do it. [*Sighs, exasperated*]

DAVID: You shouldn't have said, "I'm going downtown." [*Voice raised, replying to the sigh*]

GENEEN: [*Voice over David's higher and louder*] You're not even listening to what I'm saying!

DAVID: You shouldn't say, "I'm going downtown" and then go out and play four-square. [*Neat rebuttal*]

GENEEN: Well, David, I was going downtown. I was waiting for them to come by and pick me up. [*They make noises at each other as they stick their tongues out.*]

DAVID: You didn't stay out there very long, did you?

GENEEN: I had to go back in because I forgot something.

DAVID: You shouldn't have forgot something. [*His voice quiet, yet tenacious; he won't let her win her point.*]

GENEEN: [*Angry, raised voice and sounds sick of the argument*] David, stop it! You're *so* obnoxious.

DAVID: You told me you were going downtown, so I just told them.

GENEEN: I don't want to talk about this any more, David, because you're not getting anywhere. [*Her decision is meant to be final.*]

DAVID: Well, you shouldn't mention it [*needling her*].

GENEEN: I shouldn't do this, I shouldn't do that.

DAVID: Yeah, you shouldn't have [*quietly*].

GENEEN: It's *all* your fault [*sarcastic and self-righteous*].

DAVID: Yup. I'll prove it.

INTERVIEWER: This is the way it goes at home?

DAVID: Sometimes.

GENEEN: He's not listening to anything I'm saying.

DAVID: I am too!

GENEEN: You are not!

Make no mistake about it: these children like and respect one another. The contentiousness they display is generally short-lived. Adolescents such as these typically have parents who will monitor their squabbles, are emotionally accessible, and can serve as the court of last resort. There is no need for relationships such as these to remain static and nondemanding, as was true in the previous example in which there was a disabled parent. These children are fortunate to have parents who prevent them from becoming either so embroiled in, or so detached from, one another as to allow the momentum of their type relationship to founder. As the parents have modeled adequate conflict resolution, their children have developed a keen sensitivity to their prohibitions and wishes. In the struggle for fairness and equality between these siblings, we may also hear an echo of their parents' own dialectical processes at work. Children will often do the dance of their parents; in relationships such as Geneen and David's, that dance is based on the assumption that justice can always be gained from human interaction.

DESTRUCTIVE DIALECTIC—HOSTILE DEPENDENT RELATIONSHIPS
"We're different in many ways. We don't particularly like one another, but we need each other anyhow."

When Hegel, in the nineteenth century, wrote of a dialectical relationship, he chose a negative example, that of master and slave, to illustrate both interdependency and extreme difference (1931). In those sibling relationships where perceptions of absolute difference abound, hostile dependency, like that of the master and slave, can also occur. Particularly in the absence of other vital relationships in the family, one sibling may turn to another—whether out of fear, hate, sadness, anger, or confusion—for a sense of vitality and responsiveness. Intensely experienced object relationships in whatever form are, after all, better than no relationship; and yet it is precisely because of parental indifference, neglect, or even abandonment, that siblings will not only turn to but also heap abuse upon each other. (We will discuss this topic in depth in chapter 8.)

Why, one might ask, will children "sit still" for such a process and not disengage from one another? Each child can project onto what becomes the most available object—the sibling—all those repressed and hated aspects of the self from which one might otherwise sink into self-reproach and despair. Projective identification flourishes particularly in this type of relationship pattern, and usually these sibs say they "dislike" each other. For there to be a dialectical process, however, both siblings must need each other, have suffered some of the same parental indignities, or, at the

very least, recognize, on an unconscious level, the enormous mutual dependency of their relationship. Boundaries of difference between such siblings appear at first glance to be arbitrarily sharp, the "me"–"not me" struggles contentious, the competition always at an extreme; but the triumphs of presumed superiority can never be completely satisfying since there is so much dependency. The process is destructive, because there can be no public acknowledgment of caring, no liking, no helping of each other. Projection may flourish, but bitterness about each other grows. There are neither honorable winners nor honorable losers in such a game, but for these participants the game *must* go on.

For an example of this type of relationship, we need to look no farther than Jules Henry's masterful *Pathways to Madness* (1965), with his essay on the Rosenberg family. In the latter, we see two brothers, Irving, age thirteen, and Benjamin, age twelve, who need and depend on each other like the proverbial master and slave. Irving beats Benjamin to escape from his own fear of nothingness, to experience something outside of himself in which he can make a difference; while Benjamin endures, fights, and resists Irving's punishments and, in such endurance, experiences his own perverse triumph. Henry describes them:

> Ben is acquiescent—"Mama's boy" and Papa's joy—but to Irving acquiescence is submission, and if he can possibly escape he will do nothing to help anybody in the house. Ben is Irving's "slave," performing many little chores for him. . . . If Ben refuses, Irving beats him. Ben, however, says he enjoys these scrimmages and that he likes being his brother's slave. Irving calls using people "efficiency" and is proud of it, but he needs Ben, and even gets into his bed at night to sleep with his arm around his brother, pressed against his back, as I saw. With contempt in her voice, the mother told me that Irving has to take Ben along if he goes to the downstairs lavatory in the middle of the night.
>
> Ben is much more than his brother's slave; he is maternal, even somewhat wifely, waiting on Irving, hovering over him, accepting him in sleep. And Irving lords it over his brother and beats him up, though constantly demonstrating his own dependence. (1965, pp. 129–30)

Each of these brothers desperately lives out with each other the hope that he really matters, that each has a personal significance to the other that is unparalleled in the vacuous atmosphere provided by their parents. Irving's tyranny and dependence give his brother a reason for existing. Irving is Ben's flight from death. This type of sibling struggle begets only humiliation and defeat, not the lively face-saving challenge that a Geneen or a David can pose for one another.

Henry anticipates our own discussion of the destructive quality of this type of sibling relationship:

however, as time passes, people change; whoever was effective may begin to feel ineffectual and even defeated, and this is Irving's condition. . . . In the family he is dependent on his brother for any experience of effectiveness, and as Ben grows stronger and cannier, and therefore more effective himself, Irving's possibilities are reduced; the environment is becoming more and more impervious to him.   (P. 137)

We sense that the dialectical quality of this relationship will soon pass, that Ben will "outgrow" his need for his brother, and that he will move on to other relationships. In this vein, a brother whom we interviewed was able to say: "I feel I kind of used up all those hard lessons that I learned from my brother and that there are more important things to be learned elsewhere." These two brothers always fought as children but still maintained begrudging respect for one another. Their parents—lively, competitive, and successful professionals—believed conflicts should always be aired, had no compunctions about yelling if the children misbehaved, but also took no extra steps to insure that their two sons would like each other. After the brothers eventually grew up and left home, their get-togethers and conversations were always marked by a little extra "dig," "friendly" but extremely competitive jousts in which they derived satisfaction from scoring "points" against one another. These were scenarios that even their wives seemed to have no difficulty in joining. Although these brothers kept contact, they enjoyed each other as people about whom they could gossip and for games of one-upmanship. Unfortunately, hostile dependent relationships such as these seem all too common.

A destructive dialectic can develop into a positive one, in which the siblings acknowledge and even celebrate many points of sameness. However, many sibs who share a negative dialectic, eventually stabilize their relationship in even more destructive ways, reaching a plateau where their sense of alienation becomes extreme: they fear the recognition that they might be similar, and frozen images from the past begin to dominate so as to prevent any possibility of change.

Distant Identification

At this other extreme of patterns of identification are those siblings who feel alienated and different from one another, the siblings who are quick to say, "We have nothing in common" or "can't stand" a brother or a

sister. We have designated two such identification processes and their predictable relationship outcomes—the last of our eight types:

- *Polarized Rejection,* which creates a rigidly differentiated relationship.
- *De-identification,* which creates a disowned relationship.

Siblings of either of these types rarely "work things out" on their own,
since the estrangement is too profound. Parents who become aware of the
growing and mutual sense of resentment in their children, will usually
need to spend several years of vigilance, patient explanations, and calm
understanding if they are going to ensure that the sibling bond does not
remain negatively charged. The "go to your separate rooms until you cool
down" approach is a feeble way of offsetting the children's alienation; the
parents of children who feel this way usually carry a bitter legacy from
their own past. These sibling relationships need the most diplomacy and
delicacy to be understood and then turned in a positive direction.

POLARIZED REJECTION—RIGIDLY DIFFERENTIATED RELATIONSHIPS
*"You're so different from me. I don't want to depend on you, and I
never want to become like you."*

Ivan Boszormenyi-Nagy—with Spark (1973) and with Ulrich (1981)—
has viewed the regulation of object relations between intimates as akin to
the keeping of a ledger. Each person, according to Boszormenyi-Nagy,
maintains a psychological record of what is owed to him or her in the give
and take of any important relationship. A just relationship is, therefore,
one that is evenly balanced, in which a *quid pro quo* can be constantly
arranged. Serious imbalances in any such ledger due to one-sidedness,
deceit, exploitation, or betrayal become dishonoring influences on that
intimate human connection and mark each person as unequal and different. For young siblings, who lack the sophistication to understand the
contextual determinants of any conflict they have with a brother or a
sister, an impasse in their relationship can freeze the images of these pro-
tagonists for life. Simple, distorted, and unchanging perceptions of each
other as victim and victimizer dominate the views such siblings have in
ways that no amount of later explanations or reasoning can necessarily
undo. These indelible characterizations make for inflexible ways of relating and push the siblings farther apart. They remain a bitter residue from
childhood, cutting off possibilities of change and dialectical processes
which might otherwise bring the sibs together.

We have already indicated that one reason that siblings carry frozen
images of one another is to displace and substitute for the pain and confu-

sion suffered at the hands of parents. A more obvious reason for rigid differentiation is a sibling's oppressive, brutalizing, or insensitive treatment of a brother or a sister. In such a case the siblings form negative perceptions of one another, and their identifications are based on a polarization: neither wants to be like the other and dislikes, even hates, what he or she sees in the other. The more dominant sibling is generally contemptuous of the "weaker" sib, while the dominated or victimized sibling resists becoming like the oppressive one. Such victimized siblings are the least likely candidates to change the relationship, as they are reluctant to give up their separate identity as the "wounded one." Some of these siblings eventually come to possess a particular type of smugness and holier-than-thou attitude, precisely because of what they had to endure at the hands of their oppressive brother or sister. By adulthood, victimized siblings work hard at separating from their oppressor siblings, and often build their confidence by cultivating a personality directly opposite to that of the once-dominant sib. If the oppressor was cruel, the victim, must, compulsively, become gentle. Polarized rejection means that one still worries about having the same abhorred, reprehensible aspects as the other sibling. One still fears becoming like him or her, quakes at experiencing any of those "taboo" feelings, and needs to work feverishly to remain different.

Other victim siblings refuse to let their old victimizers off the hook and maintain moral leverage or perverse one-upmanship by still playing "one down" games. A victim sibling may slyly bring about a situation where his or her old persecutor will once again act harshly or cruelly, and, thus, through new pain or new suffering, remind that hurtful sibling that he or she has not changed, has always been cruel, or unjust, or insensitive, and probably always will be. Engendering guilt in an abusing sibling is, after all, one way of getting back for all indignities suffered in childhood. Underneath the adult mask of the victimized sibling is the implicit theme, "You owe me."

Entire sibling groups can also conspire in keeping unbalanced the old, hurtful, sibling ledger. Each person's status as creditor or debtor is remembered, marked, and serves as reference point whenever the sibling system regroups. In such circumstances as the period after a parent has died, siblings who have a rigidly differentiated relationship can add up accounts remembered from childhood, marking who was the victim and who the victimizer; who played the good role, and who the bad; who still has credit coming, and who must still pay up.

A Priest and His Domineering Big Brother: Robert and Lou. Father Robert, a forty-eight-year-old Catholic priest, asked his older brother and two sisters to meet him in one of our offices to help him resolve his dilemma about whether to leave the priesthood. Although he described his siblings as alienated from one another for many years, Father Robert desperately wanted those who remained in his family to approve his important decision. Judging by the support the siblings had recently shown each other during their mother's terminal illness, Father Robert now fantasized they might turn their helpful energies to him.

For several weeks prior to this anticipated sibling meeting, Father Robert described his anxiety and loathing of his oldest brother, Lou, now fifty-three, and told the therapist that Lou had been the family bully, the big brother who had kept his siblings in line with his fists. Even though he had a ferocious temper, he was the mother's favorite. All the siblings had been afraid of Lou. He had meted out punishment to his sisters and brother alike; no one was spared; and their parents rarely listened to the whiny complaints of the younger children.

The youngest brother, Robert, could not wait to get away from this brother and swore he would be different. Joining the seminary and becoming a priest was the perfect solution; Robert could avoid Lou, be conspicuously different, and achieve cherished status in this traditional Catholic family. After Robert took his final vows for the priesthood, he expressed interest in working with parochial school students. This gentle vocation would be the perfect foil to big brother Lou, who had become a salesman, a natural outlet for his aggressive talents. Robert, the priest, was now poised in exquisite juxtaposition to his brother; Robert had triumphed by becoming different and could, with Lou as his counterpoint, consolidate his identity. He would remain estranged from this brother for the next twenty years.

But now Robert was in danger of giving this all up, and his anxiety was profound. As the anticipated meeting was about to take place, Robert became frightened. His older brother was traveling three hundred miles to help him, and the younger brother realized he was risking a change in their frozen relationship. What would happen if Lou were to be comforting, supportive, gentle, or understanding? After all, there is comfort in knowing one's "place" and in keeping one's tightly defined identity. When the session opened, Robert began to explain himself in faltering tones. Lou, a large, heavy-set man with an impatient expression on his face, countered by asserting his "older" expertise.

LOU: [*Very emphatically*] He's got to know who he is before he takes off that collar. Because if he doesn't know who he is and where he is going before he leaves it . . . I've seen them . . . the prognosis is extremely *poor*. If he is looking for a *crutch*, he is in *trouble!* If he is looking for help from us—that sense of support—hey, I think everyone of us would be tickled pink to help him in any way we can—to help him find himself. That's the way I feel.

ROBERT: [*Faintly*] That's a valid point. What more can I add to it, really? [*Evading his brother's offer*]

THERAPIST: [*Turning to Robert*] Don't you believe your brother?

ROBERT: Yes and no. [*Warily*] Because once again, whenever I think I send out a strong signal, you . . . yet, you know . . . you . . . you won't help me, you never helped me.

LOU: [*Now yelling and red in the face*] Well for Christ's sake! . . . Why don't you ever call up and say, "God-damn it! I said something to you. Why don't you answer me?" Then I'll answer you.

Set up by his brother to attend the meeting and slipping into an old role, Lou was now very much the brother he had always been.

ROBERT: [*Rubbing his right shoulder*] I never talk to you that way. That's not me.

LOU: [*Contemptuous*] Well, why don't you?

ROBERT: Because I've never done *it* before. [*Now cowering*] You overwhelm me. You always did.

LOU: Well, you better start doing *it* now!

Both of the sisters who were present began laughing at the sight of this painful confrontation between their brothers. One of them then turned to Robert and shouted out, "Ah hah! He's still the big brother and you can't forget it!" She and the other sister then turned to Lou and began reminding him of how he had always abused, heckled, bulldozed, scorned, and dominated all of his siblings. What right, they asked Lou, did he have to expect Robert to know how to ask for help since he, Lou, had always been the bully? Robert joined his sisters in attacking the big brother. When the therapist asked why Robert was still compulsively rubbing his shoulder, the priest remembered that this was the spot that Lou, the bully, had always picked on to "pound" him. Robert's shoulder uncannily had retained the memory of what Lou had done to him. Like his sisters, Robert was recalling the unbalanced ledger of pounding and abuse. He and his sisters were now, in their own right, "pounding" the big brother. Faced with the united group of younger siblings who refused to relinquish the frozen images of previous years, Lou packed his good intentions the next day and bitterly left for home.

Patterns of Identification and Sibling Relationships

Part of the challenge for any therapist confronted with this pattern is to understand the context of the original misunderstandings that gave rise to it. Through therapy, Robert was eventually able to recognize that no one person was fully culpable for the hardships each child in that family had had to endure. The hardship and physical poverty of their home; the role of surrogate father which the oldest son, Lou, had to fill; the family's acceptance of hitting as routine; and the need to deny that they, too, could be just as aggressive—all consolidated to create the image of Lou as a hostile tyrant, keeping the others insulated from a similar self-concept. After Robert became less defensive, he was better able to relinquish his misunderstandings about his big brother, and gradually began to accept him as a peer. His dilemma about leaving the priesthood took a less compulsive course, free from the life-long pressure *not* to be like his brother.

DE-IDENTIFYING—DISOWNED RELATIONSHIPS

"We're totally different from one another. I don't need you, I don't like you, and I don't care if I ever see you again."

At the extreme end of the continuum of similarity and difference are those siblings who want as little as possible to do with a brother or a sister, and see absolutely nothing in common. They usually claim that they are "totally different," de-identify—that is, deny that there are any points of similarity between them—and disown the relationship (Stierlin 1974). De-identification° can operate both unilaterally and mutually. In families in which one child has all the emotional riches and the other is the family pauper, disowning is usually unilateral, the province of the entitled child, while the disadvantaged child remains envious and resentful. Denial and projection play a substantial role in the fixed belief that one is superior to a sibling. Strong splits in the family-embraced identities of siblings—such as the "bad boy" and the "good girl," the "well child" and the "sick child," the "strong one" and the "weak one"—contribute to eventual de-identification. Disowning is perpetuated when the de-identifying one does not protect the other sibling, avoids ever uniting with him or her, and condemns, and despises this "inferior" brother or sister, thus keeping the family fool firmly boxed into place.

A child's attempt to de-identify explains, in part, why one sibling may fight intensely with another when they live together as young children, as

---

° One aspect of de-identification has been described and studied by Frances F. Schacter and her co-workers (1976), who see de-identification as a defense against a "Cain complex," preventing murderous feelings from breaking into the open.

if to say "Get away from me." The rejection is much more severe than that displayed by the hostile dependent types who are really saying, "I *dare* you to hurt me back." These siblings reject decisively and may speak to one another only if parents force them to. Their disdain is profound; the void they create inevitably becomes permanent. Having disowned the relationship so early in life, these siblings function as if the one fears that the other has a contagious disease. The voicing of hate or detestation for a brother or a sister may express one's continued need for de-identification and does not accurately or necessarily reflect what that sibling has ever personally done to one. Later in life, when circumstances bring the two siblings together, the de-identifying one may become anxious, itch to leave, or explode in anger or frustration. Cutting off the sibling is really like severing part of oneself; in object-relations language, the hated sibling becomes "dissociated."

One older brother said of his sister:

> As soon as we're in the same room, there's a wall of tension that goes up. I get very, very anxious. And that's it. I find myself withdrawing, pulling back, becoming very, very intellectual and very, very distant. I watch her do the same thing. She'll become very nervous, smoke a lot of cigarettes, become very tense and not know what to say. . . . It's a very, very strained relationship. And I'm not sure it's something I want to change.

When the therapist asked why he didn't want to change the relationship, the brother got tense and angry and replied, "I'm not sure I know that. All I sense is that I hate her guts." This brother is de-identifying and, by making sure he sees his sister only twice a year for a few hours at a time, insulates himself against any conscious identification. He has little motive to reclaim this lost part of himself.

When both siblings de-identify, the relationship can break down completely; and, in some cases, contact may be permanently severed. Early mutual de-identification virtually prohibits close adult sibling relationships, as there has been too long a period of grievance, prejudice, suffering, and misunderstanding. Typically, these siblings have made sure that their paths would no longer cross; they often move far away, choose different, non-intersecting careers, and have little opportunity to rewrite their ledgers.

Yet an understanding of de-identification, how it occurs and affects the development of one's identity, can lead to an important insight into oneself. A determination *not* to become like a particular brother or sister

Patterns of Identification and Sibling Relationships

means that one has given up certain options of behavior and has relegated them to the other sibling. As we will see in chapter 9, every sibling, no matter how much he or she may dislike a brother or sister, recognizes that each person carries inside some part of the other.

Whether one stays tied to one's brothers and sisters, or separates from them in ways that can never be bridged, the life-long quest for a secure personal identity is inextricably woven into that of one's sibling. But other forces, particularly from the family, also dictate how siblings maintain their relationships, and capriciously enter into and alter brothers' and sisters' lives. Now we are ready to turn to these other vital matters, some of which literally involve life and death.

CHAPTER 5

Acts of Sacrifice: Loyalty and Caring

Hansel and Gretel

As small children, most of us listened to the story of Hansel and Gretel, a tale which aroused our childish fear of being abandoned by our parents.

> The children's father, a poor broom maker, has remarried after his wife's death. Then their land is struck by famine, and the father, though loving his children, falls under the evil influence of his new wife. Together he and the stepmother plan how to get rid of the children, as there is not enough food to feed them all. Three times they lead the children into a dark and dangerous forest and leave them there to die, and twice Hansel cleverly manages to lead himself and his sister back to the house, but the third time the children lose their way in the forest.
>
> Hansel and Gretel have only each other to turn to as they shepherd one another through the dangerous forest, cooperating in the face of threats, and keeping in each other's minds hopes of father, food, and freedom. Wandering hand in hand, without food, they at last come to a candy house, and begin eagerly to eat. But the house is the home of a vicious witch, who captures the two children and puts Hansel in a cage, intending to fatten him up to eat. Just in time Gretel outwits the witch and, in her turn, saves her brother. Together they spring for freedom. By a happy chance they meet their father and find that their stepmother has died in their absence. Their father is overjoyed to find them, and together they return to their cottage, there to live happily again.

Psychotherapists meet many Hansels and Gretels who have no loving or sustaining parent at home, and for whom, thus abandoned, the sibling relationship is the only caring force. These siblings' relationships and

112

Acts of Sacrifice: Loyalty and Caring

identities are intertwined, sometimes for life, because they have jointly faced traumatic psychological losses at crucial stages of their development. Mutual loyalty and caregiving for these real-life Hansels and Gretels permit both physical and psychological survival.

Intense loyalty and sustained caregiving are not based on simple strategic or temporarily convenient alliances that can easily be broken, changed, or forgotten. Unlike a momentary alliance, sibling loyalty takes years to develop and affects the loyal one's identity over much of a lifetime. Nor should loyalty and caregiving be confused with what some sociologists refer to as "sibling solidarity." Most siblings will *say* that they have enduring relationships that involve staying in touch, recognizing each other's birthdays, and meeting occasionally on the common turf of their parents' home. Sibling solidarity describes siblings who are a friendly and companionable network; but such a network may not be intensely loyal or always characterized by *committed* caregiving (Cumming and Schneider 1961).

Loyalty goes deeper, touching powerful emotions. Loyalty refers to what the American philosopher Josiah Royce called "the willing and practical and thoroughgoing devotion of a person to a cause" (1916). The word *loyalty* derives from the French *loi*, meaning "law." Loyalty involves feeling and identification with the other person; it also requires tangible action (Scharr 1968).

Many of the most loyal siblings are the oldest child in a family, and the majority appear to be older females. But birth order and gender do not always indicate who is appointed a loyal caretaker by circumstances or by family projections. Thus, while "in most societies firstborns . . . ordinarily care for, control and discipline their other siblings" (Rosenblatt and Skoogberg 1974, p. 48), in Western society, a middle or a youngest sibling can be a caretaker. A younger brother, given sufficient identification with maternal role models, can well become the nurturing, supervising "older presence" for his brother two years older. While an older sibling usually takes care of a younger, there are many fascinating exceptions to the rule, resulting from unique variations within each family's life story.

Finally, we are not talking about occasional babysitting, looking out for one's brother and sister in a neighborhood skirmish, or keeping an eye on a sibling while the mother runs to the supermarket. The caretaker, in our sense, is a "parental child"—one who acts and feels like a full-time parent, concerned with one or more siblings' total welfare, and gets little, if any, supervision or help from competent adults. Such caretaking dominates the life of both caretaker and charge to good and bad effect.

113

Reciprocal Loyalty

We conceive of sibling loyalty as being either one-way or reciprocal. In the latter, the siblings look out for one another: there is mutuality, and a repayment of help and cooperation. Since the caring goes both ways, the siblings make sacrifices willingly: these children are care*givers*. By contrast, in one-way loyalty, one child makes all the sacrifices without repayment (see pages 125–41): such a child is a care*taker*.

The following are examples of the Hansel and Gretel ideal of reciprocity and mutual caregiving.

Escaping the Witch: Bob and Stan. Bob and Stan, separated by only two years, were each other's constant companions through early childhood. The father, a creative artist, and the mother, a housewife, provided a life relatively unfurrowed by stress, and both were emotionally available. These parents fostered harmony between the boys: fighting rarely exceeded playful wrestling and friendly bickering. They were a middle-class family, comfortably settled and financially successful, and the children never wanted for parental encouragement and attention.

The father died suddenly when Bob was nine and Stan eleven, so that their mother was forced to go out to work as a business executive. But her husband's death triggered a heretofore dormant predisposition to colitis. She fell ill a year later and underwent a series of operations for cancer. During the third operation, she suddenly went into shock and died on the operating table. A family friend broke the news of her death to the boys, who had been staying with a babysitter. Orphans aged ten and twelve, they had no relatives to turn to. The father's parents were dead, and there were no uncles or aunts as their father had been an only child. The mother had but one sister, a woman who had avoided contact for years, and who made a perfunctory condolence call on Bob and Stan. After kissing them both sweetly on their foreheads, she pulled up a moving van and made off with most of the furniture. The will had been left vague, and trustees were appointed as the boy's guardians. The guardians, who turned out to be emotionally disturbed, resented and abused the children and made impossible demands of them. As the boys moved into adolescence, these foster parents criticized them and used them for the money from the trust.

During adolescence Bob and Stan felt like Hansel and Gretel in the witch's house: each maintained a conspiracy of silence on the other's behalf when the foster mother would pump one for personal information about the other. They both recognized, early in their stay with her, that she was a sadist. Each could reassure the other that her actions were irrational, and could provide the other with emotional protection. As boys (and later as young adults) they would swap stories about her vicious attacks; the story swapping united them against their common enemy. Loyal siblings verify reality for one another. In this case, the boys could certify that it was the stepmother who was insane, that neither boy had to accept her projections of badness. It is likely that neither boy as an *only* child would have emerged, from the experience with the foster mother, without major psychological injury.

Their foster parents continued to abuse them, implying that the eldest was a homosexual, and that the youngest was academically inferior, and told the boys lies about their biological parents. In an attempt to separate Bob and Stan so that they could not speak to each other at night, the foster parents assigned them separate bedrooms. The boys flatly refused and, rather than live in comfortable but separate second-floor bedrooms, chose to live together in a tiny attic room where their two beds could be accommodated only with great difficulty. By refusing to be separated, they were able to defend each other and their relationship from these hostile outsiders.

Reactions to separation were painful, as Stan, the older brother, remembered:

> Bob had to encounter a lot of things that I didn't when I was growing up. A couple of things happened to him when he was younger. [*His voice begins to tremble, and he suddenly weeps, remembering*] . . .
> He was in the hospital. I was upset. And it was like . . . [*his voice breaks, unable to speak for a moment*]—*I* was going through it. I felt that it was the worst thing that could happen to me. It was like sympathy, I felt pain for him. . . . When he has an operation or goes into any adverse situation—it, it makes me cry.

In addition, these young men, now twenty and twenty-two, chose the same small midwestern college, many miles from their home in the East. They spent most major holidays together. And they shared a fantasy that after each had married, they would buy a vacation spot together—a homestead where their wives and children could blend with them into a big, happy household.

As college students, these siblings once had a violent physical confrontation which resulted in a black eye for one and a bloodied nose for the other. The brawl, triggered by a "bossy" comment by the elder brother, continued as a verbal argument for a full day they spent together at a winter cottage. The altercation led them to discuss hurt feelings that each had harbored for several years, including Stan's rage because his younger brother had left unchallenged a rumor that he, Stan, was mentally ill. While loyalty had guided their relationship, Bob had felt jealous of his older brother's success in school and had envied his smooth rapport with pretty girls. By not stopping the rumor, Bob's envy seeped to the surface of their relationship. Now, feeling guilty for betraying his brother, he sought to make things right:

> BOB: I know you felt betrayed. All I could do was cry on your shoulder and say, "I love you and I didn't mean to say that." . . . I loved you and respected you for what you felt.
>
> STAN: We both did things we regretted. [*To interviewer*] Bob has a very dynamic temper and sometimes he doesn't have control over it and neither do I. . . . I've always considered that temper an advantage, you know, you could *really* get your feelings out, and we'd both know it was okay.

Bob and Stan had the capacity to have a battle and resolve it with a full outpouring of emotion. These brothers exemplify the pattern of loyal acceptance and mutual dependence described in chapter 4.

All for One and One for All: The Jerome Brothers. The Jerome brothers, German-Jewish and middle-class, were reared in a large midwestern city. Their early lives were characterized by good times and a relatively stable home life. The mother was economically well off; the father worked and got some support from members of his own extended family who were politically well connected. When economic times worsened, the family moved to a tough, lower middle-class neighborhood. The mother died when the boys were aged twenty-three, seventeen, thirteen, and twelve, respectively. The father became exhausted, unpredictable, sometimes violent, and emotionally unavailable, leaving the boys with only the maternal grandmother, who lived on the same street, for backup and support; now the family threatened to disintegrate. Because the father lost out in a family rift between his own eight siblings—he was the black sheep, the scapegoat of the family—economic support from his side vanished. The brothers and their floundering father were, with the exception of their grandmother, completely isolated from people who cared.

Interviewed a quarter of a century later, the four brothers were asked to reflect on their experience and current relationships with one another. Each had graduated from college, and each in his own right had become a success. Like Stan and Bob, they had suffered serious parental deprivation, and each had become the other's most important influence.

Their loyalty to each other was, to put it simply, fierce: their commitment to one another had always, and would always, come before all others. Their relationships were governed by an unwritten law that ordains that, first and foremost, "we will stick together." These were not temporary alliances but, rather, relationship agreements or contracts with a long history; and the brothers expected them to continue. As two of them put it:

> NATHAN (THE YOUNGEST): There's four brothers, going through life. Instead of falling apart, as many would do at a crisis—like the death of our mother or the crumbling of our father as a "figurehead" of the family, we didn't. We complement each other. If one is down, the others are up. At *no* time would all four of us be down, because whoever might be down at a particular time, it will be recognized by the others, and they would help to get him up.
>
> LARRY (THE SECOND OLDEST): Whether that be financially or spiritually.
>
> NATHAN: Right! Regardless of what it is. For example, I know as I sit right here, if I ever got in any trouble—the *first* ones I go to is my brothers. I don't call my father. I don't call my in-laws. I don't call my wife. I call my brothers.

These brothers communicated a sense that they would always be available to one another, that problems could be shared immediately and without embarrassment, that common values were shared, and that they could count on each other for honesty, understanding, and support. Their willingness to sacrifice shows itself in such statements as Larry's:

> If you came to me with any difficulty, you know, if it's financial, academic, or whatever . . . I'd give you my last buck. And I *mean* that, sincerely, in *spite* of my responsibilities to my children and wife. You know, I've got a lifetime to live, and I got a lifetime to make it back. I would give him my last buck.

They have tried, as adults, to stay in touch with one another. Earlier in life they had reacted with anxiety to being separated. When questioned by the interviewer, Eli, the oldest brother, recalled his emotions at the age of nine when his brother Larry went to the hospital: "You know! 'THEY'RE CUTTING HIM OPEN! WHAT ARE THEY DOING *THAT* TO HIM FOR?' That was *terrible* for me."

Eli, as the oldest, became the mentor to the other four. When, in his early twenties, he was appointed chairman to an academic department at a high school, he learned that one of his younger brothers was in serious academic difficulty, and coached him for his examinations. Eli's role as cultural and academic leader of the brothers was further established when he tutored Jack, the next to youngest brother, after the latter had transferred from a ghetto high school to a more academically demanding one. The transition had been abrupt, and Jack was in danger of flunking out. Eli had encouraged him and set an example of concern. Years later Jack attributed his own successful completion of a college and architectural degree largely to his oldest brother's help and support.

The reciprocal help and sacrifice that permeated the brothers' relationship was illustrated when Eli described what the second oldest, Larry, had done for him when their mother had died. Her death had made Eli the leader of the group of four siblings. He organized them and kept track of them—chastised them for smoking, monitored their grades, set a good example for them. His efforts were successful owing to the efforts of Larry, who helped to calm him in moments of crisis, who shared the burden of teaching the two youngest to get along, who put himself at risk in breaking up the fights of the two youngest, and even taught one of the boys to cook. Eli considered Larry an ally, a backup, an extra resource.

In their ghetto neighborhood, racial conflicts and gang fights were not uncommon. An attack on one boy was remembered and quickly avenged by the joint action of two or more of the brothers. The Three Musketeers' motto "One for all and all for one" could easily have served as theirs. Their defense of one another had been learned at home. Their father, a physically abusive man, beat them all; they learned to tip each other off about their father's moods and quietly showed support for each other when he was angry. One of the boys "enjoyed" showing his other three brothers that he could take the father's beatings without reacting emotionally in any visible way. They felt terrified by what had happened to this brother and yet encouraged that if he could stand up to their father, so could they.

All sibling groups must work out a way of handling their aggressive feelings in relation to one another. These brothers who had been exposed to (and had perhaps internalized) their father's aggression, knew that anger, unless well managed, could destructively explode among them.

Acts of Sacrifice: Loyalty and Caring

Among these brothers, as with all other reciprocally loyal groups of siblings, there was a capacity for argument, disagreement, and even outright fighting. They also had, however, the ability to forgive and forget hurts and grievances. While differences were never swept under the carpet, neither were they allowed to escalate to the point of endangering the warm bonds of the boys' relationship. Whenever the younger ones had a fight, their older brothers, sensing danger, jumped in to prop up the loser or to defuse the conflict. They all knew that their larger interest as a group could not be served if domination and unfairness were long permitted. One should remember that sibling conflict, aggression, and rivalry are not incompatible with loyalty. In fact, loyal siblings are able to prove to themselves that they can stay close despite conflict; and they have a carefully developed inner sense of where the "fair" limits of aggression are; they may attack one another, but they generally do so without humiliating. Loyal siblings, like the mythic brothers about whom Freud speculated in *Totem and Taboo* (1912–13), know how to make peace with one another, perhaps *because* they realize that they *can* annihilate each other.

In adulthood, slapstick and high jinks had replaced the primitive battling and peacemaking of childhood. Humor allowed the brothers to laugh off their differences, making ludicrous aspects of each other's personalities that less loyal sibling groups might find "bones of contention." For example, Eli patronized the fine arts and lived a fashionable and culturally sophisticated life. This difference from his equally successful but less culturally fashionable younger brothers now became a point for caustic humor, a mock battle in which they enact a seething counterpoint of macho man versus snob-*littérateur*.

Nathan, the youngest, always athletic and traditionally masculine, pointed to his oldest brother:

> Now, his "highfalutinness" till today still bugs me. He calls me up and gives me what I refer to as "high class bullshit." I sit there and say to myself, "Why is he still trying to impress me?" Really! And I can *tell* it to him too! Or as a birthday gift two or three years ago he sent me a silk scarf. His giving me a silk scarf is like me giving him a baseball glove. I will never use the silk scarf, *he* will never use the baseball glove.

At this, all four brothers broke into raucous laughter.

These brothers have become distinctly different, play different roles, have different life styles and careers; yet they "celebrate" the differences in their identities, use each other as playful foils, and remain for each other a continuing source of amusement, amazement, and curiosity.

When the youngest brother, Nathan, decided to marry a girl of a different ethnic background, he first checked with his brothers:

NATHAN: I said, look—I've been dating this girl for two and one half years and I'm gonna marry her, do you see any problems?

JACK: I told you when you told me about getting married that I'd try to talk you out of it.

NATHAN: That's right.

ELI: I said to him—I think you're making a mistake. Number one, the girl was much younger than him. Number two, I really didn't believe he was ready to marry . . . and I said to him—"I think you're crazy." And he says, "Okay, but I just want to know, would you not talk to me if I marry her? Does that end our relationship?" And I said, no, of course not.

Loyal sibling groups derive both identity and pleasure in marking their difference from outsiders by speaking a special language. The Jerome brothers repeatedly made it clear to the interviewer that he was their guest, that he was being admitted to a world that only they could really understand. They cracked in-group jokes when they were in the presence of outsiders; they enjoyed the puzzlement and discomfort that together they could cause, portrayed themselves as an exclusive club that few could enter, and attacked anyone who might challenge their underlying feelings for one another. They repeatedly made jokes about the one of their wives who found it the hardest to fit in with their brand of "special understanding." Their cohesiveness derived in part from their ability to attack outside threats, rather than to dwell on the inequities within their brotherhood. Having had such a severe father, they were determined not to become antagonistic.

Keeping loyalty alive requires energy, and some siblings from reciprocally loyal groups expend more energy than other siblings do. There is usually one key member of the group who plays an organizing, paternal and maternal role. Among the Jerome brothers, the second oldest acted to cool their conflicts and reminded his brothers of their common interest. During a three-hour meeting, he repeatedly blocked the interviewer's attempts to clarify controversial issues, interrupted him and, steered the discussion as the brothers' emotional leader—his accustomed sibling role since their mother's death. Indeed, he seemed more centrally identified than the other brothers with a caring maternal presence. He enjoyed his role as watchdog, humorist, and peacemaker, and his brothers respected him for it; but he appeared less free to "take" from his brothers than they to take from him.

Bob and Stan's and the Jerome brothers' loyalty was forged in middle childhood and adolescence. Even more extreme and compulsive forms of loyalty can be observed when children, from the earliest days of infancy, have had only one another as constant objects (see chapter 2).

The Orphans of Terezin. Anna Freud and Sophie Dann studied a unique group of six children whose parents had been murdered by the Nazis. While these children were not biological siblings, we have considered them as such because from birth, they were forced to grow up together. They formed attachments to each other long before language or freedom of choice about companionships had developed. They were reared together in the Ward for Motherless Children at the Terezin concentration camp in Czechoslovakia. Four of these children had lost their mothers immediately after birth; the other two, probably before their twelfth month. "After the loss of their mothers all the children wandered for some time from one place to another, with several complete changes of adult environment. . . . They were ignorant of the meaning of a 'family'" (1951, p. 129). Once they were placed in the concentration camp nursery, only their basic biological needs were met by adults. Lacking toys, their social activity apparently consisted entirely of play with one another. They never attached themselves to adults. When the Allies finally liberated Terezin in 1945, the children were flown as a group to a therapeutic nursery in Hampstead, England, where Anna Freud and Sophie Dann studied them. The children, at the time of this move, ranged in age from three years to three years and ten months. Striking were the total absence of rivalry and aggression among this group and their lack of trust in any adult. Like the siblings in chapter 2, they were rigidly fused:

> The children's positive feelings were centered exclusively in their own group. It was evident that they cared greatly for each other and not at all for anybody or anything else. . . . They had no other wish than to be together and became upset when they were separated from each other even for short moments. . . . This insistence on being inseparable made it impossible in the beginning to treat the children as individuals or to vary their lives according to their special needs. (P. 131)

The children chattered in German and refused at first to accept their caretakers' language (English). They used a physical language whereby they attacked, spat upon, kicked, or bit the adults—and they widely imitated one another. This physical language bound them together as a distinct and highly suspicious group.

Reciprocity, warmth, and cooperation characterized these children for the first months of their stay at Hampstead:

> When together, the children were a closely knit group of members with equal status, no child assuming leadership for any length of time, but each one exerting a strong influence on the others by virtue of individual qualities, peculiarities, or by the mere fact of belonging. (P. 132)

The children identified with one another so deeply that the special needs of any member could evoke a sensitive and helpful response on the part of the others.

> The children's unusual emotional dependence on each other was borne out further by the almost complete absence of jealousy, rivalry and competition. . . . Since the adults played no part in their emotional lives at the time, they did not compete with each other for favors or recognition. . . . They did not grudge each other their possessions. . . . When one of them received a present from a shopkeeper, they demanded the same for each of the other children, even in their absence. . . . At mealtimes handing food to the neighbor was of greater importance than eating oneself. (P. 134)

The children readily—amazingly for three-year-olds—intervened with the staff if an adult failed to see one of them having difficulty finding a toy or opening a door. The children listened carefully to each other: one who was talking too loud could be silenced by another's demand for quiet.

Any verbal aggression among the children resembled bickering rather than fundamental hatred. They never attacked each other physically but did attack the staff and furniture: it was as if each child felt every other child to be a precious extension of his or her own self and had to be cherished and treated carefully.

One child, Ruth, was somewhat on the periphery of the group and was likely to exhibit envy and rivalry. She was less willing than her comrades to make sacrifices for them, and favored adult companions at the nursery. Ruth was also, of the six, the only child with a recorded history of a strong attachment to a mother substitute before going to the nursery. We are unable to prove definite causality, but her distinct difference from the others, given this history, suggests that an early-imbued sense that adults could be trusted conflicted with a loyal bond with her fellow orphans.

CHARACTERISTICS OF RECIPROCAL LOYALTY

Reciprocally loyal sibling relationships, as in the three previous examples, have characteristics similar to those mentioned by Willard Hartup (1975) as qualities of a friendship:

- The siblings become upset when removed from one another.
- They have a special, private, code, understandable mainly among themselves, for their relationship. This private language makes them distinct from other relatives and friends.
- They protect each other from physical and psychological attacks by outsiders.
- They are cooperative and do things to help one another.

In addition, intensely loyal siblings display two other qualities:

- They resolve conflicts, contain aggression within manageable limits, and develop rituals of forgiveness and understanding. Group harmony outweighs any individual's quest for personal advantage.
- They celebrate and add to one another's distinct identities. On the basis of both role and identity, they are compatible and complementary.

THE PARENTAL VACUUM

These six characteristics of deep sibling loyalty require a basic weakness, absence, or failure of parents and the relative unavailability of parent surrogates. Thus, the more available parents are both emotionally and physically, the less intense is the attachment between siblings. As parents are absent either emotionally or physically, the siblings may be forced to reach out for one another. A variety of psychological studies conducted over the last fifty years support the notion that parental overinvolvement diminishes sibling loyalty while underinvolvement can emphasize it (Bossard and Boll 1956; Sewall and Smalley 1930; Sutton-Smith, Rosenberg, and Landy 1968).

It would be easy to conclude, then, that if parents treat their children badly, fail to nurture them, ignore them, or die when they are young, the children will be forced to form a mutually respecting and helpful society of their own. Yet not all children who have serious losses and grow up in deprivation, cherish one another.* There are countless sibling groups who neither care for one another nor go out of their way to recognize each other's existence. In some impoverished rural families in which parents have died, or which are starving, the brothers' and sisters' relationships frequently erupt in rivalry and fratricidal squabbles (Ahrensberg 1937). In extreme conditions, brothers and sisters can engage in cutthroat abandonment of each other, each desperately trying to save his or her own skin. Still other groups of siblings, under conditions of deprivation and

---

* As the reader will see in chapters 7 (incest) and 8 (aggression and rivalry), parental deprivation can also lead to vastly different, unhappy, and conflicted sibling relationships.

loss, find a parent substitute (for example, a teacher, a mentor, a thera-pist) and make only superficial attachments to siblings.

Sibling loyalty, then, does not simply form in a vacuum of parental care, although the parental vacuum appears to endow it with its intense quality. Other factors are essential for loyalty to flourish. One cannot cherish another sibling if one has experienced profound ego impairment in the first eighteen months of life. To paraphrase Margaret Mahler and M. Furer (1968), who has written about early object relationships, one whose nurturant or executive modalities are crippled, cannot fully love, cooperate, or reciprocate with other people. Reciprocity among siblings depends on having the basic needs of life met early enough. Siblings must have "role models" or examples available so that they can see and imitate nurturing and interpersonal sensitivity—qualities upon which loyalty heavily depends. The Terezin orphans related to one another in an or-phanage where they were surrounded by nurturing and kindly child-care workers.° The Jerome brothers were exposed to the kindness of a grand-mother who lived down the street, and they had had a mother who, be-fore her death, was known as firm but generous. Bob and Stan had loving parents through their early childhood. While attachment and identifica-tion may develop between children, the many positive ways of showing loyalty seem greatly dependent upon having caring adult figures whom siblings can introject and idealize.

Loyal siblings rarely allow themselves to be favored for long by one parent or relative over any of the other siblings. Among the siblings in our studies, no one was seen as any relative's "favorite," and no one was "played" against another. Favoritism breeds vicious rivalries and is anti-thetical to the growth of loyalty, as we shall detail in chapter 8. As chil-dren, loyal siblings spend enough time together to get to know each other deeply. They must also have access to one another at crucial developmen-tal stages. This access is sometimes, but not always, the result of closeness in age. Thus, Bob and Stan, two years apart, were adolescents together, attending the same high school, being abused by the same foster parents. At the time of their mother's death, the two younger Jerome children

---

° There is no documentation about the quality of care these children received while they were in Terezin. The Terezin orphans seemed to have transcended early ego impairment by virtue both of their attachment to one another as transitional objects and also of the richly warm and sensitive environment provided at Hampstead. Whether these children were in fact "ego-impaired" could be determined by restudying those who are now adults in their mid-forties.

formed a close coalition since they were only a year apart. And there was harmony between twenty-three-year-old Eli and the second-born, Larry (age seventeen) because the six years between them permitted the elder to become a warm "father" rather than a rival. Thus, Larry could act as his big brother Eli's proxy with the little kids. The matter of age spacing is not at all simple. A variety of ages allows the sibling group to organize a top-to-bottom hierarchy. At the same time, closeness in age of some siblings fosters identification and common interests.

Being of the same sex appears to foster loyalty, as children have a common ground and can identify with each other more easily than they can if one is of the opposite sex. The fact that siblings of the same sex do not have to work out heterosexual attraction with one another allows them to organize their loyalty more readily than can opposite-sex siblings. On the other hand, the sexual differences between siblings can, as with the Terezin orphans, heighten complementarity as the children play out "Momma" and "Poppa" roles. There are many routes to sibling loyalty, and each family acquires loyal structures in a unique way.

One-Way Loyalty: Being "My Brother's Keeper"

In one-way loyalty, a child carries to extremes the ideal of being *her* "brother's keeper." The "parental child," who is generally a girl,* assumes primary responsibility for brothers and sisters in childhood and often on into adulthood. Such loyalty differs from reciprocal loyalty in three major ways. First, the caretaker gives without getting. Second, the role and identity of the caretaker is locked in and rigid. There is little flexibility about who gives and who gets. One sibling bears the burden for all the others. Finally, the warm interchange that characterizes reciprocal sibling groups is relatively lacking—a lack that has negative, long-term effects on both giver and receiver.

WHY A CHILD BECOMES HER "BROTHER'S KEEPER": PAYOFFS FOR THE CARETAKER

For a child to give up her own interests on behalf of a sibling, the motivations have to be powerful. Singlehandedly to protect, teach, con-

---

*Hence, throughout this section we have used the feminine pronoun for the caretaking sibling, although boys may be in similar circumstances and take on the role.

trol, nurture, and support a younger person is, even for a biological parent, often painful and upsetting, infuriating, and emotionally depleting. A caring parent, however, has many advantages that the caretaker sibling lacks. Parents have often planned and looked forward to the time when they would have children. A biological mother has nine months during her pregnancy to attune herself to caring for her baby, and also undergoes a hormonal change that, to quote Richard Q. Bell (1974), "launches the caregiving" and lays the foundation for attachment. After delivery, there are other changes, including lactation, which release caring "instincts" in the mother—maternal responses that are stimulated even further by her physical contact with the infant.

In addition, motherhood and parenting are celebrated by society. They are virtuous roles: there are support systems for being a mother or a father, but there are few supports for being a sibling caretaker. Finally, parents are intellectually and emotionally more mature than children and thus better able to deal with their demands.

Three powerful organizing motivations activate and sustain the caretaker sibling: protecting the parents and attaining competence; cherishing the parents' image and seeking "constancy"; and seizing parental power and getting revenge. We list these as if they were separate and distinct only for the sake of clarity. In actuality, a caretaker sib can act out of all three.

The desire to keep one's parents healthy gets bound up with one's ultimate security early in life, and children will go to almost any extreme to comfort parents or to protect them from psychological collapse. One way by which a child can give the parents a sense of purpose, is by developing symptoms that energize the parents, distracting them from their own problems. Another more direct, less destructive route to preserving parents is to quiet a noisy or bothersome sibling and relieve them of having to socialize their other children. Thus, the caretaker sibling serves as a family therapist and relieves individual tensions. She also relieves marital strains. Where parents may disagree about disciplining an angry boy, a sister may appease the boy's anger in advance and thus avert parental conflicts. In addition, by organizing her siblings to clean the house, she can relieve their mother of that drudgery and of having to remind the younger children to do it. The caretaker sibling, motivated by a desire to protect a parent, is therefore always on duty. Such behavior is worried, compulsive, and driven: if the caretaker fails, the parents, and therefore the entire family, might become chaotic or could collapse.

A Protective Caretaker: Susan. Susan, the oldest of the five children of an emotionally shallow and distant father and of a mother who was disturbed, and who did little to disguise her promiscuity, provides a vivid illustration of how a protective caretaker is "made." Susan was ten when the first of her four siblings was born. Sensing at the time how over-whelmed her mother was, and noticing that her father had little time to care for either his wife or the new infant, Susan remembers:

> When my mother came home from the hospital with the baby, I made a complete dinner for the family. I mean a *complete* meal—roast beef, potatoes, and gravy. My father always told me, back then . . . and I think he was only partly joking—"The gravy is too lumpy to swallow." I don't know how I ever did it or where I learned it at ten, but every time she came home with a new kid, I had the whole house cleaned up and had prepared a special meal.

Knowing the fragility of her parents' alliance with each other, Susan dedicated herself to "making things better between them." She willingly (but with unconscious resentment) allowed her mother to assign ever more responsibility to her for changing diapers, babysitting, and cleaning the house. Susan even had to do most of the shopping, thus allowing the mother to spend more time in the afternoon and evening with her gentle-men friends. Susan also knew that if she did not make the house and siblings "shipshape," her father would discover the mess and blame her mother. By organizing her little brothers and sisters, Susan carefully guarded her mother's sexual activities from the father's scrutiny; taking care of the kids kept the peace. By the same token, by parenting the other children (which in later years included tutoring, transporting, and taking care of the medical needs of her siblings), Susan protected her father from her mother's wrath. She could become the "perfect" mother, outdoing her own mother, by acting as the protector for both of the infantile parents. Had she refused the role or run away from home, the father's coldness and neglect would have been even more painfully apparent to the mother and Susan's siblings. Years later, when she became a patient in psycho-therapy, her therapist asked her why she didn't run away from home. Surprised at his question, she pulled upright in her chair, bristling: "And just *who* do you think would have cared for my brothers and sisters?"

Susan, by sixteen, had become a competent homemaker and counselor for others, a Rock of Gibraltar for her whole family. Her experience as cook, advisor, anxious rounder-upper of stray children, soon affected her other relationships. She came to see herself as strong, invincible, and de-pendable. This perception served an important ego function: amid the horrible and hurtful marital situation in which she and her brothers and sisters lived, she was a *somebody,* an important person, perhaps *the most important person* in the home. She had little time for introspection or for feelings of nothingness or sadness. Caring for her brothers and sisters allowed her competence, dignity, and identity. Although the children often opposed her, she quickly learned how to wield power; she was a force to be reckoned with. This masterful subidentity only partially compensated for the fact that she was robbed of time to be alone, to play, to excel in sports, or to enjoy boy and girl friends. She was a deprived person but a masterful sibling.

What would become of people like Susan who do not have siblings to organize, to boss, and to nurture in order to distract themselves from the pain of being abandoned by their parents? We believe these caretaker siblings use their potential responsibilities for their siblings as a creative force for growth; to enhance their own interpersonal skills while at the same time protecting their families from further destruction. In this sense, they resemble the "Super-Kids"—children whom, according to Norman Garmezy (1976) and James Anthony and Cyrille Koupernik's (1974) studies, appear "invulnerable" in spite of being—owing to extremely poor environments—likely candidates for serious psychiatric illness. We believe that competent caretaking of siblings provides one possible path to invulnerability; and that, under certain circumstances, a child who has siblings to turn to and take care of, may be at less risk for breakdown than an only child who is all alone in trying to buffer parental conflicts. The only child has no coalition partners in the family, no alternate identity as a sibling caretaker. One absorbs parent pathology and, lacking a sibling, can become increasingly helpless—trapped in the endless process of trying to heal the parents' problems directly.° Having a sibling whom one nurtures, provides a sphere in which one can succeed. One can turn *away* from the parents who do not reward one's entreaties for change, and turn *to* a sibling who is more responsive.

The finding that the presence of a younger sibling whom one can teach also promotes a sense of competence, has recently received strong support from studies of intellectual development. Robert Zajonc writes:

> Last borns and only children share a common disadvantage: they have no younger siblings whom they can instruct in the fine areas of kite flying, puzzle solving, and the meaning of words. The chance to teach, I suggest, is an important boost to intellectual development. Older children have such opportunities;

°Although research using personality tests and social measures does not clearly support the old notion that only children are more disturbed than those with sibs (Falbo 1982), we are suggesting that, under certain conditions, being an only child is a clear disadvantage.

sometimes by parental default, sometimes by proximity in age and room sharing. Assistant-parenthood gives older childen much experience in solving intellectual problems that their younger siblings want solved. . . . It is better to have a younger sibling you can show the world to than an older one who shows it off to you.   (1976)

Cherishing the Parental Image: Sisters of the Holocaust. When siblings are abandoned by parents, or parents are suddenly removed by death or disaster, the sibling group must reorganize. Usually the most competent sibling takes over, but her capacity for caring is severely strained. In the absence of parents, this child, invoking the parents' memory, often seizes upon their wish that she take care of the other children should disaster strike the family. By acting like one or both parents, the child appeases and pleases them within herself. By nurturing a sibling, another beloved child of one's parents, the caring child can cling to a loving image of them and do as they would have done. Such parent images can sustain caretaking under the most dire circumstances. If the parents have been actively caring and encouraged a child to be so early in life, then—to the child deprived of parents—the label "my brother's keeper" takes on active significance. The child attains "object constancy" by being like the nurturing mother, incorporating her essence, and, through mothering, keeping her alive inside.

The power of the parental image to sustain caretaking is no more vividly shown than in the lives of siblings who survived the Nazi Holocaust.° Older siblings took care of their brothers or sisters, often against incredible odds and at dire risk to their own lives. These siblings clung to their younger brothers or sisters for dear life, sometimes wandering hundreds of miles through the rubble of Europe. In many cases, the parents had been killed unbeknownst to the children, who stayed together sustained by the hope that they would be reunited with their parents. To abandon one's sibling under such carnage and cultural fragmentation would be to abandon the last vestige of one's family identity and to lose one's only tie to the past and hope for the future. ·

Hilda was eight and her sister Annie six when the Nazi Storm Troopers began to exterminate the Jewish population in their city. Her sister and parents were deaf, so that Hilda had grown up as "the ear" for her entire family. Her family's link to the outside world before Hitler, now she became their lifeline. The night before her parents were arrested and deported, they, knowing the peril that awaited all of them, told Hilda,

° The authors gratefully acknowledge the help of the Foundation for the Study of the Holocaust, the Holocaust Survivors Film Project, and Laurel Vlock for making possible the study of these sisters.

"Take care of your sister, always take care of Annie." This was a role Hilda had played long before, as her sister's interpreter and voice on the playground and the sidewalks outside their home; her mother's admonition was nothing new, but these were to be the last words her mother would ever speak to her.

At a village where they were sent by friends after the parents' deportation, she and her little sister were miserable:

> I could not adjust to the wild children in the village where we lived. My sister and I kept to ourselves, and they used to poke fun at her because she was deaf. And I was very protective of her, because I had been told: "Take care of her."

They left the farm and returned to their home town where they hid in abandoned buildings, afraid to show their faces on the streets, lest they be recognized. Finally Hilda led her sister to the police and asked for their parents' whereabouts. The police put them on a truck bound for a labor camp. The girls spent several months in the labor camp:

> At that time I was nine years old, and I had my sister who was seven and a half and to whom I had to explain everything—who had to basically be taken care of. She only knew sign language and I could "sign" with her. But she didn't know how to communicate with "hearing" people, so I was really constantly having to hold her by the hand. I couldn't call her, I couldn't ever lose sight of her because in the milling of the people we could have been separated. And we were finally put on the train, and I was told I would be going to Auschwitz. And to me, of course, going to Auschwitz was just an image of my rejoining my parents.

On a train, jam-packed with people bound for Auschwitz, Hilda and Annie sat together on one suitcase for five days. The train was bombed, derailed; Hilda took her sister by the hand and, with other prisoners, began a forced march to the camp. She was still sustained by the hope of reunion with the parents, and taking care of Annie had by now become the compelling reason for Hilda to stay alive. It satisfied her need for object constancy: she was doing what her parents would have wanted. It inspired her by giving her contact with the one person who knew her, and allowed her to block out the horror that swirled around them. Hilda's contact with her sister was her only link with sanity; her cherished image of lost parents, her only sustenance:

> I had nothing to eat for a long, long time, and I fell asleep and I remember thinking life had played a terrible trick on me because I was not in Auschwitz with my parents. And I remember saying to myself, as I fell asleep, "I will *never* stop looking for them!"

As months elapsed, Hilda and Annie became emaciated, their bellies bloated; they acquired the gaunt appearance of camp victims. Yet Hilda never relinquished her search for her mother or her role as her mother's representative to Annie. Even physical abuse could not interfere with her desperate search:

> One day, I asked in perfect German, "could I please call out my mother's name," and this irritated the guard no end. But I kept doing it anyway. I knew my mother couldn't hear me but I thought somebody who knew she was deaf would tell her I was calling out her name. And I would call out her name over and over again. And by doing that, one day after the fifth or sixth time, the soldier so lost his temper he just picked me up and flung me against a stone, and I lost consciousness. I temporarily lost my hearing which was, in some ways, a tremendous worry because I had to be my sister's ears . . . I *had* to hear for her. And I was afraid I had really had my hearing permanently damaged.

Hilda had by now completely incorporated her mother's command always to take care of her sister. On two occasions, she risked her own life in order to keep her sister alive:

> I realized that my sister was being watched by the camp doctor. It was a German doctor, and he would come by and pinch my sister's cheeks, pull her ear and try to be very friendly with her. Then, one day, he said to me that he would give us oranges and chocolate if I allowed my sister to go into the hospital for a few days. My sister was perfectly well so I couldn't understand why he wanted her in the hospital, and I just was very sassy and said: "No, you are not, because if you are, I'm going to kick you." And I went up and said, "I'm serious, I mean it." And he forgot about it. Later on he said he had hoped to be able to use my sister for "scientific research."

Hilda consciously prepared to give up her life for her sister. Several months before the camp was liberated, a typhus epidemic struck the prisoners:

I had secretly kept with me a small bag of tea which a woman had given me. I was able at the time of the typhus epidemic to exchange the tea for a vaccine for my sister. I was told it was a typhus vaccine. Whether or not it was really vaccine, I'm not sure, but my sister *never did* come down with typhus. But I did get sick. And so one of the saddest things in my life is that I have no recollection of the liberation of the camp when the English came because I was totally ill with the typhus.

Significantly, during the time Hilda was sick, her sister fell completely mute and withdrew from the world.

In summary, this child was able to sustain her caretaking under the most horrendous conditions for several reasons: (1) As a young child, she had witnessed her parents being truly caring, long before they were removed. (2) She had a close relationship with her mother and was able to invoke her mother's image and values ("take care of your sister") as emotional sustenance during hard times. (3) Her sister "fed" Hilda in two ways: by being a predictable "constant" amid chaos; and by allowing Hilda to feel close to their mother and to deny the maternal loss.

The Burden of the Parental Image: Barbara. While these Holocaust sisters dramatically illustrate the power of the caretaker's identification with an idealized loving mother, there are many other kinds of family horror; and to survive them while cherishing the absent parent's image, the immature child can go to extreme lengths on behalf of a younger sibling. Barbara was one such caretaker. Unlike Hilda, she experienced intense rage at and conflict about her younger brother, Tim; only through cherishing her mother's ideal was she able to restrain herself from being violent toward him.

Barbara and Tim's father abandoned their mother shortly after Tim's birth; and from his birth, the mother would tell Barbara (then age three), "Take care of your brother, watch out for Tim." The mother, who was ill and whose life was disorganized, had communicated love and warmth to Barbara. Barbara took literally her mother's injunction to care for Tim and acted as if his welfare were her own personal cause.

When Tim was about a year old, the mother couldn't cope with the children any longer and put them in foster care. For five years, as the children moved from one foster home to another, the social workers noticed that Barbara had a comforting and controlling effect on her difficult brother. Then the children were put up for adoption, and the question was, should the siblings be placed separately or together?

A social worker's report stated at the time:

Acts of Sacrifice: Loyalty and Caring

She is very attached to her brother, and she is very eager to please adults. She has become over-responsible for his care. Even in the foster home where the foster mother tried to let her know that she was not responsible for this youngster, she mothered him to the point where the foster mother had to go *through* Barbara to get to Tim.

The social worker feared that if the children were separated, Tim would become unmanageable, and that adoptive parents might not be able to handle him without Barbara's presence and mediation.

Barbara became Tim's monitor and "schoolmarm." Deeply distressed about his hyperactivity, she watched him closely on the bus on the way to school and, though she was in the third grade and he in first, managed to stop in after school to discuss his attitude and performance with his teacher. She was truly like an anxious mother who wanted to assure herself and the teacher that she was "a concerned parent."

Barbara was always rescuing Tim from trouble. Even in the research interview, when he knocked over lights and upset the camera crew, Barbara had to save the day. She reprimanded Tim and squinted at him furiously as if to say, "You'd better shape up, or I'll kill you." This nonverbal language silenced him immediately. We in the studio understood how the foster parents felt: frustrated with Tim, relying upon Barbara. This is a common form of role induction by which adults, perceiving parental competence in a child, reinforce it—and then rely too heavily on that child.

Barbara was overwhelmed by anger and guilt when her brother got out of control. She seemed angry at herself because "sometimes I can't *make* him be good." Restaurants were particularly distressing for her. That Tim might knock over a water glass and mess up the bathroom, Barbara took as a personal affront to her "motherhood." If he got lost on the way back to the table, she would scold him, thereafter assuming ever more responsibility for his conduct. This sense of being "on duty," filled with apprehension lest Tim misbehave in the next few moments, worried and disturbed her. She was forever teaching him better behavior, lest he bring down the wrath of teachers, friends, and other outsiders. She occasionally talked to the foster parents when he misbehaved and spared him punishment by promising to speak sternly to him. At nine, little Barbara was a parent, trying to be consistent with her "child."

Underneath her sweet veneer, Barbara felt intense conflict: her mother's injunction to guard and watch Tim flew directly in the face of Barbara's yearnings for time alone, for time to fantasize and dream, off-duty time, time for separate friends, time *not* to be a good girl. Her sleep was disturbed by bad dreams in which she pictured Tim being sent, blessedly, to a different adoptive home, but when he came back to visit her in the home where she had been placed, "he turned into a monster and jumped out and scared me." She deeply wished to be rid of the overwhelming responsibility for his care; and when the social worker suggested separate placements, ultimately she agreed. She was, at nine years of age, a delightful but psychologically fatigued little girl, well on her way to a life of seriousness and overresponsibility for others. She had grown up too fast: she snatched at childhood and real play in secret moments rather than enjoying them freely and openly. In a certain sense she was a lovely and charming kid wearing patent leather Mary Janes; in another sense she was an old woman before her time.

THE VINDICTIVE CARETAKER

Any sibling who must, in some extraordinary way, care for a brother or a sister, has been to some extent abandoned by a parent. The rage that the child, adolescent, or young adult sibling feels toward that parent can be temporarily assuaged by a variety of defense mechanisms in the sibling relationship. By caring for one's siblings, one can wear a mask of responsibility and exaggerated concern and thus deny that rage. By loving and looking after a sibling, one can sublimate anger both at the depriving parent and at the bothersome brothers or sisters. One can "show up" the parent who has been neglectful, and "outparent" that mother or father.

One can also give care angrily and domineeringly. Siblings like Barbara give much but are often insensitive and bullying in their attempts to get their siblings to listen to them.

Psychological investigations confirm the aggressive aspect of caretaking. For example, Brenda Bryant (1979) concluded that, under even good conditions, older siblings get compliance from younger ones by resorting, like Lucy in *Peanuts*, to "the sweet reason of the mailed fist." The younger siblings in Bryant's study viewed the parents as much more reliable, nurturing, and understanding than their older brothers and sisters. Younger siblings often find the older ones acceptable as sitters, but the older ones are reported to be verbally and physically abusive (McArdle and Miller 1978). Normal children try to get compliance from their younger brothers and sisters; they employ power tactics that include punching, screaming, terrorizing, inducing guilt, and blackmailing (Sutton-Smith and Rosenberg 1968). Even high-school students use commands, rather than reasoning, in dealing with younger siblings (Essman and Deutch 1979). The caretaker sibling is also especially likely to use arbitrary and high-handed

134

tactics with her "children," and thus boosts both her own self-image and her power within the family.

In contrast to the sibling who idealizes or cherishes a lost parent's image, the vindictive sibling despises the devalued parent, has unconscious feelings of rage and deprivation, and seeks, by rescuing a sibling, to replace the parent. The revenge motivating such an oedipally dictated caretaker has not been resolved, and he or she has not achieved rapprochement with the parents. This sibling overidentifies with the plight of a brother or a sister, as they have experienced a common loss. By trying to enhance the "badness" of the parent, the caretaker is able to increase his or her own righteous sense of triumph and to block out disturbing thoughts and feelings, such as despair, depression, and outright murderousness toward that parent. The caretaker frequently reminds the siblings of how awful their parents could be, and thus binds them to a loyalty pact from which there is no escape.

A Vindictive Brother: Ralph. The dynamics of vindictive caretaking are illustrated in the following example of a young man who decided to "adopt" his abused and neglected little brother. The clinial psychologist was contacted by a young couple in their early twenties. Three years before, the husband, Ralph, had moved his ten-year-old younger brother out of their father's home and into his own, over the objections of the father and some of the other siblings. Now Ralph, completely supported by his wife Loretta, wanted a thorough evaluation of his brother, who at thirteen was having serious learning difficulties. Jamie suffered severe speech and language impairment and was noticeably different from other youngsters of his age.

At ten, Jamie was an undeveloped little person whose immaturities stood out in embarrassing ways. Though he appeared to be a normal, freckle-faced lad with a shock of red hair, his speech was babyish and had the singsong cadences that most children leave behind in nursery school. Speaking as if by rote, he mechanically parrotted the words he had learned from his brother. Conversations requiring give-and-take bewildered him; he would look helplessly toward his big brother Ralph who invariably bailed him out. Jamie labored to become a carbon copy of this older brother, desperately trying to wrap himself in his brother's image. The result was a droll imitation of a sibling rather than a true identification.

The clinical psychologist observed:

Jamie does not strike me as a boy who is in any way comfortable with other people's or with his own aggressive feelings. In fact, I am sure that he holds in his anger for fear of expressing it and losing loved ones. He admits that he worries about losing Ralph and Loretta. He says that when he makes "big mistakes" like forgetting to take out the trash, his brother becomes nervous and angry and yells at him. He loves his brother, but he walks on eggshells when he is around him.

Ralph was the sixth child among seven boys and three girls. When Ralph was ten, his mother died suddenly of a coronary three weeks after Jamie's birth. Following his wife's death, the father married and divorced three times. Each of the three stepmothers neglected or emotionally abused the children. Ralph felt hurt and rage that his father allowed these stepmothers to abuse them; his disappointment was especially deep because, before the natural mother's death, the father had been a strict, although effective and caring disciplinarian. Ralph had been doubly deserted: first, his mother had died; now his father had changed and abandoned him and his siblings to insensitive strange women. Because Ralph was the eldest of the last three siblings (the older siblings were already on the verge of independence or living away from home), and because he had identified deeply with his mother, he began looking after the infant Jamie and their other brother, age four.

Ralph felt most concerned for Jamie, who had been neglected from birth, and, during his adolescence, carried on a crusade to guard him, to frustrate their current stepmother's abuse, and to act like a father to the boy. Several months after Ralph and Loretta were married, Ralph brought Jamie to live with them. When the boy arrived, he was like a child who has been kept in a closet: he was underweight, unsocialized, completely unsophisticated. With Loretta's help, Ralph brought him up; the couple stated that rather than being a burden, Jamie was enriching their lives and giving them a sense of purpose and commitment.

Nonetheless, the aggressive motivation in Ralph's parenting of Jamie was played out in vindictive ways. While he did not refuse to let his brother see their father, he did nothing to encourage contact. Rigidly, Ralph insisted on near perfection in his brother, fearing that if his brother showed aggression, he might remind Ralph of how much he himself could be provoked to anger. By forcing "goodness" on Jamie, Ralph defended himself against his own sense of worthlessness, tried to prove he was a better parent than their father, but tragically proved that he was much the same kind of person as the father—rigid, domineering, intolerant of other peoples' disturbing feelings. While Ralph tried hard to nurture Jamie, he could not put his arms around him. Jamie's depression and tremendous need for nurturing frightened him, for in his little brother,

Ralph could see a reflection of himself, deprived and needy. Thus, Ralph had to relegate Jamie's nurturing to his wife; as a disciplinarian he could keep his distance and remain comfortable. Jamie loved his brother, but was dominated by the fear that he might become disloyal. The chorus of anger and disapproval that both the father and all of the older siblings were directing at Ralph for his "caregiving" placed Jamie in the position of a fearful hostage who felt obligated to his loving brother yet longed for the familiar, though emotionally unpredictable, environment of his father's home. When the psychologist raised these issues with Ralph, he at first denied them, then became angry and rigid in defense of his position. Only after much work with the therapist was Ralph able to begin to see that he could not adequately care for his brother.

CARETAKERS AS ADULTS

An adult caretaker sibling when seen in psychotherapy is often surprised to be facing a serious personal crisis. This crisis comes as a shock to all who know her for, after all, it is she who has specialized in helping a sibling or siblings and, later on, organizing the lives of sibling surrogates—her spouse, employer, children. Most of all, the caretaker's psychological symptoms come as a shock to the caretaker herself, who has never seen herself as needing help. Of older female siblings, Walter Toman has written:

> She will mediate between quarrelling parties . . . the man who gets her for good will usually find himself in very good hands . . . she may find herself consoling people over losses that are harder to her than to them . . . she is the one to whom the mourners will turn with their wails (1969, pp. 83 ff.).

And of the eldest sister of sisters:

> Property, wealth and possessions are secondary when compared to her people, above all, to her siblings, children, or those who submit to her reign. . . . What kind of man will take all that from the woman who wants to be loved by him? Only men who are somewhat passive or feminine themselves . . . they in turn may relax her sufficiently to bring her more tender, and even motherly, sides to the fore (pp. 64 ff.).

At the unconscious core, as we have seen, the caretaker sibling feels angry, deprived, and bitter that she has not been taken care of: and in a crisis, her awareness of that feeling suddenly surfaces, and she collapses. Because her self-image has always been strong and self-sufficient, she recovers from her collapse relatively rapidly.

Susan (pages 126–28) provides a vivid example of how such a person's generous inclinations lead to depletion in adult life. At twenty-seven, Susan entered a psychiatric hospital after a series of three relationships, one of them a marriage that had not worked. In each of them she played a dominant role and gave much more than she received—she even tried to form a sympathetic relationship with one man's ex-wife—just as she had as a child with her siblings. In these romantic relationships, she initially expected little from the men whose attraction seemed to be their "I'm just a little boy underneath the man" quality. All these men had been married before, and each one insisted that she care for his children while giving her little in return. The merry-go-round of giving without getting finally undid her; she became violently angry at her third lover and threatened to kill him or herself. In therapy, she admitted that all her life she had been a "sucker" and "taken for a ride." For Susan, to accommodate to others, to facilitate, to help out, was second nature, a reflex (she later owned a retail children's gift shop, where she spent six days a week, helping *others* to give). She had difficulty learning to take from her therapist, to let herself feel that she could be off duty for an hour and be the receiver for a while.

Although caretaking siblings function well for the most part as adults, and are not given to breakdowns, they have an especially fixed personality. It may require lengthy psychotherapy before such a patient learns how to receive and to allow others to give to her—how to unlearn the lessons learned in childhood with her siblings.

The Receiving Child

Milton Rosenbaum (1963), writing about sibling caretaking, has said: "Which would be worse, to be raised by a mother who is rejecting, overtly or covertly, but who is, after all, an adult, or to be raised by an older sibling?" Among patients seen in clinical practice, the child who is cared for by a sibling may be subjected to obvious and subtle abuse, both physically and mentally. Unchecked, these siblings set up a relationship that can take on the qualities of master and slave, seducer and seduced, brain and ignoramus. The enhancement of the caretaker's competence can be bought at the cost of great harm to the ego development of the receiving child. This harm can take two main forms:

Acts of Sacrifice: Loyalty and Caring

- Absorption of aggression; along with this the care receiver, enmeshed with his or her "keeper," can be paralyzed by obligation and guilt.
- Passivity and difficulty in becoming a separate individual.

As we have said, the caretaker sibling carries out her duties in a rigid and compulsive way; unable to see the child as a separate person, she feels driven to shape him or her to her own purposes. If rebuffed, she may try harder and aggressively escalate pressure, guilt, and threats. The younger sibling who loves the older one, may react by incorporating her aggression and displacing it elsewhere—upon other siblings or friends.

The care receiver is thus an "unfinished individual," who regards aggressive impulses as difficult, dangerous, or uncontrollable, and may grow up having had his or her anger censored by this ersatz parent. For the receiving child in later life, aggression is not a useful tool that she can employ skillfully to resolve conflicts.

The receiving child may become a Caspar Milquetoast, a weak and passive person who, in adulthood, seeks out relationships in which he or she constantly repeats acquiescence to a potentially violent or guilt-inducing sibling. The obligation and guilt that many care-receiving siblings experience is based on the fear that, if they challenge the caretaker's values, the latter will humiliate and reject them as disloyal. When a child suffers from a physical, an emotional, or a learning disability, an overzealous, "helpful" caretaker can promote in him or her the development of what Martin Seligman has called "learned helplessness" (1975).

Because caretaker siblings find it easier to "take over," muttering "I'll do it myself," they deprive their younger brothers or sisters of a chance to learn (Abrams and Kaslow 1976). Many caretaker siblings oversimplify their sisters' and brothers' lives, sheltering them so much that they never develop the practical sense necessary to face reality. In addition, to suppress a sibling's aggression, the parental sibling's message is: "Be passive, accept my rule, let me do it *for* you, and do what *I* want to do!" This message is daily underlined in countless little ways—with a combination of affection (desperately craved by the receiver), aggression, humiliation, and punishment. The caretaker teaches her charge to be cute, quiet, and noncomplaining.

Always a Little Girl: Rachel and Her Siblings. When a masterful guardian sister (or brother) has headed off disasters, solved problems, and autonomously asserted herself, the cared-for sibling has lived under a sibling umbrella. Once outside it and faced with having to function independently, the younger sibling may cave in and scurry back to the security of the caretaker sibling, who once again unfurls her umbrella.

Of all the decisions the caretaker sibling may make for the receiving one, the most painful is the decision to rebuff the parent and to side with the parenting sibling. While this protective alliance may save the receiving child's life, it can also produce guilt. The receiving child is thus placed in a bind, obligated now to the caretaking sibling, and afraid to voice love for the parent lest he or she lose the shield of the caretaker's love.

Rachel, aged eleven, was the blue-eyed baby in a family that included a brother, fourteen, and a sister, sixteen. In dealing with their divorced father, her siblings complained that Rachel would not think or act for herself, despite the fact that they both shielded her from the father's anger.

In one incident, they all met the father at a bowling alley, and the father began to criticize the older sibs for rejecting his affectionate gestures. He then turned his anger on Rachel. The oldest child redoubled her attack on the father; while, at the same time, the brother hurried Rachel out of the rink so that she would not have to face the father's unpleasantness. This was just one of the many "saving" missions that Rachel's siblings performed for her.

Not surprisingly, she could not speak alone to her father on the telephone or when he came to their house to visit. When he called, and Rachel answered the phone, she would greet him but then nervously give the phone to her brother or sister. This irritated them because it tended to place them in the position of having to explain Rachel's reluctance to see their father, and thus compounded their own tenuous position with him. When the therapist met with the children, Rachel seemed not to have her own voice: she looked to her siblings for answers to the therapist, just as she looked to them for answers about their father. When the older sibs, in the therapist's consulting room, criticized the father, she parroted them. Their actions, their explanations, and their thinking formed a forceful sibling ideology that she dared not change and, indeed, did not want to change. She was an anxious little girl, too well protected by her siblings, and utterly unprepared to think or act for herself in difficult relationships.

Like many children who are overprotected by siblings, Rachel got used to the feeling that others would magically make things happen for her. This "hiding" behind the caretaker, if sustained through childhood and adolescence, can become a life pattern. If the care receiver has rarely operated independently, it becomes second nature to have a sibling mediate between oneself and the real world.

Acts of Sacrifice: Loyalty and Caring

Conclusion

Does a sibling make a good substitute parent? Recent psychological investigations have demonstrated that older siblings who are approaching their
teen-age years can serve as helpful teachers (Cicerelli 1972, 1976); and it
is clear that babysitting and child care for a few hours or a few days can
be mastered by older children. Nonetheless, when there is no hope of
relief in the future, and caretaking denies a child the opportunities to live
his or her own life, the result is distinctly detrimental. We must answer
our question with a resounding No! Siblings cannot be adequate substitute
parents.

A brother or a sister can rarely, if ever, match the sophistication, maturity, or capacity for nurturance or leadership of an adult. A child cannot
impart values in the manner of a mature parent. His or her intolerance
for the emotional ups-and-downs and needs of other children is a handicap from the outset. As Brian Sutton-Smith has pointed out, in a stinging
attack on those who idealize the notion of sibling caretaking:

> While the experience of responsibility for and nurturance of the young has
> much to recommend it as a *subsidiary* educational experience, . . . we should
> not equate a desirable educational opportunity for looking after younger chil-
> dren on selected occasions with those traditional kinds of child caregiving
> which deprive the modern child of his stimulus birthright. (1977, pp. 184–85)

Three factors appear to influence the adequacy of care that a sibling
can provide for another child. The first is the *age, relative maturity,* and
psychological integrity of the caretaker. The sibling who assumes the role
after adolescence, may have fairly well-developed parenting abilities, and
thus the younger sibling is not likely to suffer from immaturity. The sibling who has had an early positive emotional experience with parents, will
be a better caretaker. The difference in the siblings' age and maturity
relates to the second factor: *the resistance to being taken care of* offered
by the younger child. The younger sibling who is, for example, resentful
of the caretaker, or is overactive, unmanageable, or disturbed, may humiliate the would-be caretaker and provoke him or her to anger and retaliation. Third, *the availability of supplemental adult resources* for organizing caretaking is a crucial determinant of whether the caretaker helps
or hurts a sibling. In some of our examples where the parents were weak
or abusive, another person—such as an aunt, a grandmother, or a social
worker or a family therapist—became involved in reorganizing the sibling

system to support the caretaker, helped her to delegate authority, and ensured that she did not abuse her power. It is imperative for a caretaker to have someone older and wiser to whom she can turn for advice, a person on whom she can unload angry feelings, and who can act as an alternative parent to the younger children, and give her a break from her slavish relation to them.

The question whether siblings make adequate parents is of ever greater importance in today's changing patterns of family life. Sibling caretaking should assume ever greater importance in the decades to come. As women and men liberate themselves from traditional family roles, with both parents or a single parent working full time, the issue of what the children are doing with each other will become more crucial. One of the challenges facing modern parents is both to help their children learn to care responsibly for their, the children's, brothers and sisters and, simultaneously, to free their children from having to assume the sibling burdens that can force a child to grow up too soon.

CHAPTER 6

The Sexual Influence of Siblings

THE SEXUAL ASPECTS of sibling relationships: this is a formidable topic. Hinted at; often suggested but seldom documented; glossed over in textbooks of human development and then bypassed, sibling sexual influence is, we have observed, pervasive. Too many patients mentioned, when asked, that it indeed has been a crucial factor in their lives. Same-sex siblings speak about playful curiosity with each other in childhood, about how they compared their bodies and imitated each other's sexual activities during adolescence, and express envy and outright jealousy into adulthood. Opposite-sex siblings tell of sexual play with a brother or a sister during the early years; of touch-and-tumble, erotically-tinged touching in pre-adolescence; of love and caring throughout life; and even of sibling incest.

That the parents are the primary familial influence on sexual identity has been emphasized repeatedly by Freud and his followers. Social learning theorists point to a child's everyday social circumstances, particularly in early adolescence, as the determinant of sexual behavior. But siblings can affect one another in this vital area of human experience for many reasons and out of many motives. We will examine in this chapter the sexual influence between siblings of the same sex and, in chapter 7, brother and sister sexual interaction. We treat the latter at greater length, not because we believe it to be more important, but—owing to the age-old incest taboo—its effects over a lifetime are much more controversial and hazardous; and what had already been written about sibling incest seemed to us to have misrepresented what each of these brothers and sisters had been through.

Biological Endowment and Identity Differences

A child's sexual development can be drastically affected by close identification or rivalry with a sibling of the same sex whom the child considers beautiful or ugly. Sexual subidentity often draws upon these social comparisons as well as upon the child's perception of a sibling's sexual expression of body functions and how that brother or sister related to other boys and girls.°

Human sexual identity develops primarily from external influence (Simon and Gagnon, 1967). Temperament and biological endowment also, however, interact in important ways with family and social events to dictate how an individual enters the world of sexual experience. This entry has been defined as sexual "'unfolding' . . . : a process made up of innumerable experiences during adolescence, by which a person becomes aware of himself or herself as a sexual being, a male or female, who relates to oneself and others, sexually, in some characteristic way" (Sarrel and Sarrel 1979, p. 19). When children are compared physically from birth on, their identities and sexual unfolding often develop inextricably, in ways that reassurance or praise cannot undo.

Beauty versus Brains—Different from Birth: Betty and Sherry. Two sisters who were only one year apart were as physically different as night and day. Betty had been a plain, gawky baby. Sherry, her older sister, was round and cherubic, the kind of baby who beamed whenever anyone paid attention to her.

> BETTY: I can relate back to when I was a baby. There's a picture of the two of us, a photograph where I'm sitting. I've got this big, long face and I was blonde as a baby and so it looked like I had no hair. And she's sitting there and she's got this long dark hair that's down to here, all curls, peaches and cream complexion, and she's sitting there all decked out, and I'm sitting there like this—dumb baby, and the whole thing was laid out like a pattern as we were growing up. She was always very, very attractive.

As the sisters went through their childhood years, Sherry's loveliness

° See Sutton-Smith and Rosenberg (1970) for a review of experiments on this topic. In one study, for example, it was shown that only boys with one or more sisters are more masculine than boys from all-boy families; the data suggest that, in the former families, boys may become more masculine as a protest against the dominant female influence. Also Walter Toman (1976) has discussed how marital sexual-object choices are forged by same- and opposite-sex sibling relationships.

The Sexual Influence of Siblings

and charm were cultivated and applauded by everyone. Betty, who remained shy and ungainly, was therefore celebrated for her intelligence:

I was very shy as a child and it probably made me more withdrawn.
And especially around her, because she seemed to have a kind of
charisma with people. She can meet somebody and in five minutes
they'll have plans for the next two weeks. And I don't do that. I'm
not like that at all. And when we were growing up, I remember I
must have been around ten years old, she said to me one day, "Well,
you got the brains, and I got the beauty." And it's stuck with me ever
since. She just cut through all the shit that had been going on and she
just laid it right on the line!
INTERVIEWER: So you still believe that?
BETTY: Yeah, I really do! It's really something that stayed with me. I
knew I'd gotten more of an aptitude for the academic than she did.
And then it became a game for me to try to develop the "brains" end
of things.

The difference in the sisters became galvanized into a certain trucu-
lence in Betty and an arrogance in Sherry *not* to be like one another—a
difference reinforced by their family and friends who always said, "You
two are nothing alike." Thus, they were becoming rigidly differentiated.

BETTY: There was also a lot of resentment between the two of us as a
function of my not wanting to do what she was going to do—my not
following what she was following. That was true all through school.
We were always involved in that.
INTERVIEWER: She provided a touchstone for what you would *not* do.
BETTY: There would be times *when I would deliberately do the opposite of what she was doing*, even if I didn't want to do it.

It was only natural that "beauty" began to attract boys, while "brains"
avoided them.

BETTY: Through junior high she dated maybe three or four boys.
INTERVIEWER: So she was an early dater?
BETTY: Pretty much, yes, but then she settled into a pattern of dating
somebody consistently and then moving on to someone else. In high
school she had the same boyfriend for four years, but in college she
dated a lot.
On the other hand I was tall and gawky, and I had braces on my

teeth from the age fifteen up to my senior year in high school. Next to my sister I really felt like chopped liver.

I can remember in seventh grade we were having a dance and a boy asked me to go to the dance, and I was terrified, I wouldn't go. And it continued that way through high school. I never dated— never! I was terrified of going out. I just didn't know how to do it.

These initial physical differences in the sisters continued to function as differentiating characteristics well into their adult lives. Sherry, "the beauty," was now twenty-seven, her sexual precosity conspicuously marked by *two* abortions and many affairs, several of them disastrous. Meanwhile Betty, now attractive and twenty-six, had had an uninterrupted, brilliant, but emotionally sterile academic career; and she intentionally left herself no opportunities for an active sexual and social life:

I think I sort of used Sherry's whole experience with sex as an excuse to even get farther away from any kind of personal relationship. And then over the past couple of years I started thinking about that and thinking, Who's the loser here? And it was always me who was the loser, and it started to really make me worry, you know? Am I after a career because that's the only thing I have to go after? But I also want emotional relationships and closeness with other people too. And I finally decided I wanted both, so I thought I've got to do something about this because I'm the one who is keeping it from happening.

While Betty was reconsidering her own conflicted position about sex, and her fixed insistence not to be like Sherry, her sister reached out to her for emotional support and shared her feelings about an unhappy love affair. Betty became sympathetic, for the first time was able to identify with her sister's sadness, but could also acknowledge to herself that what had always commanded Sherry's attention—namely, love—might also be worth having. And, no longer feeling that her sister possessed all the beauty and charm, Betty asked her for advice on how gracefully to accept a man's invitation for a date.

Other siblings, less conflicted than Betty, admire each other's charm, social grace, and sexual aplomb. They readily take cues from one another on how to maneuver in the worlds of dating, sexual experience, and, later, marriage. Siblings of the same sex often find that their *model* of how to relate to the opposite sex comes, not just from a parent, but also from a respected sibling who is close in age. Without belaboring the obvious, an attractive sibling—one who is popular, confidant, and self-assured about relationships with the opposite sex—can be a worthy model for identification, or as one songwriter aptly put it, "I wish I could shimmy like my sister Kate."

In addition, the influence of a same-sex sibling can be a potent reference point in the *consolidation* of one's sexual identity, particularly in late adolescence. This is not to say that a brother or a sister determines sexual orientation (homosexual or heterosexual), but rather that he or she can enhance and make more secure one's sense of sexual-object preference, behavioral style, gender expressiveness, and sexual feelings. This influence can come from experience as diverse as sibling seduction, competitiveness, rivalry, or modeling. The alternative to becoming different, as Sherry and Betty did, is to model oneself after a sibling by dressing and speaking in the same fashion and pursuing similar activities. Siblings can even reach such absurd levels of fusion and merging—as in a case of three *transsexual* male siblings (Sabalis et al. 1974)—as to try to copy every aspect of each other.

Same-sex siblings are not the only immediate influence; opposite-sex siblings can also be pivotal figures in the identification process that culminates in a person's sexual identity. One college student we interviewed told us:

> There actually was a point before puberty where I actually believed that I wanted to be a boy and I always wanted to wear my brother's underwear [laughs]. But then, around puberty, I started noticing boys and started . . . wanting to feel feminine and it took me until . . . actually, until my first boyfriend when I was seventeen, to really feel at all pretty and feminine and attractive to men.

This girl had another sibling, an older sister, and wavered between wanting to have the physical attributes of her idealized brother, and then those of her sister. Both of these figures for identification played an important role in giving Mary points of reference at different developmental stages:

> I'm pretty now, it took me a long time. When I look at my pictures now, I was never really all that attractive in comparison to her. When I started reaching that age where I didn't want to be a tomboy, when I wanted to be pretty, when I reached that crisis of the male-female complex, I wanted to be female and I wanted to be as pretty as my sister was. She was very beautiful and I was very jealous of her, so I had to overcome that.

147

By identifying with both of her siblings, she was able to learn sexuality from each of them, emulating her sister's graceful beauty and even obtaining cues from her handsome older brother about what to do on dates:

> Well, when I got to be interested in boys, he told me what you should and shouldn't do when you date, and how long before you should let someone touch you in such and such a place, and he would tell me a few secrets about what *he* had done. "Gee, you would do that!?" [*incredulous*] that's what I would say.

Sexual Confusion

In our clinical interviews, we discovered many siblings who experienced feelings of sexual uncertainty in late childhood and adolescence. Some people attributed part of their confusion to the influence of a sib whom they admired and unsuccessfully tried to emulate; and others, to a sibling who had so deeply offended, disgusted, or repulsed them that they needed to repudiate that brother or sister's entire mode of sexual expressiveness.

"Macho" versus "Gay": Will and Mark. Two brothers spoke painfully about their father, a depressed man who preferred solitude when he was home, and frequently and totally ignored his sons. To Mark, the younger brother, an eighteen-year-old college student, it seemed futile to complain about this devitalized father to a therapist. Everyone in the family saw the father as incapable of changing, his remoteness sustained by the mother—even though she also felt his neglect. It was possible, however, for Mark to complain with real vehemence about his brother Will, whose "macho" expressiveness both appalled and repelled him.

Will was a sexual dynamo, always gloating and boasting of his conquests and how little any woman meant to him emotionally; but in contrast to the father, brother Will at least seemed alive. This handsome, loud, aggressive, and impulse-ridden older sib always dominated any interaction between the two brothers. On the other hand, Mark, who had a gentle disposition and was extremely sensitive about inflicting hurt, was silently struggling with the question of whether he was homosexual. He felt confused by his brother's harshness to him and bewildered by Will's cavalier behavior toward girls. While Mark had not yet had a homosexual experience, the one thing that he could feel certain about was his fear of becoming like his brother. This most immediate model of heterosexuality was a cruel and driven caricature of maleness. Mark's mother also seemed to encourage her younger son's gentleness and softness, although it was clear she loved both her boys.

Dramatically opposed to one another in sexual preference, *neither* brother realized how much *both* of them were actually struggling against identifying with their father. For Mark, following his older brother's example of how to become a "man," was the second-best choice for masculine identification, but it was a poor one. Eventually Mark went to the other extreme; he overtly repudiated his older brother's interest in women and asserted his own difference through a "gay" manner of dressing, homosexual fantasies, and contemplation of a homosexual life. Although this process took several years to resolve itself, it made clear that he could become a different person from his brother.

A parent's influence on a child's sexual identity is primary; but in the second stage of the consolidation of sexual identity—late childhood and early adolescence—a sibling can tip the scales and seriously influence how an individual completes the resolution of his or her sexual unfolding.

Sexual Modeling and Pioneering

A sibling who initiates behavior, or blazes a new trail in psychological development, is said to be "pioneering."° Sexual pioneering by one child can be used as a reference point by siblings of the same sex for positive identification, modeling, idealization, and a constructive dialectic; or it can activate a destructive dialectic, rigid differentiation, or de-identification. Sexual pioneering is often innocent, gradual, and socially acceptable: one sibling may be the first to kiss, date, wear lipstick, or "go steady." A sibling who gradually pioneers, paves the way for the other children by lowering parental resistance. However, an adolescent whose sexual pioneering (for example, staying out late, taking the pill, going away for the weekend with a date) is in radical opposition to a family's scheme of values, can be marked as a troublemaker who, in the parents' eyes, may "contaminate" their younger children.

° Pioneering is often, but not always, done by the oldest sibling; a younger child who develops precociously may express signs of sexual maturity which the older sib then tries to emulate.

Delayed and Precocious Older Siblings

Waiting for the Trailblazer: Roy and Dave. The lack of pioneering can, however, delay sexual behavior in younger siblings, if they are waiting for the oldest to "do it first"—whether it be dating, sexual intimacy, or even marriage. Roy, a handsome twenty-three-year-old, spoke compassionately about his twenty-seven-year-old brother Dave, whose growth had, owing to pituitary gland deficiency, been delayed until he was sixteen, when hormonal supplements corrected the problem. Dave, a bright boy who excelled in school, had unfortunately been the same size as or smaller than his younger brother for most of their childhood. Roy poignantly recalled how bright and likable his brother was, but spoke of his own persistent feelings of sadness about the biological burden Dave carried. The family (with the physician's tacit encouragement) never spoke about it, lest he feel self-conscious. But Roy, endowed with good health, felt guilty about his greater physical riches and, even though Dave teased him by calling him "shrimp" and "little kid," knew that his brother must have been tremendously unhappy about his small stature. Roy recalled with embarrassment that Dave once asked him why his, Roy's, penis was so large. Roy also remembered that when he was eleven (Dave was fifteen) their mother said to him in a way that was both *compelling and restricting:* "Roy, I hope that by the time you go out with someone Dave will have also." And Roy went on:

> There was a lot of feeling there—it wasn't just tossed off—there was a lot of worry and concern—"Gee, I really hope by the time you start going out with girls, he will be too!" That really stuck and I couldn't forget that.

But Dave remained shy and awkward until he was twenty-four years old and, as a major figure of identification for his younger brother, contributed to Roy's own sexual dormancy. Although Dave had physically matured and grown, he was socially way behind his peers and, only at twenty-four, managed his first sexual experience by visiting a prostitute. Roy had, in a family that prized competition and achievement, always wanted to "get ahead" of his older brother; but to surpass him in the area of sexuality and dating would be to humiliate an already handicapped person whom he, Roy, admired. Therefore he did not date: girls were "just not that interesting." He had rationalized his lack of interest in sex; his fear of surpassing his brother had made him into a late bloomer.

On the day when Dave was finally able to start "having a relationship" and told Roy about it, Roy felt relieved and pleased, as if a burden had been lifted from him. Within four weeks Roy also started dating and found that he was relaxed with women and could enjoy them. Not only did he find dating easy, but the women were attractive and sexually desirable. Both brothers were pleased and could now joke over how "silly" it had been not to date earlier; and both now enjoyed a noncompetitive common area of experience about which neither felt ashamed or guilty. Each had now embarked on a natural, however long-delayed, step in the process of sexual unfolding.

In the case of these two brothers, there was sufficient mutual caring and respect in many other areas to obviate Roy's surpassing Dave sexually: to become the "bon vivant" son who was popular with girls would "show him up," contributing even more to Dave's poor self-image. But in chapters 8 and 9, we meet a number of siblings whose wish to de-identify was so compelling, as to make them oppose each other in many decisive ways, including the sexual.

Being Rushed by the Trailblazer: Marian and Phyllis. Marian had formed an early, loyally accepting identification with her sister Phyllis, two years older; but it changed in adolescence to polarized rejection. Fused by the early, tragic death of their father, the two girls also had to contend with the conflicts caused by their older brother. When their mother remarried, the girls were accustomed to keeping themselves busy; their stepfather had enough difficulty with his new stepson who was disobedient, then school truant, then delinquent, and finally drug-dependent. Marian could remember, during middle childhood, taking shelter in a favorite tree outside her house while loud, raucous, and, to her, pointless yelling about her brother went on inside. Sister Phyllis at least provided welcome relief and excitement. During early adolescence, according to Marian, Phyllis blazed a trail for both girls:

> We spent a lot of time together. There was a time when I was thirteen and she was fifteen, she introduced me to pot, drinking, taking our parents' car when she didn't even have a driver's license, staying up all night, you know—that was the kind of thing she would think was a lot of fun. I was too young for it—that was before I even had my own relationships going. You know, she would have a whole group of friends over, and she would think it was really funny to have started me on smoking pot at a very young age.

It was only natural that when Phyllis showed Marian the excitement of boys and dating, Marian would follow suit:

MARIAN: She always seemed to have a lot of boyfriends and, you know, when you're young—and I didn't know any better, I would look up to her and think, "Wow, that's great"—and just go along with anything she said.

INTERVIEWER: She was a hero for you, but one with some mixed features?

MARIAN: Yeah . . . like when I was thirteen—because she had started dating when she was thirteen and I was exposed to it ever since she started. I thought that's what I was supposed to do and I wasn't mature enough to know better.

Marian's awakening interest in boys gave the sisters a common meeting ground:

MARIAN: I know when I was in high school it used to be a big thing for me to hang out with her, to go out with her and her boyfriend.

INTERVIEWER: You were two grades apart?

MARIAN: Yeah, but there was one time where she was seeing this guy who was younger than her, maybe by one or two years, and I was seeing a guy who was older than me by maybe one year. Those two guys were friends—so there was a year when me and her used to do a lot, just socially we would go out pretty much together. When I first did a lot of things it was with my sister.

Marian's premature sexual activities were a natural outgrowth of following the path blazed by her sister. By the age of fourteen, Marian began having intercourse with her boyfriends, a fact her older sister kept track of only too well.

MARIAN: When we got older we moved upstairs, and her room was right next to mine, and she would listen through the walls in my room when I was in there with a boy.

INTERVIEWER: She told you this later?

MARIAN: Yeah, she would come in right after and say, "Congratulations!"

As Marian grew older, near the end of her high-school career, she felt the need to be very different, and the sisters became polarized. Sexual behavior that had once seemed appealing and exciting, now was "dirty" and "shameful." In aggressively switching from a positive to a negative view of sexuality, Marian was able to create a separate identity from her sister. But in departing so dramatically from her early idol, Marian became confused and depressed. Uncomfortable with the new role of the morally-superior "good girl" and disenchanted with the uninhibited sexual behavior of earlier years, Marian began psychotherapy as a way out of her dilemma.

An older child who becomes sexually active gradually and relatively normally, has a beneficial effect on a younger sibling; but the older child who deviates dramatically from family norms, can have a harmful effect on a younger one. For example, as a young woman, the third sister in Judith Rossner's novel *Looking for Mr. Goodbar* (1975) became self-destructive and promiscuous after her older sisters had made it abundantly clear that marriage could be only unhappy, and that love and sex could be disconnected.

For most brothers or sisters, the sexual influence of a sibling is not so dramatic as the ones we have just described. The influence is usually progressive, involving countless incidents over many years. Borrowing each other's clothes, asking for advice about the opposite sex, double dating, going out with a sister or a brother's friend, obtaining reassurance if a romance comes crashing apart, siblings of the same sex can be each other's most trusted confidant and most reliable ally. They usually have little difficulty in speaking about their sexual influence on one another and can often laugh at the memory of those awkward adolescent years when they were trying to become sexually secure. They can also cry or become angry in recalling the way a sister or brother made them feel inadequate or ashamed, a matter we will turn to in chapter 8.

Delving into the sexual dynamics between siblings of the opposite sex is, however, another matter. When brothers and sisters are asked to tell of their sexual feelings for one another, they usually become intensely anxious. For them this seems a nether world of unspoken feelings, hidden thoughts, guilt, and excitement never before broached with an outsider. Although poets, novelists, and dramatists have wondered about brother-sister love, clinicians and experts in human development have, for the most part, stayed far away. This is what we will now examine in the next chapter.

CHAPTER 7

Sexuality between Brothers and Sisters

I N OVID'S *Metamorphoses*, a sister Byblis writes to her brother Caunus:

> Let old men have their laws, let old men quibble
> Of right and wrong, and study up on cases.
> But we are young; our need is love, and rashness.
> We are still too young to know what is forbidden;
> All things are right, if only we believe it;
> We have examples of the gods to follow.
> And what is there to stop us? A strict father?
> Regard for reputation? Only fear!
> Not even fear, if we have no cause for fearing.
> It is easy enough to hide our stolen pleasures
> Under the names of brother and sister.
>
> (Quoted in Santiago 1973)

The sexual attraction between brothers and sisters has long been seen as either the province of the wicked or the privilege of youthful innocents. Yet therapists who listen carefully, are likely to hear that some patients have had sexual feelings for a sibling, and that more than a few have had erotic experiences with one. In many of these situations, the parents either never knew or chose not to know what their children were doing. Some of these encounters were fleeting moments of innocent looking, touching, and comparing, all in the service of childish sexual curiosity. However, some of the encounters described to us apparently grew in significance, continued over a long period of time, and occurred in an emotional context where curiosity became need, comparison became fascination, and touching became holding and loving. Finally, some of these sibling experiences evolved into what has to be defined as an incestuous relationship, where sexual intercourse actually and repeatedly occurred.

Sexuality between Brothers and Sisters

In this chapter we will examine four aspects of sexuality between brothers and sisters: playful curiosity, love, oedipal involvement, and incest.

Playful Curiosity

Ever since Freud (1905) challenged the prevailing notions about childhood being blissful and nonsexual, clinicians and researchers alike have acknowledged that boys and girls develop sexual curiosity early in life (for example, Papalia and Olds 1975). T. Berry Brazelton gives a clear example of such a process when he cites a mother who happened upon her thirty-month-old son with two other little boys:

> He was hiding behind a pair of bushes with two other boys his age. They had pulled down their pants, and were investigating each other's penis. They were saying, "I'm the doctor, you lie down." and "What's that, doctor?" as they pointed out their belly buttons and genitalia. Most giggling came out when Joe pointed to another boy's anus and buttocks and said, "Here's your b.m.!"
>
> (1974, pp. 204–5)

And another vignette familiar to many parents:

> As the children explored the doll's body, they voiced their disapproval. "Where does she wee wee?" "No hole." "Doesn't have a penis. How does he peepee?" The excitement over such communication built up, and soon the children were off and around, yelling, "you b.m." at each other. (Pp. 204–5)

Children's perceptions of sex difference continue to expand; and by the age of five or six, a child's self-knowledge of "maleness" or "femaleness" contributes to a greater security about his or her own gender (Money and Ehrhardt 1972) and to sex-role typing (Koch 1956; Brim 1958). In our interviews with adults, however, they were much less likely to recall early sexual play with siblings of the same sex than with those of the opposite sex. Playing "doctor" or "Mommy and Daddy" or actually touching a sibling's genitalia appears to be of much greater interest when the object of curiosity is different from oneself than when it is the same.° We have not assumed that sibling sexual contact is usually "no more than transitory

---

° Little appears known about sex play between brothers and sex play between sisters even in those cases where homosexuality has later become the adult's preferred orientation. To our knowledge, there is no literature on homosexual attraction between siblings. Nonetheless, it is likely that homosexual attraction and activity between same-sex siblings does exist and is rarely discussed openly.

experimentation on the part of young teen-agers—a continuation, as it were, of earlier episodes of 'playing doctor'" (Masters and Johnson 1976, p. 54).

The presence of sexual curiosity and the occurrence of sexual play between opposite-sex siblings should come as no surprise, particularly since many popular magazines and books have reassured parents that children's sexual curiosity is natural and inevitable (for example, Arnstein 1979). What exactly, however, is sex "play"? When does play become something else by virtue of *frequency, type of contact, time* spent together, the emotional *reaction* to the experience, and so on? David Finkelhor has provided a useful definition of sex play as "activities of young children of the same age, engaged in mutually, that are limited to the showing and touching of genitals, and that go on for short periods of time" (1980, p. 172). The consensus seems to be that sexual play between a brother and a sister is a normal developmental phenomenon and becomes a source of shame and guilt in the child only if parents view it as shameful, dirty, or harmful. Such worries in a child can reflect a parent's dread about sexual matters. John Mordock (1974) has described a family therapy case where the parents initially resisted recognizing sexual elements in the playful, teasing, and sometimes jealous alliance between their eleven-year-old daughter and nine-year-old son. The mother rationalized that since *she* had disliked her own brother, it was impossible for her daughter to care for and be sexually attracted to her brother.

But the daughter and son soon confronted the mother's denial with an open display of sexual teasing, jokes, and roughhousing. They revealed that the sister knew about the brother's masturbation; that the brother was stimulated by seeing his sister nude with her big "red cheeks"; that he and she openly discussed "making babies" and "having sex."

Thus, like many other brothers and sisters, these two were creating a positive dialectic, using their emerging awareness of each other's sexuality to proclaim their mutual sexual attraction. But the sexual curiosity and erotic feelings of this brother and sister were also clearly tinged with anxiety. When brothers and sisters catch glimpses of each other's bodies, they often have exciting thoughts which can make them feel guilty and confused. Unless parents have made some attempt to explain sexuality, their children are often left to their own devices, discovering sexuality through their sexual play.

This leads us to the following principle: *in the process of sexual unfolding, high-access brothers and sisters often admire, make comparisons, and engage in sexually tinged play with one another.* This behavior can stem from many motives, some of which are intensified when the children's needs are insufficiently gratified by parents. This intensified sexuality between brothers and sisters brings us to the complex question of love.

Brother-Sister Love

Out of the early days of play and attraction between brothers and sisters, love can develop. But love, based on caring, concern, and identification, often becomes romantic and sexual when the siblings wish to *bond* and *attach*. The sexual curiosity of childhood then can become more than simple comparison and exploration during adolescence. The siblings may elevate their relationship from one that coexists with other relationships to one that is primary and enduring. Yet such relationships are often tragic because they are a signal of the failure of the forces that would normally promote each child to find sexual love outside of the immediate family. The attraction of siblings to one another, natural in its origins, becomes now a double tragedy, backed by the centuries-old solemn interdiction against incest in our Western culture. In the Judeo-Christian tradition, this love is considered to be extreme and "unnatural."

SIBLING LOVE IN HISTORY AND MYTH

In spite of the Judeo-Christian taboo which has stood for centuries, sexual love between brothers and sisters is no stranger to history. We know that temptations between brothers and sisters existed in significant eras. The Greeks worshiped gods, some of whom were brother-sister pairs who loved each other and then often parted in tragedy. The pharoahs of ancient Egypt (the earliest known evidence is from the fourth dynasty, 2700 B.C.), justifying their direct descent from their gods *and* wishing to mark themselves separate from the masses, took brother-sister marriage as a sacred privilege to which only the anointed rulers were entitled. This royal privilege of brother-sister marriage appears later to have been extended to all citizens, although it is not possible to be certain of this point, since the Egyptians used the same term for siblings as for married couples (Santiago 1973). Abraham, patriarch of the Hebrew people, followed the Egyptian custom of that time and married his half-sister Sarah. Such marriages remained sanctioned until the time of Moses. From then on, Jews were exhorted to abhor such relationships, as stated in Deuteronomy, the

157

fifth book of Moses: "Cursed be he that lieth with his sister, the daughter of his father, or the daughter of his mother" (27:22). In the main, most cultures gradually came to set severe limits on the possibility of consummated brother-sister love.

With the acceptance of Judeo-Christian law throughout the Western world, brother-sister incest was codified as unlawful and repugnant. And yet the lure of brother to sister and of sister to brother has remained a potent force in sibling relationships, however unacknowledged by parents and society. To recognize sibling love and incest is to recognize that one of society's most basic taboos has broken down, that parental nurturing and protection have collapsed. Yet literature and myth have borne witness to the age-old fascination and pain of love between brother and sister. From Homer's story about Aeolus* to Ovid, whose tale introduced this chapter, to the twentieth century's Thomas Mann (1936, 1951) and William Faulkner (1929), stories of brother-sister love end in remorse, tragedy, and despair. (An exception is John Irving's recent *The Hotel New Hampshire* [1981], in which a brother and a sister have a sexual experience so intense that it is the culmination and conclusion of that aspect of their relationship.)

Just as Freud went to myth and literature for a cogent image for another unacknowledged but universal human relationship (the Oedipus complex), we have found in two stories—one from myth, the other from literature—significant insights that we later use in this chapter to analyze contemporary sibling pairs. Through them, we can begin to see that romantic attraction between brother and sister thrives when other opportunities for receiving love and nurturance have begun to wither.

MERGING AND MIRRORING: NARCISSUS AND ECHO

According to ancient Greek myth, young Narcissus saw his handsome image reflected in a shimmering pool of water. Transfixed by his reflected beauty, the youth was unable to tear himself away to attend to the everyday world, and pined away and died from sorrow over his inability to reach this reflected object of his adoration. This story has long been the prototype for the clinical and social reality of individual self-absorption—or narcissism.† Freud and his immediate psychoanalytic successors used Narcissus to explain preoccupying self-absorption and the way in which

*This epic story describes how the children of Aeolus, the god of the winds, made his six sons and six daughters marry each other.

†For example, such object-relations theorists as Otto Kernberg (1975); also see Christopher Lasch's *The Culture of Narcissism* (1978).

energy ("narcissistic energy") becomes transferred from the infant to an outer object and then back again to the infant ("narcissistic supplies").

An aspect of the myth that has usually been overlooked is that, in one version,° Narcissus's transfixion is testimony to the love of a brother for a sister. Narcissus is looking for his beautiful sister Echo, his identical twin, who has drowned in that very pool. He is not merely fascinated by his image but is also searching and attempting to recapture the sight of his dearly lost love object, the sister who is his mirror image. In this version, the siblings' relationship with each other is so vital, their love so strong, that Narcissus cannot tear himself away: unable to live without his sibling, he remains faithfully beside the pool in which she died.

Narcissus's pathetic efforts to merge with his sister doom him to failure and remind us of contemporary siblings who attempt mirroring and merging. This allegory exposes what also lies at the root of sibling love: the wish to look into the reflected image of an identical soulmate and thus to avoid ever feeling completely alone. In this fused relationship, sibling love is narcissistic, all-absorbing; and, if tragedy stalks one member of the pair, it affects the other as well. As we will see, Narcissus and Echo resemble other brothers and sisters who are unable to live without one another. Sexualization of the relationship merely bonds the siblings even closer, in a mirrored embrace of self-love.†

FLIGHT FROM TERROR: SIEGMUND AND SIEGLINDE

Such myths reflect man's discomfort with sibling sexuality. Terror is retribution for falling in love with a brother or a sister; it is "God's wrath" visited on those who break the incest barrier.

In Richard Wagner's epic operatic quartet *The Ring of the Nibelung* (1870), a pair of brother-sister twins testify to the narcissism and the hazards that befall siblings who dare to remain romantically entwined. Siegmund and Sieglinde suffer traumas in childhood when their mother is murdered, their house is burned to the ground, and Sieglinde is carried off by marauders. Many years later Siegmund wanders into the house where, unbeknownst to him, his sister has been held hostage by their father's arch enemy. As the twins behold each other, they are entranced by their dawning (but narcissistic) recognition. On seeing her, his mirror image, Siegmund calls out, "Oh wondrous vision! Rapturous woman!" Broth-

---

°*Encyclopaedia Britannica* (1947)

†We are using the term *love* in a much more restricted sense than the "caring," "affection," "liking," "admiring," or "loving" that many people say they feel for a sib. *Narcissism* and *fear* often tip the scales of such caring on the side of sexual involvement.

er and sister become lovers and try to capture some small measure of bliss and serenity for themselves in spite of their fear of retribution. A goddess, viewing them, states contemptuously and vindictively:

> My heart shudders
> My brain reels
> Marital intercourse
> Between brother and sister!
> When did anyone live to see it:
> Brother and sister physically lovers?
> (*Die Walküre*)

The twins have only one night of love and respite before the brother is slain.

This story illustrates an important idea: *Brothers and sisters will sometimes seek love, tenderness, and compassion from one another in a larger context of fear and terror.* Sexual involvement can become an island of refuge for them in a world where they feel abandoned and without protection. Thus, the sexual attraction between sisters and brothers has been seen as tragic. Contemporary brothers and sisters who become romantically entwined are, like their mythic counterparts, often driven together by the absence of adult nurturance, and by the basic need for continued contact with what is intimate and familiar.

Why have psychiatry and psychology not contributed more understanding of sibling sexuality? The most formidable and enduring of their perspectives has been provided by the oedipal tragedy and its chief advocate, Sigmund Freud. Before we can describe the cases current psychotherapists are likely to encounter, we need to re-examine some of the earlier psychoanalytic perspectives from a new vantage point.

FREUD AND HIS INFLUENCE

When Freud, guided by the disclosures of his patients in the consulting room, extended his theory of sexuality to a theory of human nature, he had to make a crucial decision. Were his patients' tales of sexual attraction to a parent based on fact, or were they—like their feelings of attraction to Freud—the products of psychological distortion, elaboration, and repression? In spite of evidence that young children were actually seduced by their parents, Freud discarded the idea of seduction and decided that hysteria was an outgrowth of the child's instinctual sexual wishes. It is now thought that Freud believed that the Victorian culture of his day could hardly tolerate the disturbing revelations that his patients were giving him about father-daughter incest, and that, to maintain his theory of hysteria, he suppressed this evidence (Peters 1976). With the benefit of hindsight, it appears that Freud's own interest in the oedipal theory of repressed sexuality would have been ill-served by placing the onus of sexual abuse upon parents. Recently other evidence (for example, Morton Schatzman 1973) has documented how consistently Freud—in favor of emphasizing purely psychological phenomena—ignored obvious facts about the real, external traumas a child can confront.

For Freud, the most important psychological struggle that every individual faces is that which destroyed King Oedipus, who married his own mother, Jocasta, and murdered Laius, his father. Freud adapted this story to describe each child's struggle: it is the parent of the opposite sex who is the child's first love; it is the parent of the same sex who emotionally bars the door to fulfillment of the child's wishes for the other parent. In Freud's opinion, the way a child resolves this struggle determines that child's entire psychological development. Once this struggle has been resolved, a person can successfully leave his or her family to seek a separate sexual destiny.

Freud also had some speculations about man's primitive past. In his classic essay *Totem and Taboo* (1912–13), he embraces the thinking of the anthropologist James G. Frazer (1910), who stated that the taming of sexual feelings toward one's own family members allowed man to turn his energies to other matters—that is, to become civilized. Modern culture could develop, as Freud saw it, only when men and women sought sexual partners *outside* the tribal group ("exogamy"). In his words, "the members of the same totem [tribal family] are not allowed to enter into sexual relations with each other" (1912–13, p. 809). He acknowledged that there is no instinctive aversion to incestuous relations, and that children's first sexual impulses are directed within the family. However, to give way to sexual feelings for one's parent is to become doomed, like Oedipus, or to fall in danger of reverting to the species' primitive past. "Incest dread" is the reaction to those still only partially repressed urges for sensual experiences with members of one's own family; the incest taboo is most severe, and the sexual wish most urgent, in regard to the child's parent.

What of siblings? Did Freud have anything to say of sexual feelings for, or erotic actions with, a brother or a sister, or about siblings' anxieties over such attraction? In *Totem and Taboo*, he portrays siblings in primitive cultures as members of a tribal horde who lust for each other but feel unbearable guilt for having murdered the father who has prevented them from acting out their feelings. Recognizing that chaos could result from giving vent to these sexual impulses, the brothers turn away from their sisters and mate instead with outsiders. Later (1930) Freud said that sibling love might exist in two forms, lustful and caring. When lustful, it is a savage residue of man's primitive tribal past; when it takes a caring form, it is a mere displacement of unresolved oedipal love for a parent. Freud implied that sibling love was basically "aim-inhibited"—a love of secondary importance deflected from the most desired object—namely, the parent.°

Freud's views about sibling love became solidly entrenched in the minds of his followers. Ernest Jones, Freud's biographer and colleague, wrote similar thoughts which, in his orthodox adherence to Freud, helped pave the way for psychoanalytic thinking about sibling sexuality to the present day.

> The characteristics of the father-daughter complex are also found in a similar one, the brother-sister complex. As analytic work shows every day, this also, like the former one, is a derivative of the fundamental Oedipus complex. When the incest barrier develops early in the life of the young boy it begins first in regard to his relationship with the mother, and only later sets in with the sister as well; indeed, erotic experiences between brother and sister in early childhood are exceedingly common. The sister is usually the first replacement of the mother as an erotic object; through her the boy learns to find his way to other women. His relationship to his sister duplicates that of the two parents to each other, and in life he often plays a father-part in regard to her (care, protection, etc.) (1910, pp. 157–58)

This became the leitmotif of the psychoanalytic theory of brother-sister relationships: if siblings are of the same sex, they are rivals for parent love; if of the opposite sex, they are the natural outlet for displaced oedipal desires. Neither Freud nor his followers described the sibling relationship in its own right, or the extent of siblings' direct feelings for one another, or the family context in which children might feel sexual longings for each other (for example, Oberndorf 1929).

Such views remained virtually intact for the next sixty years. But then in this monolithic view of sibling incest and its relationship to oedipal lust and revenge, a few cracks appeared. The most significant of these is a relatively neglected, but fine piece of scholarship by Luciano P. R. Santiago which appeared in 1973—*The Children of Oedipus*. Keeping one foot in the traditional Freudian camp, Santiago stretched with the other:

°If Freud had only looked more thoroughly into the family of Oedipus, he would have discovered that Oedipus's daughter, Antigone, loves her brother, Polynices. Antigone defies the cruel King Creon who refuses to bury her brother's body, and says, "There is no better way I could prepare for death than by giving burial to my brother." In effect, brother-sister love not *only* stems from repressed lust for a parent but can also develop out of loyalty, caring, and mutual sense of destiny.

When either or both parents are not available physically or emotionally, the siblings, lacking an object for rivalry may turn to each other instead to meet their dependency and erotic demands. What initially seems to be the "second best" love object may turn out to be "even better" than the original. The absence of authority and the greater chances of concealment (out of mutual need and fear) enhances the eventual perpetuation of the sexual relationship. (P. 7)

At last someone had begun to recognize that siblings are more than just sexual understudies for parents, and that there are distinctive features, and for some, distinct benefits to eroticizing the sibling relationship.° Santiago was alluding to the *contextual circumstances,* including the deficits in parenting some siblings might be experiencing.

Let us now summarize the oedipal container into which sibling sexuality has been poured by Freud and his adherents:

- Incestuous feelings toward a sibling are a natural residue from man's primitive, tribal past.
- Brother-sister incest is a secret rebuke of the father's power; it is, in effect, castration of the dominant male.
- By having sexual relations with their sisters, brothers replace their weak or absent fathers and become the dominant sexual male in the family.
- Daughters with incestuous feelings for their fathers can displace these feelings onto their brothers.
- Sons with incestuous feelings for their mothers can displace these feelings onto their sisters.

But this explanation appears to be insufficient. With the budding recognition that parents could be both incestuous and neglectful toward their children, the oedipal theory needs to be expanded to include the following point:

- When children's parents abandon them or no longer nurture them, the children will displace onto each other their feelings of rage, helplessness, and sexual desire; and as a result, there is a mixture of aggression and sexuality in certain sibling relationships.

FREUD'S OVERSIGHT

While Freud was a genius in his day, he can be faulted for his narrow view of sibling relationships and of sibling sexuality in particular. Intoxicated with his oedipal theory, which he extended from primitive man, to

°Even though Santiago warned about the potentially harmful effects of sibling sexual embroilment, he detoxified some aspects of brother-sister incest by pointing out how such relationships had both historical and mythological precedents.

families, to children's inner struggles, and on to all psychopathology, he had a theory of sibling sexuality right in his grasp and then let it slip through his fingers.

Sibling Sexual Influence: The Wolf-Man and His Sister. Freud's famous case of the Wolf-Man, "From the History of an Infantile Neurosis" (1918), is extraordinary because it is one of the few documented examples of the expression of sibling sexuality in early childhood. It is a rich description of how sexual preoccupation in a young man developed into an obsessional neurosis. In this instance Freud actually did describe the "seduction" of his patient by the patient's sister. When the sister was approximately five and a half years old, and her brother was three and a quarter:

> his sister had seduced him into sexual practices. First came a recollection that in the water-closet, which the children used frequently to visit together, she had made this proposal: "Let's show one another our bottoms," and had proceeded from words to deeds. Subsequently the more essential part of the seduction came to light, with full particulars as to time and locality. It was in spring, at a time when his father was away; the children were in one room playing on the floor, while their mother was working in the next. His sister had taken hold of his member and played with it, at the same time telling him incomprehensible stories about his Nanya, as though by way of explanation.   (p. 487)

The boy's neurosis presumably erupted during a summer when the parents went away, and the children had been left with an English governess. When the parents returned, "they found him transformed. He had become discontented, irritable and violent, took offense at every possible occasion, and then flew into a rage and screamed like a savage" (p. 482).

Although Freud recognized that the seduction contributed to the rage the boy expressed that summer, particularly inasmuch as he had been passive in the face of (and was, in effect, victimized by) his sister's sexual precocity, neither Freud nor the patient mentioned whether the sister continued her sexual activities with her brother during that period. The sister was also described as being aggressive toward this brother, lording her intellectual brilliance over him and tormenting him by repeatedly exposing him to a frightening picture of a wolf (which came to preoccupy him in his later obsessional neurosis—hence the name "Wolf-Man"). Later, in adolescence, he tried to turn the tables on her with further significant effects upon his character development:

> During the tempestuous sexual excitement of his puberty he ventured an attempt at an intimate physical approach. She rejected him with equal decision and dexterity, and he at once turned away from her to a little peasant girl who

was a servant in the house and had the same name as his sister. In doing so he was taking a step which had a determinant influence upon his heterosexual object-choice. For all the girls with whom he subsequently fell in love—often with the clearest indications of compulsion—were also servants whose education and intelligence were necessarily far inferior to his own. If all of these objects of his love were substitutes for the figure of his sister whom he had to forego, then it could not be denied that the intention of debasing his sister and of putting an end to her intellectual superiority, which he had formerly found so oppressive, had obtained decisive control over his object-choice. (pp. 489–90)

As he continued his explanation of the patient's personality, Freud retreated from the importance of the sibling seduction and sexual attraction to that of the primal scene between the parents (which he contended the patient had witnessed when only one and a half years old). Rather than viewing as *crucial* the interaction between sister and brother, Freud, under the sway of his oedipal theory, insisted that it was secondary and merely compounded the importance of the parent-child sexual dynamic.

Upon re-examination of the Wolf-Man case, however, we found many of the ingredients that we feel are vital to understanding any important sibling constellation, and some hints of sibling sexual embroilment similar to that of other siblings whom we have come to know. In the first place, the mother had a severe, recurring abdominal disorder and therefore little interest in the daily parenting of her children. The father was frequently depressed and often absent, due to lengthy stays at sanatoriums. The children's care was given over to multiple caretakers, some of whom were less than kind and nurturing. The children had high access to one another (there was only a two-year age difference), played frequently together, and had a prolonged period of close, mutual identification: for example, "a similar disposition of mind and a common opposition to their parents brought them so close together that they got on with each other like the best of friends" (p. 489). There was also sexual involvement: at the very least we know of the sister's "seduction" of her brother when he was three and a half years old, and of the sexual advance he made to her when he was an adolescent. Furthermore, one of these siblings, the sister, was dominant, aggressive, "lively, gifted and precociously naughty" (p. 481); her younger sibling, the brother, played a passive role in relation to her. Thus, this was not a calm, crisis-free family. The parents had serious problems; the brother was later hospitalized with a diagnosis of manic-depressive psychosis; while the sister, who was probably schizophrenic, eventually committed suicide. Although the sibling sexual embroilment was certainly not a cause of these problems, the conditions in the family indicate that the incestuous behavior was probably more than just a release of "sexual lust" (p. 494).

In our examination of the Wolf-Man case, we believe that the absence and emotional neglect of these parents played a pivotal role in energizing the natural attraction between their children. This insight led us to a hypothesis that we have subsequently seen borne out in other cases: *The emotional absence of parents can intensify the mutual dependency and the sexual curiosity of high-access brothers and sisters.*

Furthermore, as we interviewed patients who reported having been sexually attracted to their opposite-sex siblings, key points that had been evident in the sibling sagas of myth and literature also began to appear: high and early access, fusion, mirroring and twinning due to parent absence, flight from terror, and feelings of compassion and empathy for one another.

Sibling Incest

Having laid a foundation, we are ready to explore all the dimensions of incestuous sibling involvement. Lacking the heroic elements of sibling love as expressed in myth and literature, some of the contemporary brothers and sisters whom we interviewed had complicated, ambivalent, and emotionally tortured sexual involvements with each other.

In order to understand actual sexual relations between brothers and sisters, we have settled on one definition of sibling incest as differentiated from sexual play. We decided on the most restrictive definition: the sexual activity must be heterosexual, and there must be at least one instance of vaginal intercourse and/or oral-genital contact between brother and sister. In our cases, this definition excluded examples of sexual play between siblings, except when such play specifically served as a prelude to the other activities.

Since sibling incest is complex, any effort to understand it has to involve recognition of the following crucial factors:

1. The source of information about incest, and the means of acquiring that information.
2. The ages and development stages of each of the participants when the incest began.
3. The frequency and duration of the sexual experiences.
4. The general context in which the experiences occurred—including the family's ethnic, religious, and cultural values; its attitudes toward sex; as well as economic, social, and geographical variables.

5. The family system and psychological influences on the participants.
6. The type of sexual behavior and the motives for engaging in it.
7. Long- and short-term effects.

The typical clinician usually does not ask about sibling incest, and patients usually avoid mentioning it (Berry 1975). In the few studies of sibling incest that have been done, sisters have been the main source of
information (Finkelhor 1979; Forward and Buck 1978; Meiselman 1978).
We have interviewed in depth a total of seven women who had incestuous
experiences, and our psychotherapeutic colleagues shared with us testimony from eight other women.

Where were the incestuous brothers of these women or, for that matter,
any other incestuous brothers? Only two brothers, of all the men we interviewed, admitted incestuous experiences with their sisters; all the other
men we questioned denied having broken the incest taboo. Some of the
brothers we have come to know, acknowledged having had sexual feelings
for, and fleeting, stolen touches with, their sisters during early adolescence; but in the adult male, the absence of memories of incest seems
more in the service of denial than necessarily a matter of accurate recall.
In one of the few carefully conducted clinical studies on incest, Karin C.
Meiselman (1978) reported verbal testimony from eight siblings; but only
one of these was a brother. Masters and Johnson (1976) reported two cases
of men admitting to sibling incest: the sister of one man was ten years
older than he, and that of the other, seven years older; in both cases, the
effects on the brothers were long-lasting and traumatic. The psychoanalyst Robert Stein, reporting his own experience, stated that at age
twelve he was "invaded by intense sexual fantasies and desires, much of
which was provoked by my sisters" (1973, p. 92), and that he had had "an
enormous amount of repressed anger toward several of my older sisters
who . . . had excessively provoked me sexually, and then had denied it"
(p. 4). Unable to deal with both his anger and sexual feelings for these
older sisters, young Stein repressed all loving feelings for them. With the
exception of S. Kirson Weinberg's study (1955) of incarcerated sexual offenders (clearly a special subgroup, since they were considerably older
than their sisters and therefore exploitative), there is no large-scale study
of men who were incestuous with their sisters.

While men are always underrepresented in any psychotherapy sample,
there are special reasons for incestuous brothers to stay away from the
therapist's discerning ear. Meiselman agrees that brothers are likely to be
underrepresented in any incest or sexual abuse project, and that they
would be extremely reluctant to report either experience. She has several

suggestions: (1) if the brother is the aggressor, the incest does not violate the male ego ideal of being dominant, sexual, and aggressive; (2) a brother's perception of himself as victim violates his desired male image of brothers as stronger than sisters, and he would be reluctant to report the incest; (3) few people would be likely to want to believe the boy; and, finally, (4) brothers are probably less emotionally disturbed by incest with a sister: it is acceptable to them, and therefore they are less likely to seek psychotherapeutic help for it.

Brothers who report having engaged in sibling incest, or having come close to it, tend to see themselves as victimized by their older and more powerful sisters, or describe emotional deprivation and a power struggle with their fathers. We believe that most such brothers still feel guilt, shame, and fear of discovery of their incestuous experiences during adolescence. As they reach adulthood, they often phobically avoid their sisters or, upon hearing that a sister is in therapy (and therefore might tell the secret), become compulsively polite and deferential to her. One such brother invited himself to the office of one of us with the urgent and excruciatingly nervous offer, "I'll do anything to help my sister."°

The age and developmental stage of the children involved in incest is particularly important to their capacity for understanding and dealing with the experience. Children as young as five or six find sibling incest to be overwhelming, bewildering, exciting, or brutalizing. Because it occurs so early, it can take a considerable amount of lengthy psychotherapy to resolve the aftereffects. Susan Forward and Craig Buck (1978) describe a woman who, as a child of five, had been raped repeatedly by her sixteen-year-old brother. The effects of these assaults were so pernicious that she had grown to hate men, was homosexual and suicidal, and had a horrible self-image.

For more mature siblings, the incest can be less destructive. A twenty-seven-year-old dental student told of a long weekend she had spent with her older brother, when she was twenty-two. She had just left her husband, who was often hostile and withdrawn—behavior that was calculated to make her feel extremely worthless. She found refuge in her brother's home, stayed for a few days, and made love with him. There was apparently no history of incest, and there has not been any since that time. She felt no guilt and seemed to have relished the experience. The incest occurred during a period of profound loneliness and powerlessness in her life. The brother who had provided fun and relief from worry in

---

° As in the other studies, much of what we found out about these brothers came from the sisters to whom the boys turned as confidants and a source of relief from pain. These sisters clearly had a special insight into their brothers' feelings and personal concerns.

her early childhood became again, in the midst of her marital turmoil, a source of balance, stability, and contact, only this time through sexuality. Because this incest was isolated and not motivated by an unsatisfying parent-child relationship, and also because she initiated it, the sister was able to rationalize that it was what she then needed—someone to care for her in this special way in a time of crisis.

Our interviews led us to believe that certain adult women are able to undergo this experience without trauma, while extremely young children may be able to repress what has occurred. Sibling incest in pre-adolescence, however, generally has a crippling effect. It is in this stage that a child is consciously dealing with the first stirrings of puberty, sexual feelings, and physical change. These feelings can be confusing, mysterious, and delightful, but they can also induce guilt. Sexual entanglement between brothers and sisters at this point can have powerful and long-lasting effects on a person's sexual identity.

THE SIBLING INCEST TABOO: IS IT JUST LIKE ANY OTHER?

While sexual relations between siblings have been studied, the distinctiveness of these, apart from incest in other family relationships, seems to vanish; and few investigators view them as a special case, generating special effects. Anthropologists (for example, Fox 1962, 1980), clinicians (for example, Forward and Buck 1978), and sociologists (for example, Weinberg 1955) tend to describe sibling incest as having less severe effects than parent-child incest, but they often cite the former only to demonstrate the vagaries that lie behind the relative strength or weakness of the general incest taboo.*

It is clear to us, however, that the breaking of the incest taboo by siblings is special, and that its greater frequency does not mean that its ramifications are any less significant than are those of the least frequent type, that between mother and son. The magnitude of a child's experience with sibling incest appears to be in direct proportion to the *complexity* and the *subjective emotional significance of the experience.* We believe that sibling incest has profound implications for personality development because it is a basic attack on social custom and taboo and often involves such contradictory feelings as guilt, love, shame, empathy, and anger as well as the processes of identification.

It is difficult to know how often sibling incest occurs, since the sources

*The general topic of incest and the origin of the incest taboo have been described comprehensively by Gardner Lindzey (1967) and V. and A. Frances (1976) and recently by Robin J. Fox (1980).

of information about it are usually imprisoned offenders (Weinberg 1955) or mental health clinics and hospitals. Clinical institutions are more oriented toward dealing with the cases of parent-child incest, which have been referred to them, rather than with sibling incest, which is often undetected by parents. Sibling incest appears, by all estimates, to be a drastically underreported phenomenon. Finkelhor (1979, 1980), in a survey conducted at six New England colleges and universities between 1977 and 1978, found that 13 percent of the nearly eight hundred students reported sibling sexual activity of some sort, and concluded that his figures were "almost certainly underestimates."

Sibling incest has been estimated to be at least five times as frequent as parent-child incest (25 cases per 1,000 persons [Gebhard et al. 1965; Moore 1964]). Lindzey (1967) sees this as a substantial underestimate; while David C. Lester (1975), in agreeing, points out that most of research in this area has been inadequate and the studies have been methodologically weak. Karin C. Meiselman (1978) agrees that the taboo against brother-sister incest is the weakest of all, particularly in those families where the father is absent or ineffective and cannot be a "restraining agent" on his son. Meiselman indicates four probable reasons for the weakness of the sibling incest taboo: (1) It does not violate social expectations of dominance: older brothers are supposed to be dominant; males are expected to dominate females. (2) No adult-child taboo is being broken; sibling sexuality is often considered "child's play." (3) Society is more restrictive about cross-generational sexual relationships; sibling incest is not usually cross-generational. (4) Intense dependency relationships are considered incompatible with overt sexuality (the mother-child incest taboo being strongest); since siblings are not usually acknowledged as being emotionally dependent on one another, this incest taboo is once again weakest.

While the taboo on sibling incest is the least restrictive, some social scientists would argue that *all* the incest taboos are becoming obsolete (Cohen 1978). Then there are writers like sociobiologist Robin Fox (1980) who contend that sibling incest hardly ever occurs. Fox assumes that when siblings are kept apart, their incestuous impulses will only grow stronger; but that, left to their own devices, to play together in whatever way they want, brothers and sisters will eventually lose their sexual interest in each other. Such writers ignore the emotional climate that can propel siblings toward one another, and the evidence that there are siblings who do indeed have ongoing sexual relations.

Sexuality between Brothers and Sisters

THE POWER OF THE SECRET

> My parents could never understand why
> I was always so uncomfortable when I
> was in a room with my brother. We had
> this secret, but they always thought I was
> just too sensitive.

The sexualization of a sibling relationship drives it underground, out of view of the parents, and even of other siblings.° Of all the possible sibling secrets, one that involves an erotic relationship, usually remains hidden, becoming part of a sibling underworld.†

The unacceptability to most adults of public displays of children's sexual feelings, let alone sexual behavior (in spite of a begrudging acceptance that it exists), gives such a secret added intensity and power (Pincus and Dare 1978).

Unlike Wagner's Siegmund and Sieglinde, siblings who eroticize their relationship seldom initiate it simultaneously. One sibling is always a little ahead, pushing to break through the incest barrier; yet eroticization can develop and continue by mutual consent, it can become somewhat acceptable for both, or it can become free of the original motives that initiated it. The secret can always be revealed if one of the children chooses to tell someone; but the emotional payoffs for continuing the relationship tend to outweigh any that could be derived from disclosing it. Children who feel their parents have seriously failed them or hurt them, are likely to agree to continue the incest. Then the secret has enormous potency, for it reminds the children that they have a pact that the parents cannot break. Together the children are more powerful than their parents. Together they have proved themselves capable of transcending parental authority. Together they have done so right under their parent's noses! While any incest is always a "family affair" (Machotka, Pittman, and Flomenhaft 1967), sibling incest has much greater chance of successful concealment than has parent-child incest, where the nonparticipating parent's collusion is often necessary. In sibling incest both parents may be naïve, suspicious, or even vigilant against it; but if their children are determined to symbolically devastate their parents in this manner, they usually can do it. In the following case, we see that, although one sibling initiated sexual contact, it

° Denise Gelinas, personal communication, 1980.
† Finkelhor (1979), in his survey of college students, found that of those who had had a sibling sexual experience, only 12 percent had ever told anyone about it.

became acceptable to both and developed a momentum that neither child chose to slow down.

Pain, Protection, and Bonding: Patty and Shawn. Patty, an attractive, slightly overweight woman of twenty-nine, had never told anyone but her therapist the details of her involvement with her brother. No one else, not even her best friend or husband, had ever heard more than an innuendo about what childhood was really like. Patty was good, she was *very* good at using catchwords, an animated laugh, and quick humor to keep any listener off balance. Patty was skilled in pretense; she had been fooling her parents and friends for years, ever since she was six years old when she began having a sexual relationship with her eleven-year-old brother. In Patty's word's, "I wasn't real with either my brother or my parents. With my parents, I wasn't a kid, I was 'Patricia' and I was always supposed to show my brother the right way. But no one knew what I was really thinking." She always had to be wary and on her toes, a characteristic she carries with her to the present day.

Her brother had been in trouble ever since Patty could remember; when he was punished, Patty would cringe at the terrible beatings her father gave to him. Her memory of their first sexual encounter ended with just such a note.

> PATTY: It started with when I was six. There was five years difference between us . . . he would have been eleven. We'd play, "I saw your thing." That type of stuff. That was the forerunner, I suppose. One night I ran into the bathroom, he was sitting there. I didn't know he was there, and he was playing with himself, I think, and he asked if I wanted to touch it and I said yes and that's the way it got started, but we got caught. Our parents caught us.
>
> THERAPIST: That day?
>
> PATTY: Right there and then and he had the *shit* beaten out of him.
>
> THERAPIST: By your father?
>
> PATTY: Yeah, and that always made me angry. If he had been fighting and my parents caught us and said, "All right Shawn, you're the guilty one," he would get a worse punishment than I would and I used to think that it was unfair, and he would get beaten and I would get upset.

Patty closely identified with Shawn, idealizing him for a long time. When he suffered any indignity from other boys, she would go to his rescue. In these instances his little sister could be his angel of mercy:

PATTY: He was beaten up once, by this kid Billy across the street, and he went home and was crying. And I went out and beat the shit out of Billy and came home, and Shawn thanked me.

THERAPIST: How did you accomplish that?

PATTY: I had a belt and I took it off and I smashed him with the buckle.

THERAPIST: So you protected your bigger brother.

PATTY: Those were not the only times, and I still do it to this day, I do.

Patty *had* to depend on her brother. Since her mother worked and her father often found himself in financial difficulties, gambled, drank, or became involved in sexual encounters to assuage his bruised ego, Shawn was the only one entrusted with Patty's well-being. He provided her with a feeling of security when their parents left them alone, even though this feeling always coexisted with the gnawing fear that he could do her harm:

PATTY: I think I would really love to love my brother. But I don't think I *do* love him. I would like to, though.

THERAPIST: Why don't you love him? [*Long pause*]

PATTY: I don't think I trust him. And if I don't trust him, I can't love him. He frightens me. He has always frightened me.

THERAPIST: How does he frighten you?

PATTY: Physically he frightens me. He used to beat me up. He had an uncontrollable temper. He knocked me out twice when I was little by pushing my head into a wall.

Parental absence and neglect created the opportunity for brother and sister to intensify their sibling relationship:

PATTY: It was a natural thing, our bedrooms were separate but they were just door to door, and my parents would often leave and he would be babysitting and it would be easy for us to get together and do whatever it is that we wanted to do. [*Voice drops, starts to shake*]

THERAPIST: Can I ask you, what do you think about these memories as we bring them up now?

PATTY: I just feel scared, very scared.

THERAPIST: In what way scared?

PATTY: I'm almost reliving it. I'm *panicking, frightened*, because now I remember I was afraid if I didn't go along with what he wanted, that he would beat me up.

THERAPIST: During these years, you were six, seven, eight____

PATTY: ____ and nine, and ten, and eleven, and twelve. It actually went on till I went to high school and he went away.

THERAPIST: [*Referring to the brother*] So this was a secret between the two of you?

PATTY: Yes, we both kept it. The biggest fear was getting caught. That was more a threat to me than anything else.

THERAPIST: So how does that affect things now between the two of you? You don't have to fear being caught any more.

PATTY: I've lied to myself so much that I believed it never happened. I was so sickened by it.

Patty described having oral, genital, and masturbatory sex with her brother for many years. The children carried out their clandestine activities two or three times a week, only tapering off the frequency of their encounters when Patty approached adolescence. Patty ruefully admitted that there was some pleasure in having a secret world that neither of their parents could penetrate. Shawn, knowing how much Patty was upset by their parents, calculatingly used her resentment for his own advantage.

PATTY: I can't say my parents were a positive influence. I never believed anything they said. You know, if they said drinking was dangerous, I'd have to drink first because I never would have believed them. My father was running around. And I knew it and my brother knew it, and that's when my brother and I probably were closest. We knew that was a thing we weren't supposed to know, and we talked about it all the time. But Shawn used to say things like, "It's okay if we do it, look at Daddy, I mean he's got a girlfriend."

THERAPIST: Shawn would say, "Illicit sex is okay."

PATTY: That's what he'd say.

The fear of being beaten was not the only motive for Patty's sexual embroilment with her brother: She also felt great empathy with him; she could feel his pain and, in contrast to the hurtful aloofness of her parents, could make contact with her sibling:

PATTY: I felt *genuinely* sorry for him because they mistreated him. They NEVER understood him. TO THIS DAY THEY DON'T UNDERSTAND HIM. . . . And they *judge* him, but constantly judge him by *their* standards—their values.

THERAPIST: There must have been some way that they failed you badly, which made you turn to Shawn.

PATTY: Well, they *were* different from other parents. The other parents didn't mind driving, driving us one way to pick up. My parents always said, "No! You take the bus." They never went out of their way for us.

Bonded to her sibling she turned to him as a source of affection, praise, and self-esteem. He was her only model for identification:

PATTY: He was supportive of me, he was!

THERAPIST: In some ways parental?

PATTY: Yeah, if I hit a home run or a single, whatever I did, he'd say, "Good play," and that made my day. See, I didn't get that attention from my father. I think that's why I became so athletic, to get my brother's attention.

As her chief source of affection, Shawn knew that he could manipulate his little sister by ignoring her:

THERAPIST: If you didn't go along with him sexually, would he beat you?

PATTY: No, you know what he would do, he wouldn't talk to me. That made me even angrier. He would ignore me or hold something over my head. "I'm going to tell Mommy you're smoking or that you stole money from her or something like that."

Shawn also defended her, even though the parents would often punish him and then "fuse" their "bad" children together. Sex became the secret sanctuary from parental injustice and the children's retaliatory weapon:

PATTY: Shawn let me be with his friends, baseball and stuff like that. And if my parents got too hard on me, he would say something to them for which he was promptly told to "shut up" and then I would jump in and say something and my mother would say "shut up" and then we'd both be punished and sent up to bed. And sometimes we'd, later at night, get together and do things, and our parents never knew it.

Sex with her brother had other emotional payoffs for Patty. It would calm him, thus preventing the family quarrels and unleashing of passions that the little girl so detested.

In early adolescence, when other boys began being interested in her,

Patty had to disguise her sexual expertise. No one could know that she was sexually precocious, and she had to fake innocence. Deeply affected by the relationship with her brother *and* father, Patty now felt contempt for all males, including the boys whom she fooled with her pseudo-innocent disguise. However, when Shawn, her only gratifying source of emotional responsiveness, went away, Patty did become sexually active with other boys. She was promiscuous, driven by a combination of need and contempt until, at the age of seventeen, she met her husband-to-be. A quiet, unassuming lad who made absolutely no sexual demands upon her, he was able to provide the first steadying influence in her life. But Patty's sexuality was now split off from tenderness; they could not coexist in the same person. Whenever she envisioned that sex could be a part of any meaningful long relationship, she would get shaky and anxious and feel extremely threatened.

As an adult, Patty seldom heard from Shawn, since he had moved far away, but his hold over her remained. Knowing she was in long-term therapy, he occasionally called her and asked if she had shared the "secret" with the therapist:

PATTY: He can be very tender to me. I'm just . . . afraid! I almost called him last night! I'm afraid of what he might say to me or what he might do to me. He could make me go off the wall! He could say that he loves me . . . not as a sister, but as a woman.

THERAPIST: And do you love him?

PATTY: Just, just afraid. I don't have any feelings for him. I'd like to. I'm very, *very distant and . . . well, he thinks . . . well, he always used to say, "All for one, one for all, support one another."*

THERAPIST: You're still bound in by that fact.

PATTY: But what I'm saying is that up to a year ago I couldn't ever say No to him about anything, even though that's what I really felt.

The ramifications of Patty's sibling experience are extensive, affecting her core sense of security and touching everybody of significance to her. She required painstakingly steady, long-term psychotherapy to resolve the effects of the bond with her brother.

Sibling incest such as Shawn and Patty's must be understood in its family context. In this larger sense, no one is a total victim and no one is a total victimizer. Shawn needed Patty, and she needed him; in a family in which there was depression and despair, *everyone* was a victim. Siblings rarely become this sexually embroiled if there is adequate parenting. However, when there is a serious deficit in the emotional responsiveness and availability of both parents, one sibling can provide another with emotional gratification through such closeness, excitement, and involvement. Furthermore, a shared secret, like Shawn and Patty's, helps to erase the potential power each parent might gain in the eyes of their children. Keeping parents in the dark allows children to feel artificially omnipotent and grandiose. It can make parents seem, at best, foolish, or, at worst, impotent and helpless. If the love becomes eroticized over a long period of time, the bonding of the siblings becomes more intense, the struggle for separate identities more difficult, the contempt for the parents more profound.

Most of the women like Patty who complied with incest and kept the secret, tried to wear a tight façade of sweet conventionality when with their parents. Their brothers, like Shawn, often had the identity of family troublemaker; against this image these girls were usually juxtaposed by their parents as "good" or "conscientious" or "different from her brother." But these same women conveyed the impression that their parents were unavailable, narcissistic, cold, pretentious, and deadening to the human spirit. As young girls they had been terrified that they might become like their parents, particularly if they felt these mothers and fathers were unjust in dealing with the brothers. Only in the sibling underworld did these women feel free to step out from their protective façade of quiet conformity and feel really alive, experiencing an *élan vital*. A psychological split often developed in these girls between their public world of appearance and pretense and their private one of intense sibling eroticism.

These girls developed what has been called a "pseudo identity" or "false self," a mask over the secret, powerful sense of the personal identity they felt when with their brothers. The eroticized self was their core; the pseudo identity, their persona. Object-relations theorists (Winnicott 1971; Horner 1979) have discussed the implications of such a false self, which with its counterfeit behavior and public mask, serves to protect the true self from the disturbing intrusions of an imperfect environment. There are many implications for any person with such a false self, but they are particularly pernicious for the developing child who feels forced to hide his or her "real" self from parents.° The age of onset of this dynamic therefore has tremendous significance for personality development: *The younger the participant, the more confusing and potentially damaging is the incest experience.*

°We are not discussing the usual type of private experiences or "rites of passage"— things that, if known, the parents would disapprove—that adolescents often engage in, or experiment with, in order to develop a separate identity from their parents. Secrets like sibling incest have far deeper ramifications than have smoking pot, secret friendships, or even delinquent acts, such as taking the family's car without permission.

Masud R. Khan (1978) has described how one can hide oneself in just such a symptom or exist in suspended animation by escaping into one's "secret." Our own observations of siblings who had prolonged incest, suggest that every such person harbors the hope that he or she may one day emerge from behind the secret and be completely whole. One who has hidden behind an eroticized sibling relationship discovers, upon reaching maturity, that the relationship cannot be maintained as a permanent sanctuary: the price paid for keeping the secret is too great; the burden of protecting the other sibling too heavy to carry.

TWO TYPES OF SIBLING INCEST

We have already indicated that there are many types of sibling sexual contact—from experimentation to childhood seduction, to intense bonding. Some of these experiences can occur just once or continue repeatedly over long periods of time. Given this variation, it becomes useful to think of two general types of sibling incest: power-oriented, phallic, aggressive incest, and nurturing, erotic, loving incest.

Power-oriented incest is sadistic, exploitative, and coercive and often involves deliberate physical or mental abuse. Such incest need not be considered the sole province of males, although we would certainly acknowledge that, in the struggle to fulfill a sex-role stereotype of "manliness," it is more likely that older brothers will behave this way. Sisters, too, can be aggressive and can force their brothers, in a humiliating and hurtful manner, to have sex with them (Masters and Johnson 1976). Nurturance-oriented *incest, on the other hand, often occurs by mutual consent, contains many elements of erotic pleasure, loyalty, love, and compassion, and exists as a welcome island of refuge in an ocean of troubled and despairing family relationships.*°

Robert Stein (1973, 1974), eloquently writing about the "incest wound," emphasizes how the dualism of mind and body comes squarely to bear on the whole matter of incest. When power-oriented feelings predominate, love is split away; when nurturing and erotic† feelings predominate, guilt for one's sexual feelings is aroused. Stein points out that children in our

---

° To our knowledge, only one author, Christopher Bagley (1969), has actually labeled different types of incest. Although he does not discriminate between motivations and descriptions and includes all forms of incest (for example, father-daughter or father-son), he has provided some initially useful categories. He considers incest to be: (1) functional, (2) accidental or disorganized, (3) pathological, (4) object fixation, or (5) psychopathic.

† We are using the term *erotic* in the same sense that Stein does: "Following in the Platonic tradition, Eros will be used to refer to the full range of human love and passion—psychic and erotic, and not in the Freudian sense as undifferentiated sexual energies or Libido" (1974, p. 42).

178

culture are taught, early in life, to split these feelings, and that the failure to acknowledge consciously that one can both love and sexually desire one's sibling or parent (without acting upon these feelings), creates great harm to the human soul. Stein would expect loving and sexual feelings for a sibling to be the ideal.

Clearly, a pychotherapist is not likely to gain access to information about siblings who have had a mutually satisfying and erotic loving relationship. However, we believe that such an erotic-nurturing relationship is difficult to sustain; most siblings, after all, do leave one another. The cases that we are about to describe are representative. In sibling incest, there appears always to be a significant degree of anger, pathos, anxiety, and need for security.

Phallic Incest at a Critical Time: Angela and Nick. Angela was a tall, strikingly attractive, thirty-two-year-old woman whose self-assured manner began to fragment when her therapist focused on her relationship with her brother. When Angela was eleven, her fourteen-year-old brother "experimented" with her in a way that she was unable to forget. This example illustrates how even *one* such experience, if it is *exploitative and at a crucial stage of psychological development,* can set into motion shock waves that resonate for years through many areas of a person's life.

From play to incest.

ANGELA: We just happened to be home that day. Both parents were at work. . . . and we were home from school. . . . My brother, being three years older, was physically developed and more astute and aware of his sexual development than I was. It just started out as a play-thing at first and I didn't understand what was happening or why, but I wasn't really repulsed at that point. I really didn't run away or do anything like that, but as it became more involved I became very [*sighs*] scared. . . . I guess the word was scared. . . . I didn't know what was happening. . . . I didn't know how to resist either. I didn't understand why my brother would ask me to do this.

THERAPIST: Was he asking you to have sexual intercourse with him?

ANGELA: He didn't *ask,* he just did! . . . like he was experimenting on *me!* [*The scene becomes vivid for her again*]

THERAPIST: Was he making some sort of running commentary?

ANGELA: I just recall there were pieces of conversation which led me to believe that it was more like he was showing me what he could do, or how he did it . . .

Her confusion about the scene.

with the graphic description of the parts of his body. He completed the act and I didn't understand what all that was either. It never happened again after that . . . and I'd never said anything to him about it again, or to my mother, or to my father, but I *never* allowed him to get that close to me again.

THERAPIST: Do you remember feeling anxious?

ANGELA: Yes. . . . This wasn't anything that I wanted to do again. . . . I knew *that*. . . . Certainly not with my brother.

THERAPIST: Did you know about intercourse at the time?

ANGELA: No, no . . . so I didn't know that it was bad or good—or who does this kind of thing or what it all means.

Eleven-year-old Angela was bewildered by Nick's act. Still considered totally innocent and "naïve" by her parents, she felt ashamed to ask about sex, and kept her secret buried deeply inside.

ANGELA: Most of the anxiety I had was long after the act itself. . . . When I learned what sexual inter-

The shame resonates inside.

course is—"This is for procreation—you have children when you do this"—I was *devastated*. . . . I thought *I might be pregnant* . . . and this was a long time after. . . . I must have been thirteen, and I remember thinking, "Oh my God, I'm gonna have a baby," . . . and I asked my mother, "Can brothers and sisters have children together?"

THERAPIST: You said this to her in a very general way. You didn't tell her what had happened?

ANGELA: Oh no, no, no, no, God, no!

THERAPIST: And what did she say?

ANGELA: She said Yes, and I was totally devastated . . . because I thought I would now become pregnant and have a child . . . and the anxiety I walked around with for a long time after that was awful because I never discussed it with anyone after that. . . . I don't know how I realized I was not going to become pregnant. . . . Maybe it was sheer force of the passage of time. . . . I never understood how my brother could have been so relaxed and casual about such an important aspect in somebody's life and why he would have chosen me. I mean, what was the significance of *me!* [*angrily*]. . . . If he was gonna do that, why not somebody else? . . . *I thought sisters were people you took care of.*

Rage about being exploited.

Why did Angela capitulate so easily to her brother's seduction? Why didn't she fight him off, and why did she continue to keep the secret of that day buried inside her?

ANGELA: He was older and had a tremendous influence on me. Influence from the point of view that he was very persuasive. If he wanted to do something, he could by sheer force. . . . I always felt that I never wanted to anger him or irritate him or aggravate him because I would never win. [*Crying*] He'd terrorize me in every way, shape, and form all through my growing-up years.

Fear of brother's sadism.

THERAPIST: Did he used to hit you?

ANGELA: Oh yeah, he used to beat me up all the time. . . . He'd abuse me in many ways . . . verbally, physically, not to the point where I would be bruised. . . . If I didn't do something right for him, it would be the kicking and the shoving and the pushing or the teasing, "I'm gonna do to this," or "I'm gonna get you," or "I'll beat you up."

THERAPIST: What else was he doing to you?

ANGELA: Well, I felt that he was antagonizing me. When I'd say "I want my privacy," or "Let me have my own personal possessions without you stealing them from me . . . without you destroying them." . . . Those were agonizing things for me. I'd come home and go into my room where I kept all my things very, very neat, and was very proud of some of the things I had, and I'd find them broken into or my money stolen.

Brother abused her in other ways.

Because she was younger by three years, Angela depended on her older brother—a situation that the parents fostered by making him fix meals for her and take her to school. Nick resented having to take care of his little sister.

THERAPIST: It sounds as if your brother was really an important figure for you. . . . He was what we call a "caregiver."
ANGELA: What's that?
THERAPIST: Somebody who takes care of their sibling.
ANGELA: Oh yeah? [*sarcastically*] He didn't like doing it, though.
THERAPIST: It doesn't matter . . . he was the one whom you had to depend upon.
ANGELA: Yes, yes, yes.
THERAPIST: What do you think you meant to him?
ANGELA: A PAIN IN THE ASS!!!
THERAPIST: You were a little pain in the ass . . . a little burden he had to drag around with him . . . and watch out for.
ANGELA: Yup, and he hated it!

In addition, Angela knew that her brother was keenly loved and favored by her father, and this made her even more submissive to her brother. Compliance with him was an indirect route to obtaining her father's love.

ANGELA: Yes—my father loved him so! . . . Yes! Yes! I felt if he was worthy of my father's love and respect, then there must be something that I could do that I wasn't doing so that I could also get the kind of response from my father that he gave to my brother.

Furthermore, *both* parents were ineffective in disciplining their son and disagreed about discipline. Angela was convinced that had she complained to her parents about Nick, they would have done nothing.

THERAPIST: Why weren't you able to go to your parents and say, "Nick did this to me"?
ANGELA: Because they couldn't do anything. They could never control my brother. He would just laugh and run away. The *worst possible thing* that I feared was that they would do nothing. I remember times when I asked my mother, "Why do you let him get away with so many things?" She would say, "What can I do? Beat him and kill him?"

Sexuality between Brothers and Sisters

Whenever Angela did complain about Nick, the parents turned a deaf ear. Angela's mother dismissed her as an ungrateful complainer who made mountains out of mole hills.

Mother's previous ineffectiveness has taken its toll.

ANGELA: Sometimes I'd speak to my parents about things he'd already done but they didn't understand the urgency or the kinds of things he was doing to me emotionally. So when he did this thing to me that day, my mother had already accused me of being a very sensitive person to begin with. She had said, "Oh, you're just being too sensitive," or "you can handle that," or "don't get that upset about it, it's not that big a deal."

The larger context of their lives affected both Nick and Angela: the neighborhood they lived in, the type and availability of peers, the family's ethnic background, and the values surrounding the issue of sex in general. This was a family that never discussed sex or bodily functions. At age eleven, when her brother forcibly seduced her, Angela knew little about menstruation.

Now Angela told the therapist about a subsequent trauma she had experienced at the hands of her brother, and how she had tried to cope. Confusion over sexual roles, sibling loyalty, appropriate trust, and a sense of betrayal clearly stand out.

The incest had made Angela suspicious.

ANGELA: One day he brought home his friends, and they were the macho types . . . the in-trouble kids. . . . He somehow got across to me, "So-and-so likes you. Do you like so-and-so?" Now my father didn't let me associate with these boys . . . but he didn't seem to be able to stop my brother from hanging around with them either. When my parents weren't home, my brother brought them over and . . . I felt threatened, because now I felt it was "Who's gonna get Nick's sister?" "Which one will try or can achieve it or which one can accomplish this?" and I got the impression that my brother had set me up.

THERAPIST: When did this happen?

ANGELA: It was right after that incident in which he must have felt "OK if she'll do that with me . . . maybe she'll do it with *anybody.*" I tried not to be afraid. . . . I felt I knew what was coming but I didn't want to act afraid because my brother . . . instilled me with this thing—"You're a girl, and I grew up in a neighborhood of boys, and boys don't like girls who whine or cry. . . . I tried to act natural and not fearful or afraid. I just tried to see how things were going to progress . . . who was gonna make the first move. . . . When the advance was made, I just pushed the guy away so that I didn't encourage it nor act as if there was something I wanted to do but . . . it wasn't a question of asking me . . . it was a question of coming in and grabbing me and I just pushed away.

THERAPIST: Did you expect your brother would protect, honor, and stand guard over you?

ANGELA: He wasn't protecting my honor . . . he was *setting me up!!!* I said to myself why else would he allow the guys to come in the house . . . and why else would he say to me, "Which one do you like?" or, "What if he made love to you?"

Having a sister who could serve as a sex object for his teen-age pals allowed Nick to gain importance as the leader of his gang, and increased his shaky sense of power. This is clearly an example of phallic, aggressive, power-oriented incest. In the case of Angela and Nick, some important issues stand out:

- Even one incestuous experience can be extremely damaging to the participants.
- If it occurs at a critical stage of psychosexual development, it can affect the individual for many years.
- If siblings have high access and are forced into a dependent relationship with each other which they resent, incest can be initiated as an aggressive act and as an attack on the parents who created the conditions of dependence.
- The failure of parents to help a child understand sexual experience in general can make sibling incest extremely traumatic.

Two additional families illustrate how sibling incest can be initiated by other motives: oedipal feelings and homosexual fears. Both of these families give the initial impression that they are worlds apart because of vast differences in social class, financial success, and stability. In actuality, however, they share many of the characteristics of disorganization, anger, despair, and struggle for dominance and power that can motivate siblings to join incestuously. Both of these cases illustrate how siblings tried, through the incest, to achieve object constancy and protection; and in both, the pursuit of love and protection was employed as a defense against a deadening emotional atmosphere.

Father Absence and Sexual Confusion: Bruce, Faith, and Joan. When we first met this multiproblem family, the mother was a tired thirty-eight, her only son Bruce was eighteen, and the two daughters, Faith and Joan, were sixteen and thirteen, respectively. Since the father had abandoned them, the family's annual income was cut in half to poverty level. The family history suggested that the father had had a close relationship with his son and an affectionate, positive relationship with his daughters. Although marital conflicts had repeatedly surfaced, the history of sibling relationships seems to have been positive and uneventful. However, as the father's business came to require more of his time, he began to avoid his family, especially the wife and daughters. The stresses at home began to escalate, particularly after the father was in a serious automobile accident and suffered brain damage. Although his personality changes became very evident, the family tried to deny the seriousness of the accident and assumed that his behavior was entirely under his control.

Where once there had been occasional bickering and quarreling in the house, there was now constant yelling and blaming. The father had little control over his temper and exploded easily. The mother, beleaguered and angry at her husband, began blaming Bruce, as conflicts between the children escalated, while simultaneously pressuring her son to replace his absent father by being the "man of the house." Bruce, who then, at thirteen, was caught between divided loyalties and oedipal embroilment, angrily and violently refused his mother's need for a stand-in husband. Bruce started smoking pot, neglected his schoolwork, and tried to withdraw from the family fights.

As a result of the combination of family stress and actual intellectual deterioration, the father became even more unpredictable, cried easily, neglected his business, and suddenly initiated a homosexual relationship. After two years he announced his wish for a divorce, moved away, and was rarely heard from. His homosexual inclinations raised serious questions for the children about their own sexual identities and appropriate sexual roles. At this point, the bitterness and emptiness in the house became overwhelming and the mother's poor managerial skills all too apparent. Bruce began trying to act like a hypermasculine father. Although well meaning, his pseudo-parental attempts to reorganize his siblings made him act more like a petty tyrant. His mother, meanwhile, was covertly emasculating him. She claimed that he was too stupid to make repairs around the house, accused him of being immature, and would not accommodate his request for a separate bedroom, away from his sisters.

Bruce recalled that his thirteen-year-old sister Faith began to behave teasingly and seductively toward him, swaying her hips at him while undressing in their bedroom. Within a year, Bruce, then sixteen years old, began to have sexual intercourse with Faith, who seemed a willing participant. This was a nurturing, erotic incest and occurred only four times. Bruce's mother—fatigued, depressed, and preoccupied with her own miseries—closed her eyes to the transparent attraction between her children. As soon as Bruce was old enough, he left and went to work on an oil tanker. Faith, without her brother to act as a buffer in the depressing atmosphere, began being a school truant, left home, and eventually found her way to a shelter for runaway teen-agers.

On Bruce's first leave home from sea duty, he brought his little sister, Joan, a teddy bear, the first gift he had ever given her. As he handed it to her, she—to his amazement— put her hand inside her dress and began masturbating. Stimulated by this incident, brother and sister masturbated in front of each other to orgasm, on five separate occasions over the next few weeks until Bruce returned to his job. Joan, feeling guilty, reported the activity to her mother, who finally contacted a therapist for help.

The following motives were evidently at work in these children who became incestuously involved with one another:

- If a father is emotionally unavailable, his daughter(s), feeling deprived of masculine affection, may turn to a brother to satisfy these unrequited needs. If it is the mother who is unavailable, the son may turn to his sister.
- A child who attempts to assume a parental role usually lacks effective maturity and appropriate leverage in dealing with siblings; sibling incest can be an effort to exert power and obtain this leverage.
- When there is sexual identity confusion and a fear of homosexuality, siblings may turn to each other for confirmation that they can be appealing to the opposite sex.
- Sexual experiences between siblings can be thrilling, exciting, and emotionally intense and hence can be used to bring life and feeling into a home that is depressing, cold, and deadening.

Facing Fear and Maintaining Family Loyalty: Vivian and Quentin. Vivian and Quentin's mother's family had been extremely wealthy for many generations. When their mother had fallen in love with the man who became their father, everyone warned her: yes, he was handsome, dashing, full of impetuous excitement and verve, but was he dependable and stable? People were not indifferent to his manner with other women, or to the rumors that he had an illegitimate child somewhere in another state, and that his own source of income, holdings in stocks and bonds, was undependable. Also, before their marriage, relatives argued that, as a young woman who would one day inherit extreme wealth, she should be on guard against fortune hunters. Years later, and after the births of three children, when this mother left her husband after one argument too many, her relatives clucked vindictively: they had known it all along; nothing good would ever come of such a relationship; she was better off without him. No one really understood why—one year after the fourth, and final, separation—the mother still was depressed, unresponsive, and unable to relate to her children except when the maids were there to assist.

The three children—two-year-old Vivian, four-year-old Quentin, and five-year-old Lonnie—were all handsome, but Vivian was special. With fair skin, black hair, and startling green eyes, she was a miniature of her father—an obvious fact that everyone recognized. In the tumultuous month after her mother left him, Vivian's father kidnapped Vivian for one week and thus was marked as dangerous and crazy and as having a special affinity for his daughter.

The mother eventually remarried, and the father disappeared. The children's stepfather was, to the entire family's great relief, quiet, sober, eminently respectable, and responsible beyond a doubt. He devoted himself to managing the family business and, when his wife's father died, the family inheritance. Vivian referred to her stepfather as "Dad," but her two brothers resented this intruder whom they called "him." Quentin particularly was openly hostile. When his mother and stepfather finally had a child of their own, Quentin declared open warfare on this "replacement" father and avoided contact with the new stepsibling.

The household that Vivian remembered growing up in was seething with the hatred Quentin felt toward his new "Dad." Lonnie would weakly follow Quentin as the younger brother "got back" at their stepfather. Vivian's mother protested feebly against the explosions that Quentin precipitated, and Quentin whispered in Vivian's ear that she had a prior allegiance to their biological father.

The children were surrounded by such undisguised affluence as chauffeurs, maids, a splendid mansion, and two winter resort homes. Attempts to ease the tension in the family required the infusion of additional things that money could also obtain—special tutors, psychotherapists, prep schools, and finally, for Quentin, private psychiatric hospitals. Everything that could be bought was offered, but all to no avail. When Vivian was very little, she began crawling into Quentin's bed at night. She was terrified, imagined seeing monsters, but was afraid of disturbing her mother, and Quentin became a transitional object, the next best thing to a parent. Holding him made her feel peaceful and calm, and seemed to make the terror go away. But she began to develop compulsive habits—checking for dust and dirt in her room, counting the steps to the bathroom, losing control of her bladder. Her mother first yelled and implored, then took her to a child therapist. There Vivian played games but confided little. Her habits continued; her mother told her that she was "naughty," and that if she "loved" her mother and father, she would "stop." By now Vivian was eight and Quentin ten; and even though they had separate bedrooms, Vivian would get up every night and slip into her brother's bed, to be soothed by his touching of her in that "soft spot." The parents slept soundly behind their *locked* door, oblivious to Vivian's fright and to her attachment to this brother whom she loved so much.

Vivian felt some affection for her stepfather, but Quentin always reminded her that their "real" family came first and that their mother had left their own father. Her brother's ongoing influence was evident years later, when Vivian wrote:

> Part of me wants just to be her little girl and get love—but along with that comes anger at not having enough before. Then I get confused because I know I *did* get from her, though I also feel I didn't.°

Having turned to her brother Quentin for love, Vivian passively responded to all his wants, his needs, and his fears. If he wanted to tease her, she let him; if he wanted her to play strip poker, she let him; if he wanted to "hypnotize" her, she let him and would pretend to be asleep while initially he put his fingers inside of her and later his penis. The mother and stepfather, noticing that Vivian could calm her brother and was devoted to him, turned to her for advice and help. She was now the little "therapist" but inwardly she felt shame and guilt about the secret that no one but Quentin knew:

> Because I was a girl, I was dirty. Sexually active from an early age—the strip poker, the sleeping game, all my bad habits added to the feeling that I was dirty and just not a good girl—doing things that would make my parents feel ashamed of me.

° These and the following quotations are from Vivian's diary and letters that she wrote to her therapist. Written some twenty years after the events, these communications still reflect Vivian's raw feelings as a little girl and adolescent.

Vivian's guilt over her "bad" habits continued unabated, compounded by what Quentin was secretly doing with her at night. By the time she was twelve years old, she was having regular sexual intercourse with her fourteen-year-old brother. Making love with him helped fill the void the girl felt in herself:

> Last night I was trying to figure out why my mother didn't give me what I needed. I felt I was an ugly little girl with so many dirty habits. This is why, because I wasn't worth it. She gave me what I deserved. Emptiness. Silence.

The vitality and warmth Vivian felt with Quentin at night clashed rudely with the cold, tension-filled glare of day. Both her mother and her stepfather felt helpless about changing Quentin and Lonnie's attitudes or behavior. The boys were mocking, defiant, and dishonest. Once Quentin even hit his stepfather across the face. Vivian recalled how her stepfather had tried to elicit her support:

> He'd say, "Honestly Vivian, I just don't know what to do with those boys." I really felt for him. I really wanted to help. I felt caught in the middle between him and Quentin. I knew how hard my stepfather was trying and how much he was hurting. And I knew how much Quentin was hurting and how much he needed my stepfather. I saw the soft underbelly, but all he could see was my brother's hostility. Fathers are supposed to *know*.

Vivian's mother tried to smooth things out. She bought the children expensive things and offered solicitous platitudes that barely scratched the terror, anger, and shame that all three children felt:

> We could never question our great good fortune because we were "privileged," we had "everything," and we should be "thankful" and pay back our social debt by being "responsible." But the double message I could never confront my mother about was not loving me, not liking me, feeling ashamed for her ugly little girl, but she always said, "Of course we love you, dear." So I never knew what to believe, could never get a clear-cut validation of either feeling.

While the mother gave her mixed messages, Quentin gave Vivian an unequivocal message of need, availability, and attention. Sex play with him was stimulating, and he would spend time with his sister, making her feel special and privileged in sharing his secret world:

> The first time I ever saw a boy get an erection and ejaculate was my brother Quentin in our little "hypnosis" game, and that is what he said—"Now I am going to shoot scum." I was disgusted and scared, but also fascinated. He wanted me to sit on top of him but I wouldn't.

> I remember my brother once telling me about how he turned girls on, when I was about thirteen or fourteen. He said, "You know what really turns them on is not to tell them how much they excite me but to say," and he said this in a very sexy voice, "You relax me." Maybe he had something there.

The pattern of sibling incest continued until Vivian was fifteen and went away to prep school. When she was home on vacations, Quentin no longer attempted to have sexual relations with her, but he and Lonnie expressed their hatred and contempt for women through their sister. They teased her anatomy, calling her "banana boobs." When she developed acne, they called her "crater pits," and taunted her about that time of month when she "smelled." Once both brothers attempted to rape her when their parents were out for the evening. That event was crucial for Vivian, and she swore never again to be passive for her favorite brother. But her relationship with her parents seemed indelibly etched. The die was cast: she was identified as the good girl, emotionally undemanding, studious, and ambitious. The boys, on the other hand, had the identity of their biological father; they were bad, crazy, irresponsible, and slated for a worse fate than had befallen him. Vivian's words to her parents are significant, the last line particularly being prophetic:

> I feel like I have to be so cautious and controlled with both of you. Choose my words and keep an even tone of voice, only talk about neutral things or [about] Quentin, always the problems with Quentin or Lonnie. But Vivian, "Oh, she's fine. She's so mature and strong and responsible. She doesn't need us." Meanwhile, all this stuff churns around in me, underground. *I have to make up for the sins of my brothers. After all, you were kind enough to take us in!*

The case of Vivian and Quentin not only confirms our discussion thus far but also extends our understanding of the motives for sibling incest:

- Incest can provide a refuge from anxiety and provides a way to prevent total ego collapse.
- Involvement in sibling incest can provide a young child with object constancy, a person upon whom one can rely and with whom one can merge in order to feel whole.
- When a stepparent is perceived as an intruder, incest can cement a sibling relationship and serve as a reminder of familial loyalty. Such a relationship actively works against a child's acceptance of a stepparent as a figure with whom to identify or to whom positively to relate.
- When one child feels helpless to prevent the disintegration of his or her family, sibling incest provides—through cunning, strength, duplicity, and aggression—a way to exert a powerful influence on at least one member of the family.
- Other close-in-age siblings than the incestuous pair often have an intuitive sense that the incest is occurring, and tolerate or even collude in it.
- Over time, sibling incest can change from a nurturing, loving, erotic relationship to one dominated by cruelty, abuse, and physical aggression.
- An incestuous sibling relationship that changes from being loving to being hostile can reactivate previous feelings of deprivation, making the victimized partner even more vulnerable.
- When access between siblings is reduced and/or sado-masochistic overtones are accelerated, the victimized sibling may find the strength to withdraw from the relationship.°

At this point some readers may question whether many children could find themselves in situations such as those we have just described. The fact is that our culture, with its increasing rates and various forms of child neglect (overt and covert), emphasizes, as a general panacea, the pursuit of love wherever it may be found. Many therapists would, in fact, consider that all types of love always rest on a foundation of illusion, a "delusion of fusion" (Kaiser 1955), and on the "universal infantile experience of primary love" (Shor and Sanville 1978).

For many of these brothers and sisters, their sexual experience served to comfort and support their self-doubt and acted temporarily as a reassurance against annihilation by a hostile and indifferent world. Sexual contact supported the feeling of being alive, loved, and real. Heinz Lichtenstein puts it succinctly, in absolute agreement with our perception of what has motivated many sisters to stay sexually entwined with their brothers for so long:

sexuality has a special position among the other variables of development, be-

°We will not dwell here on sado-masochistic satisfaction for the sister; it is possible that Vivian felt some perverse satisfaction at doing "shameful" things with the brother as just punishment for the other things she did that the parents overlooked. Interested readers can consult Fairbairn (1954) and Panken (1973) for additional theory on this point.

cause the very core of a person's being fully himself profoundly depends on the affirmation of the conviction of his existence as an incontrovertible truth.

(1977, p. 275)

LONG-TERM EFFECTS OF SIBLING INCEST

With the evidence that we have gathered, we believe that the long-term effects of childhood sibling incest are more pronounced and dangerous in women than in men and can adversely affect a woman's functioning in the areas of trust, self-concept and identity, sex, marriage, and work.

Shattered Trust. Almost all of the women distrusted their brothers, although this distrust was not necessarily incompatible with liking them. In some cases, having been "used" and, in other cases, having been partners in a flaunting of parental authority, sisters often retain a basic suspiciousness of a brother's motives. Take the following interview, for example:

WOMAN: There's no affection between us . . . but there's no hostility either. It's not like I refuse to talk to him.
INTERVIEWER: In other words, you don't like him very much?
WOMAN: I don't trust him.
INTERVIEWER: Still?
WOMAN: I wouldn't ask him to do anything for me. I wouldn't share anything in confidence with him.

This distrust may extend to relationships with *all* men. A brother, having intruded so decisively on his sister early in life, merely compounds the vague sense of betrayal she, as a daughter, feels about her father's absence, weakness, or insensitivity. Adult men—whether lovers, husbands, friends, or therapists—usually have to pass an extremely difficult test of trust:

If somebody says they're going to do something and they don't, it's tough for me to understand that. . . . I feel betrayed. . . . I really have to work at not letting that destroy my feelings about these people. . . . My relationship with my husband, my relationship with any man, it all has everything to do with that . . . the sense of betrayal by my brother.

The sense of mistrust spills over, making some of these women anxious, and uncertain of their ability to maintain intimate relationships:

192

The types of men that I have picked, those people I set up to betray me and then say, "See you later" . . . maybe I do that in a subconscious way. I'm sure that's a direct result from my relationship with my brother in those young years, and over the years.

Self-Concept and Identity. All of the incestuously involved women suffered from a poor self-concept, although its expression ranged from being actively psychotic to compulsively self-denigrating. Although we were working intensely with a small number of cases, we suspect that most sisters who have been sexually involved with their brothers also feel disturbing aftereffects. One of the women we interviewed repeatedly referred to herself as "a piece of shit," while another said:

For a long time I was afraid that I would never make love to a man because this had happened to me . . . nobody would want me.
INTERVIEWER: That somehow you were "impure"?
WOMAN: Yes. Somehow this guilt would always be with me . . . and that for some reason it might prevent me from genuinely loving somebody or someone ever loving me.

All of the women were depressed, and there was an inordinately high percentage of substance abuse, particularly marijuana. Dissociation from herself through drugs was a striking characteristic, as if each woman wanted to step outside of who she was. This characteristic is in keeping with the previously discussed propensity to maintain a "pseudo self," to protect one's core self from exposure and intimate familiarity.

Many of these women saw themselves as victimized by their brothers and described them as manipulative.° Although many of the brothers were reported to have had, as adolescents, minor skirmishes with the law, they did not clearly fit a pattern of psychopathology. We sensed, through what the sisters said that some of these brothers were defending against homosexual fears by engaging in power-oriented, phallic incest, and speculated that they felt more secure about their "macho" image if they could be "powerful" vis-à-vis their "powerless" sisters.

Sexual Pleasure and Promiscuity. Many of the sisters who had engaged in mutually consenting sibling incest, had found the experience pleasurable and orgasmic. One woman, in detailing incest with her brother many years before, reported feeling sexually aroused. Another woman

---

° Denise Gelinas, personal communication, 1980.

said that she had never had an orgasmic experience as intense or pleasurable as that with her brother.

However, it was evident that many of these women could not have a sexually satisfying experience in a mature, adult relationship, either because their choice of partners was poor owing to mistrust (see pages 168, 177) or because their love feelings had split off from their sexual feelings. Several of the women we interviewed reported that they had begun being promiscuous in early adolescence, typically during the period when their brothers stopped having relations with them, and they continued to have frequent sexual partners. In effect, they were unsuccessfully seeking brother-substitutes. Furthermore, many of these relationships, and some later ones, appear to have been masochistic and painful. Maggie Scarf (1980) reiterates how abandonment, isolation, and depression are often precursors of promiscuous sexual experience; and Meiselman (1978) and S. Kubo (1959) report similar results. Meiselman indicates that 85 percent of her sibling sample had serious difficulties with orgasmic experience in adulthood.

That some of these women would seek affirmation of themselves through continued, sometimes exaggerated sexuality, should come as no surprise. That appears to have been one of the motives for ongoing sexual embroilments in the first place; indeed, the bond of pain and pleasure through sex with their brothers allowed for a release of both the hated and loved self-images these girls apparently previously experienced in relation to their parents. One leading psychoanalyst points out how the early and severe strains in the families these women grew up in must have paved the way for their later pattern of sexual relating with others:

> failure of this affirmative experience regarding one's existence during the early stages of development has important consequences with regard to the later emerging pattern of adult sexuality. It appears that under such circumstances, adult sexuality is placed in the service of the need for affirmation of the reality of one's existence. . . . This pattern interferes with the development of a relationship of mutuality between the individual and the object, insofar as the object is valued only to the extent to which it serves the orgastic and ecstatic needs of the individual.   (Lichtenstein 1977, p. 275)

Marital and Vocational Adjustment. In both work and marriage, these women seem to have been functioning under a strain and a handicap. As in a case that Santiago (1973) reported, the women we interviewed were able to pursue education and vocational goals, but they often required psychotherapy to "get them through." They succeeded in spite of constant feelings of depression, masochism, dissociation, and self-denigration.

In several cases, the women went through graduate and professional schools and entered the world of high attainment with superhuman efforts. They seemed determined to ensure that they would always have a tangible security base, and that the deadening neglect that they endured in their families of origin would never again be theirs.

These sisters generally considered their marital adjustment as only marginal—an estimate sometimes confirmed in our interviews with their husbands. They tended to make poor choices, often selecting men who were sexually conflicted (one woman chose a homosexual partner). They reported numerous marital problems, such as lack of intimacy, difficulties in communication, and poor sexual adjustment. Many of these incestuous siblings stayed in their marriages, for better or worse, as if afraid to admit that they might have, once again, made a poor choice in matters of love. Staying married seemed a far better alternative than being alone in the world. The love/sex split of childhood years revealed itself once again in their marriages, as these women selected men who were seemingly protective, "safe," and not sexually threatening. In our interviews some of the husbands also seemed depressed, a fact that contributed to the sense of sexual malaise and devitalization in their marriages. Few of the husbands knew of their wives' sibling incest. Of the husbands who knew, none knew the details; yet there was a general tendency for all the husbands we interviewed to be suspicious of their wives' brothers and to avoid them. Indeed, it seemed to us that the ghost of the sibling affair still hung over the lives of these women—part of their childhood past they desperately wanted to escape, and could not.

Conclusion

Neither clinician nor parent should ever neglect the *possible* influence of one sibling on another's sexuality. Parents need to be aware that sexual curiosity between brothers and sisters is natural—but curiosity can easily lead to play, and play can lead to love, or incest. Incest is more likely to occur if there is parental neglect or abandonment, so that brothers and sisters begin to need each other for solace, nurturance, and identity, or as a vehicle to express rage and hurt. Sibling incest is more likely to have long-term ill effects on sisters than on brothers. The younger the child when this relationship is initiated, the less likely he or she is able to understand it or escape from it. Sibling incest during pre-adolescence is likely to be seriously confusing or traumatic. The more information children have about sexuality, the better able they are to understand it and defend themselves against abuse. Parents who are emotionally available can assuage their children's sexual anxiety and confusion, and thus insulate them from the possibility of sibling incest. We have seen that parental neglect forces siblings into connections that they may not be able to control. Whereas in chapter 5, the Hansels and Gretels forged bonds of intense loyalty, bonds of the most disturbing sexual contact are forged when the children—lacking a satisfying alternative—hungrily and angrily use sex to substitute for the emptiness and the pain that characterize their relations with their parents.

Now we need to examine that other area where intense conflicts abound, the feelings of rivalry and aggression between siblings. We know that such feelings, like sexuality, always exist and are seldom dealt with in an entirely satisfactory manner.

CHAPTER 8

Siblings in Conflict:
Bonds of Aggression
and Rivalry

A small child does not necessarily love his brothers and sisters: often he obviously does not. . . . He hates them as his competitors, and it is a familiar fact that this attitude often persists for long years, till maturity is reached or even later, without interruption.

Sigmund Freud

N̲O DISCUSSION of siblings would be complete without considering aggresssion and its tributary, rivalry. The word *rivalry* is often loosely used. *Rivalis* is a Latin word meaning "having rights to the same stream." One child can rival another for the love or the money of a parent, for a friend's interest, for a prized family role. But many forms of sibling aggression are not rivalrous: in them, the payoff is not the possession of something that the other cannot have; but, rather, the payoff is internal, having to do with a forbidden satisfaction or the fulfillment of a deeper emotional need. In siblings, aggression and rivalry have neither simple forms nor simple causes. For some siblings, aggression and rivalry are an attempt to maim or humiliate; one may live a part or all of one's life knowing that the presence of a brother or a sister makes one physically or emotionally unsafe. At this extreme, to spend time with a sibling is to enter enemy territory, emotionally charged with murderous tension. At another extreme lie conflicts that are neither humiliating nor crippling but instead become part of a creative and interesting dialectic that strengthens the relationship. These brothers and sisters can laugh about their ancient wars, deflect a sibling's attack, and, in the process, grow wiser and more mature. Between these extremes are relationships marked by occasional peaks of murderousness and plateaus of neutrality or warmth.

This chapter highlights three main topics:

- The positive aspects of fighting in childhood.
- The ways in which parents launch crippling rivalries.
- The impact of rivalry and hatred upon personality developments.

Positive Aspects of Fighting in Childhood

Aggressiveness is a major vehicle for sibling interaction and, as such, has a broad utility for human beings (Abramovitch et al. 1979). Aggression, even when painful, represents contact, warmth, another presence. Anyone who has ever observed two brothers wrestling, will have noticed that, along with the pinches and punches, there is an enormous amount of bodily contact. As Ronah Abramovitch has noted—in a study of the natural behavior of very young children in their homes—antagonistic behavior occurs with high frequency, with patterns of attack and counterattack being the rule rather than the exception. The contact that is basic for human survival is immediately available in a near-at-hand and ready-to-fight sibling. Sibling aggression has a reassuringly predictable quality: if one punches or pinches or insults a sibling in a particular way, the retort, though painful, is familiar and expected.

During parental dislocation, aggressive contact can be reassuring. We noted in chapter 7 that, when parents are emotionally unavailable, brothers and sisters will turn to one another, using sex as the medium for obtaining desperately craved warmth and contact. Likewise, fighting, punching, even drawing blood can help emotionally starved children and adolescents to know that they are alive, by drawing a reaction from a familiar and intimate enemy. Through pain, the child obtains a rudimentary statement from others: you are alive, you are real, you are being noticed.

In one family the mother abandoned a depressed father and their three children when they were five, nine, and twelve years old, respectively. The father imported a series of "loving women" whom he touted as possible mothers, but none stayed more than a year. The children always fought, as if to say, "We have our own private relationship, and we dare you to love us despite our savagery." Their fighting peaked when the father finally met up with a woman who was warm and kind and actually wanted to bring up the children, who by this time were six years older. The siblings did all they could to hurt one another as they watched their father going off to visit another potentially undependable woman. Aggression was the one commodity in their lives which could be trusted, and it had a predictable, almost life-giving quality. The children seemed to have made a pact: "We'd rather fight than switch" (cf. Rosenberg 1980).

Another positive, constructive function of sibling aggression is that it forces the participants into a social "laboratory" where they learn how to manage and resolve conflict. Siblings know well the arsenal of weapons each possesses; they are usually able consciously to calculate, calibrate, plan, and control their aggressive actions and hostile statements. Knowing one's own and a sister's "aggression keyboard" can activate the development of competence, morality, and even of courage and creativity. Listen to any two children who are negotiating the rules of a basketball game: they will call upon a wide variety of competencies, both verbal and nonverbal.

The importance of early aggressive contact for normal social development has been documented in studies of primates observed in the wild and in laboratory settings (Goodall 1967; Suomi and Harlow 1975). The ability to deflect aggression, to use it wisely and at the right moment, to use humor, to surrender without debasing oneself and to defeat someone without humiliating that person, are all skills that children and adolescents can eventually use in relationships with peers, spouses, and ultimately their own children. The varied ages of sibling groups offer the individual a powerful opportunity to learn flexibility, play, and competence, and how to be a good sport. This kind of aggressive give-and-take is one component of the constructive dialectic (mentioned in chapter 4) that characterizes ideal sibling relationships.

As we also noted in cases of reciprocal caregivers (chapter 5), it can also promote feelings of loyalty. Children and adolescents are well aware of their need to make aggressive contact. We have found that children feel that a moderate amount of aggressive interaction *not* interfered with by the parents, is a necessary, even positive part of their sibling relation-ship—as if such aggression is an inalienable possession that marks them as a distinct subsystem, different from the parents whom they have been taught to love and honor.

A third important function of aggression in childhood is to defend the individual against imagined or real aggression. When a child is physically harmed or threatened by a brother or a sister, to respond with similar aggression can be what Anna Freud termed "identification with the ag-gressor." "By impersonating the aggressor," she wrote, "assuming his at-tributes or imitating his aggression, the child transforms himself from the person threatened into the person who makes the threat" (1946, p. 121). One can now assail the sibling who was the attacker and, in the process, reduce one's sense of being endangered. If it is a parent who makes a child afraid, the child can counter the fear of being hurt by turning the aggression onto a convenient sibling (Oberndorf 1929). We believe that children do not necessarily have to fear either a sibling or a parent to launch aggression at brothers or sisters. Siblings, as we have suggested in chapter 2, serve one another as a handy respository for all kinds of bad feelings. To pound a brother or a sister is to "cleanse" oneself and to feel, temporarily, better. The hostile 'dependent,' rigidly differentiated, and disowned types of relationship (chapter 4) often spring from just such early processes.

Being able to fantasize about aggression with a sibling can allow a child to fantasize about new behavior and may energize creativity. A ten-year-old boy had his nose bloodied by his physically more powerful and seven-inch taller twelve-year-old brother, with whom he had had an affection-ate relationship and who was actually his best and most reliable friend. (For days he had been courting this disaster by teasing the older boy unmercifully.) The week after the incident, the ten-year-old wrote the following story, which illustrates how he had to integrate his wish for revenge with underlying feelings of guilt, attachment, and loyalty.

ZAGNAR THE TERRIBLE

The wind was howling through the forest. The rain came down, drenching everyone and everything. My brother and I ran and ran, hiding from Zagnar the terrible.

Suddenly we stopped in the middle of the forest. We were lost, but we didn't have time to rest. Zagnar was getting closer and closer, coming to kill us.

We started to run again, my brother was catching a cold because his clothes were soaked. Then I heard my brother scream. I looked down at the ground. My brother was hit by an arrow. It went through his heart. "Zagnar," I said, "I'll get you." Zagnar gave me a grin, "Sure you will," he said.

Then Zagnar shot an arrow—whiz. "Ahh!" I screamed. It went right through my arm. Blood was gushing out. I was really mad now, so I took the arrow out of my arm and my brother's heart.

I made a perfect hit at Zagnar's heart and eye. He fell to the ground dead. I was happy and I was sad because my brother was dead.

Then the rain stopped and I went to the graveyard to bury my brother.

Whether children are expressing aggression to obtain warmth or to learn, or lashing out to protect themselves, clinicians should recognize that aggression between children serves many basic needs. A child should not be asked to give up aggressive contact unless adults are prepared to offer alternative ways of meeting these needs.

The Powerful Parents

In *Animal Farm* (1945), one of George Orwell's barnyard characters observes that "all animals are equal, but some are more equal than others." The same can be said of siblings. Brothers and sisters differ in age, sex, temperament, height, abilities, and emotional reaction. Even if vast differences were not created by the fateful roll of the genetic dice, sibship would be an unequal arrangement. Even if parents were able to achieve the impossible dream of treating their very different children even-handedly, each child would perceive the parents as favoring one of the other children. Achieving a feeling of *overall* fairness is the best that a parent can hope for.

American parents are particularly conflicted about being fair-minded dispensers of justice, immersed as they are in a culture that celebrates fair play, "truth, justice and the American way." Yet that same culture, while giving the underdog and the handicapped opportunities to catch up with those who are more advantaged, also extols social Darwinism and "the survival of the fittest" (Hofstadter 1959). Parents try to help each child become a distinct *individual* in a culture where being "number one" is part of a tradition of violent, individualistic pursuit of self-interest. Caught in these cultural cross-currents, American parents are often bewildered as they try to avoid favoring one child over another. Parents must rely primarily on their own childhood experiences, as they monitor their children's aggression and dispense recognition, love, and status. Each parent's conflicts, immaturities, and blind spots are exposed when he or she has to decide daily how to implement justice and fairness.

PARENTS AS MANAGERS OF SIBLING CONFLICT

Effective refereeing of children's jealousy and aggression requires mature parents who are relatively free of their own conflicts about aggression, and who apply consistent moral principles and communicate them clearly to quarreling siblings. When parents lack a stable value system by which to settle sibling disputes, or when their principles are capricious, bizarre, or arbitrary, the sibling relationship can become chaotic or even murderous. Like the marooned children who begin killing each other in William Golding's *Lord of the Flies* (1959), siblings who lack a mature parent can be forced upon one another in ways that breed destructive conflict.

Effective parents are able to use their power to enforce rules and administer consequences for violent or abusive behavior; but they also possess a finely tuned sense of when to intervene and when to "let the children work it out themselves," and are able to distinguish between a humiliating attack and ritual harassment. They have a sense of humor, respect the children's needs for some aggression and, most important, are aware of the context of particular fights between the children. Thus, it takes an observant parent to realize that one child may attack another out of fury at having been humiliated the day before on the playground. As careful monitors of feelings and sequences of events, effective parents are not easily confused by sibling conflict. For example, the mother and father of two squabbling youngsters had been reprimanding the older for screaming at the younger, and feared that the former was taking advantage of the other. Then these parents began to listen carefully and realized that the younger (a spirited and somewhat manipulative boy) loved to see his brother incur the parents' ire. They finally realized that their younger son was the true culprit, because he specialized in making their older, passive boy lose his temper. Reversing their course, they stopped objecting to the elder child's attempts to deal with his bratty younger brother, and even suggested to him that he toughen up by refusing to play with his younger brother until the latter stopped taunting. Such parents make the time and have the energy to monitor their children's behavior as well as gauging the impact of their *own* actions upon the children (Ihinger 1975).

Ineffective parents appear to fall into two groups: those who *avoid* (or suppress) conflicts, and those who *amplify* them.

Conflict-Avoiding Parents. Some parents station themselves, like Solomon the Wise, at the center of their children's conflicts, continually setting themselves up as a source of mediation. It can be gratifying to a parent to decide who is right and who is wrong (although such tactics usually encourage the children to repeat episodes of the same argument). By arresting conflicts between the children, the parents can also quell their own fears about aggression. Fearing that children's conflicts will escalate, such parents negotiate *for* the children when, in fact, the youngsters may be capable of arriving at their own solutions. The result is to deprive the children of the birthright of learning, on their own, to work out their problems. Because conflict is a major language of normal sibling relationships, parental interference—ill timed, overreactive, overinvolved, all wise—can undercut the problem-solving capacities of children and adolescents. Many conflict-avoiding parents are *oversensitive* to sibling conflict and spot it too readily. Ever on guard, they try to extinguish it through appeasement, cajoling, and sometimes anxious outbursts of their own. Leaping into action, they may appear angry; but their anger covers an anxiety that worse anger will break out.

When parents anxiously or angrily interdict their children's fighting, they run the risk that the children may express anger in secret and forbidden ways. Siblings' conflicts *belong* to them, but many parents find it difficult to respect the boundaries of those conflicts. Many siblings "freeze up" and feel uncomfortable around their brothers and sisters because the parents have never allowed them to discharge or resolve angry feelings. One woman, an accomplished and attractive actress, was a fraternal twin. At birth her brother was one pound lighter than she; and the parents, projecting their own fears onto the boy, worried that the daughter would have superior strength. They were constantly vigilant, making sure that when the children were infants and toddlers, she would not hurt him in play. Among her earliest memories is the picture of her mother admonishing her: "Don't be so tough with your brother, be *careful!*" The overt and covert message from the parents was always: "You have superior size, stamina, intellect, agility, personality. Beware that you don't squelch your brother. You can be dangerous because of who you are." Years later, as a patient in psychotherapy, she remembered feeling guilty and inhibited when she and her brother entered the same room. "We lived our lives in a gigantic goldfish bowl with our parents nervously looking on. I was afraid to even bump him." Having to hold back with her brother made this woman's sibling bond tentative and uncomfortable. For her, aggression with peers and the *fair* uses of power were terrifying. She relished aggressive and murderous roles on the stage for reasons that she did not quite understand. Her psychotherapy was aimed at helping her realize that she need not be ashamed of expressing aggresssive feelings with other people who often seemed "beyond touch."

Other conflict-avoiding parents underestimate the hurt and pain that their children inflict on each other (Kaufmann, Hallahan, and Ball 1975). While this observation stems partly from the fact that sibling conflicts are often transacted secretly away from the parents' purview, many parents do not want to be reminded of any aggression whatsoever. They "see no evil, hear no evil, speak no evil" and, with heads firmly stuck in the sand, fail to perceive obvious aggression. Ignorance of their children's fighting provides temporary bliss, as the parents label vindictiveness as "teasing," humiliation as "kidding," abuse as "a little wrestling." Hoping that the children's arguments will disappear, they salve old emotional injuries of their own by being unobservant.

Conflict-Amplifying Parents. A very different set of parents unconsciously encourages sibling conflict by subtly egging it on. Some parents simply overlook the escalating spiral of aggression and retaliation, repeatedly failing to notice that one sibling is taking advantage of another, or assume that "the kid is tough and he can take it." As Adelaide Johnson and S. A. Szurek (1952) have pointed out, some children can act out their parents' angry feelings—impulses that the parents forbid themselves. One child may beat upon another for hours without a parent's intervention—a lack of intervention that is a green light for one child to injure another, either physically or psychologically. At some level this aggression satisfies a parent's deepest needs. The extreme manifestation of this tendency to amplify conflict occurs when the parent hates one child and covertly encourages the second child's attack. Kay Tooley (1977) has observed that

> the older siblings were acting out mother's (only slightly) unconscious wish to be rid of the younger children—a rather drastic form of maternal rejection that must have been manifest in many other ways in addition to the murderous acting out of the older sibling. . . . The attacks included such experiences as attempted drownings, poisonings, and setting fire to clothing.

Tooley also reported how a five-year-old boy was terrified by his eight-year-old brother:

> Mrs. J. recounted without much evident concern that over a period of a year the older boy had tried to drown Allen in the bathtub; pushed him down the stairs; cut his head to the degree that he required a dozen stitches to close the wound; and had set fire to the family home.
>
> Mrs. J. further reported that she was often tired and left the three younger children in the elder boy's care. She never disciplined the children, she said. When she gets angry she just feels that she is going to kill someone and so does nothing. Mrs. J. reported several dreams about killing her children and her husband. . . . Mr. J. had withdrawn . . . from effective involvement with his wife and children.

Siblings in Conflict

Sibling abuse, engendered by parents who amplify conflicts, is probably widely underreported. Such parents often rationalize their children's aggression as normal horseplay. The distinction between normal power tactics and abuse in sibling relationships remains vague and undefined by the courts. It is often reported that periodic bullying, force, and threatening appears to be the norm in childhood sibling relationships: older children use raw power to get their younger brothers and sisters to comply, and younger children get back at their older siblings in covert ways. Given the fact that many aggressive encounters occur every day, a parent can easily express dislike of a child by failing to prohibit violence between children.

FAVORITISM AND ENTITLEMENT

It has long been observed that the academic attainments of earlier-born children tend to be higher than those of later-born ones (Galton 1874; Altus 1965; Zajonc 1976). Eminence—whether one becomes Nobel Prize winner, National Merit scholar, or college professor—appears related to one's being the oldest or the only child in a family, presumably because of the greater value and attention given to first-born children, both economically and psychologically. It thus comes as no surprise that parents tend to expect more of a first-born child than of second, third, or fourth children. First-borns are nudged toward independence and self-sufficiency and are disciplined earlier in childhood (and more harshly) than are their younger brothers and sisters. This can begin when mothers suddenly withdraw their affection from their first son or daughter when the second child is born. For example, M. K. Taylor and K. L. Kogan (1973) watched the interactions of mothers and their oldest child a few months prior to the delivery of a second child, and then again, several weeks after the birth. In this study, each mother's emotional response to her eldest had changed dramatically: she was "emotionally flat" and less interested, and her reactions were forced and labored. Robert Sears et al. (1957) noted that later-born children were treated with more spontaneity and unconditional acceptance by parents than were earlier-born siblings. Still other studies portray mothers as more possessive and anxious about their eldest child's performance and as more relaxed with second-borns. James J. Conley (1981) speculates that the uterine environment for first babies is different, making these babies more sensitive to anxieties. In addition, the mothers of first babies may be biologically more reactive to these sensitive first-born children than to children born later. From these studies, it is possible to conclude that the position of both first-born and later-born children have their respective and distinct advantages and disadvantages. More is expected of the oldest child, and he or she goes a bit farther in life. The oldest is subjected to more anxiety and harshness than is a younger sibling, who is more lovingly accepted by the parent.

Favoritism occurs in all families. But in well-functioning families, children are favored for different characteristics. Or, they are favored on different days, or at different periods of their lives, so that *on the whole* no child clearly prevails. Most parents become aware of their favoritism, admit it, and consciously attempt to balance it before one child begins to monopolize family favor. Ideally, the parents consciously try to anticipate and compensate for the fact that their attention is taken away from an older child when they bring a newborn home.

In a classic study Freud (1909) observed the jealous reactions of Little Hans to the "mysterious" birth of his sister Hannah. Hans was ignored by his mother, and the sudden appearance of a baby sister made him feel worthless and angry. However, the father, an unusually concerned papa for turn-of-the-century Vienna, provided interest and support for the son, took careful notes about his behavior, and even took him for a visit to Dr. Freud. Hans soon repressed his rivalry for Hannah, partly because his emotionally available father took the sting out of his "dethronement."* A father's early intervention to give the older child extra support can substantially buffer that child's jealous reactions to the mother's favoring the newborn. It need not be the father who supplements the disenfranchised child: it can be a grandparent, an uncle or an aunt, or another sibling; or when the father favors the newborn, the mother can even the balance.

Balance corrects favoritism, and its influence can be observed in studies of the effects of family size upon rivalry. M. Sewall and R. Smalley (1930) and David Levy (1937) investigated aggressive behavior among siblings of different family sizes. They found that the larger the sibling group among young children, the less able are parents to give large amounts of time to any one child; the children accept the situation as a fact of life and are less inclined to fight or to depend on adults to settle disputes. A similar result was described by Bossard and Boll (1956) who interviewed the adult members of large sibling groups. Fewer than 20 percent of the respondents felt that there were serious sibling conflicts during childhood and adolescence; and while most of these respondents remembered inequities, quarrels, and hurts, they had learned, like the loyal siblings we described in chapter 5, that their parents could be neither manipulated nor monopolized, and that no one child could be favored. Parents who

---

* This case is usually cited to show how a child's fear of his father exerted a pernicious influence and resulted in Little Hans's developing a phobia. The father's helpful influence in enabling the boy to deal with the sister's birth usually goes unnoticed.

realize that they have to respond to a variety of children, tend to distribute their attention evenly, and hence promote in their children a constructive "We're all in this together" attitude—as in the film comedy *Cheaper by the Dozen* (1950). In addition, in a large family, there is a greater chance of one's developing a close friendship with at least one other child, and there is always at least one person to play with. This is not to portray an unrealistically rosy picture of large families. Children from large families *can* become very aggressive to one another if parental or financial deprivation is severe. If the children are underorganized or unsocialized, aggression can be the major theme of their relationships (Minuchin et al. 1967).

In some families, the children are entitled and unchallenged from birth; while in others, the interplay of fairness and favoritism becomes the overriding issue. The varieties of favoritism and the struggles surrounding it are endless and depend on the unique structure of each family. Famous studies of the jealous reactions of young children displaced by the birth of a child (*Journal of Abnormal Psychology* 1949) have established that jealousy and its handmaiden, envy, are normal but transient emotional reactions, and that parents can do something constructive about them. Making the older child "part of the experience" and letting him or her become mother's helper are virtually standard practice in American families, who turn to such experts of child development as Benjamin Spock, Louise B. Ames, and T. Berry Brazelton for help in dealing with a newborn child. By the time adolescence begins, a child's jealous reactions to the birth of a sibling have usually subsided and been forgotten, as is confirmed by surveys (Yamamoto 1979) of children's fears. By the time a child gets to sixth grade, for example, the birth of a new baby is ranked low on a list of events that most eleven- and twelve-year-old children view as upsetting.

Under certain conditions, however, jealous reactions can spiral to dangerous levels which dominate the life of a family for months and even years. Let us examine the distressing experience of one happy and well-functioning family that was thrown off balance for more than a year owing to the acute jealousy activated by the adoption of a four-month-old baby girl. We will describe this case as it unfolded before the parents' eyes, and then detail the reasons for the uncontrollable jealousy of their oldest child, who was three and one-half years old at the time of the adoption.

Throwing "Baby" Out the Window: Kathy and Bonnie. One afternoon four-year-old Kathy's mother heard the child say to her twelve-month-old baby sister, "I want to throw Bonnie out the window." The mother smiled and thought, "A little sibling rivalry," and went back to preparing dinner. Then the next week she caught Kathy hoisting Bonnie up to the window "so the baby can see outside." Kathy had her mother's permission to pick up the baby: in fact she had been allowed to hold the baby from the moment Bonnie had been carried off the plane at the airport, where she had been flown from an orphanage. But now Kathy was opening the window, raising her sister high above the sill. The mother, a woman known for her warmth and calm ways, firmly took Bonnie from Kathy but, not wanting to plant destructive ideas in the four-year old's head, said nothing. The next morning at 5 A.M. the parents were awakened by the shrill screams of the baby. The father hurried into the nursery and found the crib empty. Across the hall, Kathy had taken Bonnie in bed with her and was trying to feed her a bottle filled with Listerine. The baby had been crying more than usual during the last few days, and Kathy had complained that she was too noisy. "Why did you give her this?" demanded her father. "You *know* it tastes bad." Kathy replied that she wanted to wash the baby's mouth out so Bonnie "wouldn't cry so much."

Over the next six months Kathy got worse. She smeared Q-tips with toothpaste and painted the baby's gums. She gave the baby bear hugs with an intensity that frightened the parents. She became preoccupied with the baby's every movement, appointing herself as guardian and mother. Just after Kathy's fifth birthday (Bonnie, eighteen months), the mother found her giving Bonnie a spanking with a hairbrush for "being so messy." A week later she found Kathy with a blunt scissors taking "pretend" snips at Bonnie's fingers. Several days later Kathy put Bonnie on the potty chair and threatened to spank her until she "made B.M." Having recently achieved a shaky mastery of the urge to soil her own pants, smear food, and suck her thumb, Kathy was now rudely reminded that these had become someone else's privileges, and she became vengeful and vindictive.

Kathy did other alarming things. She wandered away from the house at night and, after walking down a highway, was returned by a neighbor to her distraught parents. She jumped off walls she knew were too high, and set her mother into paroxysms of apprehension. She took risks such as walking dangerously near the father's lawn mower—something that she had been told many, many times not to do. She bit the skin around her fingers, so that her mother worried about infection.

Up to now the mother and father had considered themselves effective parents, but they began to worry that this little girl, who had been such a joy, might have a character defect, or that they had failed as parents. The first four years of Kathy's life had been "terrific." A much-wanted child, she and her mother were closely attached. The mother, whom her friends considered an example of a completely committed parent, had reveled in her relationship with Kathy. Being Kathy's mother had been a joy; they had traveled to museums and parks; the mother's play was stimulating. Time with Kathy had both quality and quantity. This mother had willingly given up her own career as a reporter for a newspaper to enjoy childbearing and bringing up her family, knowing that she could free-lance while the kids were growing, and later return to work once they were launched in school. The father, a successful entrepreneur, appeared to be a warm, committed husband and parent.

The parents called upon a child psychologist for help. In his first encounter with Kathy, he quickly confirmed that her overwhelming jealousy and rage toward her sister was indeed the central problem, and he shared the parents' concern that Kathy might harm her sister. When given the Rorschach Ink Blots (a projective test), her thoughts appeared tinged with rage and with attempts to be a perfect little angel:

> A turtle: someone poked holes in his back.
> A monster: he's growling.
> Two girls: little angels.
> Two pigs trying to get to the top of the mountain to eat something.
> Paint, spilled on top of a baby.
> Spiders. And a gun.

Kathy was bright enough to understand her parents' prohibitions; her conversational fluency made her appear closer to seven than to five years old; and the nursery school teacher considered her to be brighter, better behaved, and more mature than most of the other children. Yet Kathy appeared totally enslaved by her mounting feelings of anger and jealousy. She stated, with hardly any probing: "I love my sister, but she's a pain. I wish she wouldn't be alive. I wanted a baby sister, but now I think she should go back on the plane." Despite her quickness, Kathy's intellectual energies were being sapped, and her mind wandered easily. Her drawings were scribbles; and on an intelligence test, she turned in a surprisingly mediocre performance. The psychologist was puzzled: "a little sibling rivalry" was to be expected, but why had it expanded to include the possibility that Kathy could seriously harm herself and her baby sister?

The first clue came during a family diagnostic session. The mother put baby Bonnie on her lap, while the father and Kathy took separate chairs. As the psychologist and the parents began discussing recent events, Kathy made a beeline for her mother's lap and jumped up on her knee. The mother, with some discomfort, held her wiggling eighteen-month-old in one arm and her fifty-pound five-year-old with the other. As the father ignored this struggle, the psychologist told the mother to ask Kathy to go back to her own chair. It took four requests from the mother to get the child to comply (grudgingly), and Kathy scowled and turned her body away. When the psychologist asked her if she was angry, Kathy unleashed a storm of accusations, saying that she hated her mother. "You don't love me!" she howled. The mother's assurance that Kathy was loved equally with Bonnie simply spurred Kathy on. She left her chair and reclaimed her mother's lap; and the mother, backing down guiltily, accepted her and smiled at the psychologist. Here was a major clue, the psychologist realized, to the puzzle of this child's anger. Paralyzed by her tyranny, these parents were unconsciously allowing her "to get away with murder" and vent her hostility. In their next meeting, the psychologist tried to learn why the parents were ignoring the obvious.

This mother, herself the eldest of five siblings, had been severely deprived by her own mother, whose psychotic depressions made her unpredictable and unavailable to her child. Kathy's mother thus had grown up like the caretakers we described in chapter 5: for her, caring for her children was a way of caring for others and became a lifeline, making her feel nurtured. She consciously wanted her children *not* to be burdened by maternal anger or selfishness, and compulsively tried to make certain that all her children's moments were happy. Furthermore, the circumstances of the adoption, and other events, over which the parents had no control, had played a part in creating the present dangerous situation. The mother, who had wanted to have a second child two years after Kathy was born, had developed uterine difficulties and was advised to adopt rather than conceive another child. To a woman with five siblings of her own, the idea of not giving Kathy a sibling was "almost unthinkable."

The mother's efforts to undo the injuries of the past increased with this second child's arrival. With only one child she could consciously give everything. With two children, however, she unthinkingly assigned to Kathy the caretaker role she herself had played for her mother. Months before Bonnie's adoption the mother would hold Kathy on her lap and tell her: "When we get you a baby sister, you're going to be my special helper." Thus, to an impressionable age, Kathy learned to feel responsible—a result quite the opposite of what her mother had consciously intended! The father's background dovetailed with the mother's: having had an aggressive and unstable father, he had vowed to be a peaceful parent, and succeeded so well that he became paralyzed and guilty at his daughter's aggression.

From the moment Kathy and her parents put baby Bonnie in the old infant seat Kathy had used only three years before, it was clear that this family had, to use the father's expression, "gotten lucky." They had been handed what the mother said was "the most gorgeous baby we had ever seen." The baby instantly *smiled* at everybody. On the way back from the airport, the family stopped at a McDonald's where waitresses raved about Bonnie and ignored Kathy. This was the first of a long series of unequal comparisons between the fetching Latin, dark-eyed Bonnie and her older, less magnetic sister. The sensitive mother tried hard to balance the attention. On baby Bonnie's first night at home, the mother, though exhausted, stayed awake to play games with Kathy and succumbed to her demands to read Babar and Dr. Seuss to her. Thus was laid down a pattern of compulsive balancing which played into the little girl's greedy desires.

Soon after Bonnie's adoption, two traumatic events served to increase Kathy's insecurity and concern about losing her mother's love: the mother had an automobile accident and was hospitalized. Kathy, who before this time had never spent more than an afternoon away from her mother, began to wonder if her mother would ever come home. The little girl had had no preparation for this sudden separation, had never stayed overnight with a grandparent or a sister. She began dreaming of robbers and woke up screaming. After ten days the mother returned from the hospital but, several months later, was rehospitalized with head pain—an absence that reactivated Kathy's fears. Left without her mother to reassure her, and having only the rudiments of a conscience, Kathy had to monitor her own aggression toward the baby. Simultaneously she had attached herself in a primitive way to little Bonnie, in the manner described in chapter 2. Bonnie had become a "transitional object" for Kathy, who clung to her for dear life, while at the same time wishing her gone.

Kathy did *not* kill or maim Bonnie. The parents, after the therapist had pointed out how they were giving in to Kathy's whims, set firm limits and finally slapped her on the bottom—something that calmed her and showed her that the parents could give her external controls until she could fully develop a conscience. They insisted that Kathy come to *them* to report her sister's immaturity rather than taking it upon herself to be a disciplinarian. And, in the psychologist's office, Kathy unloaded some of her fears about losing her mother, and went away, buttressed by the reality of her mother's good health. In the last meeting with the psychologist, Kathy—who by this time was five and one-half—had begun attending an all-day kindergarten and felt like a big girl. The all-day separation of the children had done both of them "a world of good," the mother reported. No longer biting skin from her fingers, Kathy appeared free of serious worry or guilt. The mother told the psychologist that Kathy was *really* growing up. Bonnie had bumped her hard in the forehead with a wooden doll and had bruised her, drawing blood and tears. Kathy cried but did not hit back, realizing it was an accident, and reported the incident to their mother. As the meeting came to an end, the psychologist caught his last glimpse of Kathy still struggling to form a conscience, as she dropped little dolls into the dungeon of a play castle and told them: "You've got to listen to your mother or you can't come out to play."

In this case, the parents wanted to give both children equal recognition and attention. But when parents make one child their favorite, that child may develop an identity based on a sense of privilege, power, and entitlement. The effects of such early dominant experiences upon identity are clearly demonstrated in the life of Sigmund Freud, the founder of psychoanalysis.

An Entitled Brother: Sigmund Freud° Freud stood at the top of the pecking order in a family of five younger sisters and a brother who was ten years his junior: Anna, Rosa, Marie, Adolfini, Paula, and Alexander. Among Freud's earliest memories were guilt feelings resulting from murderous thoughts he had directed at another brother, Julius, who died at the age of nine months when Freud was nineteen months old. Freud noted that the fulfillment of these death wishes aroused in him a lifelong tendency toward self-reproach. (In chapter 10, we will discuss the disturbing effects of sibling death in greater detail.)

The father's first wife had died more than a generation before, leaving Jacob Freud with two sons, Philip and Emmanuel, Sigmund's half-brothers, twenty and twenty-three years older, respectively, than he. Emmanuel, who lived close by, had a son John, who was a year older than Freud and became his playmate. In recalling his childhood, Freud reiterated that the development of his character had been conditioned by his ambivalence toward John, his nephew and peer:

> Until the end of my third year we had been inseparable; we had loved each other and fought each other and, as I have already hinted, this childish relationship has determined all my later feelings in intercourse with persons my own age. My nephew, John, has since then had many incarnations which have revived first one and then another aspect of character and is ineradicably fixed in my conscious memory. At times he must have treated me very badly and I must have opposed my tyrant courageously. (Jones 1953, p. 8)

The relationship between Sigmund and his sister Anna appears never to have been particularly friendly, but the reasons remain a mystery. Ernest

° This discussion appeared in lengthier form, in "Freudian Siblings," *Psychoanalytic Review* 67 (Winter 1981): 493–504.

Jones associated Anna's birth with a crisis in Sigmund's family life. In the following description, note the particularly negative feelings of Sigmund and the striking parallels to Freud's description of Little Hans's jealous reactions to the birth of *his* sister at a similar age:

> The problem of the family relationships came to a head with the birth of the first sister, Anna, when he was just two and a half years old. How and why had this usurper appeared, with whom he would have once again [a reference to his brother Julius's birth] to share his mother's warm and previously exclusive love? The changes in her figure told the observant child the source of the baby, but not how it had all come about. And at the same moment, when his mother was in bed with the new baby, his Nannie disappeared.   (Jones 1953, p. 9)

Freud's warmest sibling relationship was with Alexander, ten years his junior; and it perfectly suited Freud's temperament. He could dominate easily and be looked up to by his brother, without having his authority challenged. Shortly after the younger boy's birth, the family turned to young Sigmund and asked his opinion of a suitable name. He picked the name "Alexander," and it was instantly adopted. Alexander traveled with Freud in the latter's young adulthood. Together they took walks and went to the baths, always with Alex dutifully and with good humor carrying his older brother's bags. The alliance between Alexander and Sigmund lasted throughout their lives, but it was based on the shared assumption that Sigmund would be in charge.

As sisters came into his life, he became a parental and paternal child. Perhaps because Jacob Freud had been shaken by the failure of his business and played a rather weak role in the family, Sigmund became the brother who essentially supplanted the father in dealing with the other children. Freud was the classic first-born who thrived by dominating: when he could not dominate, he tried to eliminate or ignore. As the eldest and the most favored (they knew he was a genius: his mother, Amalie Freud, called him "my golden Sigi"), he was treated with a respect that verged on deference. His sisters, abetted by their mother, learned early to look up to him and to stay out of his way.

Sigmund considered himself superior to his siblings, with Alexander the single exception. In Freud's brief autobiography (1935), he mentions only his parents, omitting his sisters and brothers. His experience with them in middle and late childhood confirmed his feelings that brothers and sisters could be dominated. To Freud they were something of a bother, people to be tolerated or who owed him admiration (Bank and Kahn 1980-81).

Because the entire family recognized young Sigmund's special talents, unique measures were taken to protect him from having to take responsibility for the younger children. His sister, Anna Bernays, recalled in an ambivalent memoir:

> No matter how crowded our quarters, Sigmund always had a room to himself. There was a parlor, a dining room, three bedrooms which the rest of us shared, and a so-called cabinet—a single room separated from the rest of the apartment. This cabinet, long and narrow with a window looking out on the street, was allotted to Sigmund. (1940)

This sister recalled that Freud was much more involved with friends and intellectual companions than he was with his sisters and brother:

> During his teens he did not join us at our evening meals but took them alone in a room where he poured endlessly over his books.

He occasionally tyrannized his siblings, showing toward them that sense of privilege and entitlement that first-born males seem destined to live out. His mother did little to prevent his tyrannizing of his sisters. Sister Anna continued her memoir wistfully:

> When I was 8 years old, my mother, who was musical, wanted me to study the piano and I began practicing by the hour. Though Sigmund's room was not near the piano, the sound disturbed him. He appealed to my mother to remove the piano if she did not wish him to leave the house altogether. The piano disappeared and with it all opportunities for his sisters to become musicians.

For a girl to become a socially attractive young woman in the Vienna of the late nineteenth century, playing the piano was virtually a necessity. Finally, Anna recalled, "In our bedrooms we used candles, and Sigmund an oil lamp."

Thus, Freud was "anointed" by his mother, easily overcame his passive father, and positioned himself at the head of a sibling group in which no one could question his dominance and special status. His experiences as a brother influenced not only his theory of siblings (which emphasizes rivalry, jealousy, and domination at the expense of other, more cooperative traits), but also his relationship with rivals and equals in the psychoanalytic movement. According to Ernest Jones (1953) and Paul Roazen (1975), Freud had to dominate those who were his intellectual equals. His personal autocracy in the psychoanalytic movement flowed naturally from the autocratic role that he had played out among his siblings. His younger brother, his only male rival, was his worshipful follower. In this light, Freud's struggles with his fellow psychoanalysts Alfred Adler and Carl Gustave Jung, his ruthless domination of one of his potential rivals, Victor

Tausk, and his refusal to compromise intellectually or socially as leader of the psychoanalytic movement, all make more sense as a reflection of sibling dynamics than as simply one of his relationship with parents.

We live in an era of psychological awareness of favoritism, beyond the imagination of most nineteenth-century parents. In the next example, one mother tries to cope with the differences between two very unequal children.

Worried Balancing and Comparison: Adam and Mark. In a family of four children, Adam, age ten and the oldest, had been born with cerebral palsy,° and Mark, age nine, was entirely normal; there were also two younger siblings, a boy of three and a girl of two. The father was unassuming and quiet but provided objectivity, humor, and a definite voice of calm when his wife was overwhelmed by anxiety about how to handle their damaged child. The mother appeared bright, positive, and warm. She had given up a successful nursing career to become a proud and dedicated full-time housewife and mother—a role that she obviously enjoyed. The only area of child rearing where she appeared to have conflict was in the management of her reactions to her two, very different older boys.

When Adam was born, and the mother was anguishing over her damaged infant, a bright young neurologist had counseled her: "You must treat him normally whenever possible." In spite of Adam's slow development, she doggedly decided to fight with all of her resources for him. With her husband's support, she worked with Adam, obtained specialized physical therapies, and expected the best of him. By the age of ten, he had become a child whom everybody considered amazing: a well-adjusted, sunny youngster who, when we tested him, doggedly persevered at any task where he had the barest chance of success. He was the crowning achievement of his mother's life; and, from almost everybody who knew them, she received ample credit for Adam's "having come so far."

Mark, a year younger, had no physical handicap. Yet he was a more dependent child who appeared to lack his handicapped older brother's self-starting tendencies, and whose will-power, by comparison, seemed weak. Although it was Adam who limped physically, the mother panicked because Mark was limping psychologically. What the mother did not realize was that Mark had long envied the attention and sympathy she was lavishing upon Adam. Mark craved this attention: by failing and faltering in his own way, perhaps someone would give him equal recognition. To the child psychologist who saw him, Mark's actual ability appeared to be

---

° The problems of being the sibling of a handicapped youngster have also been described by Helen Featherstone (1980).

in the high average range—considerably above Adam's. The mother wished that Mark, her well-endowed son, had more of valiant Adam's emotional strength; to her, contrasts between the two boys were many and painful. The mother said to us:

> Mark is easily hurt, sensitive to what other people think about him. Adam will tell kids to go jump off a cliff, while Mark will come home wounded. Mark can go in to the doctor for a routine thing and blow something minor into a huge trauma! He hasn't had a hundredth of the medical problems Adam has had. Adam is a fantastic patient; he cooperates even when it hurts.

The mother's anger at Mark (and at herself for not being able to make him use his potential as she had been able to make Adam use *his*) peaked when Adam, in spite of all his efforts, was kept back in fourth grade. He was now in the same grade as Mark, but in a different class with a different teacher. Now the children's differing temperaments and abilities were painfully magnified:

> MOTHER: What bothers me the most is that I feel awful for Adam! He was really giving his work everything. And Mark would bring home papers with "excellent" written on them and they were *trash!* And I'd say: "Don't bring those home to me. This isn't as good as I know you can do!"
>
> INTERVIEWER: How do you explain this to Mark?
>
> MOTHER: It's hard to explain. What can I say to him when he says: "You're happy Adam got a C—what's wrong with my getting a B?" How do you explain that to a kid?
>   I feel like shaking him sometimes, and saying: you've got a normal brain and a normal body: USE IT!

The boy's mother anguished over the inevitable comparisons between them and feared that Mark would soon outshine Adam:

> "I think about eighth-grade graduation, how people will compare them. I think about when Mark says, Well I'm going to the Naval Academy," and Adam says, "Well, I'm going to work at the five-and-dime store." The comparison is always there. It really scares me.

Constantly making sure that Mark's superior physical and intellectual power never upstaged his limping older brother, the mother got angry at Mark for "inventing" his own little disabilities—underachievement, overblown reactions to physical illness, mild depression—devices he used in order to gain her love. She was aware that she had given Mark mixed messages and might thereby have made him anxious: "Use all your potential, *but* don't compete against your older but handicapped brother." In preventing Mark from aggressively topping his brother, she realized that she might be reinforcing his passivity. Thus, she hesitated when Mark showed an interest in joining Adam's Cub Scout Troop:

> Adam has been in Cub Scouts and he's loved every minute of it! He is so happy there! It was so wonderful—it did my heart good! Now what am I going to say when Mark wants to join the same Cub Scout Pack? I hate to see him take the glow off of this for Adam. Right now Adam is the one who marches off proudly with his little blue uniform.

Despite her many worries, this mother is still thoughtfully but anxiously trying to balance the great inequalities between her children.

MARITAL WARFARE AND SIBLING CONFLICT

Children are keen observers of their parents' attitudes and actions. The statement that children learn what their parents live describes how many siblings live out, in their relationships, the aggressive themes expressed by the parents (Steinmetz 1976). When there is marital conflict, and parents are hurting each other, the children sometimes turn to one another for support and solace. But a long-standing war between parents may result in long-standing conflict between siblings. Parents who are getting along with each other can more readily defuse sibling conflict.

Children are rivals for their parents' affection, and parents often compete for the allegiances of their children. A parent who feels unloved, let down, or hurt by a spouse, may look to a child for support against the offending spouse, who is thus left out in the cold. To whom will this parent turn? Most likely to one of the other children. In parental conflict, an only child can be torn apart, as in Frank Gilroy's play *The Subject Was Roses* (1962), where a young man tries to be loyal to both warring parents. But in families of two or more children, at least one may be asked to take sides with one of the parents.

If a divorce takes place when children are young, they have less choice about taking sides and can more readily be used as parental pawns. However adolescents and young adults have a greater capacity to steer clear of the maelstrom of the parents' conflict.

Taking sides with parents can poison the children's relations with each other in several ways. First, a sibling who is loyal to one parent, and who effectively monopolizes that parent's personality, may make it difficult for another child to identify with the good qualities of that parent. Second, the opportunities for the siblings to form cordial and supportive ties are reduced, since each child may be a proxy for one of the parents in their conflict.

Proxies for Warring Parents: Melanie and Cliff. The issue of sexual identification is highlighted in the unhappy effects of divorce on two adolescent siblings, Melanie and Cliff. Melanie was twelve and her brother Cliff, ten, when it became clear that the parental tensions that had prevailed since they could remember, broke out into open conflict. The mother would bring home her lovers, leave evidence of her lovemaking, get caught by the father—and there ensued violent fights and arguments in front of the terrified children. In time, the father won the loyalty of the daughter, and the mother won the sympathies of the son. In the breakup and relocation of the family, each child chose to stay with the parent of the opposite sex. Thus, there were two new "marriages": between father and daughter, and between mother and son. And there were two "divorces": the old one between the parents, and a newer one, between brother and sister.

Late in adolescence, Melanie, age nineteen, and Cliff, age seventeen, were each possessed by one and *only* one parent. On her periodic visits to her mother (across town), Melanie would sit and watch television, barely communicate, and go into a sullen rage when Cliff tried to draw her out. He felt bad that his mother was being hurt by his sister's indifference. Melanie's rage at the mother for failing the father and for old infidelities was so great that she barely noticed Cliff's friendly overtures to her. She rebuffed him as though he had all along been their mother's partner in the crime of wounding Daddy.

Cliff's visits to his father were brief and unhappy. The boy's general behavior, school difficulties, drug experimentation, and free-living style was viewed by the father as reflecting his fallen ex-wife's behavior. When Cliff departed from his father's house, he left behind traces of his own contempt—a broken light bulb, dirty dishes in the sink, a soiled bathroom. He knew that his father would berate Melanie for not keeping him in line; after all, she was the housekeeper and should know how to influence her younger brother. Melanie would then scold Cliff for getting her in trouble. She sniped at him over the phone and refused to defend him whenever their father exploded in frustration.

These siblings' relations almost completely mirrored the unfriendly relations between the parents. Cliff, more than Melanie, wanted to reach out and improve his relationship with her: he appeared to reflect his mother's attitude that she could somehow forgive and forget the hurt she had suffered with her husband. But Melanie wanted little connection with Cliff, and thus loyally reflected her father's "holier-than-thou" attitude toward the woman who had betrayed him. We were struck by the bland neutrality of their relationship. Cliff told us, "I'll tell you about my Mom. Melanie can tell you about Dad." Whatever warmth may have existed in early childhood seemed almost impossible to recapture now.

Thus, an antagonistic sibling relationship mirrors an antagonistic marriage. Children can identify with some core attitude of each parent, take sides, and re-enact the marital war.

Struggles for Superiority in Adolescence and Adulthood

As children grow up, the time comes when their parents can no longer balance their notions of the relative individual worth of each child. Increasingly, the siblings must find their own balance, negotiating with each other about complex issues of equality, superiority, and inferiority (Ferguson 1958). As we suggested early in this chapter, rivalry can be a major vehicle for ego development and identity resolution in childhood. The process continues throughout adolescence and adulthood.

Helgola Ross and Joel Milgram (1982) suggest that adolescent and adult siblings have considerable power to help or hurt each other's sense of personal worth in three areas:

- Achievement and success.
- Sexuality and beauty.
- Social relations with peers, outsiders, and other siblings.

Siblings endlessly compare themselves with one another in these arenas, and the process is heavily tinged with jealous concerns about superiority and inferiority. Now the struggle between closeness and distance is interwoven with a fight to see who's better, who's on top.

In regard to the relationship between any two siblings, these three areas—achievement, sexuality, and social relations—are never separate

219

and are always to be thought of as in dynamic balance with one another. Rarely does one sibling dominate completely in all three. If triple domination has occurred for many years, the dominated sibling will feel severely inadequate and like "a nobody." Usually siblings realize that a brother or a sister "controls" one, or perhaps two, of these areas (as if they were actual territories); and thus the other sibling may feel impelled to seek distinction and superiority in the remaining area.

ACHIEVEMENT

Superiority in Separate Domains: Frank and Eric. Frank was always surpassed by his achievement-oriented older brother, Eric, and thus became a very different person from him. At twenty-nine, the younger brother had just finished college and had still not settled on any clear vocation. Savoring his ability not to be like his brother, Frank told us:

> Eric got his Ph.D. at twenty-four and became a tenured professor by the time he was thirty. Work, work, drive, drive *hard.*
>
> Me? I've dropped out of school three times, studied Zen in Idaho, worked construction. I tried hard to become like him, and he even made me a research assistant in his laboratory for a year. I've always fooled around compared to him. He was always mildly disgusted with me.
>
> He gets a little threatened when I do something in his area. He can't tolerate me when I'm "more." I have talent, but I just don't have the same will-power as he does. He says: "If I could get you to put it all together, you could go beyond me." I just cannot do all the things he could do! It's like I've got nothing in my hands. He can say, "I have been appointed professor, I wrote this paper, I did something concrete—what are you doing with your life?"

Never able to measure up to the driving, demanding Eric, Frank became only marginally successful in the world of work; but in sexual and social relationships, he became everything that his nose-to-the-grindstone elder brother was not.° Frank's enormous charm endeared him to many people. He loved women and enjoyed their company and was sought out by women who were considered stunning. His brother related superficially to women and set aside little time for friendships or family. Eric's

---

° Frank's identity was set in opposition to his brother's success and, as such, became negative in certain respects. This is not, however, the case with all brothers and sisters. For example, Milgram and Ross (in press) interviewed the brothers and sisters of famous persons and discovered that these obscure people often basked in the reflected glory of their well-known siblings.

snooty condescension (although mixed with caring and mentorship) forced Frank to seek his own areas of success. For a while he envied his brother's identity as a brainy academician and tried to catch up with him, to become his brother's image; but the image never fit. Finally Frank came secretly to value his marginally successful and half-baked academic identity which, though it pained him when he compared himself with his brother, also gave him the identity of one who could be "his own man." When we asked him what he could give to his brother, he replied, "I could teach him the art of relaxation and the art of being human."

Despite the painful dialectic they sustained, these men had both heavily invested in keeping the relationship the way it was. The older still saw it as his mission to improve the younger. The younger allowed him to do this to a certain extent and then would contemptuously fall just short of becoming as successful. In this way Frank showed that he was really his own boss and could spoil his brother's wish to make him become a star.

Such relationships of older and younger siblings are supported by cultural expectations. One of these expectations is for the younger brother to acknowledge and appreciate the accomplishments of the older. In this case, the younger had repeatedly robbed the older of the pleasure of turning him into a success. This was one area where he could *make* the older brother fail! Conversely, the older always implied that the younger one was "perhaps a nice guy" but really worthless when it came to making it in the world where achievement counts. These brothers continue to care about one another, each realizing that the father never did and never will provide solid male identity. Their bond is energized by their sniping dialectic. Frank gains identity as a social winner (but vocational loser), and Eric gains identity as a high-powered success (but a social loser).

Many other factors can come into play as siblings struggle for superiority in the area of academic attainment and vocational success. Foremost among these is whether they are both males, both females, or a male-female pair. It is particularly painful, in the context of sex-role expectations of excellence for men and average performance for women, when a sister's achievements far outstrip those of her brother, especially an older one. A younger girl who surpasses her brother in academic achievement and career, often must conceal her greater success from her brother who has been overshadowed by someone who is "supposed" to be inferior.

SEXUALITY

Adolescents and young adults are always vulnerable to attacks made upon them by their siblings, but nowhere are they more sensitive and impressionable than in the realm of sexuality. Between the ages of eleven and twenty-one, sexual feelings, attitudes toward one's sex, and sexual attitudes toward others can develop in either a healthy or an unhealthy sibling context. (We have already noted the positive effects of sexual pioneering in chapter 6.) Because siblings have an intimate knowledge of one another's treasured sexual secrets, they also have the power to crush one another with a mere comment or an allusion.

We noted in chapter 7 the erotic, nurturing motives and the power-sadistic motives which can propel siblings to make sexual contact. In adolescence, however, the need for superiority over one's sibling peaks and can reach its zenith via sadistic verbal attacks that have the distinct aim of laying low one's brother or sister. The attacker has several motives, including: the desire to feel superior when one feels inferior or the need to ward off one's homosexual feelings for the attacked sibling, or the attempt to achieve distance between a brother and a sister to whom one is attracted, either heterosexually or homosexually. The attacks can be subtle, such as a girl's telling her sister that she's welcome to borrow her bra—"though of course it will probably be too big" (said in an extra sweet tone). Or the attacks can be obvious: humiliating a brother or a sister in front of esteemed peers; "making out" with or stealing a jointly prized boy or girl friend; standing passively by, silently withholding support, while a sibling is insulted or taken advantage of by members of the opposite sex; or by repeatedly implying that a brother or a sister is sexless or, even worse, a "queer," a "whore," a "slut."

Many siblings refuse to recognize or validate a brother or a sister's emerging sexual interests or powers and, in so doing, deny them the much-needed recognition that they are normal sexual human beings. Some women (and men) pride themselves on having married a man (or woman) handsomer than the one a sibling has married, or on having had more and better children or more of the favored sex. Or a woman may gloat that she is able to conceive a child while her sister remains barren. In short, the treacherous sexual waters are mined with countless possibilities for sibling betrayal. Especially when one sibling is dependent upon another for esteem, attacks on the former's sexuality can create psychological wounds that last a lifetime.

SOCIAL RELATIONS

Many adults recall the bitter feeling of being excluded by two of their siblings who paired off privately. Rivalry for the attention of a third sibling (or for a friend who is prized by *both* siblings) can persist through adolescence and into adulthood.

Triangles are unstable human configurations; sibling groups of three or more individuals can foster cutthroat rivalries. As we pointed out in chapter 2, a child who cannot attach him or herself successfully to a parent turns to a sibling as a transitional object. If two siblings are rivals for the love of one prized and valued sibling, however, someone must come out the loser. A sibling who is unable to attach him or herself to parents, seeks compensation for unrequited love by anxiously allying with the brother or sister who shows the slightest sign of interest, and this is often done at another sibling's expense.

Leaving One Sibling in the Cold: Elaine, Greg, and Janet. Elaine's parents were away from home a great deal during their children's middle years—a time of stress, as the parents fought to reach the top of their professions—and she was left as a mother substitute for her little sister, Janet. This was a situation that Elaine hated but never complained about. The little sister was the mother's favorite; and when the mother came home tired from work, she would play with the delightful younger girl, causing Elaine to sulk and feel jealous. Even more painful was her father's absence. Although he loved her, he was available only in the late evening and during brief weekend interludes. Elaine was in a difficult bind: she was acting as a mother substitute to her sister whom their mother favored; she wanted loyally to be a good substitute parent to Janet and to free their mother from tension; and at the same time she was not getting parental support or nurturance. The one family member who was available and consistently warm was her brother Greg. In this situation she did everything she could to make it impossible for her sister to possess their older brother. As Elaine reported when she was in her early twenties:

ELAINE: Greg and I are *so* close, and there's so much tension between Janet and me. So that puts him in the awful position of being a middleman who has to break up our arguments, at least it used to. And he used to play little kid stuff with her, and wrestle playfully with her. . . . I always resented hearing them squealing together. I would tell myself that I had no right to feel that way, but he could see by the tone of my voice afterward. He enjoyed being with her and he enjoyed being with me. She resented me and my special relationship with Greg, too. . . . She would get cut off by me. And he couldn't take the pressure of having to be equally nice to both of us. It got so bad that he'd just go for the night to a friend's house [*speaking sadly*].

Yeah, I was really rotten, I wanted all of him, and that put him in a tough position.

This young woman's rivalry with a younger sister for her brother's love became a blueprint for Elaine's developing sensitivity to triangular situations in her everyday social world. Such blueprints, as we suggested in chapter 2, can be drawn very early in life and can last for life. Helgola Ross's interviewees in old-age settings (1982) told her that rivalries and hurts had become "frozen in place" from as early as the age of three and were still vividly experienced in old age, affecting the elderly person's feelings about himself and prejudicing his ability to trust intimate relations with other people.

Mechanisms for the Containment of Sibling Aggression

Given the bitter jealousy and anger that can prevail between brothers and sisters, it is a wonder that siblings don't kill each other. Most sibling conflicts get to the brink of disaster, and then, somehow, they pull back and defuse the explosive situation. Why do siblings contain their conflicts without doing more damage?

Geographic separation at the end of adolescence provides a helpful safety valve. Because ours is a "neolocal" society that encourages young people to seek jobs regardless of where one's family of origin is located, siblings find it convenient to avoid direct contact after the early adult years. Our mobile society also allows siblings to work out distinct identities in separate territories. The actress with a fraternal male twin, whom we described earlier (see page 203), moved across the country to get away from conflicts she had with her brother. Such lack of contact reflects no lack of feeling but is, instead, an energetic neutralization of anger, guilt, and competition.

Many siblings in our study initially reported bland or neutral feelings about their brothers and sisters or seemed so confused about their feelings that it was hard to know what they really were. Other siblings portrayed themselves as bewildered and lacking in insight, stumbled for words, and lapsed into stereotypical catchphrases or employed hopelessly convoluted abstractions when it came to talking about their relationships with brothers and sisters. Such neutrality or confusion, especially when the siblings have had considerable access to one another, can serve as a defensive maneuver designed to keep disturbing feelings from being resurrected. Melanie Klein (1975) believed that confusion can serve as a defense against explosive rage, and also mentioned *devaluation and contempt* as major mechanisms for reducing the disturbing experience of jealousy and envy. One deflects a sister's hurtful impact by saying: "She is worthless anyway, so how can she disappoint me, we have nothing in common." (This mechanism is similar to the disowned identification mentioned in chapter 4.) The opposite of devaluation is *idealization*. By idealizing a brother, one can avoid feeling and facing vengeful thoughts that might tarnish one's own cherished ideas of brotherly kindness. An understanding of how siblings mitigate their hostile feelings involves an understanding of the type of identification that has existed between them. A sibling's willingness to harm or humiliate depends upon whether identification is close, partial, or distant. In the extreme case of identical twins, where one person is a beloved and narcissistic extension of oneself, conflict is generally kept to a minimum, since harm to the twin is harm to oneself. The process by which siblings become different (partial negative identifications mentioned in chapter 4) allows siblings to become "opposites" in many major personality and interest areas. Thus they avoid conflict, having divided up emotional territories and roles.

De-identification (see chapter 4) leads to a "disowned" type of sibling relationship where siblings feel totally different from one another and reject one another completely. By de-identifying with a sibling, one avoids intense sibling rivalry: thus, "if we have nothing in common, we cannot even compete against one another" prevents angry feelings from escalating (F. Schachter et al. 1976). Parents participate in teaching siblings to de-identify with one another since they, too, fear the outbreak of hostility between their children (Schachter et al. 1978).

When positive identification is not strong enough to prevent hurtful conflict, adult siblings may make peace by relying on their *common identification with a cherished parent*. Many siblings resurrect their parent's hope that they have a good relationship, and interpret attacks on each other as an attack on family solidarity. They agree tacitly not to fight, each knowing that the other has a special power to make one's life a miserable "balance of terror" and thus defy the parents' wish for a peaceful, united family. The need for constancy and continuity, particularly after parents have died, appears to be strong enough for siblings, who have had some positive identification with the parents, to minimize their differences (Masterman 1979). However, if one sibling was scapegoated by a dead parent, and if the other monopolized that parent's love, there is no reason for either sibling to place family solidarity above angry self-interest. Sibling relationships that have been very negative and polarized before a parent's death, will become more negative afterward; if positive, they will then become even more positive.

Restitutional efforts and *richness divestment* also serve as conflict controls in hostile and rivalrous adolescent or adult sibling relationships. Many entitled or "superior" siblings have been favored by family, fate, or their own hard-won successes. One may worry about offending a less-advantaged sibling, who may feel jealous and angry that the other has made out so well, married so well, had such nice children, gotten such good jobs. The successful one can feel especially guilty if he has purchased his success at the expense of a sibling toward whom he was supposed to show a loyal and charitable spirit.° Managing riches gracefully so as not to give the impression of piggishness, rapaciousness, smugness, or (heaven forbid!) triumphant supremacy can be a practical and artistic problem (Goffman 1973).

Evening the Balance: Diana and Helene. In everyday relationships, restitution and richness divestment can be performed by steering away from encounters that are likely to make a sister or a brother feel undone. Diana had become an excellent pianist, surpassing her older sister, Helene, whose dreams of becoming a professional performer had been dried up by realistic appraisal of her average talents. The sisters' relationship as children had been marked by close attachment and identification. They had totally agreed never to cause each other anguish. The now-accomplished musician never invited her older sister (who had become a journalist) to her performances, fearing that "this would be like rubbing her nose in my success." "I didn't want to get you upset," Diana said when they met in a therapist's office. Not letting her older sister see her perform was a great detriment because Diana valued her sister's comments and criticisms of her, Diana's, abilities above anyone else's. But Diana was still sensitive about outshining her sister as she had done fifteen years earlier when, at a gala performance of the orchestra they both played for, she was touted as a star while Helene faded into the woodwork. The image of her sister crying silently backstage was still guiltily etched in Diana's memory. She did not want to make things worse. When she finally did invite Helene to a major recital, Diana went out of her way to express doubts about herself, complained that her career was in the doldrums, and insistently asked Helene for advice about her relationship

° Recognizing this principle, a Connecticut Superior Court judge has ruled that an eleven-year-old brother had to donate his kidney to a sister who was dying of renal disease—on the grounds that if the girl were to die, the well sibling's chance for an emotionally healthy life could be ruined by the guilt of *not* having made the donation.

with her boyfriend. By divesting herself of her "riches," Diana made restitution to Helene. Helene, in return, said that she found Diana "most touchable" when she presented herself as a "pitiable mess."

Satisfactions in Sibling Aggression

Why would anyone allow oneself to be rebuffed, rebuked, abused, or humiliated by a brother or a sister over months, or even years, when one is free not to associate with one's sibling? Whenever conflict between siblings persists over time, both participants obtain secret and powerful gratifications from the struggle. These satisfactions are not immediately apparent, but they can be determined by a thoroughgoing study of the siblings' previous emotional experiences with one another (Henry and Henry 1942; Marscak 1968).° This hypothesis can be useful when we search with our patients for answers to such questions as: "Why do I keep reaching out to my sister, only to have her kick me around and ignore me?" "How come I keep acting like a sucker with my brother? Why won't I ever learn he doesn't care about me?" In short, what makes the pain of continued sibling conflict worthwhile? And why don't abused siblings make a "total break" with their oppressors? By giving the sibling "enough rope to hang himself," the apparent victims in our next two examples actually confirmed their cherished identities as more self-controlled and "better" than their impulse-ridden brothers.

Payoffs for Both Brothers: Charlie and Marty. A successful restaurant owner's wife poured out her exasperation to a psychotherapist, while Charlie, her husband, sulked in silence. Why, she demanded, had he given his brother half the partnership in the restaurant when Marty had done nothing to deserve it? Why had Charlie helped his brother build a beautiful home, when the brother had "stolen" several thousand dollars from the family business and squandered it on worthless property in Florida. Why was Charlie the one who took his mother in, while brother Marty didn't lift a finger! Why did Charlie work eighteen hours a day, while Marty came in whenever he pleased? "Charlie!" she screamed at him. "Why do you take his insults day in and day out and then come home and take it out on me and the kids?" She burst into tears and

---

° These concepts about the disturbed but comfortable ways in which two siblings' identities may fit perfectly with one another are similar to those described by Henry V. Dicks (1967), William J. Lederer and Don D. Jackson (1968), and Augustus Napier and Carl Whitaker (1978) in their studies of unhappy married couples.

sobbed quietly, while her husband uncomfortably avoided her eyes and looked down at the floor.

Charlie grudgingly gave the therapist information, as if trying to stonewall a brother relationship that had many secret meanings. When Charlie was eleven and his brother Marty sixteen, their father, a severe alcoholic, died suddenly. This left Marty in charge as the man of the house, a job that he took seriously. He quit school, went out to work, and gave his earnings to their mother, providing clothes and even the food for his younger brother. Charlie remembered that somehow Marty bought him a bike for his thirteenth birthday, a thrill he never forgot. Yet, simultaneously, Marty was a bully of the first order: he dominated Charlie and downgraded his then-marginal academic accomplishments, beat him physically, and humiliated him. Thus Charlie was both indebted to Marty and despised and feared him. Until they were in their late twenties, Marty seemed to be making lots of money in real estate and sporting new cars and flashy clothes, while Charlie was always mired in questionable ventures and never made it past eleventh grade.

Then a reversal occurred. Marty's life began to deteriorate. His first marriage dissolved. He lost his job. He was twice arrested for breach of peace and drunken driving. At thirty-five he was in bad straits. Meanwhile his younger brother's life was rising, confounding all who had known the two of them. He bought a restaurant and married a competent and responsible woman who tried to help him overcome his immaturities and nurtured him. When Marty, now on the skids, came and asked him for a job, Charlie too generously consented and, over his wife's protests, took his brother into partnership. Yet from the day of this association, Marty treated Charlie like an underling and junior partner, robbing him of time, money, dignity, and status. Marty seemed once more to be the domineering older brother. One day Charlie, egged on by his nagging wife, socked Marty in the jaw but later weakly apologized that he had "gotten up on the wrong side of the bed."

As Charlie allowed the therapist to know him more intimately, it became clear that he received both internal and tangible satisfactions from this inferior role that he allowed himself to play vis-à-vis his big brother. By never really insisting on any changes in his brother's demeanor, Charlie "gave him enough rope to look stupid with." He colluded with his brother's disturbing behavior by not drawing a line against it and, in this way, made himself look better. Charlie felt that, despite all the brotherly abuse, he *owed* Marty "so much" that he could never stand up to him and certainly never disown him. The image of a shiny new bike twenty-five years before, and all the other debts he owed Marty, were enough to make him discount any past and current abuse. By remaining indebted to Marty, and thereby "inferior," Charlie also got a great deal of attention and emotion from his wife, as she endlessly reminded him of his superior virtues compared with his "self-centered" brother. His wife hated the anxiety that her husband brought home from the business; but at the same time it allowed her, a proud and dominant woman, to nurse her husband's wounded feelings—a role that secretly satisfied her, too. Deep satisfaction also accrued to older brother Marty: he could be supported by his brother in business and pretty much do what he pleased. For a fellow who had had to become the man of the house when he was sixteen, it felt like a much deserved vacation.

"I Love Billy and Billy Loves Me": A President's Brother. The acceptance of abuse and embarrassment from a sibling was dramatically played out in a national arena during the spring and summer of 1980. It was Jimmy Carter's final year as President, and an important summer lay ahead for him; he faced a tough campaign for re-election against Ronald Reagan.

From the moment of his inauguration, Carter's advisers had been worried that younger brother, Billy, would embarrass the President. Previous presidents, Lyndon Johnson and Richard Nixon, had taken precautions to ensure that their brothers would stay out of the limelight, but Jimmy Carter refused in the case of Billy. Maureen, their sister, was a nationally known religious healer and, during Carter's presidency, made no controversial statements that in any way embarrassed him.

Not so with Billy. Over a four-year period Billy got into one scrape after another. He appeared dead drunk at news conferences and social gatherings. He assailed his brother's triumph at Camp David by making anti-Semitic remarks at a time when the President needed to retain Jewish loyalties as the campaign for a second term approached. There was the disclosure that Billy had received $220,000 in cash for acting as broker for the sale of a quantity of discounted Libyan oil to a Florida importer. Billy's life seemed to be a shambles. He had recently been hospitalized for alcohol detoxification, and a bank was threatening to foreclose on his $300,000 home. Joan Beck, a columnist for the *Chicago Tribune*, opined (Wednesday, 30 January 1980):

> How sad to be a Billy Carter, psychologically caught in a good brother-bad brother bind, unable to live his underachieving life in backwater peace and privacy because he can't escape from the edges of the spotlights focused on his overachieving brother.
> Without the constant comparison with Jimmy's born-again righteousness and public triumphs, who knows whether Billy might have avoided the temptation

to drink too much, to make self-parodying public appearances for pay or to try to win a new financial stake playing over his head in the hardball league of Arab and oil politics . . . ?

As the damage and embarrassment to Jimmy Carter progressively worsened with Billy's contemptuous and unrepentant conduct, the President did nothing whatever to rebuke his brother. "The President doesn't have any control over him—quite the contrary," a senior White House aide observed (Terence Smith, *New York Times* News Service). When questioned about his brother's behavior and lack of regard for him, President Carter smiled and said of him: "I love Billy and Billy loves me" (*Newsweek*, 25 August 1980). The only rebuke that the President made publicly was the mild statement that he should not be considered responsible for his brother's comments. Through the whole affair, which dominated the headlines for several months, the President was self-effacing and forebearing and did nothing publicly to restrain his brother, nor did he rally their family to do so.

Fourteen years separated these brothers who, according to the same issue of *Newsweek*, were "virtual strangers in an otherwise close-knit family." By the time Billy was eight, Jimmy was already preparing to graduate from the U.S. Naval Academy. In 1953, Billy, age fifteen, stayed on the farm to take care of their dying father. Upon the father's death, Jimmy became the family head and received his inheritance in farmland, while Billy received a cash gift which he soon spent. When the money was used up, Billy asked Jimmy for a job at his peanut warehouse, and Jimmy treated him with no special favor, as if he were just another employee. Billy had a stint in the Marines and then attended the University of Georgia, where he flunked out. When Jimmy was elected Governor of Georgia, the family offered Billy a chance to run the business. Here, for the first time, Billy was a success, and the business prospered. But when Jimmy was elected President, he put the business in a blind trust. Billy tried to buy the business but was turned down. This move effectively robbed Billy of a positive personal identity: he had no job—it had been taken away from him. It was at this point that his public misconduct seeped into the open and embarrassed his brother. According to close friends, Billy felt that his life as a functioning person was over. What did he have to lose by attacking his famous brother, whose success had been Billy's undoing as a man? President Carter's forgiving attitude is typical of the kid-gloves approach used by some entitled siblings who feel guilty about having succeeded at a sibling's expense. Already concerned that he had always overshadowed his younger brother, and possibly fearing that

230

any attempt to discipline him might result in devastating retaliation, "superior" siblings like Jimmy Carter allow conflicts to be perpetuated by maintaining silence and showing forbearance.

The Carter brothers, locked into mutual misery, were playing out life scripts that apparently provided as many satisfactions as discomforts. Just so are other siblings compelled to reaffirm their identities in contrast to each other: one playing the part of a reprobate who can do what he or she wants; the other, a Sunday-school teacher who can reach for ever-higher levels of dignity and righteousness. The actions of each reaffirm the identity of the other.° Such a relationship bears some of the classic and tragic features of the unhappy relationships between disturbed siblings and their well-functioning brothers and sisters, as we will observe in the next chapter.

° There are, of course, limitations to this kind of second-hand analysis, for it relies entirely upon the limited and selective information about the Carters that was picked up by the national press corps. We present this discussion to the reader with caution. A full understanding of any family rests upon extensive information gathered about the lives and experiences of all family members. Nevertheless, we feel that our views on satisfactions in sibling conflict may cast light on these two brothers' relationship.

CHAPTER 9

The Embroiled Family: "Well" and "Disturbed" Siblings

> To pity the unhappy is not contrary to selfish desire; on the other hand, we are glad of the occasion to thus testify friendship, and attract to ourselves the reputation of tenderness, without giving anything.
>
> *Pascal*

MILLIONS of Americans—young, middle-aged, and elderly—are hospitalized each year for such diverse problems as alcoholism, depression, and psychosis, while others are arrested, jailed, or live out marginal existences on the fringe of society. Still other people are mentally retarded or become disabled later in life, and are so emotionally disturbed that they can never lead socially normal lives. Most of these people have brothers and sisters, yet the relationship between them has rarely been addressed by mental health professionals. This oversight is surprising because many people who enter the helping professions—doctors, psychotherapists, nurses, teachers—have helped as children with a sibling in serious difficulty. In this chapter we will note the special ways in which the identity of each sibling contributes to the establishment of another sibling's disturbed or well self-image, and answer such questions as: How, and to what degree, does one become involved in the life of a troubled sibling? What fears, sensitivities, and conflicts are typical among the so-called well brothers and sisters of disturbed individuals? Is their wellness more apparent than real? Do well siblings cause some of the problems of their less fortunate brothers and sisters? Do they ever have a positive influence?

Let us acknowledge at once that *well* and *disturbed* are entirely relative terms,° which we use to refer to functional differences between people. We attach three meanings to the term *disturbed sibling*. First, the sibling's difficulties have commanded unusual attention from the family for many years. Second, the sibling's difficulties are accorded more importance and seen as more serious by the family than are those of the well siblings. Third, a disturbed sibling, in contrast to his or her brothers and sisters, has required extraordinary services from medical doctors, mental health professionals and/or law-enforcement officers who have been brought into the picture because he or she cannot function at home or at work.

It is the central thesis of this chapter that a well sibling derives a distinct and satisfying subidentity from having a deviant brother or sister. The disturbance and inappropriate conduct of this sibling, although upsetting, provides ego satisfaction, because it forces the "normal" child to become competent and even superior in the eyes of the parents. *The disturbed sibling also derives a distinct identity, albeit an unhappy one, from the contrast with a well brother or sister.*

The parents play a crucial role in assigning these contrasting identities and richly reward the well sibling for acting well and for stabilizing the family. Parental arrangement of the sibling relationship determines whether the well sibling will be compassionate and involved, on the one hand, or critical, distant, and cold, on the other. Differences are reinforced and amplified over many years, so that two distinct and nonoverlapping personalities are formed. Children are mythologized as different and then actually drift miles apart: soon they cannot enter each other's distant worlds.

° There are many perspectives on what constitutes emotional disturbance or "abnormality"—moral, psychological, situational, or phenomenological. These issues are reviewed by such writers as David Rosenham (1973), Thomas Szasz (1963), Jay Haley (1969), Erving Goffman (1973), and Daniel Miller (1982). The clinical examples cited throughout this chapter are based on cases of serious and chronic emotional problems or physical illness. There is a great range of emotional and physical problems. We believe that our examples are relevant to those "mid-range" difficulties involving neurosis, milder illnesses, minimal retardation, and brain damage; but further investigation of these "mid-range" sibling difficulties is needed.

Well siblings must balance two divergent identifications: identification with the parent and identification with the disturbed sibling. No well sibling can be neutral, since genuine emotional neutrality is impossible in family relationships. The result of this struggle between split attachments, mixed identifications, and divided loyalties will be a choice in which the well sibling must side with someone. The well sibling often de-identifies with the disturbed sister or brother and manifests a complete allegiance to the parents. All of the well sibling's activities are in the service of protecting the parents' interest. Far more frequently seen in clinical practice are those siblings who act as family mediators, identifying both with the parents and with the failing sibling. These siblings witness the wounds that the parents and the disturbed brother or sister are inflicting on each other, and—in carrying the woes of the entire family on their broad shoulders—try to heal everyone. In the clinical examples in this chapter, we shall examine the struggle of the well sibling who tries to become a family therapist at home.

Three structural characteristics of a sibling's severe disturbance should be taken into account. The first is the age and developmental stage of the other, well siblings when the disturbance becomes manifest. The importance of the age and the stage of the well sibling has been established in several clinical investigations of children with physical illnesses, including: Thesi Bergman and Sidney Wolfe (1971) in a child orthopedic setting; Frances K. Grossman (1972), in the area of mental retardation; and Maria Carandang et al. (1979), who studied the impact of diabetic siblings upon their nondiabetic brothers and sisters. Some severe disturbances, such as autism, in a brother or a sister are a fact of life with which a well child must always cope. Other disturbances become manifest only in adolescence or in early adulthood. Younger children find it difficult to express their dismay with words. Older children can be more articulate and can understand what has happened if parents try to explain it. At each age a child will interpret disturbing sibling behavior according to his or her current developmental stage.

The second, and related, issue is the *rate of onset and chronicity* of the disturbed sibling's problems. Some problems come on without apparent warning, and a sibling changes almost overnight from being well to sick and then, relatively quickly—after a six-week hospitalization, say—resumes healthier functioning. This kind of disturbance allows more sympathy than does a chronic illness which pounds at the family for years, draining everyone's energy without relief. Far more prevalent are disturbances that have a slow rate of onset and last for years. Lacking a clear point of beginning, and seeming endless, few people can say, "At this

234

point in time my sibling became disturbed." This situation actually makes it more difficult for the sibling of an aberrant person to deal with the latter's mental problems. There is *no* clear cause, no moment when the person is struck with a disease. The awareness of a good relationship turning bad ferments gradually, as the family grows ever more miserable. Disturbance does not appear to be a *thing* that one can combat, or a *force* that can be named and that one can "cope with." Months and years go by, and members of the family slowly come to realize that the different child is not just different, not just difficult, but is deviant. If the disturbance lasts many years, hopelessness, pessimism, and cynicism can paralyze the sibling relationship.

Finally, the *degree of embarrassment or stigma* resulting from the way the disturbing sibling broadcasts misery, affects the willingness of a well brother or sister to help out. Parents have little choice even when their child has sorely embarrassed them, but siblings have a range of choices. It is easier to extend oneself to a sibling who is depressed than to one whose florid psychotic break is expressed by winding up completely nude in front of a church on Main Street, trying to crawl into the cradle of the infant Jesus in a nativity scene. Guilt by association depends on whether the family perceives the sibling's behavior as socially disgusting or socially acceptable.

How Parents Arrange Relationships

Parents define their children's roles and draw up a blueprint for relations between disturbed and well children early in these children's lives. In the following example, we will see how a mother groomed her younger daughter as a loving helpmate for a retarded son while, at the same time, assigning her older daughter a distant and rejecting relationship with him.

Denise and Her Retarded Brother. Denise was the second of four children born to a physicist father and a housewife who later became an educator. Denise's older brother, Andy, had already married, leaving Denise the oldest of the remaining children. Henry, her other brother, was nineteen; and there was a sister, Elaine, seventeen. Henry had enraged Denise ever since she could remember. A year and a half younger than Denise, Henry was handsome and, in family photographs, looked strikingly like her—a phenotype that covered their profound difference. For Henry's retardation was much more extreme than his good looks indicated; Denise's IQ was sixty points higher. Henry attended a special school for the handicapped in a nearby community; but it was clear that he could never fully care for himself. He was easily disoriented if anyone in the family changed a routine, came home late, or asked him to adjust. Many of his expressions were droll, silly, or inept, and he kept making mistakes—such as forgetting to turn off the burners on the stove.

From the time Denise was able to talk, she had avoided and ignored her retarded brother, and later bitterly rejected him. She viewed him as a spoiled brat whose abilities had never been properly developed. She freely admitted that there were many moments when she had wanted to kill him. Even at twenty-one, her approach to Henry was curt and condescending. Denise's intolerance stood in jarring contrast to her sister Elaine's sweetness, patience, and devotion. For Elaine, Henry was a friend, a person she could love, a mind to be developed. Elaine was proud of her brother where Denise might be ashamed; she was gentle where Denise was irritable.

How had these two daughters come to synchronize solicitous "goodness" and unconcerned "badness" in dealing with their handsome, defective brother? When we asked their mother to remember their growing up, she supplied a narrative with the easy manner of a person who knows the unvarying roles and fixed identities that her children have played a thousand times on her family's stage. She first revealed how her own sibling experience drew her close to Elaine, the caregiver, and made her pull away from Denise, the unhelpful child. The mother had enjoyed a fond relationship with both her brother and her sister. Their growing up was permeated by loyal rather than rivalrous themes. Thus, when Elaine seemed warmly drawn to the damaged baby, and Denise rejected him, the mother was inclined to promote the quality in Elaine that she had cherished in her own sibling relationships. Disappointed and angry when Denise rejected Henry, the mother began to view Denise as "inhumanly cruel." This thought became a prediction and, eventually, a fixed part of Denise's relationship with Henry. After all, the mother had never seen siblings be cruel, and a daughter of hers must never do what she, herself, had never done!

From the start, the mother had observed differences in each daughter's reactions to Henry;

> Each girl had a different reaction to Henry. Denise was never interested in him, even when he was born, and she was only eighteen months older than he was. *All* of her focus was on brother Andy, who was

three years older than *she* was. She just *wanted* to be with him all the time, she wanted to emulate him. If he went out to play, she wanted to go out and play. She tagged after him everywhere. Henry was a passive baby, slept a great deal, and she wasn't interested in him. She wanted to be with Andy, to do what the big kids were doing, and to push ahead.

The mother, fearing that Henry would interfere with the budding relationship between Andy and Denise, kept Henry separate and thus relieved Denise of responsibility for her embarrassingly overactive little brother. On the other hand, Elaine seemed to have an affinity for Henry. By the time Denise was in first grade, the mother found herself alone at home with helpful little Elaine and wild, destructive Henry. When asked about this time, the mother replied:

> By the time Henry was six, we had a diagnosis, and by this time Elaine was three. Rather than putting her in nursery school she went every day with us to the cerebral palsy clinic, which lasted all morning. She was smaller, so she was easy to take along. She still says the first years of her life she grew up in that cerebral palsy center, tagging around with me and Henry.
>
> Elaine had accepted Henry from the first, almost as if she was born knowing somehow she was going to take care of him. We used to joke that Elaine was born with an umbilical cord attached to Henry. They were absolutely inseparable, so that it was quite a trauma for both of them when she was thirteen and he was sixteen, and we had to tell him that he couldn't go off to be with her and her friends.

Elaine's earliest memories were of Henry, of comforting him. As a younger child, she grew up in helping centers, seeing help given to this boy whom her older sister ignored. Giving help to Henry became Elaine's second nature.

The powerful parent helped determine these two very different ways in which her daughters related to their troubled retarded brother. Even after the mother's influence waned, Denise and Elaine continued to play their sibling roles, selecting vastly different college experiences. Denise pursued a major in English at a liberal arts university and dreamed of a brilliant career, while Elaine attended a vocational college to pursue a mission she had had since early childhood—to become a special education teacher of retarded, emotionally disturbed youngsters.

The Well Sibling's Role

The decisions whether and how to be involved with a disturbed sibling depend on the extent to which the well one identifies with the parents or with the sibling. The following cases will illustrate how identification with a sibling must be weighed against competing loyalties to the parents.

In the next two examples we will see how two young men, desperately seeking to protect their parents and a disturbed sibling, tried to buffer the extreme tensions within their respective families, and became, in the process, competent.

Loyal to the Parents: Patrick. For years Patrick had shepherded his older sister, Annie, to psychiatrists' offices or bailed her out of harrowing close calls when her drug habit indebted her to unsavory men who wanted to cut her face or break her hands if she didn't pay up. Now, at forty-eight, she had bounced from a hospital to a shelter for indigent and delinquent women. She had lost what once had been a genuine beauty; over the years she had become dumpy, lusterless and rundown. Now she pleaded again with Patrick, her brother, to pull her out of the mire. Burdened with his own responsibilities to his wife and newborn son, Patrick was exhausted and sick at heart after spending a depressing weekend with Annie. And, again, she was having a devastating effect on their parents, who implored him (for the thousandth time) to rescue the black-sheep older sister. "Nobody," his mother had reminded him, "can talk to Annie the way you can."

He sat at his typewriter and pounded out a letter with such fury that his hands shook.

> Dear Annie:
>
> I have finally decided to tell you how I am feeling about you. I owe it to you. And I must do it for myself.
>
> I don't *ever* want to see you the way you were last weekend. Read that last sentence again, because I truly mean it! I refuse to be a witness to your self-destruction, and I refuse any longer to collude with you. You are an addict again, and therefore no one can be of help to you. I see no evidence that you are trying to help yourself, and things are going from bad to worse. My help and support have obviously done you no good. You continue to lie to me, to use me and punish me and other members of this family.
>
> Your behavior is so outrageous that I wouldn't have you in my house for twenty-four hours the way you are now. I don't know why the folks put up with it. You seem hell-bent on trying to destroy everyone close to you. Do you *like* dragging people down with you?
>
> We don't know how much time Mother and Dad have left; but it's about time they were free of the burdens of their children so they can have some fun

and make their earthly peace with each other and with God. Don't continue to make them part of *your* self-destruction! Or me either!

Everyone in this family has suffered a lot for you, out of caring and love and a desire to help. But no one's help will do any good until you want help.

Start by getting out of that house. Build your own life! If you did it in prison, you can do it from a rest home. *Work* at building up your injured right leg. Go to doctors who can really help you, rather than just feed you drugs to support your habit. Read. Develop some interests. All you do now is eat, sleep, watch TV, take medicine, and fall a lot.

Can't you see what you're doing, or don't you care? Well, I care! I care for you, for me, for Mother and Dad. When you can prove that you have chosen to live rather than die—then, and then only will I be of whatever help I can be. Until then, I wish you'd forget you ever knew me.

If this letter sounds harsh and uncaring to you, read it again. There's a lot more love in it than I think you realize.

I wish you the best of luck in the difficult days ahead. But it will take much more than luck! The choice is yours as to what the days ahead will bring.

Love,
Patrick

He reread and mailed the letter, surprised, relieved, and even pleased that he had finally discharged feelings he had harbored for twenty years. But it was too late. He received a doctor's phone call the next day: Annie had been found dead of an overdose of sleeping pills.

Patrick, long-suffering soul, had acted as his parents envoy to his sister for twenty-five years. Like a seasoned career service diplomat, he had calmed his parents, imploring his sister to change, asking for understanding and reason from all of them. Letters of comfort from Patrick to his parents filled his mother's drawer: many were eloquent; others soothed; while other notes tried to distract the mother from her worry about Annie by calling attention to his own successes. Until the day of his break with Annie, he had tried to be the good guy who could pick up the pieces after a family explosion. This was an ancient role, performed without thinking: he cared for everyone, especially for his parents. For him caring and mediating was a natural, reflexive, automatic way to be. He had done this as long as he could remember:

PATRICK: My role in the family was sort of to keep everything light. I can remember Annie and my mother yelling at each other and a very unhappy time for me. And I remember feeling sorry for Annie that she was sick and she had a number of operations—but basically I think I took my folks side to a great extent.

I was trying very hard to keep both sides afloat. But I really got to know my sister as a sick person.

239

THERAPIST: Was there any kind of a boost for you from playing this part?

PATRICK: Absolutely! There were times I can remember my mother saying to me? "You have a way with Annie."

They would encourage me to go and find out Annie's feelings about something—or "Why don't you take Annie's dinner up . . . she'd like to see you." I can remember her saying at times, "Oh, I'm glad you came rather than mother." I can remember my mother saying things to my aunts and uncles—"I don't know what I'd do without Patrick."

In fact, there were periods of time, in fact years of my life, when I used to say that—well, my sister's illness is unfortunate for her, but it has been fortunate for me—in terms of giving me a very special place in the family. And also, when she was in the hospital I would be on my own a great deal more. And I also saw that as a fortunate accident.

THERAPIST: Because your parents would be visiting?

PATRICK: Yeah, I would be on my own a lot and allowed to have a lot more independence than either my brother or sister had. I grew up pretty fast in some ways.

Siblings like Patrick may feel simultaneously sorry for and angry at the parents *and* at the disturbed sibling. But the determining factor is their deep feeling for their parents. They try for approval as they position themselves between the parents and the disturbed sibling, and valiantly try to save the parents. The payoffs can take many forms, including increased respect from parents for being such a "good child" and heightened independence because parents' energies and attentions are directed toward the sick brother or sister.

The liberating effects of the "well" role are also shown in the leadership that the mediator sibling can assume in relations with other siblings in the family. Sometimes others defer to the involved go-between child. Patrick gained status with his eldest brother (eleven years his senior), who was relieved that his kid brother was being such a helpful force in the family and thereby giving him, the eldest, more leeway to leave effectively. A low status in the family hierarchy can make a sibling eager for any opportunity to prove his or her importance and usefulness.

Patrick enacted this role for many years. Only when the father became terminally ill did this son finally abandon his role as family mediator. The feeling that Annie had failed the family, making his parents' lives miserable, was now framed in the context of "so little time." Patrick, more somber as he faced middle age, no longer needed to help Annie to prove his own importance. Now that he was being robbed of a relationship with his father, he realized more painfully than ever that he had never received anything from his sister. He consciously blamed her for having ruined their father's life and their parents' opportunities for happiness.

But there is more to this story. The erosion of Patrick's commitment to his sister was an inevitable result of the fact that he had never identified with her in any positive sense. They were seven years apart in age; there was the gender difference; in addition, their early years together were not enlivened by close identification, access, or play. She had never been his caretaker nor had she been a person to whom he looked up in any way. The sense, but not the substance, of bonding between them had never developed. Patrick was serving a family role, one that affected him deeply; but he was a loyal brother only in that his devotion to Annie was a way of expressing loyalty and affection toward his parents. His closeness and responsibility, without deep attachment or identification, had no momentum of its own and, for its continuance, depended upon his parents' and older brother's encouragement. Now depressed and exhausted, he could no longer shoulder his self-proclaimed role of his sister's helper and angrily threw her over; his dying father dominated his attention. When Annie died, he grieved bitterly but briefly, relieved by her exit.

Divided Loyalties: Jack. A person who identifies both with a disturbed sibling and with their parents, has conflicting loyalties. Unable to detach themselves from the parents, siblings like these sail a careful, nervous course between the twin whirlpools of the parents' need for support and the disturbed sister or brother's hunger for friendship.

Jack and Martin were the third and fourth, respectively, of five children. Their father's motto, daily underlined for four of the children, was "You've got to help Martin, he's needy." In mid-adolescence, Jack realized that there was one chief way he could make it in this family, and that was to be recognized as the helper to this brother. Yet he also enjoyed Martin, played sports with him, and used him as a sounding board for his own struggles. Martin admired his older brother, Jack, and preferred his company.

Martin was always the problem child in this upper middle class family. For years he had been at loggerheads with the blustering but weak father, an old man who made enormous and irrational demands upon him. Martin's underachievement, hostility, and drug abuse in high school was the behavior of a troubled boy trying to tell his father to back off. Jack had long ago fallen into the rigid role of overinvolved and helpful son, shuttling diplomatically between his brother and his parents. Sensing his father's apprehension about his brother Martin, two years younger, he learned early that Martin never seemed to be making it in their father's eyes, and felt sorry for him.

In Martin's freshman year of college, he suffered his first psychotic episode. Jack temporarily kept the news from the parents and took on the lion's share of responsibility. He rallied the eldest siblings to have Martin, heavily sedated, transferred from the college infirmary to a private psychiatric institute near the family home. Jack was the one who said that money was no obstacle: "Martin has to have the best of care." Throughout this terrible time Jack was exhausted, drained, and depressed, as he had had to take a lot of time away from his new job. In contrast to his brother's ferocious outbursts, Jack appeared competent, helpful, and remarkably calm.

The following excerpts are taken from a joint interview after Martin had been released from the hospital, and Jack himself had decided to enter psychotherapy. Note how Jack's identity, like Patrick's, became clarified and subtly benefited from his having involved himself in his sibling's difficulties. The identities of the two brothers, well and disturbed, seem now to be firmly fixed:

THERAPIST: Jack, how do you explain this role you've had with Martin, kind of being his therapist, and mediating between him and your other brothers and sisters, and your parents?

JACK: Everyone in our family felt there was always something wrong with Martin—it was like "Jack, you've got to help him." I guess it's a role I chose for myself. You see, I never had a position in the family. I felt I had to carve something out for myself. And that's what I did.

THERAPIST: You mean, you wouldn't have been significant in this family if you hadn't played such a strong guy trying to help Martin with his problems?

JACK: Sure. My older brother was always "Mr. Cool, Mr. Status," just because he *was* the oldest. Then there was my sister, six years older than me—she was favored because she was a girl and had tons of status, which I couldn't stand. I was in the middle, and I wanted a lot. I wanted something. I wanted approval. I wanted to be a member somehow, but I didn't feel I counted for very much.

[*To Martin*] I was even your social worker back in school! Wanting to make sure that you were okay. I wanted to get you into Little League baseball, running, anything that would help you solve your problems. . . . Whatever it was, I was always trying to make Martin fit in some place.

The Embroiled Family

For all its benefits, this rigid role demanded that the older brother be on the alert whenever his brother got into trouble. Yet Jack would not voice to anyone that he felt Martin to be a burden. He, Jack, was, after all, healthy, responsible, and well! To complain of Martin might undermine the entire structure of his identity.

Martin came to expect that Jack would be called whenever he, Martin, was in trouble, and he appreciated Jack's friendship. He found Jack's concern more palatable and less judgmental than his parents', whose response was worry and overindulgence on the mother's part, bullying and bellowing on the father's. But by his second hospitalization, Martin had begun to resent his older brother's incessant and compulsive help. For Martin, this help carried a condescending and humiliating message: namely, that he was a pitiful person who could never fend for himself. He told us: "People keep trying to take care of me and protect me. That's assuming I'm weak. And maybe I'm *not* so weak! That really gets me angry! Because I don't know how, in this family, to say I'M STRONG!" Significantly, Martin was eventually diagnosed as manic-depressive. During his manic period, he had visions of being the strongest man in the world, a person who needed no one's help, especially not that of his brother Jack!

Martin received an unusual chance to show his strength for the first time when, in a dramatic reversal of roles, Jack, who had been experiencing severe pressure from his new marriage and conflict with his work supervisor, collapsed with signs of acute anxiety and depression. We illustrate from an interview obtained six weeks after Jack first experienced his confusion. Here, in contrast to previous interviews with these brothers, where Martin was the identified patient, Jack was now submissive, tearful, his facial expression grim, his body movements jerky and tense. In previous meetings, Martin was the focus as the impaired sibling, and Jack had been the crisp, intelligent, forthright older brother. Now their lives seemed more equal, and Martin seemed more creative, more direct, not at all manic or depressed, and he held his body erect, in contrast with his fallen brother's slouch. One would hardly have known that Martin was the brother with the multiyear history of serious psychiatric difficulty and hospitalization. Now Jack was the one who cried frequently, sometimes seemed out of touch; while Martin was articulate, on target, open, in touch, *and* the supportive, helpful one whose voice communicated both warmth and support to his brother. For the first time in their lives, Martin could reciprocate; and the opportunity to be strong appeared, temporarily, to remove him from his role of "weaker, crazy, younger brother." The fixed and rigid "well" and "disturbed" role assignments had flipped completely, as Martin joined the therapist in helping his brother.

We begin with the part of the interview where Jack described his own collapse. Many of his symptoms were similar to those that brother Martin had displayed during his last hospitalization.

JACK: I had a hard time sleeping. And I was wondering who I could talk to. I was talking to my wife incessantly—nonstop. I was really high. Just *high*. I felt my head was going to float off into the trees some place and never come back, and I was thinking and thinking. I had been in touch with Martin, and he had been telling me how our parents had been on his case again and he couldn't stand them. And *then* I started thinking: Wow! Martin's going to go crazy *with* me. It's going to be great, we'll both go crazy. I had never thought of that before! I'll call him up, and we'll lose our minds!

THERAPIST: So you called Martin?

JACK: I think so.

MARTIN: You called me up, and you said, "Marty," and then you burst into tears.

JACK: That's right, I did.

MARTIN: And I just said, "Hey, man, take it easy, take it easy."

JACK: [*Begins to weep, laughs, relieved, reliving the moment, reaches for a glass of water*]

MARTIN: [*Moved*] Oh, Jack . . . I just wished I could have been there at the moment. It was so frustrating for me to be just a voice, unable to make contact, to not hug you.

THERAPIST: What feelings did you have, Martin, with your brother calling you, telling you, "I'm going crazy."

MARTIN: I just think it was something like, wow, I can help this guy! I was in a position . . . I knew I could help. I felt VERY STRONG! [*Again, as in the earlier interviews, makes fists*]

THERAPIST: Did you feel his strength?

JACK: He was like an oak tree.

It was the first time I had experienced him like that. I had respected Marty for being the only one in the family to be outspoken to Dad and for having the balls to be different, but I had never seen the other side of him, I guess. Jeez, it was an emotional night!

MARTIN: You called me a second time, and I suggested, "Jack, do you want me to be there?" You said, "Yes," and BOOM, I was there.

THERAPIST: [*To Jack*] What was your reaction when he walked in?

JACK: It was great! He knew *everything*. He even knew how worried my wife was and that he shouldn't upset her. He knew how to talk to me—it was real natural.

MARTIN: [*Proudly*] I guess I sort of molded myself to the situation.

Although he had been assigned the role of guardian and family mediator, Jack was eventually able to shed the rigid lockstep of being too normal. This allowed his brother Martin to realize briefly that his well brother could fail, and he could at last be the strong one in the relationship. In contrast to Patrick, Jack's loyalties were split. He was a more genuine help to his brother and was eventually able to take as well as to give, because early in their lives they had empathized and identified with each other. Jack and Martin's definition of their brotherhood was changed forever by this natural crisis, one that corrected the fixed, frozen images of the mythic strong one caring for the fantasied weak one. But Jack and Martin were now on new ground, uncertain soil they had never tilled before. They were replacing the fixed certainty of a "well-sick" relationship, where the well one had been burdened but celebrated by the family, and the disturbed one had been helped but humiliated by having to receive the ministrations of the appointed go-between sibling. The brothers had found a new and untested kind of equality and respect and the opportunity for a positive dialectical relationship. Jack was still receiving covert messages from his parents to "look after Martin" and found it difficult to resist slipping back into the old entitled pattern. By the end of the interview, now that identities and roles were being shed, uncertainty prevailed:

THERAPIST: Jack, what's the chance you can get out of the social worker role with Marty?

JACK: I really don't know. It's something that I *want* to do, but I'll have to reprogram myself.

MARTIN: Yeah. You say you're finished being my director, and then you don't follow through with it! [*Skeptical, angry*]

JACK: There's a lot I'm realizing I don't understand about you, Martin.

Each man had benefited from the disturbance of the other in the family economy of rewards and recognitions. Could they now relate as equals, each being strong *and* weak, neither having to play upon his sibling's weakness to boost his own self-esteem?

The life stories of Patrick and Jack are parallel in that both acted as go-betweens, trying to calm disturbances in both sibling and parent. Both Patrick's and Jack's lives were burdened because of their mediating roles as resident family therapists; but each had a distinct and separate identity, a piece of turf that was all his own. But there are differences also. Patrick's identification with his sister was, at best, negative and rigidly polarized; his involvement with her hinged on his emotional connection with his mother and father. Jack and Martin, however, had had enormous access to one another as boys, shared angry feelings about their father's inadequacies, and had a positive and partial identification with one another. When identification between siblings is partial and positive, it also has the greatest potential for flexibility and change. Thus, Jack's and Martin's roles could be reversed.

What about siblings who are even more deeply attached to their siblings? As we shall see in the next example, when parents have allowed enmeshment to occur, the disturbed sibling's demands interfere with other's own chances to grow up.

Forever Enmeshed: Christine and Dominique. Christine's relationship to her sister Dominique, eighteen months older and overtly disturbed, illustrates how, for twenty-five years, their lives had been entangled and had thus interfered with Christine's development as a separate person.

Their parents, simple, hard-working immigrants, had always relied upon and used Christine as their ego, their agent, the one to deal with Dominique when she acted peculiar: they set few limits on their children's mutual involvement. Dominique soon came to expect that Christine would rescue her from disaster.

To outsiders, theirs was a relatively amicable, close childhood, and they were one another's constant companion and favorite playmate. But in actuality, fusion was being encouraged. They slept in the same bed until they were teen-agers, and were treated by their parents as equal in age and *expected* to keep each other occupied. The experiences of the two sisters were not differentiated. Excessive merging and mirroring was occurring between these siblings whose parents were emotionally unavailable and physically exhausted. Slowly Christine began to notice that she was different from her sister. Increasingly Dominique was mean and aggressive to Christine, and the latter could not understand why. Her overlapping identification and blurred relationship with her sister was being replaced by apprehension, anxiety, and a wish to stay safely away from her.

In most children's eyes, the emergence of emotional problems in any member of a family is not a sudden event:

CHRISTINE: I guess it was in the middle period of our growing up, ten or eleven, that my aggravation and disillusionment with her as a good person began. I decided that she had a lot of traits I didn't like. Until then I don't remember anything I didn't like about her. I was getting the responsibility that she wasn't following through with. If my mother said she should take the money to the electric company, she'd forget or mess up. I realized she wasn't responsible, so I would eventually do it. My parents would ask me.

She did many aggravating things too. In sixth grade it was a major catastrophe in school for me—she'd take the clothes I'd pressed and wear them [*speaking angrily*].

Once she reached adolescence, the momentum of the change in Dominique accelerated. Rather than being a constructive trailblazer for her sister, Dominique frightened their parents by her wild life style. The result was that the intimidated parents increased their restrictions on Christine, their younger daughter, who had never challenged them at all. Christine explained:

Whatever mistakes my parents made with my sister, they tried to make up with me. If she could do something at fourteen, I couldn't do it until sixteen. How could I complain—they loved me so much!

I'd say to my mother: "Why are you doing this to me? Why can't I go to the dance?" And she'd explain: "You see what happened to your sister? We won't let that happen to you."

The embroilment between Christine's mother and Dominique created a pained, worried home, where Christine witnessed both parents suffering with her sister. Christine could not also cause her parents pain. And it became clear to her that she would have to differentiate from Dominique: She would take the cues that Dominique offered and do the opposite.

Dominique countered by offering neither kindness to Christine nor interest in her welfare. Dominique's sexual activities became embarrassing, as she began drinking and hanging out with a wild crowd. Christine cringed as teachers and friends began to withdraw from her, wrongly assuming that she was like her sister. As Dominique's little sister, her own reputation was in danger of being tarnished; boys whispered that she, too, was "an easy lay." Finally Dominique was expelled from the school where they were students together in their junior and senior years. Christine heaved a sigh of relief; now she didn't have to fight the daily battle of proclaiming that she was a well person. Her life at the age of seventeen was already constricted as her sister sapped the energies of the entire family.

At the next stage of Christine's development, Dominique's conflict with the parents sent further tremors into the younger sister's life. Although Christine felt more secure about being different, she found it hard to break away from her suffering family. She compulsively tried to help Dominique, hating her at the same time for being demanding and acting crazy. Six months after Christine left home for college in the Midwest, far from the entanglement at home, Dominique, who had already gone to the West Coast, had the first of many psychotic breaks. She was arrested and forcibly restrained in an emergency unit of a hospital, screaming that she was suicidal and threatening to kill people. Christine, on returning home, found her parents secretive, anxious, and quietly on the verge of hysteria. Since the parents had always dealt with stress by denial and obfuscation, Christine was once again left to figure on her own the meanings of her sister's behavior:

> My parents were acting bizarre—nobody would tell me what my sister had done. She was in a local hospital at this time and allowed out for temporary visits, and she was talking strangely. I remember asking my mother, "What has she done? What is she going to do?"
>
> And I got answers like, "If we all stick together and be patient, God will help her to get over this and she'll be herself again."
>
> I changed my plans for the summer and stayed home instead of working far away at a beach resort. I gave up the summer to help and support. But it got worse!

Dominique was now embarked on a series of crises—hospitals, therapists, more hospitalizations. Christine was grateful to go back to school. The professionals had their hands full. What more could she do?

Her sister's emotional problems dominated most of Christine's waking moments and sometimes occupied her troubled sleep. She felt terrible that Dominique was in a hospital. When would this end? What had gone wrong? At night she would awaken with her sheets soaked with sweat after dreams of violently attacking and being attacked by Dominique. Maybe she had hurt Dominique; maybe Christine was the one who started Dominique on her downward spiral.

> CHRISTINE: The summer after Dominique's breakdown, I went back to college, trying to concen-

> trate, but I was worried. I didn't *care* what happened to her, but I was just furious that my mother and father had to suffer.
>
> THERAPIST: Did this interfere with your social development in college?
>
> CHRISTINE: It did. Dominique was getting *all* the benefits of my mother and father's full attention, and I was preoccupied with what was happening to her. And I was very aware that the support to make my own transition was *not* coming from my mother or my father.
>
> I then proceeded to get myself pregnant.
>
> THERAPIST: Your getting pregnant was a *reaction* to that?
>
> CHRISTINE: I took care of everybody except myself that year. And I *let* him get me pregnant. I knew this was no mate for me. But I married him right after I actually saw, for the first time, my sister having a full psychotic break. At that time, I felt my boyfriend was providing me with so much fun. He was alive! I didn't think of the problems I had at home or with Dominique when I was with him.

Although as an adult, she lived 150 miles away from the psychiatric hospital to which Dominique had been readmitted, Christine still conducted her life on the edge of her sister's crises. Christine had struggled to get free; but, obligated to her parents, she felt guilty about her sister's misfortune and was unable to set boundaries around her own life.

Thus, a well sibling's life is seriously affected by embroilment with a disturbed sibling. One may, like Denise, become a hard-boiled martinet in protest against the family's overinvolvement with a retarded sibling. Or, like Patrick and Christine, one may desperately try to rescue disturbed parents and drowning siblings and, in the attempt, enhance one's own identity, but also run the risk of great suffering and of having a sibling's problems interfere with one's life. Or, like Jack, one may come close to being engulfed in a sibling's problems but manage, as an adult, to reconstitute the childhood empathy the two siblings have shared. Siblings like Jack are, in our clinical experience, rare. Most commonly, the well sibling sees, in a disturbed brother's or sister's eyes, a frightening shadow of what he or she might have been or might still become, and flees.

Disturbing Mirrors of the Self

Well siblings, however, may not be so well off after all. When a clinician encounters any two siblings who are differentiated as "well" and "disturbed," the first diagnostic question should be: What kind of identification has prevailed in their relationship? Locating the relationship along the continuum from "fused" through "disowned" (see chapter 4 and table 4.1, p. 85) will indicate the degree to which the well sibling will be likely to share the plight of the disturbed brother or sister. Relatively undifferentiated siblings share symptoms, while siblings who have separated psychologically go their separate ways.

SYMPTOM CONTAGION

At the extremes of closeness, we find siblings whose emotional lives are fused and blurred as if they were one person. Many cases of *folie à deux*, or shared madness, involve siblings of the same sex whose fates are inextricably linked (Potash and Brunell 1973; Wikler 1980). The deep sharing of symptoms and thinking patterns in *folie à deux* is understandable in light of the ways in which high-access siblings, who have been neglected by parents, can deeply merge, mirror, and twin with one another.

Near-simultaneous breakdowns of identical twins have appeared periodically in the literature for years (for example, Benjamin 1957). In childhood, when close identification between children is especially strong, the spread, from one child to another, of behavior patterns, values, and psychopathology is observed by parents and psychotherapist alike. Sometimes the spread of symptoms is simultaneous: more frequently it is phased months or years apart, taking on identical or parallel forms. Symptomatic imitation can involve almost any behavior pattern seen in child guidance clinics, such as hyperactivity, stealing, lying, using drugs, school phobia, and suicidal patterns. It can also show itself in the deep-seated similarity of personalities.

In a case of two girls who developed anorexia within two years of one another (Shafi, Salguero, and Finch 1975), the elder stopped eating entirely near the anniversary of her younger sister's hospitalization. Two years earlier, her younger sister, then eight, had been diagnosed as anorectic. Through starving, both girls objected to their father's authoritarian style and their mother's disturbed way of handling closeness, and protested against a marriage that was not functioning well. As the elder girl's crisis unfolded, her younger sister, who was fast becoming an expert on anorexia, began to spend more time with her. Like the twins described in chapter 2, the girls told each other their most intimate concerns about their weight and their parents. Their shared experience with anorexia nervosa allowed them to form a subsystem that the parents found impenetrable.

The symptomatic identification between siblings also serves dramatically to change the unhealthy homeostasis of the family (Minuchin 1974). Siblings find strength in unity; and in some sibling groups, the "sick" child enlists or is joined by a closely identifying brother or sister in order to shout to their parents: "There's something terribly wrong in this family!"

When symptoms seem to spread from one child to another, many parents experience the sharp edge of failure, sensing they have lost control of those they love, that their children are in unison upsetting the delicate balance of family rules, values, and relationships. Siblings who join each other symptomatically, are powerfully testing the parents' abilities to lead and to nurture intelligently. These siblings are often deriving many satisfactions from each other, sharing adventures, defying the parents, daring to do the forbidden. But parents usually view one child as a "bad" influence, and believe that his or her contagious or insurrectionary potential should be contained, extinguished, neutralized, or quarantined. The parents may try to insulate their well child by sending him away to a residential school, by encouraging him to have a separate set of friends, or by assigning the children to separate activities or giving them separate bedrooms. Well children are far from innocent, as they often relish the bad behavior of their black-sheep siblings.

A Golden Boy Sets Up His Brother to Be a Black Sheep: Max and William. Max recalls the double life he led with his brother William, who was seventeen months older than he. As boys, Max and William roamed their neighborhood, little kids in the world of backyards and swing sets, and as a team they dominated other kids. When William was challenged, Max would aggressively join the battle, even at great risk to himself. But inside their home, their relationship marched to a different beat, since Max would never dare side with his brother against their mother, who had usually begun drinking scotch by the time they came home from school. Keeping silent as the mother flayed William, who taunted and defied her, Max was "good as gold," emphasizing at every opportunity his sanctimonious difference from his wicked brother. His silence became the backdrop for ugly, bruising conflicts between the mother and her scapegoat son. The father, a high-powered executive, was rarely at home and, when he was there, was usually demanding and hard on everyone.

In the sequence that follows, it appears that William expressed *for* Max, through defying their mother and delinquent activity, a spectrum of angry attitudes and feelings which Max, sweet fellow that he was, would have been terrified to admit. Max never tried to restrain his brother's angry behavior; his silence gave ample permission to William to conduct warfare on behalf of both of them.*

> MAX: The battle was usually between mother and William. Frequently it was precipitated by a fight that William and I would have. Then of course I would look like the "good person," and I'd get off pretty free, and he'd look like a villain. And he resented that like hell. Oh, I'm sure I set him up, lots.
>
> William was more vocal about our family, about our mother's being drunk much of the time. It was harder for me to admit it. So in comparison, in my mother's view, I became even more "the child who could make it." As William worsened, there was more and more pressure on me to succeed.
>
> And he would rebel almost every time that he was told he was not eating properly or his manners were terrible. What I would usually do was obey them. I'm sure that from the start he thought he was worthless. And I think at the same time he was seeing me as a person who was being loved and was obeying. That made him even more angry, I'm sure.

In high school Max, hiding behind his brother's hell-raising badness and his own avowed goodness, secretly reaped the benefits of being the brother of a delinquent. William, who was in public school, had joined a street gang; Max, coming home from an élite prep school for ten weeks in the summer, joined William, unbeknownst to their parents:

> MAX: It was a very fast, exciting life! We'd chase cars down back streets, throw cherry bombs out the window—just incredible stuff. So what I realized was that the only way I could keep any control was to hide in this boarding school.
>
> THERAPIST: Meanwhile, William is running around town tossing cherry bombs?
>
> MAX: [*Laughing heartily*] That's exactly it. What I set up was a pattern which allowed me some fun in the summer when I was home from school, run around with William and toss bombs, then turn right around and go to school, study hard, do the success story routine.

---

* Adelaide Johnson and S. A. Szurek (1952) established that parents can find vicarious gratification for their own forbidden desires in the acting out of the child. Parents give subtle permission for their children to break society's rules and standards. A similar process occurs between child, adolescent, and even adult siblings.

The Embroiled Family

Max led a double life with the assistance of his disturbed older brother who, as the only constant male figure, led him through this rite of passage and allowed him clandestinely to express his anger. When the brother was finally arrested and jailed, Max was concerned but distant, detached, almost clinical, trying to "have perspective" about the brother whose problems proved to Max that he, by contrast, had truly matured. From that point on, Max severed his close bond and really became the golden boy of this family by becoming a physician.

FEAR OF MENTAL ILLNESS

Every well sibling we have interviewed has, at one time or another, feared the possibility of becoming like a seriously disturbed brother or sister. Some siblings do not dwell on this fear, while others allow themselves to be haunted and dominated by the possibility that they could wind up in serious trouble or in a mental hospital. When an affected person announced that he or she has a disease that is known, or thought, to have genetic components—such as lupus, heart disease, cancer, or diabetes—the siblings may panic and make an unnecessary visit to the doctor's office. Even diseases that have no genetic tie can frighten a well sibling who has identified over a lifetime with a brother or a sister, and who may feel that they always have had and always will have a common fate.

Studies of the genetic aspects of major mental illnesses lend support to the notion that schizophrenia, manic-depressive psychosis, and alcoholism are more likely to appear in the siblings of individuals so diagnosed than in the general population. For example, the risk of being schizophrenic for unrelated people is 1 to 2 percent; while among brothers and sisters of schizophrenics, the risk is increased fourfold to between 6 and 8 percent (Rosenthal 1971). In well-replicated studies of the incidence of schizophrenia in twins, the concordance rates (that is, the chance that *both* will be schizophrenic) for identical twins are always three or four times higher for identical twins than for fraternal twins. The greater similarity in genetic inheritance, physical appearance, and "twinning" behavior, the higher the risk for similarity of health and illness. Other studies of non-ill but moderately troubled siblings frequently indicate a higher rate of mental health referrals than in unrelated pairs (see Gallagher and Cowen 1976). Whether siblings tend to become disturbed because of common genetic factors, having been subject to the same parental influences, *or* whether the siblings have so influenced one another that both become troubled, the fact remains that siblings of seriously disturbed individuals run a higher *statistical* risk of being disturbed themselves.

In a major study of the brothers and sisters of mentally retarded children, Frances K. Grossman (1972) observed that young adolescents are particularly preoccupied with the possibility of being like a damaged brother or sister. These early teens, as well as a college-age group of normal individuals, appeared most worried about being like a retarded sibling if the sibling was *not* severely retarded and if there were few physical differences between them. The more alike they looked, the more fearful was the well one of also being defective. Frightened siblings like these often try to flee the imagined contagion and will do anything to distinguish themselves as different. They often try to cultivate habits unlike those of a troubled sibling and, in adolescence, feel compelled to protect their "reputations" and try to convince their peers that they are *not* like the troubled sibling.

The age and the stage of vulnerability of the well child is particularly relevant when it comes to adopting the disturbed sibling's style. Children can be especially vulnerable depending upon the developmental task they are facing. An eleven-year-old girl had a brother who was retarded and had been institutionalized. She displayed learning disabilities of her own that accentuated her fear that she, too, was retarded. She lived out these fears in her play and everyday activity, acting "dumb," making unnecessary mistakes, and playing the part of maladroit "klutz." Convinced that she was tainted with her brother's retardation, she said, "I can't do things any more; I think my mind is broken" (Grossman 1972). Despite her sophisticated ability to talk with adults, this girl seemed determined to fail in life and did not respond well to psychotherapy. She was finally institutionalized, the victim of her total identification with her brother's defects. Such a total collapse as hers is rare. Most children and adolescents arm themselves with evidence that they are very, very different from their defective siblings, and point out to friends, family, but especially to themselves, that they are not vulnerable.

It sometimes takes a personal crisis, pushing an individual to the breaking point, to force the perception that one, too, could wind up like a failed sibling. A successful medical school professor who used work to avoid disturbing feelings and ideas, described to his therapist his sense of heightened vulnerability to emotional problems, as a result of his brother's collapse in a frenzy from overextending himself and the latter's psychiatric hospitalization. The professor, asked by his therapist if he had ever thought that he might break down, replied:

The Embroiled Family

Oh, wow, you bet! [*With great feeling and emphasis*] At times when I'm working a lot, extended out to the limit, mark papers, do research, teach, get home to my family and am beat and stretched out. I just feel as if I'm at the edge of not having any control. And then the thought of my brother would come to mind. I mean, I guess anyone with enough stress could crack, but it could be a predisposition. And I have my brother's tendency to extend myself without acceptable limits, beyond the point of realistic attainment. And then he went under—and to this day he's never been able to come back.

This is not to suggest that a sibling is the only influence that makes one fear being "extra vulnerable." The failure of a sibling almost always occurs in a context of parental conflict and failure—a context in which all the children are vulnerable. A sibling's collapse simply sets off the alarm bell. To be close in age to, and to share both a common history and genetic material with, one who has failed is to be a risk. One bright psychiatric resident whose brother had had several psychotic episodes, confessed:

I sure hope that I'm not too much like my brother because I wonder: Am I getting into this field because I really need help for myself? Am I going into this business because I'm crazy? Am I going to inflict a lot of my own garbage onto other people?

Parents who have had a seriously disturbed sibling, often fear that their own children will repeat the troubled lives that they, the parents, witnessed years before. A parent who is hurt by the actions of a child in ways that parallel or resemble those of a failed brother or sister, may fearfully (and irrationally) conclude that history is repeating itself, and anxiously watch the child for other disturbing similarities to that failed sibling. This anxiety can take constructive or destructive turns.

A mother began psychotherapy because she found herself violently angry and on the point of abusing her slightly hyperactive little boy. As therapy proceeded, one of the roots of her extreme sensitivity to his behavior was exposed. A caretaker sibling with *three* younger brothers (the same number of children she had), she had been saddled with the complete responsibility for their welfare. All three boys were difficult, ran over her like Mack trucks, and did not heed her discipline—a fact that she was blamed for repeatedly when her hard-working, overburdened parents came home to a house that had nearly been destroyed by their rambunctious sons. Her *eldest* brother, in particular, was seriously disturbed and "hyperactive," and set fires, and she frequently had to search the neighborhood for him during his escapades. It was little wonder, knowing this, that she had been extremely disappointed and apprehensive when her first child was a boy. She tried twice more for a girl, each time deeply disappointed as she was presented with the mixed blessing of another male infant. It was only the understanding of her traumas as a sibling, and insight into her parents' failure to monitor what her brothers had done to her, that allowed her to cope with the irrational rage she harbored toward her eldest son. After she came to understand the sibling roots of her attitude, she was able to take a more constructive and rational approach to her child.

PROJECTIVE IDENTIFICATION

One can have violent or fearful emotional reactions toward those others who *most* remind one of upsetting aspects of oneself. Projective identification is different from embarrassment; for were normal siblings simply embarrassed about a disturbed brother or sister, they would not want, with disgust and compulsion, to pull away from that sibling, nor would they rigidly fortify themselves behind arbitrary barriers of normalcy. After all, some children live out their early lives together, in a secret world, where each of their primitive identities are exposed, where neither child has to put on the restrained, social mask that they have to do for the mother or father. But as an adult one may be surrounded by the accouterments of normalcy and wish to deny a former affinity with a disturbed sibling who still may carry out the forbidden feelings and activities that in childhood and adolescence thrilled both siblings. The well sibling knows that the disturbed sibling realizes that he, the titular well one, was also once imperfect and possibly almost as crazy, dependent, weak, omnipotent, depressed, or sexually unlicensed as the disturbed one. But some well siblings must, through cleverness, deceit, or camouflage, keep wrapped in the mantle of wellness. Only the disturbed sibling is privy, as no one else can be, to a set of secrets about a "polished" brother or sister who has managed to stay out of difficulty. A disturbed sibling often harbors resentment and anger at being, in effect, abandoned by this former partner in pathology.

The well sibling who sees his or her old forbidden self writ large in brother or sister, unconsciously disowns that part of himself or herself which is still being mirrored by that sibling's behavior, and says in effect, "You are the bad person I once was, you are what I can't stand about me." The haughtiness, superiority, and condescension of the well sibling tip the clinician off to this process of projective identification in which, as James Framo says, "the close other can become a structural part of the

The Embroiled Family

self. Whenever two or more persons are in a close relationship they collusively carry psychic functions for one another" (1972, p. 289). This is especially true for relationships between previously closely entwined disturbed siblings and their brothers and sisters who have now become "golden" boys and girls.° Exposure to a disturbed sibling reminds the well one that he or she may not have traveled very far from home after all.

"She's Such a Needy Person": Art and Lois. At the beginning of our interview with Art, a lawyer known for his commitment to public causes, he described that in his private life he was a "taker" and "living on the pleasure principle." He had married a woman who until recently had waited on him hand and foot, and who subjugated her needs to his. He had so arranged his life that he had been favored by almost everybody who knew him, including his parents, who not only cherished him but gave him a sense of entitlement. Although these words were tossed off almost as an aside, they turned out to be the central feature—the self-professed quality of "being a taker"—upon which was based Art's repugnance for his sister Lois, younger by eighteen months. At thirty-five, he had images of Lois that still filled him with loathing and an inarticulate disgust—feelings that this sensitive, perceptive, professional man felt helpless to combat. The sister, a former alcoholic, and a consumer of psychotherapy for many years, had from birth sustained a serious lung disease which required extensive treatment and special handling. Now she had gone back to school and picked up an accounting degree, and had settled down with a mature woman friend with whom she appeared to have an affable, stable, and possibly homosexual relationship. Lois was beginning to grow and to grow up; but to Art, her presence, even the thought of her, remained unspeakably upsetting. He had felt this way about her when they were small children, when she wanted to tag after him and his friends; she had seemed to him then like a sickly, ugly albatross with whom he had been saddled. Her disease had made her into a child who was coddled by the parents, and for whom Art, as a five-year-old, was expected to show special understanding. When they were small children, she had spoiled his life by becoming the center of nervous conflict in the family.

ART: I can't stand to be around her without being overwhelmed [*cring-*

° Henry V. Dicks (1967) described the process, in married couples, by which each person lodges in the intimate other, forbidden, bad, or split-off parts of oneself—a process that satisfies both partners because for each, the intimate other is the perfect representation of an old, and therefore predictable, emotional relationship. If they knew each other intimately as children, siblings who engage in such trading of selves, can do so with even more power than can couples.

ing as if disgusted]. She's a very needy person, a *very* needy person, always taking.

Her problems are *so* manifest! She's so dependent! When her therapist goes on vacation, she almost commits suicide! Earlier it was the sense she always gave me that she was so helpless and dependent, that really enraged me. The expectation that she wouldn't have to do it herself. My reaction has always been—well, do it yourself. She has always expected that she wouldn't have to struggle with these issues.

INTERVIEWER: Were you free of dependency yourself?

ART: I guess not. I guess I had my own dependencies in those days, choosing to come home. I guess I didn't want to acknowledge that— maybe I dumped some of that onto her.

INTERVIEWER: Could you possibly see in what was going on in her, a bit of what was going on in yourself?

ART: Probably [*slowly, reluctantly, as if he had doubts*]. I know I had the wish that she'd go away and let me be alone and get my needs met. But every time I wanted to get MY NEEDS met, she was always popping in the door saying, "Don't forget about me, what about me, what about me?" [*disparagingly, angry, sarcastic*].

INTERVIEWER: It sounds as if being near her was awfully unpleasant.

ART: I've been able to change my relationship with every other person in this family except her! But I'm not sure it's something I *want* to change.

INTERVIEWER: Why?

ART: [*Tense, angry, avoiding*] I don't know. I'm not really sure I know. It's the regressiveness in her. Her immaturity bothers me. I want her to be *different*. I want her to be put together better.

INTERVIEWER: But didn't you say before that she'd gotten a lot out of her therapy?

ART: Yeah, probably. I mean, sure, *objectively*. TO A LOT OF PEO- PLE she *is* pretty together.

Despite the fact that Lois does nothing now to "engulf" him, he has to stay perpetually on guard with her, vigilantly keeping her at a safe distance, lest the forbidden parts of himself become too visibly mirrored.

The Price of Being Normal

Being normal and remaining normal in a family where emotional disturbance threatens to embroil everyone, requires one to cut off relationships and to establish rigid personal boundaries. The consequences of maintaining such rigid boundaries has been recognized in numerous clinical investigations. For example, C. F. Hoover and J. D. Franz (1972) studied thirty schizophrenic patients (adolescents and young adults) and fifty-seven of their nonschizophrenic siblings. The central finding: most well siblings retained their sanity only by keeping themselves out of the family orbit—in a "safe place" with secure boundaries. Those who became entangled with the sibling's interaction with the family, functioned poorly and developed personal difficulties. Hoover and Franz noted that it takes tremendous energy to *stay* free of the sucking force of a family that is involved with life-and-death conflicts. Many siblings had to erect *rigid* barriers and isolate themselves from the entire family. In some siblings this need for a firm boundary allowed them to function in jobs and marriages, but they appeared to the investigators to be rather drab people who had purchased their freedom "at the expense of greater depth of character and personality, a depth which derives from the ability to perceive . . . life's contradictory experiences."

In another study, the adolescent and young adult siblings of schizophrenics seemed to function well but appeared constricted emotionally, as if afraid to give anyone a glimpse of their insides—something that their psychotic brothers and sisters had no difficulty doing. Using art therapy productions and interviews as the medium for comparing the schizophrenic with his nonschizophrenic brother or sister, the researchers observed:

> We were untouched by the sibling. . . . Our inability to involve ourselves emotionally with these siblings had its counterpart within their families. These offspring seemed to be less involved with the family difficulties, more detached from the family's distress than their hospitalized brother or sister. Some of them who participated in family therapy sat in silence, albeit an intense and watchful one.　　　　　　　　　　　(Day and Kwiatkowska 1979, pp. 58–59)

In dissociating themselves from family conflict, the well siblings appeared conventional, appropriate at all times, but uninvolved, and, to an extent, unimaginative. It seemed to the investigators that the well siblings presented themselves as silhouettes that would not come to life, perhaps because of the risk of becoming involved, as had a schizophrenic sibling, in the family's crazy interaction.

As we have pointed out, aggressiveness is one natural way through which siblings communicate. But when one sibling is defective, or is *seen* as defective and needs special treatment by parents, the well child must learn to inhibit, to refrain from aggressive taunts and actions. To establish himself as "well," he must give up and suppress these vital angry parts of himself, or submerge or hide them, lest he further injure his vulnerable sibling. Further, the well sibling learns not to rock the parents' boat, not to roil already troubled waters. Inhibition of anger also means that other forms of spontaneity—such as kidding, humor, and "messing around"—get squelched. The relationship between disturbed and rigidly avoidant siblings is serious and drab and lacks playfulness.

A well woman in her thirties, whose older sister had recently undergone several psychiatric hospitalizations, bitterly remembered a childhood in which there was no room for *her* anger, since her disturbed sister had monopolized it:

> I couldn't stand for them to yell. My parents wouldn't be as hard on me if I did the same bad thing as my sister, so I found myself trying to take the blame for her. If Mom would find out that she screwed up and I was pretty sure she was going to get hit, I'd say that I did it, because I didn't want there to be screaming and punishment.
>
> INTERVIEWER: Who were you protecting?
>
> PATIENT: *Myself!* Because I couldn't stand this disharmony in the family, and my sister would balk at everything they wanted. I still can't stand it, and I'm thirty-two years old!
>
> I finally got angry and said to my sister, "Listen, this is my life! I'm not going to have you stop me!" And when I went out the kitchen door, I slammed it, and my mother yelled at me: "How *dare* you slam that door!" And I thought, Oh my god, I can't even slam the door but my sister can act like a nut and scream at the top of her voice. And my mother went upstairs to comfort her because I had raised my voice for the first time in my life.

Siblings like this woman often express a wish to be able to go crazy, to let out feelings, to become as violent and expressive as the disturbed sibling. They envy the license shown feelings, all the while wrapping themselves in the mantle of normality. When anger is suppressed and not discharged at the fragile sibling, the well sibling is left with the sense that he or she can never really level in an open aggressive way that might feel good and clear the air. To show aggression toward a damaged sibling is to defy the parents and to be a disloyal child. Thus aggression, in the context of the sibling's disability and special needs, is expressed and experienced, by the well sibling, as "unclean," as a "dirty something" to be discharged in secret when the parents are not looking. Rather than invigorating the relationship with the give-and-take of insults and punches, easily dished out and quickly forgotten, the well sibling must be wary of hostile impulses toward a sick brother or sister, or risk being charged with kicking the crippled and hurting the handicapped. The well sibling, being presumed to have many riches and advantages, is expected to show restraint, charity, kindness, and loyalty. Being a true-blue Boy Scout is, of course, impossible; and well siblings may vent their damned-up anger in sneaky and violent ways.

A successful businessman, for example, reminisced about growing up with a sister, two years younger, who had been born with a defective kidney. From their earliest days, he remembered her as vulnerable; when her bad kidney was removed, she cried out in pain, eliciting parental injunctions to her brother to "be careful not to hurt her." This brother went on:

> She was a pain in the ass, that's what I felt she was. She was coddled and all she would do was cry and, of course, I would be expected to be more responsible. She was never happy.
> I was secretly furious with her in so many ways. When we were left alone, I remember having punched her a number of times and being very ashamed of that. Then I'd be very concerned because she would turn black and blue very easily.
> She would develop hematomas. My evidence was left behind me. Then I'd whisper—"Don't tell Mom or Dad." Then she'd blackmail me.

EMOTIONAL CUT-OFF: "LET ME GET AWAY AND BUILD MY OWN LIFE"

As we have said, brothers and sisters are sensitive observers of each other's lives. Noting the pain and emotional carnage caused by a sister or a brother's bind with the parents, well siblings draw their own conclusions. The realization that "If it happens to my brother, it can happen to me," may spur the well child to make an exit from the family; and this child is allowed to escape because the parents are so involved with a troubled child. Many well siblings have left families where one child has a demonstrated psychosomatic illness, such as anorexia (Minuchin et al. 1978) or inflammatory bowel disease (McMahon et al. 1973), or where an adolescent or a young adult is being seriously disruptive.

Leaving the family and staying out of it by setting effective boundaries is a lifelong struggle for the siblings of profoundly disturbed individuals. For example, Roger had long wanted to cut himself off from his brother Gus, who was younger by thirteen months and was mentally ill. There were two other brothers—four and five years younger, respectively—one of whom was retarded (Down's syndrome). Roger described his feelings:

We hated that retarded brother. He was banging his head against the wall, he wasn't toilet-trained, we were teasing him. Life was one big crisis. One brother retarded, another with visual disturbances! I remember my mother begging me to take Gus to school. "You have to take him to school!" I refused. I was furious that I should have to take care of him.

It was like—the ship is sinking! Every man for himself! When he was sent away, it was a relief.

After completing medical school, Roger was still disturbed by his family's pressuring him to get reinvolved with Gus, who had by this time been a patient in several mental hospitals:

I decided to leave the country and study abroad, to flee this position of responsibility. I'm the only successful one of my generation. Therefore, it will fall on my shoulders to take the responsibility for my mentally retarded brother, the schizophrenic brother, and a mother who is depressed. One of my fantasies is to leave this whole kit and kaboodle behind, and they wouldn't even be able to call me on the phone. Christ! Keep away! I'm trying to build a successful life!

Roger went on to complete his training as a psychiatrist.

"Drawing the line" with a disturbed sibling can become particularly difficult in midlife as the parents age and weaken, and as that sibling turns to a well sibling, imploring: "Be my friend, get me out of here!" (Samuels and Chase 1979). For most people, it is impossible to do a job well and care for home, children, and spouse *and* for a chronically unpredictable, unstable sister or brother. Two sisters—the well one aged forty-five, the problematic one aged thirty-nine—discussed this difficulty with one another several weeks after the younger sister's husband had committed suicide. The younger sister had been hospitalized years before—an unhappy event that prompted this comment from the well sister:

OLDER SISTER: You came back from London and had a nervous breakdown. There was a hospital only ten or fifteen minutes from my house, and I definitely did not want you there. I was having a tough enough time just holding down my own life, and I felt it would create a dependence that I was not able to handle. So you ended up in another hospital, much farther away, which was better for everyone.

The Embroiled Family

You would have loved to live with us or near us and have me help you through that very hard time. I was *not* willing to do that!

YOUNGER SISTER: Yes, I would have liked very much to have lived in town, where you were.

OLDER SISTER: And I knew I couldn't handle that! It's like being in a whirlpool, or quicksand, you just back away.

The "ghost of insanity" can hang over even the most educated individual and can also affect the way in which spouses of well siblings form relationships with their mates. From married couples, clinicians elicit exchanges such as the following:

INTERVIEWER: So, what's it been like for you, being the wife in this situation?

WIFE: It's been really up and down. I wasn't at first very supportive, and I'd just say to my husband, you've got a crazy family, my family is much more normal. That's why we moved away for a couple of years, you know, to England. His brother was so crazy and the whole family kept trying to get us to rescue him.

I was also afraid that my husband would have a psychotic breakdown if [*turning to her husband*] they influenced you enough.

HUSBAND: [*Completely amazed, hearing this for the first time in the eight years they had known one another*] You've *never* said that to me before!

WIFE: Your family's problems were too close for me to say it to you. [*Reminding her husband, conciliatory, afraid she has wounded him*] We're both concerned about how schizophrenia can be genetic. It does bother me to think there is a heavy load of schizophrenia in your family, that it's *in* your brother. That places a burden on me to make our relationship very stable.

Another woman spoke of her troubled sister:

But how can you forget about someone who comes to every family get-together? Every family event—Thanksgiving, Christmas, Easter, birthdays were tense. It all revolved around: Is she well? Is she in the hospital? Will she freak out on Christmas Eve? She went absolutely bananas when I got married. And she went crazy when my daughter was born. The bigger the celebration, it seemed, the bigger the occasion, the worse she would behave.

It's very edgy now when she visits, my husband and children are on pins and needles. And that's the pattern. That's been it for the whole of our lives.

Even when these troubled people are not acting disturbed, they are frozen in an image of the way they *used* to be, of the way they *might* become. Often hurt by being excluded, they cannot understand why their brothers and sisters seem so cold, and why they are invited in a lukewarm manner to come "just for a few days at Christmas."

The Well Sibling's Sense of Responsibility

Many well siblings ask themselves, "By what right do I live a relatively normal life when my sibling suffers so much?" The Hiroshima survivors have never led full lives, as if expiating for the sin of breathing, loving, and living while their compatriots perished, and experienced what Robert J. Lifton (1967) has called survivor guilt. The survivor guilt of the well sibling takes a vastly different form and has a different texture because his sibling, while not actually dead physically, may be deteriorating emotionally or physically, with death likely to be imminent. And, unlike the Hiroshima survivor, the well sibling's wellness has, in many instances, been predicated upon and taken its energy from the disturbed sibling's continuing failures. The impaired sibling may be a sacrificial lamb—the focus for many of the parents' troubles that the well sibling might otherwise have shared.

As well siblings go off to seek their own fame and fortune, they appear to forget their brothers or sisters. The disturbed sibling feels let down and envies the well sibling's comparatively greater opportunities. One brother, who had been a drug-using, underachieving black sheep, remembered how he felt abandoned when his brother left home to attend a topnotch university:

I stood there at the airport, and I realized that I was the only one left in the house. Now I was the only one to blame. So, it was all on me then—left in that miserable house, knowing there was nobody else. Not that Dad ever smacked you, since I had been getting all the abuse anyway. When your plane went down the runway I saw my home base flying away. That's when I realized I was going to suffer for the next three years.

The Embroiled Family

Gustave Newman, after studying younger brothers of three schizophrenics, concluded:

> There was guilt over "letting" the older brother bear the brunt of the parents' demands. This guilt was expressed in their conception of the older brother as a sacrifice—a mine sapper or a blocking back which each felt as making him culpable for the brother's illness.
>
> Closer examination of the younger brother's experience of guilt permits the following condensed approximation. "Since I benefit by my brother's illness, I am responsible and guilty; since I see his illness and need for help, I am guilty within myself if I remain passive; and if I take action, I violate the family rules and am guilty." (1966, p. 151)

Newman continued:

> These younger brothers of schizophrenics chose a path of self-determination *with guilt* rather than choosing the pathological passivity of their older brother.

Guilt over one's advantages is not the only manifestation of the bad residue of such a sibling relationship. As we have discovered, the well sibling often neither likes nor respects, and has frequently resented and devalued, the disturbed sibling and considered him or her a fool; yet these feelings directly contradict the ideal social notions of brother-and-sister-hood. Furthermore, we are all taught that we should not entertain these invidious feelings about people who are "less fortunate than we are," in this egalitarian society where the underdog is supposed to be given more than a fair chance. This is a "catch-22," to be sure.

Guilt over angry *feelings* is often combined with guilt for hostile *actions* that may actually have harmed the weaker sibling and been instrumental in making that unhappy brother or sister slip a few steps farther into difficulty. Many people feel acutely guilty about having directly contributed to the problems of a brother or a sister.

Guilty Survivor, Guilty Rival: Roger and Gus. Roger, the psychiatrist we have already cited (pages 261–62), was mythologized by his family as "tough as nails," while his brother Gus was viewed as "very soft." Yet when they were boys, the soft brother, who later became chronically psychotic, was more attractive than Roger, who was jealous of him. Envious of his greater popularity with girls, Roger was particularly pained once to find his younger, but sexually more precocious, brother on the couch making love to a pretty girl—something that Roger did not yet have the courage to try. In other contests he could not stand the fact that Gus was soft, and that it was this very gentleness, softness, and helplessness that won him more attention from the girls in high school. Roger's bullying of his brother, which had gone on for years, was difficult for him to remember when the research interviews took place, and unusual blocking for someone who was a mental health professional and whose sibling was only thirteen months younger. Roger had taken advantage of his brother; in spite of knowing how easily hurt his brother was, he often pressed on every sensitive nerve:

ROGER: I remember my exploiting him in some ways—borrowing money that I never paid back.

INTERVIEWER: He wouldn't stand up to you—you could get away with it?

ROGER: Yes, and he never would press the issue. "Can I borrow some money from you?" "Sure." Then, my never paying him back and him going along with it—kinda allowing me to exploit him.

INTERVIEWER: You both shared the knowledge that you could steal and he wouldn't fight you.

ROGER: I can't remember. I can't remember. My memories of him aren't sharp like they should be. I think that I have gaps in empathy when it comes to him.

We had beds that faced one another, and we slept with our feet facing each other. And we would wake up with my kicking him, and then I would start a fight with him. That happened practically every morning during a certain phase. He would kick back and then I'd have good excuse to jump on him.

The rivalries of earlier childhood, now in the context of the disaster of the disturbed sibling's life, raised painful questions for Roger, who suspected that he had contributed to his brother's low self-esteem. What if he had been kinder? His trouble "remembering" protected him from acknowledging the full extent of his aggression and his guilt.

WORKING OFF THE GUILT: FAILED ATTEMPTS AT RESTITUTION

Some well brothers and sisters live their whole lives silent about their guilt, while others try to make reparations. One may be motivated to equalize the obvious inequities between oneself and a sibling, sporadically swooping into the sibling's life or trying, with an urgency bordering on desperation, to energize the professional healers into whose care the sibling has been entrusted. By getting involved in the health system, often angrily blaming the psychotherapist or the hospital for impotence and a failure to care, the well sibling tries to demonstrate good intentions. When Roger learned that his brother had to be hospitalized again, he thought:

> What hospital should he go to? Would our local hospital be good enough for him.? No! He can't go there, it's not fit for him? He's got to have the very best, even if we spend thousands on it. My professional standards are high, and my brother has got to have the best. It can't just be the local therapist. Send him to Carl Whitaker, to Virginia Satir, to Austen Riggs, Mayo, or Menninger!

Once family therapy had begun in the hospital, he eagerly participated. When his brother accused him of previously neglecting him and of being unkind, Roger felt relieved that now he could make restitution.

Another go-between, Jack (see pages 241–46), who had taken charge of his brother's treatment after a drug-induced psychotic episode, told of his own confusion and anger:

> What the hell *is* this? This is my brother, and he's locked up in a nut house! I couldn't stay out of it, and I finally went directly to his psychiatrist, and I said: "Look, doctor, my brother's going crazy, my family's going bananas! What *are* you going to do for us?"
> But the guy didn't do a fucking thing, not for me, not for my brother or my family. Nobody knew what to do or how to take any responsibility.

The frustration of these siblings who want to help, but cannot do so, was movingly articulated by one patient who, in exasperation, wrote the superintendent of a large hospital:

> To what extent do my brother and I have responsibility for our sister, or does responsibility rest with our parents who are elderly?
> I believe your hospital is guilty of a shameful and unforgivable act. Someone is accountable for the lack of concern, the neglect of doctors to inform us of progress or the lack of it. No one has kept us abreast of the use of drugs which she has been given over the years. Is this situation only one of thousands like it?
> Now that our sister is living at home, why have you no solutions to our dilemma? She obviously cannot be maintained at home. You cannot continue, can you, to expect that our parents can cope with a situation for which even qualified and trained professionals have so far

failed to find solutions. Is *this* the way you answer the needs of society? What insight or guidance can you give me so that I can do something more useful than to wring my hands. We are now talking about fourteen unsuccessful years of treatment. Our pleas for you to re-evaluate our sister have fallen on deaf ears. And we are angry!

RESCUING ONE'S SIBLING

One might wonder whether any siblings can effectively commit themselves to rescuing their sisters and brothers, and to improving their troubled lives. Does a well sibling ever form an alliance with a disturbed sibling? Does a well sibling ever see life from the disturbed sibling's point of view, rather than staying neutral, siding with the parents, or tepidly getting involved for a few hours? The answer is a *very* qualified Yes.

Alliances are most likely to occur when the sibling being rescued has a worthy cause, and when the problems of the distressed sibling do not carry a heavy stigma. Thus, there is rarely a rescue where the distressed sibling has been engaged repeatedly in behavior considered outrageous. When the sibling is considered dangerous, there might be a temporary rescue, but never one where the rescuer devotes months or years to a disturbed sibling. To be rescued and supported, the disturbed sibling must behave and contain his or her pathology within limits that may stress but must not stigmatize or embarrass the rescuer. The rescuer has a life to lead, and the rescued sibling must respect this or risk the loss of the newly caring sibling's support.

Even under the most ideal circumstances, a well sibling who has a partial, positive identification with a disturbed sibling, may be able to provide support for months, but not for years. The *partial* quality of the identification is crucial: if the siblings are too close, stress escalates; and if they are too distant, the welcome quickly wears out. The coalition between well and sick typically serves important needs of both. The strong sibling provides the weaker one with much-needed friendship and gains in the process a change to rework personal issues that he or she has left dangling by avoiding the parents.

"I'm Having Trouble Being a Mother": Julia and Melanie. Julia, older than Melanie by six years, grew up in a cold household with a depressed and immature mother and their bitter, sarcastic, suspicious father. A loveless home, expensive but unfurnished emotionally, it became a harsh and sterile setting for growing up. The parents' angry marriage set the tone for a home where parents and children were rarely touched or embraced.

The Embroiled Family

The father threw epithets at Julia as she became an adolescent; their relationship deteriorated to "hardly speaking" by the time she was fifteen.

Julia excelled in high school, finding the recognition among teachers and friends that she lacked at home. She vowed to go to college without a dime of her father's money; and by the time she finished her education, she was more than $15,000 in debt. Yet she was glad to be free. She broke contact with her parents: in fact, she knew that to contact them was to let herself re-enter a web of psychological hatred and misery that could destroy her. In her final two years of college, Julia began receiving distressed, panicky calls late at night from Melanie. Secretly phoning her sister, unbeknownst to her parents, Melanie told horrible stories of humiliating and untrue accusations her father was pointing at her. Hearing about her sister's suffering, Julia felt her own emotional wounds reopening, as though she and Melanie were one. The abuse increased; the phone calls to Julia continued. One day Melanie went to school with bruises on her back.

Julia became Melanie's only lifeline. A visit to a family therapist failed to prevent the next stage of the drama. Melanie was badly beaten and kicked down a flight of stairs. The therapist did not report child abuse; and Melanie, who felt utterly abandoned by the therapist's passivity in the face of brutality, turned even more desperately to her older sister. Julia took matters into her own hands, picked up her sister's belongings, and—over the parents' protests—removed her from their home. On the way out, Julia said, "You'll never lay a hand on Melanie again!"

Melanie moved to the town where Julia lived, in a different state. Julia mothered her, fed her, held her when she had nightmares of being beaten. Julia's health began to deteriorate, but she persisted and comforted her sister. At this point Julia, who was twenty-four and held a managerial position with a major corporation, enrolled Melanie in a preparatory school. On top of her $15,000 debt for her college loan, Julia committed part of her $18,000 current income and borrowed an additional $8,000 to pay for her sister's schooling. Julia visited Melanie every weekend. These encounters were a comfort to Melanie, but they left Julia feeling depleted and drained. Her efficiency at work suffered. Her social life came to a complete halt; her life suspended. Julia felt ill at ease with her new role as savior, part-time psychologist, and fellow sufferer. Uncertain whether to treat her sister as guest, patient, or boarder, she began to resent the needy girl's unstated insistence that she supply what their mother had failed to give them both. Melanie, uncertain of where her home really was, also generated confusion when she was there, sometimes offering to help, at other times lolling around the apartment while dust and dishes accumulated.

Finally, Julia consulted a psychotherapist about Melanie. "I love this kid," she declared, "but I'm having trouble being a mother." Saviors like Julia are sustained in their zealous efforts by their personal outrage against the injustice that has been inflicted on a sister or a brother. Lacking previous experience ministering to a damaged sibling, they sooner or later overtax themselves, and their own mental health begins to suffer.

The mental health system in America, despite its discovery of family psychotherapy during the last two decades, rarely addresses the needs and feelings of adult well siblings like Julia. It exacerbates their impotence and offers few constructive alternatives to their guilt-ridden attempts to care for their brothers and sisters. Since siblings are not considered vital influences on each other in adulthood, therapists often focus only on spouses or parents and ignore the well sibling's guilt and savage self-reproach.

Siblings like Julia, who go above and beyond the call of brotherhood and of sisterhood, are numerous, but rarely do therapists make use of their ability to provide a healing touch and simple kindnesses that can never be purchased from a professional. Well siblings can be allies for the therapist who realizes the power as well as the limits of the sibling bond, as we will discuss in chapter 11.

CHAPTER 10

Siblings as Survivors: Bonds beyond the Grave

There are two parties to the suffering
that death inflicts, and in the apportion-
ment of this suffering, the survivor takes
the brunt.

Edwin Shneidman (1973)

IT HAS BEEN SAID that death ends only a life: it does *not* end a relationship. This statement is especially true when a sibling dies in childhood, adolescence, or early adulthood—an untimely death whose unhealthy consequences can endure long after the last farewell at graveside. Sibling death can create what has been called "the senseless arithmetic of adding newly warped lives to the one already tragically ended" (Cain et al. 1964). The dead sibling's legacy can be a force for sickness and stagnation or, under beneficent circumstances, can serve as an inspiration for maturation and creativity.

In this chapter we will show that the loss of one sibling can be crucial for the personality development of another if the siblings' identities have been interwoven during their lifetimes. We will first examine how parents grieve for the dead child, how—by facing or evading their past relationship with the deceased—they provide a model for the survivor-children. A second, all-important force in sibling grief is the type of previous identification between the children: how did the survivor feel about a dead brother or sister in life?

Edwin Schneidman wrote that death can be "appropriate to the individual's time of life, to his style of life, to his situation in life" (1973). But, in the Western world, when a child dies we do not feel that the death is appropriate: we feel that the child has died before his or her time, that it is a tragedy. This attitude is a fairly recent historical development. While the death of a young person has never been easy for families, children were once not expected to live for long and had a high mortality rate.° One historian put it this way: "Childhood was simply an unimportant phase of which there was no need to keep any record. . . . It was thought that the little thing which had disappeared so soon in life was not worthy of remembrance. . . . One had several children in order to keep a few" (Ariès 1962, p. 38). Only in the last hundred years or so, as infant and childhood mortality have steeply declined, has the idea of death in childhood or adolescence become charged with emotion. In a world of antibiotics, miracle surgery, and average life expectancy exceeding seventy, today's siblings, along with other family members, are shocked when a brother or a sister dies, and lack any kind of preparation for becoming survivors. To the modern sibling, the early death of a brother or a sister has a more devastating impact than ever before because one is likely to have only a few siblings rather than many. In a two-child family, to lose a sibling makes one an only child. If one's identity is interlocked with only one sister or one brother, it will be dislocated by the loss of that sibling. With no other sibling available to continue the identity process, the survivor is truly bereft and has for a partner in the dialectical dance for self-definition only the dead sibling's ghost. As the reader will see, the dance is no pretty *pas de deux* but likely to be a *danse macabre*.

Parental Influence on the Grief of the Surviving Siblings

From the moment of a child's death, the parents have many decisions to make in connection with their living children. In what manner shall the

---

° In the late nineteenth century, as many as 200 out of 1,000 infants under the age of one year died from dysentery, pneumonia, measles, diphtheria, or whooping cough. In 1925, the figure fell to 75 infants out of 1,000 and, in 1976, to only 15 per 1,000 (Nelson et al. 1979). Among children aged five to fifteen, the death rate per 100,000 children declined from 264 in the year 1920 to 41 in the year 1970. Today deaths from appendicitis, tuberculosis, and rheumatic fever are virtually unheard of.

children be told of the death, and should the parents inform them together? Should the children be asked to attend the funeral, or should it be up
to each of them to choose? How much information should they be given
about the death? How much detail, if the details are horrible? If there is a
wake, should the children go? And what will be the effects of seeing a
brother or a sister lying in an open casket? These are only the initial
decisions for parents. As weeks and years go by, the parents will determine—by their conduct, by what they do and say and by actions *not*
taken, words left unsaid, tears unshed—how their surviving children remember the dead child. Remembrances made, remembrances not made
are all taken into account by the surviving children. The family stares at
countless cruel reminders of an ended hope. Should they display the dead
son's picture in the living room or enshrine it in a room nobody uses?
Should the dead daughter's toys and bike and clothes be discarded, or
should they be freely used and worn as hand-me-downs? The fatality of
the sibling casts a shadow across the parents' wounded forms and thence
upon the children.

The situation of a young person's death is loaded with opportunities for
the parents to fail to assist their surviving children in healthy mourning.
The parents have many tasks. They must grieve and yet maintain a marriage; they must explain their grief to the minister or rabbi and well-
intentioned friends. They must buffer the loss for their *own* parents who
suffer the special bereavement of grandparents. They must get back to
jobs where work is piling up and co-workers' patience is running out.
They have little time and energy for their surviving children.

Who helps these children who had their *own* feelings and special attachments and conflicts with the dead sibling? It has been aptly said that
the surviving sibling becomes a double orphan, losing not only a sister or a
brother but also an emotionally available parent. But the death of a child
typically produces much unresolved grief, because parents rarely have an
"objective attitude" about their offspring. It has long been observed that
parents "ascribe to the child all manner of perfections which sober observation would not confirm. He is to fulfill the dreams and wishes of his
parents which they never carried out. . . . Security is achieved by fleeing
to the child" (Rieff 1963). This observation leads us to an important concept which helps explain the parental orchestration of sibling grief. *If a
part of the parent has died with the child, that parent, who was narcis-
sistically invested in the child, will be likely to mourn unhealthily and
involve the other children in that pathological grief.* It thus becomes an
all-too-easy step for parents to center unresolved grief on surviving children, who are immediately at hand, and in whom they have already emo-

tionally invested. When a spouse dies, there is no other spouse living in the same home; loss is a constant presence. But parents can deny the loss of one child by displacing affection and projecting onto the other children. Surviving children run a high risk for developing a pathological relationship to the parents *and* to the ghostly memory of the dead sibling.

Foremost in the mind of the bereaved parents is the issue of their own guilt and self-reproach. One mother whose son died of a brain tumor at seventeen, expressed the feelings of many parents who struggle with self-recrimination:

> Missing him now, I am haunted by my own shortcomings, how often I failed him. I think every parent must have a sense of failure, even of sin, merely in remaining alive after the death of a child. One feels that it is not right to live when one's child has died, that one should somehow have found the way to give one's life to save his life. Failing there, one's failures during his all-too-brief life seem the harder to bear and forgive" (Gunther 1949, p. 258).

To outlive one's child is to defy the order of nature, to tamper with the existentially dictated sense that all things will grow and die in the proper season. To realize, through the death of a child, that nothing of oneself will be perpetuated is to experience guilt *and* an aching sense of incompletion. Many families never really bury their dead child. The ghost lives on silently, sometimes in the form of "replacement children," sometimes in the form of scapegoated children who distract the parents from feeling that they have somehow permitted their child to die.

After death the following three pathological processes can ensnare survivor siblings in their parents' unresolved mourning (Krell and Rabkin 1979):

Parental Process	Effect on Surviving Child's Identity
Silence and secrecy	Being haunted by the dead sibling
Preciousness and overprotection	Being fearful or counterphobic reactions
Substitution and replacement	Resurrection of the dead sibling—living two lives

SILENCE AND SECRECY: HAUNTED SIBLINGS

Some families impose upon the surviving children an unspoken rule of silence. Albert C. Cain and his co-workers observed:

> The child's parents often clearly would not allow the remaining sibling to talk about the event. . . . The parents were fearful of being swamped by even fur-

ther affects beyond those already overwhelming them. The dead sister who only last week walked among them now becomes a ghostly presence. She must now be avoided, her name must not be spoken, she is an "untouchable." (1964)

Whatever bonds, whatever conflicts the surviving children may have experienced while their sibling was alive, must be sealed off. Many children learn from their wounded parents that to raise up a dead sibling's image is treacherous or disloyal. Bereavement must remain a private matter; one must stifle or choke back sadness, anger, or happy remembrances. Entombed within this conspiracy of silence, the family tries to regain its balance, and life goes on "normally," in the pretense that the death has never occurred.

The central motive of these silent, haunted families is the avoidance of blame. The question of blame faces every family member:

> Parents and child come to share a powerful bond through the spoken or unspoken feeling that, if any one of them had somehow acted differently, the child might still be alive. The guilt maintained by these unrealistic beliefs remains intact and intense, with each individual locked in a struggle with his own conscience and unable to share such painful feelings. (Krell and Rabkin 1979, p. 473)

The remaining child interprets the parents' unwillingness to talk about the dead sibling as an unspeakably angry accusation that somehow he or she is at fault. When a child's relationship with a sibling was conflicted before the sibling's death, the parental silence has crushing force. The parent keeps silent because, "It would upset our remaining child to talk about it," and a child keeps silent because, "It would upset my parents to talk about it." Constricted in circles of mutual protection and self-protection, the sibling never fully faces the loss.

If the dead sibling was the apple of the parents' eye, the mother and father may go out of their way *not* to allow that child to be discussed, lest they make damaging comparisons with their remaining child or children. Such a situation bursts into the open in Judith Guest's characterization of the Jarret family in her novel *Ordinary People* (1976). Conrad Jarret, the central figure, is the less-cherished, surviving sibling of an older brother who could do no wrong. After Buck drowns while sailing with Conrad, the mother becomes cold and unloving to Conrad, and the father relates to him as superficially as possible. Conrad finds that he can neither replace Buck nor live down the mother's silent invidious comparisons. Stalked by his brother's ghost in a household where sad emotions are suppressed as signs of immaturity, he struggles alone with his guilt: he fails in school and attempts suicide. His life is saved, eventually, by his contact with an outsider—a psychotherapist who challenges the family's secrecy and silence. Because the therapist refuses to let Conrad keep his stiff-upper-lip façade, his anger and secret guilt at having participated in his brother's death are unlocked and finally brought into the open where he can discuss and resolve them.

The need for openly shared grief, and for full communication by the surviving children, with each other and with other family members, has been documented both clinically and in carefully conducted investigations. In one study of a group of young women who had experienced a recent death of a brother or a sister, open communication within the immediate family about the dead person was the critical issue affecting the survivor-sibling's mental health. If the family suppressed communication and pretended that life had not changed, there was a greater risk that the remaining sibling's mental health would suffer (Pomerance 1973).

In psychotherapy, siblings usually play down the impact of a brother or a sister's death, on the assumption that therapists are interested only in relationships with parents. Thus, patients often state a sibling's death as an unemotional simple fact and then go on to describe other, apparently more pressing life circumstances. A child's low-key portrayal of a sibling's dying can fool even the most astute clinician who, unconsciously colluding with the patient's denial, allows the trauma to be overlooked. Sometimes the death is never even mentioned because the clinician fails to ask: "Did you ever have any brothers or sisters who died?" In clinic settings, intake workers often write such antiseptic notes as: "The patient is one of three children, the youngest of which died of meningitis." When parents state, for example, that they and their surviving children have gotten over their child's death, psychologists should be skeptical.

PRECIOUSNESS AND OVERPROTECTION: FEARFUL AND COUNTERPHOBIC REACTIONS

The death of one child is a family catastrophe. The fear that their remaining children could also be snatched by death can, thereafter, dominate the conscious and the unconscious life of some parents who become conspicuously overprotective. If a child has died of a brain tumor, every headache of the remaining child becomes an alarm and requires a trip to the pediatrician; if a teen-ager dies in an automobile accident, the parents may restrict the surviving sibling's access to automobile travel. More typically, the parents set no obvious restrictions but subtly communicate that the business of living can be fearful and dangerous, that the point of life is to escape illness or injury; and the "precious" child becomes a frightened, timid individual. Living enclosed in a protective bubble, afraid of their own motions, cautious to the point of fearing any risks, these parents stifle their children's healthy strivings for separateness. These children become dedicated to proving that they can escape a sibling's untimely end. In adolescence some of these "bound" siblings try desperately to break away from the sibling's specter. Spitting at danger becomes its own fascination; they counter their own fears and the family's protectionism and take unnecessary risks. The need to prove themselves invulnerable dominates their adolescence and early adult years, as they live down the possibility that they will share a sibling's fate. They appear fascinated with motorcycles and with dangerous skiing and often risky outdoor adventures. If the survivor has had psychopathic traits before the death, he or she may get into dangerous scrapes, courting arrest or getting expelled from school.

REPLACEMENT AND RESURRECTION: LIVING TWO LIVES

Many survivor-siblings must live two lives—their own and that of a dead brother or sister. Searching for the lost loved one, as Erich Lindemann has noted (1944), is a normal part of grief, wherein the survivor looks actively for evidence of the deceased and seeks the embodiment of the dead person in people or objects. In the near-at-hand brothers and sisters are countless possibilities for the parents to embody the dead child. The parents (with friends and neighbors) appoint a living child as the dead one's embodied representative, with the task of picking up the torch dropped by the dead sibling. Some children are conceived specifically as a way of replacing a dead child; and from the moment of conception, such a child's identity is linked to the one who has passed away. From birth the child is compared openly or subtly with the dead one: the way she smiles or parts her hair; whether he likes pizza or strawberry shortcake, or plays baseball or does math as the dead child used to do.

These resurrected children have assumed the burden of living out two identities, one's own and that of someone who no longer exists. One must become an image, a myth, and form a bond with a person whom one's parents now consider a saint. How can one hate a person who has had the misfortune to die untimely? How can one despise a person who no longer exists but invades one's every private moment? This relationship with the dead sibling can become an insufferable burden, leading to confused identity and symptoms of failure. One such sibling was Jack Kerouac, the titular father of the Beat Generation, whose identity was merged with that of his brother Gerard, who died when he was nine and Jack was four.

As a small child, Jack was as burdened by his mother's pain as by the loss of his brother; the route to his mother's heart was to comfort her by sanctifying Gerard's memory. In *Visions of Gerard* (1963), he remembered his pity for his bereft mother, whose teeth fell out one by one as Gerard lay dying. Everywhere Jack looked for the rest of his life, he saw Gerard whom he pictured as God's anointed: If only he could become like his brother! If only he could *become* his brother! Later in his life Kerouac came to believe that Gerard was truly the author of the books he, Jack, had written, that he was Gerard incarnate, that his own existence was proof Gerard still lived. Jack never fully separated his own identity from that of his dead brother (Pollock 1978).

This fusion of two children's identities is a common manifestation of replacement siblings. Parents' attempts at resurrecting a dead child in the form of a living child meet with strong resistance as the latter rebels against the dual existence and listens to his own strivings to be himself. The living child's failure in some important role or function in which a dead sibling succeeded, is the most usual indication that the former is attempting to get rid of the latter's "harassment."

Circumstances of a Sibling's Dying

The kind of trauma inflicted on the survivor-child depends upon the manner of the sibling's death. Among the many circumstances affecting the survivor's relationship to the death, the clinician should determine four facts: the horror of the death, how long it took the sibling to die, the degree to which the death could have been prevented, and the age of the survivor.

THE HORROR OF THE DEATH

A survivor who has witnessed a sibling's death, may be unable to forget or even to speak about critical death images: An eight-year-old boy who helplessly watched his three-year-old sister being buried alive by a truck dumping tons of sand, had been haunted by this memory for over twenty-five years. A fifteen-year-old girl discovered her older brother, whom she had idolized, in the woods behind their house, mortally wounded by a shotgun blast. A college student last remembered his brother painfully gasping in a hospital bed, his face lost beneath an array of tubes and

bandages. These gruesome images, while forcing the survivor to relinquish the dead sibling, are deeply wounding. So horrible are they that the
survivor who seeks help in psychotherapy may sidetrack the therapist; and
the latter may collude in this avoidance by not getting the patient to
speak of memories that he, the therapist, might find disturbing. Full expression of these traumatic memories and full catharsis can be an essential
component in the work of mourning.

Some children and adolescents hear at second hand of a sibling's death;
or a sibling may die far removed in a distant hospital, which the young
surviving child has been prevented from visiting; the fact that the sibling's
death was not seen, being filtered through parental reports, leaves matters
entirely to the survivor's imagination. Such deaths lack visual finality.
Those survivors who have not witnessed the death, are spared the horror
but tend to deny the loss. This denial is especially true of younger children who may believe that the dead sibling has gone on a long trip. When
the parents, protecting both themselves and their children, give sparse
information about the death, young children's imaginations, fueled by
projection, fill in the details. In less grim (but equally excruciating) circumstances, the sibling dies peacefully—as an infant in crib death—and is
found by a brother or a sister who believes the baby has simply gone to
sleep.

HOW LONG IT TOOK THE SIBLING TO DIE

Related to the horror of a sibling's death is the length of time it has
taken him or her to die. For many young people, the end comes neither
sweetly nor suddenly, as a child may be slowly crushed by a devastating
illness such as leukemia, cystic fibrosis, or cancer or neurological degener-
ation. In *prolonged* death, the well sibling has time to prepare for the loss,
but suffers the long absence, both physical and emotional, of one or both
parents and, while the sick sibling suffers, attempts, sometimes guiltily, to
live a normal life. More often than not, one becomes like many of the
siblings we described in chapter 9, who feel angry, helpless, and frightened as the ripples of a sick sibling's life begin to trouble their own. One
is, for the time being, assumed to be functioning "just fine" by parents
who are engaged in a life-and-death struggle on behalf of a dying child.
This situation both forces independence on the healthy siblings and de-
prives them of care. The parents whom the well child does see, are exhausted, dazed, and short-tempered and in need of care; yet those same
parents will find energy, time, and smiles to hold the hand of the child
they know will not be alive next year. The parents essentially must put

"first things first" and, with time running out, feel about the well child: "I'll take care of you later." Thus, the well sibling must put aside his or her own needs and assume a caring role with the victim sibling and the emotionally taxed parents. Tangible responsibilities—caring for younger brothers and sisters, cleaning up the house, or getting off to school—all can serve to burden the well child and to increase his or her underlying resentment about the sibling's illness. The well child truly becomes a parental child. In prolonged sibling death, the well child is very much at risk for psychological disturbance; and if positive identification has existed between the sick child and the healthy one, the latter worries about the possibility of also falling ill.

The following interchange was part of a psychotherapy session between eleven-year-old Andy, suffering from leukemia, and his older brother Greg:

ANDY: [*Tearful, sad, small, squeaky voice*] I wish I was killed . . .

THERAPIST: Why?

ANDY: Then I wouldn't get all the needles.

THERAPIST: Can you tell us about what happens when they give them to you, Andy?

ANDY: *Sharp* pains.

THERAPIST: Where do they stick you with the needles?

ANDY: [*Pointing to his hand and back*] Here, and here, and here, for a spinal tap and a bone marrow.

THERAPIST: [*To Greg who has been very involved and is looking intently at the therapist*] Does it surprise you to hear your brother say he wishes he were dead?

GREG: No. Not after seeing what he's going through [*very sadly*]. I sometimes go with my Mom to the hospital when he's getting a bone marrow. They jab him with needles, and he's got to wear that pump on his body. I can see why he screams so loud. I wouldn't want that to happen to me.

As his brother sickened, it became harder and harder for Greg to go to the hospital. He was horrified by what was happening to Andy. He had other feelings, too. He rarely spoke about it, but he resented the fact that his brother was relieved of doing housework when he, Greg, had to do his normal load. And he had to be careful when playing with his brother, lest he bruise him or rip the skin where the fluid pump had been attached. Slowly, his brother, who had been his ever-present sidekick, faded as a playmate and sank morosely into a twilight reverie, ignoring everyone, eyes blankly fixed on the television.

Siblings as Survivors

COULD DEATH HAVE BEEN PREVENTED?

"What might I have done to cause my sibling's death?" "What might I have done to prevent it?" These are the usual questions that face the survivor who wonders if he or she has passed the test of being a brother or a sister's keeper. If the death is unresolved and undiscussed, the surviving sibling can remain under a cloud of suffering and self-accusation. The majority of deaths in the fifteen-to-twenty-five-year-old age group, James Lynch (1979) points out, are caused by accidents, suicides, or homicides and can therefore be considered potentially avoidable. In most cases, there exists a gray boundary between actual complicity in a sibling's death and genuine inability to prevent it; and this grayness makes it even more difficult to come to terms with what happened, and why. The boy who watched as his little sister was buried alive, was standing fifty yards from the sand truck, unbelievingly, transfixed, staring as if he were watching an event on the television. The impossible was happening before his eyes, and he couldn't move. Then he raced to save her seconds too late. Convinced that he had not tried hard enough, he blamed himself for failing to prevent her death. In the same way, Conrad Jarret, the surviving brother in *Ordinary People,* can never be sure that he tried to the limits of his endurance to save his brother, Buck, when their sailboat overturned in a storm. The sense that the death *might* have been prevented becomes part of a shameful and crippling legend for Conrad, as for many other survivor-siblings. Occurring against the natural substratum of one's periodic wishes to be rid of a sibling, such a "potentially preventable death" can lead one to deny one's own rights to existence.

Suicide is a special case of the issue of preventability, for it is an accusation, as angry as it is silent, against the brothers and sisters (along with the parents) who have all failed to make the suicide *want* to live. The legacy of unanswerable hatred sticks in the throat of the survivor of suicide; and, for the ambivalent sibling who all along has had to struggle with hateful envious thoughts, wishes, actions, and words toward the dead person, the suicide leaves a specially bitter residue. A survivor who has closely identified with a sibling suicide should unequivocally be considered at risk for psychological disturbance (Holinger 1977).

THE AGE OF THE SURVIVOR

Younger children are more likely to misunderstand or distort a death than are older children and adolescents; below the age of ten, magical attributions and fantasies about the dead sibling can go unchecked as can corresponding ideas about the responsibility of the survivor-sibling.

The death of a sibling leads to fearfulness, irrationality, and ego impairment. One fourteen-year-old girl remembered nothing of her baby brother's crib death; yet what she had heard made her selectively fearful and unrealistic when handling dolls and babies:

> After that day, I would never again play with dolls the size of a baby. . . . What if I had been taking care of that baby? . . . Most of my friends babysit. I usually don't, especially if the people have a small baby. What would happen if the baby died while I was watching it? (Sahler 1978, p. 281)

This young girl concluded that perhaps she had some monstrous, contagious power that had to be concealed. Another child had always *believed*, as a fact of his existence, that the crib death of his eight-month-old brother (he was two at the time) had occurred because he left an aspirin bottle near the baby's crib. The belief persisted for years, despite clear evidence given him by the mother that the baby could not have reached the aspirin, and that the autopsy showed no evidence of toxicity. Parents may believe that a young child has actually understood the death when, in fact, the child still believes that the departed sibling has gone on a long trip, lives on as a ghost who can visit secretly at night, or is just taking a long nap. These distortions must be exposed and corrected if the living sibling is to mourn completely. Older children and adolescents are *not* invulnerable to sibling death. Teen-agers are more capable of understanding death. However, adolescents are especially sensitive about their own rapidly changing bodies and worry about being weak, puny, or ugly. When a sibling's illness causes damage or disfigurement, the healthy adolescent's bodily concerns may become particularly acute.

Previous Identification and Pathological Mourning

It will be remembered that there are eight patterns of sibling identification, as outlined in chapter 4. In the middle ranges of identification, two siblings enjoy a positive and flexible dialectic constituting an ideal that allows each a separate sense of self and, at the same time, a feeling of being the same. When a brother or a sister's death occurs in the context of this "constructive dialectic," the sibling can do the normal work of mourning: that is, by testing reality in many ways accept the fact that the loved individual exists no more. Constructive dialectical sibling relationships permit this mourning to run a full, expressive, and uncomplicated course.

Siblings as Survivors

But many sibling losses in childhood, adolescence, or early adulthood have painful complications. It takes all of childhood, adolescence, and, in many instances, years of adult life to resolve the sibling relationship or to fashion a constructive dialectic. Thus, when one's sibling dies before one is twenty-five, the dance of distance and closeness is aborted, and mourning takes a strange twist. The death of a child can leave the parents with a treasured legacy; but when one immature being leaves another, there is always ambivalence, and it therefore becomes hard really to let go. Two factors can complicate sibling mourning. If the previous identification with the dead sibling has been too close or fused, the death jolts the survivor by depriving him or her of narcissistic supplies. Thus, if the dead sibling provided a pleasant and flattering mirror of oneself, the loss of that mirror can be devastating. At the other extreme are siblings whose relationship has been polarized and rejecting, and between whom hostility has prevailed: the survivor's mourning will conflict with anger and guilt.

In the old three examples that follow, we will discuss sibling mourning as a result of two distinct identification patterns: (1) a fused relationship based on early attachment and poor differentiation; and (2) negative identification and rivalry.

MOURNING BASED UPON FUSED RELATIONSHIPS

When the siblings have an undifferentiated relationship, each one serving as an extension of the other's self, death makes the survivor a psychological amputee. Siblings who merge, mirror, and twin with each other (as described in chapter 2) are particularly vulnerable, because the loss of the object *feels* like a loss of self. When the sibling has flatteringly confirmed one's existence at the deepest level, death produces "phantom sibling" symptoms—just as people who have lost a limb experience "phantom limb" symptoms. The survivor literally believes that the sibling lives, despite evidence to the contrary.

Phantom Sibling. The "phantom sibling" symptom was dramatically illustrated by Deborah who, at twenty-eight, lost her brother, one year younger than she. They had become a loyal Hansel and Gretel in a childhood where both were abused by the father and neglected by the mother. He became her baby when she was four, and remained her only constant person throughout childhood and adolescence. As young adults, they married and then divorced within a year of each other, and shared an apartment after their divorces. The strength of this sister's undifferentiated attachment to her brother was exposed when he died in an automobile collision. The following conversation with a therapist took place four months afterward:

283

DEBORAH: I keep *seeing* him—there's this reddish light around his face—I'm upset. . . . It's too awful to face.

THERAPIST: Maybe if you can talk some of this over with me, you won't have to hallucinate about him.

DEBORAH: [*Long silence. She shakes, visibly.*]

THERAPIST: Are you picturing him right now?

DEBORAH: Yes [*very softly*].

THERAPIST: Tell me about him.

DEBORAH: Everybody knew how close we were. They wouldn't let me get near him at the funeral home. I wanted to be there when they embalmed him, I wanted just to touch him. They were afraid I was going to kiss him in his casket. Oh! [*She begins to sob.*] I couldn't *talk* to him. I couldn't *pray* with him.

THERAPIST: He's still alive for you?

DEBORAH: I refused to believe he was dead. It still is hard. I keep looking for him. I met this guy by accident in a diner and he started talking to me, and I was having these visions of my brother. He had a very similar smile, same personality, he was rejected by his family the way my brother was. He became my brother for a while, my brother lived through him.

THERAPIST: Your brother—he was like you?

DEBORAH: Same eyes, same hair, same complexion. . . . We were look-alikes. I loved that about us.

Narcissistic gains mirrored by her brother had ceased, but she maintained them by keeping him alive and searching for him in other men.

At age fifty-nine, having outlived by a decade his identical twin Frank, George Engel, a distinguished psychoanalyst, described (1974) his struggle with his brother's death, and his own subsequent heart attack, which occurred near the anniversary of his brother's coronary (see chapter 2, p. 41). Because they were twins, the diffuseness of ego boundaries and their merging as one, during life, gave them the omnipotent advantage of being able to deceive others about which was Frank, which was George. With Frank dead, George was, for the first time, deprived of his alter ego: he felt naked, strange; from time to time the amputation of his twinship paralyzed him. His subsequent fascination with his own possible death involved the possibility of recapturing the lost part of his identity which seemed to have been lowered into his dead brother's grave. After Frank died, George Engel reported that he periodically experienced "an extraordinary sense of confusion about who was who and which one had died." When a colleague addressed him as Frank, George did not correct him and responded as though *he* were his brother. Few siblings are as attached as George Engel and Deborah whose brother's image haunted her waking life; but these examples dramatically demonstrate that when there are bonds of strong attachment, and personalities have been merged, mourning will produce a disturbing crisis of identity.

MOURNING BASED ON NEGATIVE IDENTIFICATION AND RIVALRY

In some sibling relationships, bitter death wishes have been the dominant motif. When vindictiveness and hatred have provided inner satisfaction in the days, months, years before a sibling's death, the survivor's mourning will be shot with guilt. Young people will go to almost any lengths to reduce this type of guilt, and among them are several maladaptive reactions. °

The guilty survivor can become, suddenly, prone to accidents—falling off bicycles, getting into car accidents, careless use of tools and machinery, to name but a few of the ways in which the survivor-child punishes himself for having had "death-dealing" wishes. One child gets into scrapes he knows he cannot win, allowing his persecutors to beat him bloody; or another child acts up in school, sets fires, steals in broad daylight. Nearly any form of acting out will suffice as long as it brings a temporary halt to the child's terror of being a guilty murderer. The child's central motive is to be stopped and controlled, to get others to relieve his or her guilt and to validate the overwhelming sense of badness. Antisocial reactions are not uncommon. One boy who had been unaggressive and mild prior to his sister's death, became, in second grade, the menace of the playground. In the months before her death, he had also begun to entertain sadistic fantasies toward her—a dramatic change from the positive dialectic that had characterized his earlier feeling about her. He developed in six months the reputation of a malicious trouble maker and a finely tuned knack for making the toughest children dislike and pummel him. Attempts to discipline him backfired and routinely had no other effect than to relieve him. This pattern continued unchecked for five years until his family learned that he was blaming himself for his sister's death. Sadly, by the time the origin of this boy's social aggressiveness was discovered and explained in psychotherapy, he (gasping underneath an avalanche of rejection) had been labeled a "misfit" by exasperated teachers, family members, and school chums, who all thoroughly rejected him.

° For a more extensive discussion of the self-punishing aspects of sibling grief, see Cain et al. 1964.

More subtle self-punishment may be manifested by failing or giving up, as in poor scholastic performance. As the guilty survivor's grades fall, teachers write such comments as: "Sarah's concentration has not been good this marking period—she seems to be daydreaming." Or the child's feelings may masquerade as a "learning disability" in reading, spelling, or arithmetic; parents and teachers may collude by not exploring the emotional basis for the decline and by suspecting organic trouble or an unbalanced diet. By going to school, the survivor feels daily confronted with the question whether he dares to surpass someone who has been robbed of the chance to live and flourish. If the siblings were only a grade or two apart, if they were linked in the minds of friends and teachers, there will be countless little reminders of their relationship and their competition. The comparisons they used to make with one another in grades, sports, and friendships in the common proving ground of school will be painfully apparent as the surviving sibling seeks to "make it." To succeed in school means to surge ahead in life; school failure can be part of an unconscious constellation of wishes to refrain from adding insult to a sibling who has already been outdone by death. We would expect late adolescence and early adulthood to be particularly vulnerable times for survivors, for this is the period of awards, scholarships, trophies, college placements, choice of career, and other life choices. Now survivor guilt and depression take their toll, as the survivor wrestles uncomfortably with the desire to achieve.

Depressive reactions can numb the guilty survivor-sibling so that one feels neither guilt nor anger. We have observed patients in adolescence and early adulthood who, after the loss of an ambivalent relationship with a sibling, become physically and emotionally numb or glazed: they seem to be speaking from behind a darkened screen. These survivors cannot get past the haunting sense that they, too, may meet and deserve their sibling's fate, and that they have less than a full right to a happy existence. One's body often complies with these depressive, life-sapping scripts. Psychosomatic ailments—including severe headaches, sleeplessness, skin rashes, back problems, undiagnosable gastrointestinal difficulties, and exhaustion—are other masks worn by guilt. Patients present themselves as rundown and marginally sick; and in myriad ways, their bodily infirmities ensure that they will not surpass the dead sibling.

Some survivors fear that they will not live beyond the age at which the sibling died; others are convinced that they will meet a similar end. Depressive, and even psychotic, anniversary reactions to a sibling's death are not uncommon in the years immediately after the death (J. Hilgard 1969).

Destructive Ramifications of a Sibling's Death

Sibling death does not cause psychopathology; but it can become a potent organizer of disturbance *in* the survivor or *between* the survivor and the parents. Immaturity or disturbance in family members may be unmasked by sibling death. When death alters the structure of the family, its members learn whether the dead child was vital to its psychic economy: if the child's life kept the family members balanced, then his dying will destabilize them. Other family dislocations, relationships, and stresses must always be taken into account when weighing the impact of sibling death. If the family was antisocial or depressed *before* the child's death, these problems will become exaggerated: the family's ability to develop healthy restorative mechanisms has been arrested, and the child's death fixes unhealthy and even destructive patterns both in the individual and in the family.

THREE SIBLINGS REACT TO A BROTHER'S DEATH

In the following example we will see the different ways in which the death of an oldest boy interfered with the personality development of three surviving siblings. At the time of Matt's death in a boating accident, he was eighteen. His surviving siblings were: Tom, fifteen; Holly, thirteen; and Sam, eleven. Fifteen years later, they became involved with a family psychotherapist who requested that they meet with him to discuss the crippling depression that had forced Sam, the youngest, to seek help. In this family each individual's personal development had become uniquely arrested with Matt's death.

Long before Matt's untimely death, the members of this family rarely spoke to one another about their feelings. They were already having difficulty being intimate, and Matt's death drove each person even farther into a settled way of cutting off love and caring. The father was a loving yet angry man who terrified the children; they viewed him as sitting on a throne where he was feared and silently hated. While seeing him as self-centered and unkind, they saw their mother as an unexpressive soul who prattled on about details of household life and rarely allowed any of the children to peer inside her insipid exterior. When Matt died, both parents' defensive styles of dealing with feelings became even more pronounced; and subsequently they communicated less and less while simultaneously increasing their expectations of perfection for the three surviving children.

Rivalry, Blunted Anger, and Despair: Tom. Matt and Tom, three years apart, had had a negative and polarized relationship with one another. Tom felt that his parents overrated Matt. In death, Matt seemed even better to the parents than he had in life. The parents now wished that Tom would compensate them for the loss of their cherished oldest boy. Tom was given the expectations but not the nurturance to sustain him enough to surpass the brother he had envied, admired, and disliked. Tom's reaction to this comparison was despair: and when, near the anniversary of Matt's death, his mother let slip the wounding comment "Matthew was a thousand times nicer and more responsible than you've ever been," Tom realized that his parents would allow him no room for error. Overhearing his mother endlessly telling Sam, the youngest child, what a "marvelous boy" the deceased Matt had been, he went into a shell. He kept his mistakes to himself and lived as though strapped tight with iron bands. He recalled that era of his life as a time when "I began thinking crazy thoughts"—thoughts so bizarre that, when he admitted them years later, he was certain that had anyone known what he was thinking, he would have been committed to a hospital.

Tom fled the family and, after college, broke all contact with it for two years. Then he suddenly reappeared, making occasional trips home, but staying for only a few hours at a time. None of the emotional issues that had driven him from the family were ever discussed. His stance with his parents was to be "on top of things" and to appear impervious. His only significant tie to family was with Sam, his younger brother, whom he dominated and treated as a boss might treat a subordinate.

Haunted by the Loss of an Ideal: Holly. Holly was thirteen when Matt died. He had been the person she admired most: because the parents had been cold and critical of her, she had adopted Matt as a stand-in parent. Five years older, Matt was her connection with the exciting world of young adults, her gateway to emancipation. Upon his death she lost the one purely affectionate relationship she had ever known. She was already under fire from the father—and now that her tie to Matt had been destroyed, the father's stings went deeper. She fought back and defied him; he reacted by beating her down, both physically and mentally. Holly broke contact with her family and, after high school, rarely came home. Her willingness to trust males, never strong before, was weakened by her brother's death. Despised by her father, abandoned by her dead brother, she thereafter avoided attachments to men and held herself back in relationships. At twenty-eight years of age she had concluded that men were not worth the risk. Pushed into silent ways of disconnecting herself from a depressed mother and father, and unable to derive much enjoyment from either of her surviving brothers, she asked little of anyone.

Passivity and Brother Worship: Sam. Of the three surviving siblings, Sam had the hardest time adjusting. At eleven, he not only experienced the loss of Matt, but, at a young age, witnessed his parents' suffering and observed the troubled reactions of Tom and Holly. When Tom threw off the role of replacement child, the mantle of the dead Matthew fell readily on Sam's shoulders.

When he first contacted the therapist, Sam had been feeling acutely depressed for a year. The death of a good friend had triggered a tailspin from which he could not pull out. Sitting across from the therapist, he was at twenty-six a picture of hesitation and fearfulness, with his glazed eyes and continual half-smile. His indecisiveness had begun to affect his relationship with a lovely woman he had been dating: she could not understand why he showed so little initiative, and she was growing impatient waiting for Sam to grow up. After all, his future had appeared bright; he had graduated high in his class from a good college and had received enthusiastic encouragement from mentors to follow his first love—writing plays. Now, four years after graduation, he still had not made a step toward graduate study, but was frittering his time away as an underpaid assistant in a day-care center and spending his evenings playing the jukebox at a local tavern. Sam lacked the confidence to leave home, to assert himself in life. He tried writing poems about death but rarely had the energy to complete them. His was a bland, compromised existence.

As the youngest child of this family, Sam had always been expected to be the cute "good little boy"; and when his father became emotionally volatile after Matt's death, Sam clung to his identity as a passive nice fellow, hoping not to jar the parents' fragile adjustment, trying to compensate them for their disappointment at the lives that his older siblings, Tom and Holly, were pursuing. Since Tom and Holly had so visibly disconnected themselves from the family, Sam felt that it was his responsibility to stay near his aching, uncommunicative parents. He never made waves, took few risks. "I'm stuck," he told his therapist, "and I don't see any way out of it."

With Matt dead and his parents being emotionally unavailable, Sam looked up to Tom, four years his senior, as a model. The process that we described in chapter 4—"I want to become just like you"—was the watchword of Sam's early adolescence, as he desperately clutched at his baseball-playing, rock-music-loving older brother's image. Tom was clearly the boss; Sam, the worshipful admirer, was willing to play the game according to Tom's rules. Tom reinforced Sam's passivity by dominating him, and this domination continued through their adult years. Yet Sam, seeing that his older brother was, in the latter's own way, not embracing life, had adopted, in him, a passive model: he had chosen to worship someone whose identity was not a strong model for adult functioning. The only male models available to Tom had failed him: a brother who had died, a father who frightened him, another brother who feared life and dominated him. Living in Tom's shadow, and grasping unsuccessfully at Tom's unfulfilled life for guidance, Sam had failed to become "his own man."

MASS-MURDERER'S IDENTITY

We hesitate to introduce among the cases of people whom we have treated or interviewed that of the mass-murderer Adolf Hitler; but he is of interest to this discussion as the shadow of sibling death loomed over his early life to a striking and, in hindsight, sinister degree.

Fivefold Replacement Sibling: Adolf Hitler. The early life of Adolf Hitler, as described in Robert Payne's biography (1973), exemplifies the way in which sibling death can bring forth latent problems in the development of an individual. Adolf Hitler was the sixth child of Alois Hitler. At first glance, theirs would seem to have been a typical turn-of-the-century Austrian family, in which the father, a rising bureaucrat in the customs service, provided well for his second wife. She and Alois tried three times to celebrate their marriage with a child, and three times they failed: Gustav, Otto, and Ida all died before the age of two. When Adolf was born in 1889, he was in a sense a *triple* replacement for three dead infants. He became his mother's pride and joy, for he allowed her to prove that she could at least bear fruit. Adolf's birth was celebrated for other reasons. His older half-brother, Alois, their father's namesake, was obviously headed for trouble and was in constant opposition with the forbidding father. Adolf was the prize; Alois, the black sheep. Alois finally left the home, discontinued his schooling at age sixteen in 1898, and went to England, where he was arrested early in 1900 and jailed. A letter from the mother (in *Adolf's* handwriting but dictated by her) has been preserved: it chastises Alois and excoriates him for his mistakes. The father, having written off his first, bad son, turned to Adolf to fulfill his paternal hopes and dreams. Then, in the winter of the same year, Adolf's brother Edmund died at the age of six, of measles. This death, combined with the three previous deaths and the failure of the father's namesake, devastated and demoralized the Hitler family, which had fallen on hard times: the father had retired from the customs service and had undertaken to farm a barren unyielding piece of land. Adolf, on the verge of puberty, had two more siblings to replace.

Siblings as Survivors

Crucial Dates for Young Adolf (born 1889)				
Gustave Dies	Otto Dies	Ida Dies	Edmund Dies	Alois Arrested
1887	1888	1888	1900	1900

Evidence is scanty, but the historian Robert Payne believes that Hitler's mourning for Edmund may have been complicated, even tortured. His bedroom overlooked the cemetery wall behind which Edmund was buried; and eleven-year-old Adolf was frequently seen, by neighbors, sitting on the wall staring into the graveyard. We have no actual record of what went on in young Hitler's mind, but he appears to have undergone a radical personality change during that year. From an outgoing child who whizzed through his subjects and had been no disciplinary problem in the early years of school, in the year of Edmund's death he became a brooding misfit, a spiteful, defiant troublemaker, who despised authorities and seemed to relish the cascade of criticism and punishment he brought upon himself. He began drawing and fantasizing and, for the first time, ran into conflicts with his father, although the boy's grieving mother clung tighter to him. Torn between fulfilling the father's angry demands to be a perfect replacement sibling and the exiled Alois's call to be impulsive, Adolf Hitler turned inward and became openly hostile to everyone's expectations. His status as a replacement child (five times over), in the context of an already overclose maternal relationship and a strict father, can be seen as a major organizing factor in the development of Hitler's sadism and his arrogant claim to superiority and invulnerability.

Positive Resolutions of Sibling Death

Not all sibling deaths contribute to such tragic results as Matt's did for Tom, Holly, and Sam, or to such monstrous deeds as did the deaths of Hitler's siblings. The surviving siblings' outbursts can be healing and force the parents to face their own grief. A mother recalls:

It took my living son to show me a great deal about death and accepting grief. . . . I hadn't planned to drive down the street I had chosen, nor had I planned on the snow or the two bickering children jailed with an intolerant mother in a car doing last minute holiday shopping. But that street . . . took us past the cemetery where a small marker is a reminder of that child that was. The announcement by my daughter that we were passing the cemetery was almost one of retaliation to her brother, an attempt to even the score of the backseat hostilities with some special knowledge. And the announcement brought silence, a silence that was broken by the sudden demand of my son to stop, to turn into the cemetery and to see his brother. It was a turn I made with reluctance; we so rarely stopped there any more. . . . It wasn't enough to trudge through the snow and locate the tiny grave. He asked to see his brother, and wanted to do just that. To see him, to touch him. . . . When it was finally clear that we couldn't see the body, a series of relentless questions began. "Why did he die?" "What did you do?" "Why couldn't you save him?" "Why my brother?"

All *my* questions coming back to haunt me. All the questions of any parent who has ever lost a child. And the snow became mixed with tears, mine and his, as we stood there. I cried for him, that young son caught in unexpected grief for a brother he never knew and would never know. And I cried for the daughter who somehow survived our inadequacies . . . and I cried for that child who would never grow up. And I cried for me. (Sahler 1978, pp. 287–88)

Adults can use the children's honest, though sometimes stifled reactions as a force for change, for healing. As the surviving children struggle with their relations with a ghost, they can motivate their parents to complete the work of mourning.

The loss of a family member can activate a person's capacity to adapt and lead to mastery and creativity (see Eisenstadt 1978). In a similar vein, George H. Pollock has commented that mourning can be viewed as a "liberation" process: "In a sense . . . the positive outcome of mourning . . . is creativity. . . . The creative genius is not a direct result of the mourning process, but the creative product may . . . show evidence of its presence in the theme, content, style or purpose" (1978).

Using the life of writer James M. Barrie, Pollock illustrates how mourning for a sibling can spark creative efforts. On the eve of older brother David's fourteenth birthday—at the time James Barrie was seven—David suffered a skating accident, fractured his skull, and died of intracranial hemorrhaging. From the moment of his death, the mother became an invalid, taking up almost full-time residence in her bedroom. She neither recovered from this son's death nor ever faced the fact that he was gone. James, more than anyone else in the family, felt the impact of his older brother's death, and took it as his mission in life to help his mother forget the dead child's image. He became a jokester and, to cheer her up, began writing stories, which he read to her at her bedside. He was the only person who could make his mother laugh, and gained a distinct identity by being her consoler. Writing was his only way of laying claim to the attentions of a mother whose thoughts lingered at David's grave. Thus, organizing his life around mother and dead brother, Barrie wrote (and tried out on her) plays and the children's classic *Peter Pan*, which he subtitled *The Boy Who Never Grew Up*.

Siblings as Survivors

The death of a brother or a sister, of no matter what age, forces the group of siblings to reorganize their roles and relationships to one another and their parents. Under certain circumstances, the death jolts the surviving brothers and sisters into being alert, sensitive, and actively concerned as never before. Such concern can be catalyzed, especially when the remaining siblings feel that they might have prevented the death had they only been more caring.

Judy Harris was thirty-five when her mother phoned her from Iowa to tell her that Darleen, a younger sister in a family of five girls and three boys, had just been found after having strangled herself in the family's barn with a hank of clothesline. Darleen was only twenty-six. She had been withdrawn and depressed for a year since a breakdown and mental hospitalization. A shroud of secrecy had been drawn around what was really wrong, and her seven brothers and sisters had written occasional letters but had failed to realize the seriousness of her troubles. At the time of her hospitalization, they were shocked, because she had had few problems during childhood, had been a "straight A" student, and was an accomplished and original musician.

The other seven siblings had enjoyed, over the years, a positive dialectic that allowed closeness and separateness; but when problems arose, they avoided contact. Darleen's violent, self-inflicted death aroused guilt in each of them. Searching for answers to the terrible tragedy, Judy began making phone calls to her next-in-age sister, Betsy, more frequently than at any time in years: with her Judy could share her guilt that she had not done more. Suddenly the sibling group came alive to one another, and Judy began worrying about Betsy, whom she feared might have the same suicidal tendencies as Darleen. The two sisters began to show an interest in a black-sheep brother who had been abusing drugs for years. Feeling the full impact of their possible responsibility for Darleen's suicide, they realized that a second tragedy could occur, and that they had to try to prevent it:

JUDY: We fear for each other. Whenever we see any signs of stress in each other's lives, we come right to the point now, *as we never did before*. We ask, "What's bothering you—what can we do?"

INTERVIEWER: For example?

JUDY: Just last week my brother lost his job. The girl he had been living with split up with him—and she had been his mainstay. I think within twenty-four hours he was so bombarded with calls from all of us that he probably got help getting things sorted out on the phone. The boys have their own special hotline and we have ours. But anything we feel is as serious as this, there are immediate calls between the boys and the girls. My brother Jake called me and said, "I heard from Betsy this morning . . . that she had been on the phone with my sister-in-law. Betsy and I have really *found* each other lately, we call back and forth and can now really bare our souls to each other."

Following Darleen's death, the family started having reunions, big get-togethers involving more than thirty people, including siblings, spouses, and children.

Music was Darleen's life, so it now plays a big part in all our get-togethers. It provides a lot of comfort for all of us. My brothers all play guitars and all sing folk music. This also has to do with Darleen—she taught them all how to play. My youngest sister, who was ten when Darleen died, also learned from her—she's now entertaining professionally in Florida with the guitar, and singing the songs. . . . She has completely imitated Darleen's style, and she sings for us at the family reunions.

The siblings' partial identification with Darlene held up to them a disturbing mirror of their own suicidal possibilities. Their guilt about her death became a creative force, helping each of them to forge a more nurturing identity.

A sibling death, especially the death of "the most responsible" child, can force the surviving children to face reality more forthrightly than ever before. Some adolescents and young adults *must* contribute to their parent's emotional well-being now that a dead sister or brother is no longer performing this function; others, who have not lived up to their potential, "floated through life," or considered themselves inept, can be forced to mature and take charge of their own or others' lives—to become a caretaker.

Conclusion

What, then, are the practical implications of our discoveries about sibling death? In the chapter on psychotherapy (chapter 11), we shall discuss the kinds of intervention that a psychotherapist can make in the lives of survivor-siblings and their parents. Psychotherapists, however, are healers of last resort. Little is now being done in the United States to help surviving children face the death of a brother or sister. Well siblings are considered to hinder the efficient conduct of a hospital. The hospital team assumes these unknown children to be doing well, attending school, and playing happily.

We believe that this lack of attention and care must be corrected, because during and after a sibling's death, the surviving child is very much at risk, for both psychosomatic and emotional disturbance. Hospital-based social workers can educate parents about the management of well children and can help the parents to support these children more effectively and honestly during a terminal illness or a sudden death. To achieve this end, the hospital physicians, pediatricians, and family doctors and psychologists who practice outside the hospital, must be in good communication with the social work services inside it. Responding immediately after a fatal diagnosis, and seeking follow-up contact with the family for months after the event of the death, health professionals, led by the family doctor, should reach out vigorously rather than assuming that medical responsibility ends when life ends. Contact should also be made with the surviving children's elementary school or high school, so as to achieve a sensitive and responsive handling of social and academic problems.

It is our firm conclusion, based on our own and many other clinical studies, that survivor-siblings of all ages should be worked with individually, with their parents, and in support groups of brothers and sisters.° In addition, their parents must be helped to cope with their own loss, so that they can be relieved of the need to replace a dead child with one who lives. Leadership must come from the medical and psychological community in organizing such healing opportunities if we are to enable families to free themselves, their children, and future generations of the silent but destructive ghost of a person who has died too young.

° Hopeful beginnings have been made by such organizations as the American Cancer Society and the Candlelighters, who sponsor educational and supportive groups for adults and children.

CHAPTER 11

Psychotherapy with Siblings

> I hold this to be the highest task of a bond between two people; that each should stand guard over the solitude of the other.
>
> *Rainer Maria Rilke*

AS LIVED by each individual who is a brother or a sister, the sibling experience dictates some of the grandest and some of the meanest of human emotions. The whole range of human feelings enters into this relationship, whose complexity defies anyone to dictate how and what it ought to be. That there can be *no standard, unitary sibling bond* will by now have become obvious to the reader: the permutations are endless.

But what, then, is the role of the psychotherapist who, more than anyone else, dares to presume the bond any two siblings should have with one another? The psychotherapist, as a chronicler of important personal events in the modern world, may have supplanted priest, historian, theologian, friend, or parent at the crossroads of significant emotional experience, and is able to focus on two vital human abilities that determine a person's life: the ability of individuals to live separately and independently of each other and, simultaneously, their ability to enjoy closeness, intimacy, and dependency in harmonious relationships. The sibling bond affects both of these capacities, by determining the issues of separateness and relatedness as they arise during childhood, and how they will continue to affect the individual as an adult. The challenge for the therapist is to find out the nature of each sibling bond, whether it is close or distant, and how it was forged, and how responsive it will be to psychotherapy.

Psychotherapy with Siblings

The therapist, like the archeologist, needs to understand the sibling relationship as it was conducted in the past, and, as dramaturgist, to examine and possibly even to rearrange the sibling bond as it exists at the time of psychotherapy.°

It is important to remember that the sibling bond, like any other vital relationship, is comprised of all kinds of transactions. Whether for the individual patient remembering a brother or a sister, or for a group or groups of siblings sharing common experiences, or for a married couple with each spouse still having a vital connection to a sibling, or for families with parents and children, the therapist can utilize sibling-specific concepts to explain, to highlight effects, to interpret, to communicate messages, and to execute desirable change. But the working principles the therapist uses always have to be tailored to the dynamics of the particular problem or issues that affect the sibling bond. Anorexia nervosa requires a different approach from depression, and the approach for "unhappiness" is different from that for delinquency.

We consider that just talking about sibling experiences is an insufficient form of intervention, just as may occur if the patient is asked to talk about experiences with mothers and fathers. But knowledge of important sibling transactions and a sibling-specific diagnosis help determine whether brothers and sisters can work cooperatively to become allies for their common benefit. The sibling relationship requires a case-by-case approach, without any prior assumptions that "brotherhood" or "sisterhood" is positive, compassionate, loyal, or reliable. Once a therapist recognizes the potential importance of siblings, it is up to him—be he a psychoanalyst, behavior therapist, family therapist, gestalt therapist, or any other kind of intervener—to deal with them according to his own approach. We hope to provide a map that allows for an orientation, not for a specific way to do therapy

Some siblings have so de-identified or stabilized into negative patterns that bringing them together will only prove fruitless, frustrating, and destructive. Some hate each other, carry around a weighty ledger of grievance that they refuse to give up, or rely for their own identity on behaving diametrically different from a sib—and, alas, will always do so. Indiscriminate grouping of siblings only creates therapeutic problems. Bonds of love and caring are always relatively easy to deal with and are likely to yield positive results; bonds of hate and hurt are always relatively

° There are an enormous variety and many schools of psychotherapy practiced today. This chapter provides information which can be used by therapists who see patients on an individual basis and by those who treat families. We are intentionally avoiding the controversies that are often created when proponents of either approach attempt to justify the relative strengths of their philosophies over those cited by proponents of the other schools.

intractable and may defy the most ingenious therapist. Sibling waters can be treacherous, and family therapists in particular—since they often invite to sessions all the immediate family members—should tread with care and a discerning eye. Sensitive questioning and well-planned moves become the order of the day.

Some published references by therapists have attested to the use of siblings with behavior therapy and group therapy approaches. Behaviorists (Arnold 1976; Lavigueur 1973; Resick et al. 1976; Leitenberg et al. 1977) have attempted to use the brothers and sisters of adolescent patients to help administer positive reinforcements, while a few group therapists (for example, Coleman 1978, 1979)° have put siblings together in groups. The reported results appear mixed; and since there were no apparent attempts to evaluate the nature of the sibling bond before intervention was initiated, the only moderately positive results are due probably to some of these sibs disliking or being disinterested in one another. Other factors also interfered. In some of these studies, well siblings of seriously disturbed adolescents were asked to help in residential-treatment situations where treatment time was limited. In other cases, an immediate crisis (such as drug abuse) was used to "pull" the siblings in for help. Once the crisis passed, or the siblings went their separate ways, the sibling "solidarity" appeared to break down or was of only minimal benefit, unless some attempt had been made to create a positive relationship that would endure with insight-oriented therapy.

Problems for the Psychotherapist

While children are often referred for therapy because they are fighting with their brothers or sisters, adults sometimes have to bear their sibling indignities without much sympathy from other people. "Brotheritis" or "sisteritis" is usually not the complaint for which help is sought. Unless the therapist is prepared to probe in this area of a person's life, adult patients are unlikely to bring it up on their own.

We were amazed when we began this project to find that the most traumatic and highly charged sibling experiences that our patients had had (incest, suicide, abandonment, psychotic episodes, caregiving, and so on) were never touched on by the other therapists whom these patients had seen. Ruth M. Lesser (1978) and Alberta B. Szalita (1968), in discuss-

° Also personal communication from Patricia Daly, 1980.

ing patients who were dissatisfied with previous analytic treatment, also underscore that the previous therapists neglected and, in some cases, totally ignored the sibling relationship. There appear to be many reasons for this unfortunate, long-perpetuated problem of neglecting siblings in therapy.

SIBLING AVOIDANCE BY THERAPISTS

Contemporary psychotherapists—analysts; neo-Freudians; ego psychologists; gestalters; group, marital, or family therapists—are, for the most part, taught nothing about sibling relationships. No cohesive body of information—no support for investigating the sibling bond—has been given them up to now.

The most highly regarded of psychodynamically based therapists—Sigmund Freud, Harry Stack Sullivan, Frieda Fromm-Reichmann, and others—never used sibling-specific concepts. We have already pointed out Freud's sibling bias and the theoretical legacy of sibling rivalry, discord, and hate that he helped create. There have, up to now, been no outstanding models for sibling-focused therapy with a positive view in mind; and training analyses for future psychoanalysts usually neglect major sibling events (Lesser 1978). The vertical parent-to-child vector is so deeply embedded in dynamic theory that master therapists ignore the parallel, peer-related, horizontal vectors of sibling-to-sibling relationships, and instruct the next generation of therapists in the same manner. In addition, most therapists have little support from related disciplines to begin snooping about in the sibling underworld.*

Furthermore, most therapists enjoy the role of authority, and some may even unconsciously exploit it. Parent-transference, rather than sibling-transference, interpretations are inevitable if the therapist views himself as parentlike, wise, beneficent, and omnipotent and the patient as childlike, helpless, confused, and dominated by infantile feelings. Heinz Kohut (1971) observes that analysts who are too demanding that patients give up their symptoms, are usually older siblings whose own sense of a grandiose self focuses on maintaining ethical superiority over younger, "sibling"-like individuals.

In addition, love and caring by the patient for the therapist are tricky

---

* As we have pointed out in chapter 1, personality theories are overwhelmingly "parentogenic." Studies of child development for fifty years focused exclusively on mother influence and, only in the 1970s, began to include fathers (Biller 1971; Lynn 1974; Lamb 1976; Parke 1979). It is just in the last few years that child-development specialists have observed the triadic interaction of mother-father-child (Clarke-Stewart 1978; Fagot 1978), and a few look at reciprocal interaction between siblings (Lamb 1978).

elements in the psychotherapeutic process and often create apprehension in the therapist. We do not mean neurotic, distorted, transferential love, but we mean the deep, human attachment to the person of the therapist who is showing concern, compassion, empathy, respect, and caring for the patient. The caring by the therapist for the patient is often a crucial factor in whether the patient gets better or stays symptomatic. Carl Rogers (1951), in writing about the therapist's unconditional positive regard, and I. H. Paul, in his *Letters to Simon* (1973) describing therapist compassion, focus on these as central aspects of successful individual psychotherapy. These therapists, by *explaining how* and *why* they care, and how they may sometimes hold negative feelings, are often more like siblings than parent images or pseudo parent-ideals (Whitaker and Malone 1953). By demythologizing themselves, they afford more opportunities for "twinning," as Kohut would put it, and facilitate direct challenge by the patient. The "love" or caring in this context becomes more difficult to manage but is also rather that of two equals than of parent and child. Therapists who are reluctant to face such a direct challenge, which comes from a patient's caring for them, are likely to slide into, or hold onto, parent-transference models that keep the patient "one down" and themselves "one up" (Haley 1963) and also keep the patient waiting for the beneficence of an interpretation, or wise saying, or acceptance from on high. The patient's collusion in this process—by being weak, helpless, confused, desperate, amnesic, or shamefacedly manipulative—feeds this inequality, prevents change, and often stagnates the therapy by perpetuating a parent transference in which the patient refuses to face the fact that therapy must end. The "neutral" position of some analytically oriented psychotherapists, who remain fairly silent during the sessions, will also often stimulate a parent-child dependency state. A therapist's active stance can, on the other hand, bring the sibling dynamic out into the open.* Siblinglike relationships, if the therapist permits them, are more egalitarian, promote faster change, and deny the patient the illusion that he or she can be protected or nurtured "interminably" (Freud 1937). Family therapists, in condemning individual psychotherapy, often belittle the slow pace and dependency the patient assumes in that one-to-one model; but if the therapists begin also to think in sibling terms, it is possible more quickly to resolve transference, resistance, and the rate at which the patient changes.

---

* Later in this chapter (pages 302–5) we will comment on how the silence of a therapist can also help induce sibling transference.

Psychotherapy with Siblings

Among family therapists, strategists such as Jay Haley (1963, 1976) and Salvador Minuchin (1974) view power as the central force in family relationships. Abuse of power and confusions about the hierarchies and rules that sustain power are viewed as creating problems for individual family members. Haley explicitly states that children should have the least power in normal families; and in his form of family therapy, the therapist restores strength to the "rightful" hands of parents. The sibling relationship is either not mentioned, or is viewed by strategic family therapists as an obstacle to what they see as the rightful power of parents. Family therapists often also employ power tactics of their own (manipulation, giving directives, unbalancing, constructing realities, challenging, setting boundaries, imposing paradox, and so on) in order to create change (Minuchin and Fishman 1981). The message is clear: *parents* and *parentlike therapists* should have power and strength; children and, consequently, sibling relationships are weak. The sibling bond is rarely explored by these therapists. It is no wonder that brothers and sisters have little to say about their relationship in this type of therapy, if the person who is in the best position to validate what is safe, appropriate, and desirable—the therapist—stays completely away from probing this connection.

We should like to speculate about another factor that contributes to the avoidance of sibling issues by psychotherapists: their birth-order position. Many therapists are *first-borns*. Many studies point to the economic and educational advantages first-borns have over later-borns: psychotherapists, with their extensive schooling, have been the beneficiaries of their first-born position. As we pointed out in chapter 1, while arguments have raged for thirty years about the legitimacy of birth-order effects, there is some agreement about the so-called dispossession theory. First-borns (including psychotherapists), while more advantaged and entitled, are anxious and insecure because, many of the devotees of birth-order effects would argue, they were "dispossessed" of maternal attention by their later-born siblings, kicked out of the nest and pushed into accelerated maturity and self-sufficiency by their busy parents. While this "dispossession" may create budding academic stardom in first-born psychotherapists, it is hardly the stuff from which springs a therapeutic tolerance for younger siblings or an appetite for building sibling bonds in therapy.°

° It would be interesting to compare the birth-order position of therapists with that of their individual patients, to see whether contentiousness or cooperation marks the therapeutic relationship. Would a first-born therapist do better with a first-born patient than with one farther down the birth-order continuum?

SIBLING TRANSFERENCE AND SIBLING COUNTERTRANSFERENCE

Transference reactions—a patient's distorted perceptions of the therapist that echo that patient's reactions to significant figures in his or her
past—have always been the bedrock of individual, psychodynamic therapy. They are the basis on which the therapist can differentiate a patient's
distorted reactions from valid reality testing, and the glue for the thera-
pist-patient relationship. Concepts of transference always include feelings
about mothers and fathers (Kernberg 1980; Langs 1977; Searles 1959); but
for all the reasons we have named, siblings rarely come into view.

Countertransference—the emotional, sometimes unconscious reactions
of the therapist to the patient, reactions based on the therapist's own life
experiences (Snyder 1961; Rabiner et al. 1971)—can be utilized benefi-
cially to facilitate therapy; or it can sit, an obstacle, right in the path of
change. Art, the bright lawyer we described in chapter 9, tended to disapprove of any female clients who formed an overly dependent bond with
him. A first-born son, whose next younger sister was troubled, sickly,
parasitic, and had been foisted on him to take care of, Art described the
visceral reactions he felt toward female clients who clung to him for advice and help in ways that seemed burdensome and unending. While Art
had tried to avoid taking on such clients until his avoidance was pointed
out in his psychotherapy, he saw no connection between his sister's old
dependency and the gut reactions of annoyance and despair he occasionally felt when advising other needy women.

Some therapists seem at midlife (thirty-five to fifty-five) to have become casually "insensitive" to the difficult issues gnawing at siblings in
the families that they see or in individuals whom they treat. As adults,
having grown professionally successful, and no longer in active conflict
with their own siblings, such therapists seem to have actively repressed
the personal memories of the conflict-laden years of childhood and adolescence. They can easily gloss over sibling "rivalry" as "normal," excuse
the fighting between brothers and sisters as a "phase all kids go through,"
and try to calm parents whom they, the therapists, see as "excessively
worried." A therapist who is given sibling concepts to work with, *and* an
opportunity in supervision to bring up some of the material from his own
personal sibling experience, becomes sensitized to the sibling dynamics in
his patients.

Other therapists keep aware of their sibling experiences in childhood,
drawing from these in ways that add to their therapeutic strength. One
therapist told us:

My brother paired with me against our father—he needed that—and I was ten years younger. Not that he did it openly—but he got his warmth from showing me great brotherly and parental care. Thus, he modeled a kind of rescuing of me and I identified with that and have been rescuing ever since.

Then this therapist let us know that watching his siblings fight it out from the safe sideline of his youngest position gave him diplomatic and problem-solving skills:

I was the family "bystander"—never caught in the feuding positions others got into. I used my position as the baby of the family to remain the one person always able to communicate with everybody.

Family therapists, confronted by families and sibling relationships, often join the sibling subgroup to create change, and sometimes act out patterns of behavior that are vestiges of ways they acted in their own families of origin. One family therapist was surprised at discovering that he always sided with the teen-agers against the parents. In supervision, he began recalling how much he and his brother had shared the wish that they could get back at their parents for what they, the children, felt were injustices and indignities. Countertransference and transference reactions are not just phenomena of dynamically oriented individual psychotherapy. The often unconscious reactions of patient to therapist and therapist to patient are present in group, marital, and family therapy—but are more tangled and often seem complex or too circuitous to track. The therapist must always probe a sibling dynamic for its potential to produce strong emotional reactions. Such reactions stand out clearly when either patient or therapist has had a striking sibling experience: there may be a resonance of sibling images that can affect the whole course of therapy. These sometimes appear even when the therapist is relatively silent; the patient may then begin to project the image of loving or sadistic or gentle or hateful brother or sister onto the therapist. At times it is useful for the therapist to remain fairly neutral, commenting little about these sibling transference reactions, letting them build in intensity until they become clearer and are free of the parental issues about which patients always seem to be more conscious. Not surprisingly, under the trying demands of the therapeutic encounter, the therapist may also have a sibling countertransference reaction.

Specific Sibling Transference Reactions. The patient who has an aggressive, compulsive need to compete with the therapist, has often received the brunt of a destructive sibling's tyranny. The therapist, as a natural figure for envy and jealousy, often draws the ire, even the rage of such a once-dominated sibling. Or the therapist may feel a patient's recurring need to provoke the therapist's anger, as if to re-create an all too familiar dynamic in which the other person, the therapist, is bound to retaliate; thus is fueled a dialectic of hurt, anger, disappointment, remorse, and then hurt and anger again. The old adage, "It's safer to fight than love" finds ready fulfillment in this type of sibling transference.

Then there are those caretaker siblings who essentially hate their position of dependency in therapy. Wanting to be in control, cherishing the powerful core of autonomy around which their identity has been created, they surrender all of this temporarily, when they begin therapy, to the assumed wisdom of another adult. The therapist is usually the first adult in their lives to whom they can admit dependent feelings, only to be quickly relinquished as soon as they discover aspects of the therapist that they assume need giving to and caring about. Being a caretaker is after all central to their core. The therapist *qua* sibling is someone they too often try and look after, relinquishing their own needs in session, bringing him gifts, showing premature progress, asking the therapist how he feels, accommodating themselves in the session to whatever topic he wants to bring up, and subordinating their own moods and needs to those of the therapist so far as they can intuit them. Self-sacrifice by such patients is always a paradoxical and clever way of maintaining control, and the therapist has to be wary of succumbing to such patient interest.

Incestuous siblings seem to project and re-create, through transference, the old dynamic of secrecy, mistrust, anxiety, and sometimes love of a sibling. Mistrust of men was *the* issue for one such woman. She remained in therapy for four years, intellectually acknowledging her need to work through the issue of mistrust. Yet she was fearful and anxious about the caring she felt for the therapist, about her fantasy that they would one day make love, and that then she would feel betrayed as she had been by her brother. Another female patient tried to lose herself in the symbiosis of her sibling transference. Brother love in childhood had been her secret sanctuary from what she perceived as a hostile, angry, and deceptive world. To imagine losing herself in love for the therapist and fantasizing that he had the same wild, rebellious, crazy streak as her brother had had, was her vehicle, her new sanctuary, her current refuge from a world that still seemed to her to be threatening and treacherous.

Well siblings—those brothers or sisters who often stand out in contrast to a disturbed sibling—may engage in an interesting reversal in therapy. One may project one's own good self, unconsciously, onto the therapist, using him as a temporary ego ideal, and reveal that one also has some of the same reviled, denigrated characteristics of one's disturbing sibling. In wanting to have the therapist's help, and even to be exonerated by the therapist, such well siblings often try to make him be the same good, forgiving, kind brother or sister that one still views oneself as being. Splitting of good and acknowledged parts from bad and repressed parts occurs in such patients; and the therapist has to avoid being the idealized angel that the patient wants also still to be, or the reviled devil that the disturbed sibling was too often seen to be. Such patients often engage in rigid splits of good versus bad guys. The therapist must avoid being the repository for one or the other side of this projected sibling dynamic. Under these circumstances it is sometimes wise for a therapist to admit, in the therapy sessions, his own human feelings and his negative and positive reactions to a patient; therapist and patient are equally human.

DEALING WITH RESISTANCE

What we have been describing as transference reactions are also a form of character resistance (Horner 1979)—the patient's way of blocking the productive course of therapy by relating to the therapist in *specific*, characteristic, rigid, historically determined ways. These character resistances are usually dealt with by interpreting to the patient the ways he or she is still relating *as if* the therapist were a sibling. There is another form of sibling resistance, one based on the more *general* nature of how most people have been a brother or sister. These are the sibling experiences that have not been verbalized, and therefore have not been evaluated, that stir ambivalent feelings, and that stayed out of the purview of the patient's parents. Thus, there is a natural resistance to these experiences being spontaneously and easily dealt with in therapy. We are using the term *resistance* much differently than do psychoanalysts, who describe a patient's general resistance toward establishing a collaborative relationship with the therapist (Langs 1977). Sibling-specific resistance is a natural outgrowth of this elusive relationship and can be dealt with in a variety of contexts and ways.

Many patients seem conflicted about *how* to describe their previous sibling experiences. They often feel guilty about some of these raw events that they engaged in as children, and that now seem inconsistent with their high ideals and their self-concepts as adults. In describing past events with brothers and sisters, a patient usually starts out with empty and trite language: "We fought," "She was a stranger to me," "We had nothing in common," "We were always close," and so on. We have found that it is enormously helpful to teach our patients something of the rich variety of possible sibling experience. For a patient to hear about other siblings—what they did and did not do with each other—first, relieves tension and, then, helps to unleash a flood of memories, gives the patient permission to talk about what he or she has never talked about before, and obviates some of the guilt carried from the past.

In *group therapy*, it often helps for the therapist to point out how members are relating to each other in ways that may be a residue of their sibling roles of old. In *marital therapy*, couples, whether seeking divorce or a closer relationship, usually keep their siblings tucked away in the distant background. It is expected in marriage that each partner's primary loyalty is to the spouse; hence, there is conflict if one is also still loyal to a brother or a sister. Resistance to focusing on a sibling can be overcome by the therapist's pointing out the circumstances in which sibling loyalty arose, how much it was determined early in life by one's parents. The spouse's jealousy usually subsides if the therapist puts the sibling relationship in its proper context.

In *family therapy*, it is sometimes helpful to draw the children aside, away from the eyes and ears of their parents, if the therapist wants to overcome resistance and know about sibling dynamics. Young children and early adolescents often resist exposing their disagreements, lest their parents disapprove, or lest their own feelings run wild, with the danger of savage retribution. These children sometimes respond with noncommittal grunts, shrugs, smiles, or dumb stares at the impertinent questioner. This is, after all, one way children can have power over their parents: to keep the secret of their sibling transactions away from parental control, even if the children are not sure of the responses they will elicit. Once parents have left the room, however, a group of impassive, truculent, resistant, nonverbal siblings can become animated, taking on life as distinct individuals who are delightfully frank with the therapist.

Assessing Sibling Issues in Therapy

The therapist should always gather information about a patient's early development, the early caregivers, important childhood events, the nature of family interaction, and, above all, the actual emotional tone of the family. The therapist should expect confusion, inarticulateness, avoidance, indifference, or that common selective amnesia that people have about their siblings, and thus needs to probe carefully but persistently in the initial assessment of sibling dynamics.

The issues the therapist should raise will vary depending on a patient's age, and the problem presented, and on whether the therapist is dealing with a family, a sibling group, or an individual. The following are the essential issues:

ACCESS

What has been the amount and the quality of access (see chapter 1) between a patient and his or her sibs? High access creates a much greater awareness of the sibling bond; these are the brothers and sisters who have known each other on a "gut" level. Low access will mitigate against close identification and any "felt" sense that the sibling relationship was, or still is important. Three major areas are important to explore in order to obtain a clearer understanding of sibling access: these are feelings, factual information and memories, and the kind of interaction among the siblings. The therapist must ask each person how he feels about his brothers and sisters and whether there is a sense of distance or closeness between them. If the siblings are present, agreements and disagreements over these respective views ought to be explored, and factual consistencies or inconsistencies noted. The therapist can usually begin to ascertain the strength and the quality of a sibling relationship by the amount of factual information each sibling provides and how he or she seems to feel about it. Since most people look on sibling conflict as normal, it is usually easier to obtain candid statements of mutual dislike or lack of interest than it is in most other family relationships. Basic questions to ask are: How much time did (do) you spend alone or together with a sibling? And, if together, were (are) you then only in the company of your parents? Do you remember significant past events that affected you and your sibling? And if you do, in what detail? What kind of interaction was there between you? Did (do) you share rooms, beds, clothes, privileges, and household chores? How did (do) you deal with crises in your sibling's life—and he or she with those in yours—particularly during your younger years? This question is important if the siblings are close in age and of the same sex. By such questions, the therapist may determine the degree of access that the siblings have had to one another, and the strength or the weakness of the sources of projective and mutual identification at the time of therapy.

THE SIBLING CAREER

Another major issue to investigate in early sessions is each sibling's career: that is, how similar the siblings' experience has been, and whether their early development was parallel. This issue includes the following variables: (1) economic changes in the family, (2) parental work patterns, (3) places of residence, (4) marital patterns, and (5) developmental milestones in language acquisition, physical capabilities, and intellectual performance. Siblings close in age often have similar careers, with twins having the extreme example of parallel life experiences. A close-in-age set of siblings, who have lived in the same house and community, gone to the same schools, and had the same economic status, whose parents never have divorced, and who have developed at similar rates, can be considered *similar* and joined in their sibling careers. Their access is usually high. On the other hand, a brother and a sister who are eight years apart, *and* whose father's economic fortunes have changed drastically can be considered *dissimilar*. He, the older, attends an inner city school and hangs out with rough kids; she is sent to a prep school, rarely sees her brother who, by the time she goes off to an Ivy League college, has already moved far away and rarely comes home: these exemplify dissimilar siblings. A wide age spread between sibs increases the chance of dissimilar careers.

When there is high access between siblings, and their life experiences have been similar, they are more likely to be fused, to identify closely with one another, and to be loyal to one another. Siblings further apart in age, of different sex, and with low access are more likely to have dissimilar careers; and there is less identification and less loyalty for a therapist to count on in interventions. Sibling careers and access always interact in various ways.

IDENTIFICATION PATTERNS AND CHANGE

On the continuum of sameness and difference as indicated in chapters 3 and 4 the therapist should check whether there is a dialectical or static quality to the relationship, whether the siblings have served each other as models for identification, and whether there are conscious feelings of similarity or dissimilarity. The therapist should try to discover whether identification is at the core, the subidentity, or the persona level, by asking such questions as: Did you like each other? What didn't you like? Was it always this way? What made it change? Why do you think your brother became different, and did this cause you any problems with Mom or

Dad? Did you talk about the things you didn't like in each other? What made you feel you could no longer rely on your brother (or sister)?

The therapist can understand sibling dynamics by examining the psychological change in a patient, and the ways in which this change may have affected the sibling relationship. If change leading to problems in one child is rapid, and symptoms are severe (for example, when a previously quiet adolescent develops paranoid thinking and bizarre behavior), a too closely identifying sibling may also become symptomatic—a kind of echo, which can perpetuate and intensify the problems of the disturbed sibling with whom the well one is still fused or blurred. These are the *folie à deux* sibs (see chapter 9), whose similar problems are easy to spot in the first few family sessions. If change in one sibling is perceptibly slower but symptoms are moderate in severity (such as the personality changes that accompany a child's repeated school failures), the well sibling who is still twinning and merging, tends to be sympathetic but is often conflicted about whether to stay close or become distant from a brother or a sister. These well siblings initially appear to have no special problems. They tend to hide in the first few sessions, uncertain whether to stay silent or speak up.

When slow change is accompanied by severe symptoms (such as a deepening depression in which the youngster stays in his room and then has to be hospitalized (see chapter 9), the closely identifying well sibling can experience a profound sense of loss and resultant feelings of mourning. In these cases, the sibling who is not the identified patient is often eager to help, recognizes that he or she has many of the same feelings as the disturbed brother or sister, and wants to be helped, too.

Estranged, rigidly differentiated siblings react quite differently to their symptomatic siblings. If change is rapid, and the symptoms are severe, the well sibling often realizes angry feelings, avoids or scapegoats the disturbed sibling, protests loudly against therapeutic involvement, and therefore requires much more subtle, indirect maneuvering by a therapist to become a helpful ally in family therapy.

When the change in the sibling has been slow, and a brother or a sister's symptoms are moderately severe, non-identifying siblings can feel more secure about being "different" and are often initially willing to help, although their patience tends to wear thin. A therapist's expectations of sibling loyalty will usually cause these more estranged siblings to refrain from indicating their lack of involvement by stating that they "just don't care," by not showing up for family sessions, or by actually sabotaging the therapist's intervention and strategies. Ambivalent sibs have to be encouraged to be cooperative, and the therapist should approach them, saying,

"I just need to know a few things about Jim's background," or "I know you can tell me a lot about Jim. Can you come for a few sessions to fill me in?", and so on. Thus, the therapist can set the stage for involving siblings who de-identify or initially resist owning a share of the family's problem. The rate at which one sibling has changed, and the degree of his or her identification with the other, will help determine many of the therapist's strategies.

In our opinion, extreme patterns of sibling identification, whether close or distant, always require careful scrutiny. Since these begin early in life, the patient may be at a loss for words to explain to the therapist the sense of "sympathetic vibration," or lack of it, that he or she feels for a sibling.

LOYALTY AND TRUST

The therapist always needs to know whether there was loyalty between siblings; and if so, how it created expectations of caring, love, protection, and fairness. Loyalty, as was pointed out in chapter 5, often stems from very different sources. Was it based on one-way caretaking or reciprocal caregiving in which everyone derived benefit? The therapist should ask about those times when a sibling came to the rescue—or failed to rescue, leaving a brother or a sister with the sinking feeling that if that sibling was incapable of help, perhaps no one else ever would help. One younger brother, growing up in a sterile home, grew bitter about his big brother's refusal to protect him from their parents' imprecations. The younger brother began to rationalize that it would be best never to count on anyone. His parents were either "busy" or "tired" (but he loved them); his big brother was "peculiar," "selfish," and "aloof," and sometimes betrayed him to the parents. The younger brother, growing up isolated, had no choice but to develop the tough bravado of a self-reliant, self-sufficient, self-made man. He married a woman who mirrored his distrust and self-sufficiency; and when the marriage tottered, he went into couples therapy reluctantly, finding it difficult to accept the premise that a therapist could be trusted. No therapist could be "brother" to him; he had not even seen his own brother in four years and felt no loyalty. Even though the marriage was threatening to break at any moment, the therapist had to avoid being like the brother: he was extremely gentle, careful in his confrontations and interpretations so as to not embarrass the husband, and avoided siding with the wife or giving any other sign of "betrayal." Therapy took a decisive, positive turn once the husband admitted his dependence on the therapist (who was the same age as the older brother)—a condition that this man had never been able to enjoy. Working through his sibling transference and his damaged feelings about trust opened the gates for change.

Loyalty ties will also determine the availability of siblings for family therapy. Rigidly differentiated or de-identified adult siblings have their own "busy" lives and can rarely be counted on for therapeutic involvement. If a patient mentions a loyal sibling, the therapist should consider using the sibling as a future resource: for example, the sibling may be called in for one session to supply important information, or relied on as a "consultant" to help develop a therapeutic plan; or the therapist may create therapeutic tasks in which sibling alliances and relationships are an organizing feature of the entire therapy.

SEXUALITY AND AGGRESSION

Sexuality and aggression, (see chapters 6, 7, and 8), always require sensitive handling by the therapist. One's feelings about fairness, justice, equality, anger, and love may have sprung out of the sibling relationship in these two vital areas of human experience or, in the case of children, may just be surfacing. The therapist has to get beyond glib or inarticulate descriptions of "fighting" or beyond understated—or, more likely, unstated—communications about sexuality. Sibling rivalry is easier to talk about; but the therapist should ask about the extent and kind of past aggression, about its immediate effects, and about whether there continues to be a residue of rancor, hate, shame, or guilt. Once the therapist understands the roots of aggression, he can help redistribute power, teach parents how to discipline appropriately, and reward cooperation.*

Sexuality takes more time to uncover. Our own experience has been that the therapist must gain the patient's trust as a prerequisite for obtaining valid information about any of the relatively conflicted aspects of sibling sexual experience. Early on, a patient usually gives clues to whether he or she is holding any secrets; discomfort shows in the hesitation or the rush to answer, in the body language of conflict, in the wavering voice or look, in sharp, pessimistic attitudes about sex and love. If broached through questions—asked by the therapist in a gentle, understanding manner—any area of secret conflict such as sexuality, can begin to give the patient relief, breaks the bond of perverse loyalty to the sibling, and

---

* Significant progress has been made in recent years by behaviorally oriented researchers who teach parents how to reward their children's cooperation with one another, and not to reward sibling aggression. When sensitively applied by the therapist, and when parents are genuinely cooperative, excellent results can be achieved (Patterson 1980).

creates opportunities for a different type of sibling bond to emerge. But sibling experiences with sexuality are usually so fraught with anxiety that the therapist must persist, asking in a particularly gentle way.

DEATH

In chapter 10 we described the weighty legacy shouldered by survivor-siblings. The therapist should always ask whether there have been sibling deaths in *any* generation; and if so, how they affected the family. What was the cause of death? Was death unexpected and catastrophic, or slow, expected, and insidious? How did the family mourn? With elaborate ritual, such as a wake or the sitting of *shiva,* or in the antiseptic, compartmentalized manner that social critic Jessica Mitford has called the "American way of death" (1963)? And what were the long-term aftereffects?

Every child plays an important and separate role in his or her family; and when that role is vacated by death, there is an enormous temptation for *role reassignment* to occur. Parents may attempt to dull the pain of their loss by having the surviving children do the household jobs that the dead child was always expected to do, whether the job was walking the dog, washing dishes, or babysitting. Or role assignment can include more important, and subtle, functions: a child may become the new family healer, comedian, athlete, serious thinker, tension-reliever, or the new proud loving and living representative to the world of the best qualities the family can still offer. The therapist should always ask about changes in the apparent roles of surviving siblings brought about by the trauma of sibling death, and how these changes might still be operating in the survivors over the years. One sixteen-year-old girl, whose own birth had followed, by two years, the tragic crib death of an infant brother, cried out to her parents, "I'm so tired of hearing and knowing about that dead baby! Please let me live out my own life." Children never totally "recover" from a sibling death—but they do need to develop and grow, unfettered by legacies of guilt, sadness, horror, and helplessness (Masterman 1979).

THE PARENTS' SIBLING EXPERIENCES

A sibling relationship always occurs in the crucible of the larger, multigenerational family system. The therapist, therefore, needs to ask about each parent's sibling alliances, the nature of the family's projection process, and the manner of relating experiences as they occurred over two, and sometimes even three, generations. The reasons that each child becomes celebrated or ignored, favored or "disfavored," singled out or grouped by parents, must be understood in terms of each parent's sibling relationships. How did the parents like their brothers and sisters? Where and how did they derive their image of what the sibling relationship was supposed to be? And are they still imposing this image onto their children? An individual's birth-order position can sometimes determine the way he or she later enacts a marital relationship (Toman 1969). Birth order, however, never operates in a simple way. Deaths, illnesses and emotional crises all interact with birth order to create patterns of affinity or distance.

Sibling-Specific Techniques in Individual and Family Therapy

EXPLORING SIBLING LEGACIES

A therapist can sensitize a family to the patterns of sibling relationships it has inherited. Parents tend to impose on their children the template of sibling relationships that served them in their youth, on the assumption that what is good or bad in one generation is equally so for the next. Two parents who have had vastly different sibling experiences tend to clash over the meaning of their children's interaction, each spouse imposing on the other his or her notions of "normal sibling relationships."

For example, a family contacted a child guidance clinic about the poor relationship their fifteen-year-old daughter was having with her six-year-old brother. According to the father, the boy was being "abused" by his sister; she seemed contemptuous of him, complained about his being "spoiled," thought he was "obnoxious," and hated babysitting for him. The mother did not worry; this was "normal"; it would all "work out in the end"; and besides, she just "knew" her daughter loved her son. Thus, these parents were stalemated about what to do about the so-called sibling rivalry of their own children. What were the sibling experiences that fed the impressions of these parents? When the therapist asked this, the mother said that she loved her own brother as much as her parents, she visited him constantly, shared confidences with him, and denied that there had ever been animosity between them. The father, on the other hand, was a male Cinderella: his two older sisters had scapegoated him, ignored him, and when he had graduated from college, had neither attended the commencement exercises nor sent any word of congratulations. He had not visited either sister in five years and, for all an outsider could see, had no siblings. Only when the therapist was able to elicit from these parents their vastly different sibling experiences, were the parents able to understand and break the stalemate involving their own children.

An Individual Therapy Case: Jim. For some people, their sibling legacies become submerged, requiring probing by a therapist to bring them back into awareness. Although they may seem a distant and faded memory, they can send ripples of influence over a person's current life, enriching or enfeebling current relationships.

Jim, a handsome and poised thirty-eight-year-old, spoke to his therapist about his striking inability to acknowledge finally that his marriage was truly over. Jim's wife had left him three years earlier; and although the couple was childless, and he had had many opportunities to date attractive women since the separation began, Jim felt "numb" and grimly waited for his wife to "make up her mind about what she would do." Jim's stoic acceptance prevailed in spite of his acknowledgment that his wife told him little of what she was thinking or doing, and that he often felt depressed and helpless thinking of her. The therapist probed further; had any other episodes in Jim's life given him similar feelings? Jim recalled none, citing successful relationships with girl friends in college before he married. The therapist asked about siblings. Yes, Jim said, he had a younger brother and a younger sister, and then softly added that he had had another sister, Nancy, three years younger than he, who had died of leukemia when he was eleven years old and she was eight. The therapist pressed on, asking the patient to describe what it was like in the family as the sister lay dying. What had Jim done during this terrible, draining period? Jim began to describe the frightful circumstances: how he had been a good boy, fatalistically accepting the inevitable result but feeling angry and helpless that his beloved sister could no longer live as he was able to live; how he had said nothing, not burdening his parents with his complaints since they were already so burdened. Jim was the one who heated up the meals at night, who straightened up the bedrooms, vacuumed the house, and stoically accepted his and his sister's fate.

The therapist pointed out how Jim was dealing with the erosion of his marriage in much the same way. He again was enduring loss impassively; he again had not complained; he again seemed numb, helpless, and despairing. Jim sat as if thunderstruck. He then remembered how he had unthinkingly begun to do the vacuuming for his wife in their home; how—by beginning to cook the evening meals—he had tried to assuage whatever might be troubling her; how he had said nothing, mourning the decline of this relationship just as he had mourned the slow and inevitable decline of his sister and the loss of that relationship.

Psychotherapy with Siblings

During the next month in therapy, Jim began to realize how much his current life had been affected by his sister's illness and subsequent death. The sibling legacy had remained, casting a shadow over this survivor-child, rendering him just as helpless as he had been as a faithful brother and obedient son. Jim, unburdened by his telling of his sibling's demise, was now able to take a convincing stand with his wife. He asked for several meetings with her, tried to explore her feelings, and, when it became apparent that their relationship could no longer be salvaged, began dating another woman and took steps to finally emerge from his impasse.

CHANGING THE SIBLING BOND

Once the therapist understands the nature of the sibling bond and how it came into being, he has to determine whether it requires changing. A satisfying, reasonable, and flexible sibling relationship allows separateness and differentiation from one another without isolation, and cooperation, closeness, and intimacy without enmeshment. In chapter 4, we stated that siblings who have a constructive dialectic with each other, will have a dynamically independent relationship. We hesitate to define exactly what a "normal" sibling relationship is, but a therapist should be able to spot relationships that hinder development, create conflict and difficulty, destabilize the family, or cause psychological damage. For example, a younger brother was plunging headlong into disaster with his wife because of his older brother. Even though the older had bullied his kid brother and beaten him up when they were teen-agers, the thirty-two-year-old young brother insisted on being loyal and protective to the big brother, whom he now employed, let live in his house, lent thousands of dollars to, and literally bailed out of jail. The older brother had been arrested several times for pulling several minor holdups. Now kid brother could be "one up" on big brother. He could act morally superior, could offer aid, refuge, *and* lecture his brother in a style that seemed more *in loco parentis* than brotherly, and could even risk losing his wife, who was enraged that their good name (an unusual Irish name which was easily identified) was being affected, and that her home was being invaded by this troublemaking brother-in-law. Therapy uncovered her husband's covert need to dominate his brother in retaliation for the hurt and pain the former had endured twenty years earlier, enabled the marital relationship to regain its rightful place, and made it possible for the wife to have an equal voice in determining who would live in the couple's home.

In another family two teen-age brothers, only thirteen months apart, acted like Tweedle-Dum and Tweedle-Dee in defying their parents.

Their mother was an overly conscientious person, who spent her weekday evenings acting as the union delegate on behalf of her hospital co-workers. The father, a successful salesman, was on the road four nights a week and rushed home on Friday nights to relieve his exhausted wife, who greeted her husband with tales of distress about the "boys." Being a loving husband, the father punished his sons, grounding *them*, sending *them* to their room, cutting off *their* allowance, denying *them* privileges, and, if *they* showed no remorse, refusing to speak to *them*. The more the father related to his sons as if they were a set of Siamese twins, the more the boys thumbed their noses at Dad, snuck out of their house, drank excessively, took his car without permission, and joked and laughed with each other at his feeble authority. The therapist helped the parents to set clear rules, but he also refused to let the brothers sit together in sessions, told them that they were very different individuals, and that since no one family session could do justice to their collective needs, there would have to be alternating sessions—one focusing on the older's needs, the next one on those of the younger brother. Each brother was allowed to comment on the other's problems and needs in the alternating sessions, since it was acknowledged they were close; but one could not speak for the other, and both had to remember that each was an "individual." Once the process of differentiation was under way, each boy felt he could speak for himself and each began laying claim to separate roles in the family; the older became more the physical worker, active helper, and strong "silent" one; while the younger became more the quiet, studious, "gentle" one. The parental process of fusion had been interrupted.

CALLING IN CONSULTANT SIBLINGS

It is usually natural and commonplace to ask all the children in a family to attend family therapy sessions. Once children grow up, leave home, and move apart, however, it is not easy to gather them together for a sibling's psychotherapy sessions. Nonetheless, a therapist can try to arrange for siblings to come for a session when they congregate for a holiday. In other situations, any brother or sister within a two-hour drive can usually be persuaded to attend at least one session, and the only excuse needed is for one sibling to let the other(s) know that he or she is in therapy, and that the therapist needs their help. The consultant role can easily be filled by most brothers and sisters, no matter how distant the sibling bond, since the therapist should say only that he is looking for "information." He can ascertain whether siblings will become therapeutic allies after they participate in a session.

Psychotherapy with Siblings

Objective Older Brother: Bert and Jerold. Bert, a sharp, successful, senior executive at a major insurance company, was respected by his colleagues for his interpersonal skills and his ability to keep his staff enthusiastic and productive. For all of his smoothness, Bert was wary, even awkward with women. Since his divorce, he had been able to attract a bevy of women friends who were attracted to his "softness," to his ability to express his "feelings," and to a certain gentleness of manner which they often said contrasted with the other men they dated. But Bert found it difficult to sustain a relationship with any of these women; he would often get "depressed," as he put it—a certain lassitude of mood which he took to be an important cue that the relationship was problematic and probably should be terminated. After all, he had gotten "burnt" by his first wife whom he had married after a hot summer romance while he was preparing to leave for graduate study at a prestigious southern university. This was the same school his older brother Jerold had attended, and Bert had planned to follow in his footsteps. By marrying, Bert was able to abort this plan, particularly since his new wife, an aspiring studio artist, "hated" the idea of having to settle into the dreary grind of graduate student life in a sleepy southern town.

Now, twenty-two years later, the therapist called the older brother in as consultant. What was this "depression" of Bert's, and did Jerold know anything about it? The older brother explained his own moods, that he, too, frequently felt "depressed," that it was a family characteristic for everyone to be moody, and—beautiful women notwithstanding—that no one in the family had ever seemed particularly *sad* or *troubled*. In this Jewish working-class family, with both parents spending seven days a week in their store, "moods" were just a part of life. Of women? Jerold respected his younger brother's concerns but sincerely reminded Bert of the age-old grimness of life, of the cultural necessity to prevail and endure in the face of hardship, which this family had always had, and of a certain Jewish forbearance required of all of them by their father and mother whenever things were difficult. The older brother's personal revelations and reminders of the cultural and social heritage of depression did much to relieve the younger brother of his oversensitivity to the meaning of his depression when it came to women. Obtaining a broader perspective from this concerned, but more objective sibling helped both therapist and patient to conclude therapy, and for Bert to sustain more satisfying love relationships without premature and undue anxiety.

It is especially important not to abuse the consulting sibling's role. If the relationship has been hostile, distant, or disowned, it is wise not to ask that potentially destructive sibling to be more than a temporary consultant, unless the therapist is dealing with a clinical emergency, when he needs help from whomever will give it.

UNFREEZING MISUNDERSTANDINGS

We have already indicated (pages 74–75) how the language of young siblings can engender misunderstandings and "freeze" resentments. Frozen misunderstandings are at the heart of rigid, polarized, unhappy relationships. One can smugly assume that one is better than a brother or a sister—an assumption based on incidents from long ago that neither sibling can accurately recall. A middle-aged man told of remembering how his grandmother, the oldest of her clan, and her youngest sister gossiped over their middle sister, who lived just three floors above them in the same apartment house. These two sisters swore that they would never speak to their middle sister, and had not, in fact, done so in over many years. What a superior air to this sister they assumed, and what profound umbrage they communicated to the boy about what this sister had done or said to them long ago when they were all young girls, a continent away from where they were now living. Here they could juxtapose themselves and their grievance against each other, just as they apparently had done in childhood. The frozen, silent misunderstanding between these old sisters lasted right up until the grandmother's death years later, when her surviving two siblings—the man's silent great aunt and the talkative one—finally spoke to one another at her funeral. All his growing-up years he had been told of how bitter his grandmother felt about her silent sister, and how bitter the silent aunt felt toward his grandmother. At his grandmother's funeral, the man was finally introduced to his silent and mysterious great aunt. When she gave him a kiss without uttering a word, he felt her need to maintain the frozen, silent rift: even with her sister's grandson, she refused to break the perverse bond of sibling silence. The silent great aunt died ten years later at age ninety-two, and her great nephew was never able to discover the original cause of the old sibling rift. The old sisters undoubtedly had derived solace and object constancy, however bitterly experienced, from carrying part of their old childhood dynamic, unchanged, into their new country.

Family therapists can try to break up these frozen misunderstandings by gathering siblings together, obtaining everyone's version of a grievance, and pointing out the perverse satisfactions the siblings derive from feeling "hurt" and carrying "the pain." If such measures are insufficient, the therapist can create "rituals of forgiveness," much like acts of atonement, which can help wipe the slate clean without necessity of explanations, and permit a fresh beginning. It is best that these rituals be accompanied by some physical, visible act, which can punctuate the old grievance, separating it from the new once and for all, and can be solidified or even "celebrated" in the presence of the therapist. In one family of warring siblings, the therapist invited the elderly parents and instructed them to gather their children into a huge group bear hug, which then broke into a laughing, half-embarrassed chorus of giggling and tickling by the siblings. In another family, the therapist brought a bottle of champagne into the office, and everyone solemnly toasted the new beginning.

INTERPRETING DEVELOPMENTAL CHANGES

When one sibling grows and develops into a different kind of person than he or she had previously seemed to be, the change can come as a sharp and painful jolt to a previously calm and amicable friendship (see chapter 3). What may be good for one sibling may often occur at the expense of another, who is left bewildered, shocked, angry, or disappointed. The therapist can help a sibling by explaining the change, redefining it as a normal, necessary, expectable happening. Thus, it is imperative that a therapist know the expected stages of child, adolescent, and adult development so that he can help the patient to distinguish unusual developmental changes from those that are a part of growing up.

A frequent dislocation in sibling relationships occurs when one child enters adolescence while the other is "left behind" in childhood. A sister, thirteen, and a brother, eleven, had enjoyed a close identification for many years; but suddenly the rules of their relationship changed, and the girl would have nothing to do with her pudgy little brother. She ridiculed his friends, refused to play with him, and spent her free time listening to music in her bedroom with the door locked. The brother began fighting with her, pestered her, tried to humiliate her at every opportunity. Behind this aggressive front, he felt angry and rejected. He wondered what he had done to cause her to turn away from him, and secretly blamed himself.

The therapist joined the boy by agreeing with him that he had indeed been rejected, but emphasized that older siblings often behave as the sister was doing, and that at certain times each sibling had to go his or her separate way. This interpretation helped the boy to realize that his sister's rejection was not his fault. He began to recall that some of his friends also complained about having trouble with older siblings. Once this matter had been clarified, the boy was able to address other pressing matters, including the fact that he had few friends of his own and had been hanging on to his older sister to help fill a social void.

In another family, a three-year-old boy began hitting his fifteen-month-old sister. The worried parents described their surprise at the sudden onset of these attacks, especially since he had previously been mother's sweet helper. Why was this taking place, the parents wondered, and was there something "wrong" with their son? After watching the children play, the therapist observed that from the perspective of the three-year-old boy, his fifteen-month-old sister could indeed be very vexing. Within seven months, the baby had changed from a relatively immobile, smiling, and cooing bundle of joy into a highly mobile, biting, mischievous creature who was fully capable of destroying her brother's carefully constructed block towers. To the parents, the psychologist pointed out these normal developmental changes in the younger child and reassured them that their older child's responses were not inappropriate. He explained that the three-year-old did not have the cognitive ability to understand his younger sibling's changes. He also reminded the parents that three-year-old children typically engage in rough-and-tumble play and assert their rights and privileges (Blurton Jones 1972). This information helped to relieve the parents' anxieties. They were now conscious that, from their son's point of view, the baby could be perceived as a pest (they saw her only as "cute"). They also became sensitive to their three-year-old's need for private space and special activities and, as a result, arranged for him to enter a play group. The clarifications about normal behavior and suggestions for handling the sibling relationship enabled these parents to manage their children's interaction more effectively. As the boy felt more confident that his parents would control his baby sister, he became increasingly gentle and could admit he loved her.

The gamut of any sibling's emotional reactions to developmental changes invites probing and interpretation from the therapist. By pointing out the process of normal healthy individuation, children and parents can be helped to understand what they can expect, and to realize that none of life's relationships is impervious to change.

EXILING SIBLINGS

In the usual clamor and clash between individual family members that marks normal developmental change, a child can become too important a force. He or she can stabilize events all too smoothly, can become an indispensable mediator (acting as a buffer between every member and the urgent demands of each), or can act like an overworked executive whose splendid efforts allow everyone else to take off vital time. Such parental children (see pages 132–34, 137–38), by pre-empting this important role for themselves, can become so burdened that their own development is stunted (Ackerman 1966; Minuchin 1974). They often develop into a helpful or bossy identity, so that no one else assumes any personal responsibility for themselves: the caretaker sister or brother can be the appendage superego. Good, obedient, docile, depleted, and passive, these loyal caretakers often need to be rescued by the therapist, so that they can grow. Helpfully exiling such children by providing useful socialization experiences away from the rest of the group (for example, sending them to camp, arranging a new job, sanctioning a "vacation" for them) can positively destabilize the whole family, forcing everyone else to re-examine their previous roles.

In other situations, the closely fused alliances between sibs may be preventing their personalities from developing: some children act in tandem as if they have a common mind, as if what is good for one is good for the other; and neither can act without the approval of the other, the symbiotic partner. Or a brother or a sister can act the role of family terrorist, driving everyone into a state of heightened fear and anxiety. As lightening rod for everyone's apprehensions, the family terrorist makes everyone jump to his or her tune—pushing the parents into immature or insensitive responses, confusing the siblings, or causing unfortunate, undeserved splits into "well" and "sick" sibling identities. Separating the children by sending one away can break up the log jam of confusion or passivity and give the family therapist new opportunities to become an important force for change.

The symbiotic set of sisters in chapter 2 proved that, united, they could defeat therapists. Marilyn, the fourteen-year-old patient with anorexia, depended on her sister, Vickie, a buffer, to resist all outside attempts to get her to eat. When the therapist insisted that the buffer sister be sent to summer camp, everyone, including the parents, protested. This became a condition for therapy: either the buffer sister had to leave for two months, or the therapist would terminate treatment and refer the family elsewhere. The family finally gave in; the buffer sister was exiled; and the anorectic sister was left to struggle with the therapist, who, supporting her individuality and "courage" at "standing alone," got her to resume eating. When Vickie returned from camp, she revealed that she had had a wonderful time and was looking forward to the next summer's experience as well.

In another family, a previously rebelling oldest daughter now sat quietly in her room while the parents hammered out scheme after scheme to get her "moving." They considered buying a family restaurant, leasing a franchised store, starting a family catering business—anything to get their oldest child on her feet and out in the world. The father left his position in the South to move north in the hope that this daughter, who had ballooned in weight by one hundred pounds, would get out of her room and begin to do productive activities in a new environment. Worrying about this daughter prevented the parents from dealing effectively with their other two daughters. The other girls hid their own concerns, feeling superior to, or not as "troubled" as, their silent, immobile, fat sister. In family therapy, the therapist challenged this older sister's position as the one who captured most of the parents' attention and worry. It was time to move her physically out of her room and let the other daughters get the brunt of parental preoccupation and anxiety. The oldest took the therapist's advice, gleefully anticipating what the parents would do now that she was going into voluntary exile. After three weeks, she had moved into her own apartment with a roommate, had a part-time job of *her* choosing, and had begun to diet. The parents then announced that they had had enough of worrying, would be "damned" if they would switch to being preoccupied with their other children, and left town for their first vacation as a couple in twenty-four years. The two youngest also made decisive changes: the log jam was broken!

RALLYING THE SIBLINGS

When the therapist senses that a sibling bond is positive, he can bring siblings in for sessions to rally around a troubled brother or sister. Especially when there are three or more siblings, these get-togethers can achieve a certain momentum and create a dramatic statement of support by the sibling group for the one who is in difficulty. The heightened sense of cooperation and mutual identification by the entire troupe (which may be collectively more positive than their individual feelings for one another) usually conveys great support and gives the patient the sense he or she is not alone. In this sense, sibling rallies are like miniature network assemblies which orchestrate help around crises (Speck and Attneave 1973). These siblings often provide practical suggestions, even offer financial assistance, or admit to similar, if not greater, problems. If the siblings are young, rallies often focus around strategies for dealing with parents. The therapist in such cases has to reassure the parents he is not siding with the kids but will function as a neutral but concerned go-between (Zuk 1971).

When sixteen-year-old Cathy, who had been acting out sexually, was referred for family therapy with her two brothers and parents, she looked like an anxious, confused child, chattering helplessly, and frequently jumping out of her chair in agitation during the initial sessions. Her brothers knew all too well the virtues of remaining silent and siding with the parents in their exasperation with their daughter. Yet when the therapist arranged for the three children to come in alone, things changed dramatically. Coached by the therapist to offer help, not censure, the brothers gave advice, provided information about the parents' difficulties which Cathy had not known, and promised to support their sister whenever the parents bore down on her too hard. For the first time, the brothers revealed some of their own sexual escapades, sympathized with their sister for being singled out as a scapegoat, and noted how they identified with her in other ways. When the parents met with their children in the next session, they expressed surprise at the new unity among the children and acknowledged that Cathy had been acting less jittery, and that all of the kids had been more spontaneous and easy-going and seemed happier than the parents had seen them in a long time.

REHEARSING THE SIBLINGS

Rehearsals are similar to sibling rallies but make more use of role-playing techniques. Under the guidance of a family therapist, siblings are often able to encourage the expression of new behavior with each other, based on their intimate common familiarity with the parents or other family members. Siblings can double, play auxiliary ego, use role reversal, or simply share important issues in practice and anticipation of what they hope will occur outside the sibling sessions.

Many of these working principles are illustrated in the following case (see also Kahn and Bank 1981) in which—during individual therapy sessions—an unhappy woman became aware of her neglected "baby" status and of her yearning to be closer to her older sisters. Subsequently, by meeting as a sibling group with the therapist, the siblings worked out new mutual understandings with one another. They then faced the parents at the end of a psychotherapeutic intervention designed to help the youngest sister, the "baby" of the family, finally achieve equal status.

Changing the Sibling Bond: Maureen and Her Sister. Maureen, twenty-nine years old and unmarried, sought psychotherapeutic help for recurring cycles of depression, occasional suicidal thoughts, dissatisfaction with her work, and a unsatisfactory sexual life in which she had developed almost no intimacy with anyone, yet considered herself "homosexual." Maureen was an elementary school teacher, as was her mother.

Since graduating from college eight years earlier, Maureen had roomed with a much older woman, about whom she said she "cared." While identifying herself as homosexual, she seemed to do so by default, since both her fantasies and her behavior reflected only an inhibited, vague awareness of sexual preference. In her relationship with this roommate, she played a role more like a clinging, symbiotic child than an adult. Actually she did little confiding in this woman or in anyone else. She always felt passive, distant, and resigned. Maureen acknowledged that she was emotionally dependent on the male principal of her school—her employer of eight years, from whom she accepted friendly "advice"—but had no other adult friends. She was approximately one hundred pounds overweight, kept to herself, and did little to enhance her appearance. Maureen had siblings, but they seemed to be in a shadowy background, playing no active role in her life. She lived near her aging parents, closer than did her three other sibs, all married sisters and older than she. All the family members lived within a twenty-five mile radius of each other. As the baby of the family who was always quiet and nondemanding, Maureen had never been taken seriously by her older sisters—Barbara, age thirty-two, Gail, thirty-five; and Sally, thirty-six. Even when they experienced crises in their adult lives, Maureen reported functioning like a helpless bystander, sympathetic but without the ability to assist them.

Therapeutic Step 1: Exploring sibling relationships in individual therapy. The therapist began seeing Maureen in weekly individual sessions. In spite of her almost schizoid life style, she rapidly developed a good working relationship with the therapist, but her manner was waifish, dependent, and childlike. She described her relationship with her sibs as "pleasant," but they knew little about Maureen's core self. Although they had been somewhat accessible to one another in childhood, there had been little vital contact since, and Maureen's identification with them seemed faint and distant. They were all described as having recurring adjustment problems. Since they had so many "burdens," Maureen felt reluctant to "impose" on them, except for infrequent, brief visits. Now that her sisters were married, she had become even more of a spectator, looking from the outside in, as they led their lives and had families of their own.

She was a dutiful child to her parents, never criticizing them and rarely making demands. Although the older sisters had had their crises, Maureen, by contrast, was a "nice" fat girl, who rarely bothered anyone. Both mother and father were described as caring, concerned parents who, Maureen felt, had done their best in raising the children. They seemed to be beyond criticism, despite the therapist's inquiries about discordant notes in the patient's relationship with them. Maureen identified more closely with her mother, who had allowed her daughter to know her as a person. The father, by contrast, had been a remote, overworked executive whom Maureen had idealized, but with whom she had never interacted in meaningful ways. She described attempts in pre-adolescence to be with her father, but these seemed to have been sabotaged by her mother's enveloping and oversolicitous interference. Maureen seemed totally confused about how to relate to her father now that she was an adult, and had no awareness of how her sisters dealt with Dad. She didn't have the vaguest idea of how to speak to him or how to examine her own feelings about him. She passively accepted her own and her family's view of herself as an unobtrusive youngest daughter, who expected little and of whom little was expected. Her faintly felt anger was never shown in this rigid arrangement of family roles.

After twelve individual sessions, the therapist felt that Maureen had established a passive-dependent relationship with him not unlike her previous relationships. The therapy began to take a tone similar to the sibling connections Maureen had developed: it was calm, resigned and uneventful. Maureen's sibling transference was becoming evident: she asked for little, constantly inquired if she could "do something" for the therapist, and seemed "grateful" for the attention he was giving her in spite of her paying for the therapy. The only point at which the therapist felt that Maureen expressed strong affect was when he told her that she was living her life as "the baby of the family." This role, she finally admitted, was one that she had resented for years, and in which the sisters seemed to collude with the parents. Now she began being more critical of the therapist; in the next few sessions she began asserting her opinion, once reminding the therapist that he had contradicted himself in one of the previous sessions. Her newly critical stance was one she admitted she had never been able to accomplish with her bossy older sisters. She had purposely suppressed her irritation toward her siblings, fearing they would reject her. The aliveness and resentment that these issues sparked dictated the therapist's next move.

Therapeutic Step 2: A visit by sibling consultants in which resentments are expressed. At this stage of treatment, the therapist arranged for Maureen to ask her three sisters to come in for a session. Invited to participate as "consultants" in order to help their "troubled" sibling, the sisters admitted that their relationship with Maureen had come to an impasse and was worth working on. Maureen expressed dissatisfaction with her role as the baby of the group; the sisters replied that she showed her feelings and her presence so seldom that they had never known she was troubled.

But probing revealed other difficulties in the sibling group. They began to admit resentments, grudges, and frozen misunderstandings that they all had held toward one another over the years. Especially surprising was the admission that Maureen and Barbara, whom everyone had thought were close (as the two youngest, they were supposed to be close), were in fact "distant." Similarly, Gail and Sally, a year apart, were not the natural friends that they had seemed to be.

The meeting ended with the sisters' apprehensions and resentments having been brought into the open. Since they had achieved this so rapidly, the therapist recommended that they meet in one of their homes to continue to discuss their misunderstandings. Maureen continued her individual therapy. She told the therapist he was becoming like a "brother" to her and she was feeling more equal. After four weeks the therapist was surprised and delighted to learn that the sisters were now meeting regularly for three to four hours every Saturday. These get-togethers seemed to have become like sibling rallies with the focus off Maureen and on the problems they all faced. These included attempts to undo the frozen misunderstandings from the past and to explore the coalitions that now prevailed. For the first time Maureen reported feeling like an equal.

Therapeutic Step 3: A sibling rally in which new sibling bonds emerge. At this point the therapist arranged for a second sibling session in which the pursuit of "sisterhood" was to be negotiated. The following excerpt illustrates how the sisters pursued the constructive dialectic that must characterize healthy sibling relationships:

Attempting to undo the frozen misunderstandings.

GAIL: I don't want to be Sally's neighbor—I want to be her sister. I don't want to meet you for lunch, I don't want to hear about your tennis lesson. I want to know you—I want to know what you are really thinking

SALLY: But I feel we have—we have discussed the kids, we've discussed our husbands, we have talked about all kinds of problems we have and everything.

GAIL: Well, I feel for a while we did—but not for a long time, a long time.

SALLY: I think it all started with your problems with Jim [Cathy's husband] last year. I think I didn't

know how to sit and really talk then. I had some
problems that seemed trivial to yours, so I wasn't
going to sit down and bother you with mine.

THERAPIST: Where did she let you down?

GAIL: I don't know. I just felt all of a sudden every
time I talked to her, I didn't know what to say
any more because, when I said something that
was vital to me, she just sort of ____ "Oh really,"
you know, sort of a neighbor kind of attitude—
where maybe she cared inside, but she wasn't letting me know that she really cared, and I just felt
I couldn't open up any more.

*Searching for
a sense of
"sisterhood."*

After this discussion, in which they admitted having been hurt, the
sisters began to attain a real cohesiveness, and all four began speaking to
each other as adult women with a common stake in life. Maureen became
an equal and held her own in the subsequent meetings. She announced
her homosexuality to her sisters. They had sensed her sexual confusion
many years before, and they now seemed relieved that Maureen's "secret" could be openly shared. Maureen drew courage from their
acceptance.

It was now five months since individual therapy had begun and two
months since the first sibling session. Maureen was becoming less depressed and had begun dieting in emulation of her slimmer sisters. She
began feeling more alive and, in her individual sessions, was becoming
more curious about mature sexual relationships. Her dreams and fantasies
were no longer ambiguous and immature and now included both heterosexual and homosexual content. She began questioning her empty and
passive relationship with her roommate and expressed discontent with her
job.

The sisters continued to meet regularly both with and without the
therapist. The mother now joined her daughters in what had become the
weekly leaderless sibling rallies. Now that the sisters had become a more
cohesive group, the stage was set to begin full family sessions with *both*
parents present.

Individual therapy sessions were now reduced in frequency and alter-
nated with the sibling and the full family sessions. At the second full
family session, Maureen, encouraged by her sisters' acceptance of her secret, announced to both of her parents that she considered herself a homosexual. Confronted by the presence of mutually supportive sisters, the parents expressed no apparent rejection or even surprise. By the third family

327

session, Maureen, because of the empathy and support of her sisters, was finally able to confront her parents about the parental neglect she had experienced as a child:

THERAPIST: [*To Maureen*] I don't know why you have decided to use your appearance and your sexuality as your battleground—but I think you were plenty angry as a kid, and they disappointed you in some ways, and I think you were very angry about it.

Another sister identifies.

BARBARA: It makes me wonder about me, too—if I have the same problem. Anger directed at all of us, or at Mother and Dad. What do you mean?

THERAPIST: I think Maureen has to answer that.

GAIL: I want to know why Maureen is crying now— why she feels very upset.

Sister allies with therapist. Maureen confronts her father for the first time.

MAUREEN: [*Crying*] I think I had a lot of anger—I think I was, you know, just shut off. I really don't even know how to talk about it or to say it, but I really don't even know how you feel about me Dad [*sobbing*].

FATHER: I always loved you, Maureen.

MOTHER: You still don't know?

FATHER: I get mad at you sometimes—but I love you.

MAUREEN: I feel it more now than I ever have, Mother. But there were so many years we fought and fought when he just stood back— I just felt like nothing [*crying*].

She finally is able to articulate her confused identity.

Like I was just kind of a *pawn* between you and he [*sobbing*]—or I was his little *boy* [*gasping*] or *something* that I couldn't be. I couldn't [*sobbing*], I just couldn't tell you how I felt. And it's only been since we started these family sessions that I felt him sending more feelings toward me, but before that I just didn't know how he felt.

FATHER: I had a lot of good feelings for you.

MAUREEN: I didn't know whether I was just somebody nice to talk to about the football game, Daddy, I know, but some things don't mean love.

Mother resists the change in Maureen.	MOTHER: You said you were getting along so much better with Dad, you had a much better relationship with Dad.
	MAUREEN: Right, exactly right.
Therapist facilitates the confrontation.	THERAPIST: [*To Sally*] Would you let her sit next to Dad. [*Changing of seats: seating Maureen next to her father*]

The mother, Joan, then countered with a birth-order explanation to ward off responsibility for any of Maureen's problems and, characteristically, to shield the father from blame:

> MOTHER: Might I also say to Maureen, sometimes, inasmuch as you were the youngest, it might have been, as you know, sort of an overprotective thing that Dad was doing. The others were growing up, and they were getting married and going out, and you were the youngest—so all the attention was focused on you, perhaps not in the right way—but in a way to see that you were brought up properly and didn't get into trouble, and so forth. Maybe it wasn't just directed in the proper way, or something. I think it's the same as with the oldest child. If there is a large area of time between an older child and a younger one, the oldest one is the focus.

The therapist blocks the mother's defensive use of a birth-order explanation and then proceeds to validate Maureen's view.	THERAPIST: Joan, Joan [*shaking head*], Maureen is really saying that there was something going on between you and Bill [the father] in those years. Granted this was a long time ago, O.K. Maybe after everybody cleared out, she was left to be the only one to be the buffer between you and him. She was shuttling back and forth, *confused*, about whom to defy, whom to protect, whom to align with.
	MOTHER: But in what way, I can't—I really can't_____.
Having been comforted by her sisters, Maureen is able to continue.	MAUREEN: Do you know what it was like when I lived at home, Mother? It was horrible.

Maureen, no longer weeping, is now firm and emphatic.

The " baby" of the family bore the full brunt of the marital conflict.

MOTHER: I remember, you were in high school_____ .

MAUREEN: It was horrible. It was terrible. It was just awful, and I was having so many problems then. That was when I first decided on my own that I was a homosexual. And I was really in a lot of trouble. I couldn't talk to either of you. You were bickering back and forth. I know that you and Dad bicker, it's a thing that people do, but it used to grate on me. I couldn't talk about anything, we were fighting all the time. He and I would have a fight, and you would come in and slap me or tell me not to talk to him like that, or something else, and we really never really fought it out. We never really sat down and said "Hey, let's talk about this. We're people." This is the way I left home. I couldn't wait to get out of the house. I have to be blunt with you, I couldn't wait! It was a couple of years later when I finally said to myself, "Yes, I miss them. I'm sorry—well, I'm not sorry I'm not living with them. I'm having a good time living on my own," but I still didn't know how you felt, how I really felt about anything. I didn't know how Daddy felt about me or how, whether I was *even a human being* or a *female person* in his eyes. I just felt like a *thing,* and it was a terrible feeling. It was a bad place for me to be. I just had no place to turn.

The poignancy of these statements was remarkable to everyone, as if Maureen was, for the first time in her life, becoming a person.

Later in the session, the sisters successfully parried their mother and father's collusive attempts to avoid discussing feelings. Just as they had supported Maureen in their sibling rallies, they now came to her rescue as the father first evaded, and then finally expressed, his love for his daughter:

This keen observation by a sister frees the family therapist from his

CATHY: Can I interrupt a minute? I see something here that I never realized before, but have noticed more and more in sessions. Whenever Maureen directs a question to Dad, Mother answers for him.

330

confrontational work and allows the family confrontation to proceed more naturally.

THERAPIST: Yes, she does.

GAIL: And Maureen and Mother end up talking, and Mother and Dad never really____

FATHER: That's because she [*referring to his wife*] is able to express herself much better than I can.

GAIL: That's not it. Maureen and Mother can talk, Dad. *But you've got to talk to Maureen, you have got to tell her. No, Dad*____

FATHER: I talk to Maureen.

The sister has become Maureen's advocate.

GAIL: Mother can't answer for you. Mother can't say, "This is how I feel—I don't know how Dad feels—" this is now the time, Dad. You've got to say, "Maureen, this is how I feel." This is what Maureen wants to know—not how Mom thinks you feel, but how *you* feel.

FATHER: I don't know how I feel. I can't express how I feel. I know how I feel. It's been a love for Maureen. I like to do things for her. I have done a lot of things for her. I can take her places and do things like that. And to me it's just a way of living. I know that we have had a lot of troubles in the past—and they were partly her fault and partly my fault. That's over the dam now.

THERAPIST: It's not over the dam.

GAIL: Not for her.

THERAPIST: The river is flowing, but it's still the same river.

Another sister offers support.

BARBARA: She wants to know how you see her now.

FATHER: I'm just telling you how I feel—I love *all* of you. What else am I going to say?

Gail continues to mediate as the go-between.

GAIL: Tell her.

FATHER: I just told her.

GAIL: Tell her again.

He finally validates Maureen.

FATHER: Maureen, I love you. Give me a kiss, will you? [*He reaches for his daughter, who comes to him from her chair. Long hug, giggles from others*] I could've told you that yesterday morning, too.

GAIL: Why didn't you?

*Again third-
oldest joins in.
Referring to her
weight loss.*

BARBARA: Tell her every morning.

FATHER: I'm not going to tell you to sit on my lap yet, but I will in another couple of months [*laughs*].

MAUREEN: I tell you, that's the first time I ever told my father I loved him! I think that's the first time I ever told my father I loved him! [*Exhilarated*]

FATHER: This has been the *underlying* feeling for the last few years. We never have to——

*Now all the
sisters agree that
love was rarely
expressed, and no
longer hold their
father solely
responsible.*

SALLY: That was always a very hard thing to say in our family.

FATHER: I could never say it in public. I say a lot of things in private I would never say in public.

SALLY: Hugging each other and holding hands and things like that. I never remember *us* saying it back and forth to each other.

GAIL: Grandmother never said, "Gail, I love you," or "Barbara, I love you," either. That was never a thing that the family gave to us. Even though we all knew it. It was never anything verbal.

Maureen's issue with her father was now revealed as one part of a larger problem in the family system. Later Sally spoke for herself as well as for her sisters:

SALLY: We are a family of things. To show our love for each other we have, through the years, given things to each other or done things for each other. But we haven't put our arms around each other or just said, "You are a really neat person, and I really love you. I'm here if you ever need me."

Shortly after this confrontation session, Maureen decided to begin a completely different career, one in which she had supervisory responsibilities, in contrast to the passive role she had previously played in her work. She lost seventy pounds over the next six months and began to develop an intimate relationship with another woman whom she first considered a close friend and whom she could hold her own with in discussions and decision making. The relationship steadily developed and appeared to be mutually satisfying. Eventually Maureen took an apartment with her friend and said that for the first time in her life she was happy and felt like a "worthy human being." She frequently saw her family and now was welcomed in each of her sibling's homes.

Termination and Maureen's outcome. One year after treatment began, the individual sessions were reduced to every other week and then monthly. The family sessions occurred every three months. These served to consolidate the gains achieved earlier. The sisters continued to meet regularly by themselves and, now that the ground had been broken, invited both their parents to join them in ways that were both affectionate and productive. Seventeen months after therapy had begun, and fourteen months after the first sibling session, Maureen terminated treatment. Annual follow-ups by the therapist over the next five years revealed that Maureen was still functioning well. She had maintained her relationship with her friend, they had purchased a home, and Maureen reported being the dominant decision maker about financial matters. Along with this stable and meaningful relationship, Maureen maintained close relations with all her sisters and her parents. Indeed, she had moved from the periphery of the sisterhood to its center. She was looked upon as the "leader" of the family, the one who organized family get-togethers and could be counted upon in crisis. She expressed great satisfaction about her work, intimate relations, and self-concept.

The gains achieved by Maureen were helped enormously by the changes in her siblings' feelings about one another. These sisters had initially focused on Maureen's symptoms and then subsequently addressed all of their shared concerns. Uncovering sibling dynamics in the individual sessions, and then employing siblings as consultants and organizing rallies with them, allowed mutual differences and past frozen misunderstandings to become resolved. Once this happened, the patient was able to address her father, knowing she was more fully understood and supported by her sisters. Faced with such a unified sibling group, the parents were forced to abandon their usual tactics of denial and evasion and to redress old grievances by being helpful and accepting. Without the support of the sisters, who now positively identified with Maureen, it is doubtful that the therapist could have facilitated as successful and rapid a resolution of the client's problems. The family's old idea that older children should have more power and dominate, and that younger ones are weaker and should be passive, no longer seemed relevant or had any determining effect in this family.

Conclusion

In spite of past misunderstandings and contemporary obstacles in the form of commitments to spouses, parents, children, and friends, many siblings can be brought together to resolve their differences. By uniting in order to help a sister or a brother, siblings of all ages can more successfully challenge the usual patterns of defense of one or both parents. The collective force of a united sibling group, working under the guidance of a family therapist, can rewrite the rigid roles family members play in their ultimate social system. Because of the increased respect and acceptance a person receives from his or her siblings, there can be positive personality change.

Not all siblings can be brought together to resolve differences and to rally support for the one who is "in crisis." The therapist must be careful not to assume that all siblings can easily be united and that brothers and sisters can always be supportive of and cooperate with one another. Whether they can depends entirely on how the sibling bonds were forged. We believe that the therapist will find it most helpful to probe the actual relationship and discover any serious grievances before attempting to bring siblings together. In individual psychotherapy, a great number of sibling issues can emerge in the course of treatment. When using a family therapy approach, a number of sibling-specific techniques can be employed, but to rally siblings in the cause of someone they envy or hate, to ask them to cooperate when rifts exist, will only compound hurt in an already injured group of siblings. In carefully selected groups of brothers and sisters, a therapist can rally them to struggle for mutuality and equality. By uniting, after mutuality has been achieved, siblings, regardless of their ages, can deal effectively with defensive parents. Once the hard work of becoming a reciprocating group of equals has occurred, siblings can enjoy a constructive dialectic. The sibling relationship can work as a force for the betterment of relationships among all family members and can help each person function more effectively in life.

Epilogue

The man turned away from the grave, where his mother now lay beside his father. The last shovelful of dirt had been scattered, the last goodbyes had been said, the last of the family friends had paid their respects, and now he was left alone with his two sisters.

He felt a great desire to hug them and tell them they should always stick together. Then he thought of the huge sacrifices his older sister had made caring for their mother in this long year of her last illness; while, from the sidelines, his younger sister watched passively, full of platitudes, but at the same time complaining that *she* couldn't be expected to pay for any of the hospital bills. Anger wrestled with sorrow as he followed his sisters out of the cemetery. He'd be damned if he'd speak to his younger sister after all her carping as their mother lay dying.

Suddenly it occurred to him that he wouldn't have to speak to her if he didn't want to, now that both of their parents were dead. He knew he'd always want to see his older sister, they'd been close since childhood. But the younger one? What did he owe her? What, indeed, did the three of them owe each other? Should they gather together regularly, as their parents had always exhorted them to do, as if they loved and respected each other, as if they were obliged to, as if they were linked in some way?

This brother was not alone in his musings. Each of us who is a sister or a brother must, consciously or unconsciously, decide—when the second parent dies—whether and how to continue actively to recognize the sibling bond. Like Rebecca and Lillian, with whom this book opens, siblings in some way or other decide whether to maintain their ties in spite of—even because of—past family turbulence. Although the sibling bond may be the ultimate parental legacy, the day soon comes when parents are no longer there to dictate, orchestrate, nurture, or embitter their children's relationships. Now each child is free to choose: Whether to keep alive and lively the sibling bond, to sustain it by helping brothers and sisters, by gathering together at Thanksgiving, to reminisce about their childhood, trade Mother's recipes, regale each other with Father's jokes, or admire the treasured heirlooms that once adorned their parents' home, now divided among the brothers and sisters. Or, whether to sever the sibling bond, to turn away from some or all of one's brothers and sisters, to remain politely distant, never communicating in any deeper way—to set, once and for all, a frozen misunderstanding.

Still—whether one celebrates or denies the sibling bond—as long as one has a brother or a sister alive, there is always another human being who has known one as a child, who has experienced one in a unique and intimate way over which one has had little control, who has been a mirror, however distorted, of one's childhood and youth—someone, in short, who has been a child of, and has shared, the same parents.

Over and over, the people whom we interviewed spoke of wanting more control of an ongoing sibling relationship, of wanting to know how to interpret it, how to predict its course. Parents who understand this crucial human relationship can improve upon it and help their children to have richer and less difficult sibling experiences than their own may have been. Adult siblings who understand the sibling bond may be able to act in ways less compelled by irrationality and find more constructive ways of dealing with their feelings about each other.

But the broadening of knowledge about the sibling bond—how to shape it, how to change it—is just beginning. We hope that our ideas will inspire further thought and investigation of this, one of life's most powerful human relationships.

It is our hope, too, that this book will enable our readers—be they therapists or teachers or siblings or parents of siblings—to become aware of the complexity of the sibling bond and to deal wisely with its surprises, its frustrations, and its potential for joy.

BIBLIOGRAPHY

Abelson, Robert P. 1981. "Psychological Status of the Script Concept." *American Pscyhologist* 36(7):715–29.

Abramovitch, Ronah; Carter, C.; and Lando, B. 1979. "Sibling Interaction in the home." *Child Development* 50:997–1003.

Abrams, Jules C.; and Kaslow, Florence W. 1976. "Learning Disability and Family Dynamics: A Mutual Interaction." *Journal of Clinical Child Psychology* 5(1 [Spring]):35–40.

Ackerman, Nathan. 1966. *Treating the Troubled Family*. New York: Basic Books.

Adams, Bert. 1968. *Kinship in an Urban Setting*. Chicago: Markham.

Adler, Alfred. 1928. "Characteristics of First, Second and Third Children." *Children* 3(14 [issue 5]).

Adler, Alfred. 1959. *Understanding Human Nature*. New York: Fawcett Publications.

Adler, William. 1980. *The Kennedy Children: Triumphs and Tragedies*. New York: Franklin Watts.

Ahrensberg, Conrad. 1937. *The Irish Countryman*. Garden City, N.Y.: Natural History Press.

Ainsworth, Mary. 1972. "Attachment and Dependency: A Comparison." In J. L. Gerwitz (ed.). *Attachment and Dependence*. Washington, D. C.: Winston.

Ainsworth, Mary D. Salter. 1979. "Infant-Mother Attachment." *American Psychologist* 34(10):932–37.

Ariès, Philippe. 1962. *Centuries of Childhood*. New York: Vintage Books.

Aldous, Joan. 1978. *Family Careers: Developmental Change in Families*. New York: John Wiley.

Allen, Martin G.; Pollin, William; and Offer, Axel. 1971. "Parental Birth and Infancy Factors in Infant Twin Development." *American Journal of Psychiatry* 127:1597–1604.

Allport, Gordon, 1955. *Becoming: Basic Considerations for a Psychology of Personality*. New Haven: Yale University Press.

Altus, William. 1965. "Birth Order and Academic Pimogeniture." *Journal of Personality and Social Psychology* 6:872–76.

Altus, William. 1966. "Birth Order and Its Sequelae." *Science* 151:44–49.

Anthony, E. James; and Koupernik, Cyrille, (eds.) 1974. *The Child in His Family: Children at Risk*, vol. III. New York: John Wiley.

Arlow, Jacob. 1960. "Fantasy Symptoms in Twins." *Psychoanalytic Quarterly* 29(2):175–99.

Arnold, J. E.; Levine, A. G.; and Patterson, G. R. 1976. "Changes in Sibling Behavior following Family Intervention." *Annual Review of Behavior Therapy and Practice* 4:535–45.

Arnstein, Helene S. 1979. *Brothers and Sisters: Sisters and Brothers*. New York: E. P. Dutton.

Bagley, Christopher. 1969. "Incest Behavior and Incest Taboo." *Social Problems* 16:505–19.

Bane, Mary Jo. 1976. *Here to Stay: American Families in the Twentieth Century*. New York: Basic Books.

Bank, Stephen; and Kahn, Michael D. 1975. "Sisterhood-Brotherhood Is Powerful: Sibling Sub-Systems and Family Therapy." *Family Process* 14(3 [September]):311–37.

Bank, Stephen; and Kahn, Michael D. 1980–81. "Freudian Siblings." *Psychoanalytic Review* 67(Winter):493–504.

Bank, Stephen; and Kahn, Michael D. 1982. "Intense Sibling Loyalties." In M. Lamb and B. Sutton-Smith (eds.), *Sibling Relationships across the Life Span*. Hillside, N.J.: Lawrence Ehrlbaum.

Bell, A.; and Weinberg, M. 1978. *Homosexualities: A Study of Diversity among Men and Women*. New York: Simon & Schuster.

Bell, Richard Q. 1974. "Contibutions of Human Infants to Caregiving and Social Interaction." In M. Lewis and L. A. Rosenblum, *The Effect of the Infant on Its Caregiver*, vol. I, pp. 1–20.

Benjamin, H. P. 1957. "Simultaneous Occurrences of Psychotic Episodes in Monozygotic Twins." *AMA Archives of Neurology and Psychiatry* 78:197–203.

Bergman, Thesi; and Wolfe, Sidney. 1971. "Observations of the Reactions of Healthy Children to Their Chronically Ill Siblings." *Bulletin of the Philadelphia Association for Psychoanalysis* 21:145–61.

Bernays, Anna. 1940. "My Brother, Sigmund Freud." *American Mercury* (November), pp. 334–40.

Berry, Gail W. 1975. "Incest: Some Clinical Variations on a Classical Theme." *Journal of the American Academy of Psychoanalysis* 3(2):151–61.

Biller, Henry B. 1971. *Father, Child and Sex Role*. Lexington, Mass.: D. C. Heath.

Blechman, Elaine. A. "Are Children with One Parent at Psychological Risk: A Methodological Review." *Journal of Marriage and Family*. In Press (1982).

Blinder, B. J. 1972. "Sibling Death in Childhood." *Child Psychiatry and Human Development* 2(4):169–75.

Bloch, Donald, ed. 1973. *Techniques of Family Psychotherapy*. New York: Grune & Stratton.

Blurton Jones, N. 1972. "Categories of Child-Child Interactions." In N. Blurton Jones (ed.), *Ethological Studies of Child Behavior*. London: Cambridge University Press.

Bossard, James H. S.; and Boll, Eleanor S. 1956. *The Large Family System: An Original Study in the Sociology of Family Behavior*. Philadelphia: University of Pennsylvania Press.

Boszormenyi-Nagy, Ivan. 1965. "A Theory of Relationships: Experience and Transaction." In Ivan Boszormenyi-Nagy and James Framo (eds.), *Intensive Family Therapy*. New York: Harper & Row.

Boszormenyi-Nagy, Ivan; and Spark, Geraldine, M. 1973. *Invisible Loyalties: Reciprocity in Intergenerational Family Therapy*. Hagerstown, Md.: Harper & Row.

Boszormenyi-Nagy, Ivan; and Ulrich, David. 1981. "Contextual Family Therapy," In Alan S. Gurman and David P. Kniskern (eds.), *Handbook of Family Therapy*. New York: Brunner-Mazel.

Bowen, Murray. 1966. "The Use of Family Theory in Clinical Practice." *Comprehensive Psychiatry* 7:345–74.

Bowen, Murray. 1970. "Toward the Differentiation of Self in One's Own Family." In James Framo (ed.), *Family Interaction: A Dialogue between Family Researchers and Family Therapists*, pp. 111–73. New York: Springer, 1972.

Bowerman, C. E.; and Dobash, R. M. 1974. "Structural Variations in Intersibling Affect." *Journal of Marriage and the Family* 36(1):48–54.

Bowlby, John. 1969. *Attachment*. Vol. I in *Attachment and Loss*. New York: Basic Books.

Bowlby, John. 1973. *Separation: Anxiety and Anger*. Vol. II in *Attachment and Loss*. New York: Basic Books.

Bowlby, John. 1980. *Loss, Sadness and Depression*. Vol. III in *Attachment and Loss*. New York: Basic Books.

Brazelton, T. Berry. 1974. *Toddlers and Parents: A Declaration of Independence*. New York: Delacorte.

Brim, O. G. 1958. "Family Structure and Sex Role Learning by Children: A Further Analysis of Helen Koch's Data." *Sociometry* 21:1–16.

Bronfenbrenner, Urie. 1970. *Two Worlds of Childhood*. New York: Russell Sage Foundation.

Bryant, Brenda K. 1979. *Siblings as Caretakers*. Paper presented at the annual meeting of the American Psychological Association, New York, September 1979, as part of a symposium entitled Lifespan Perspectives on Sibling Socialization.

Bryant, Brenda K. 1982. "Sibling Relationships in Middle Childhood." In M. Lamb and B. Sutton-Smith (eds.), *Sibling Relationships across the Life Span*. Hillside, N.J.: Lawrence Ehrlbaum.

Burlingham, Dorothy. 1952. *Twins: A Study of Three Pairs of Identical Twins*. London: Image.

BIBLIOGRAPHY

Cain, Albert C.; Fast, Irene; and Erickson, Mary. 1964. "Children's Disturbed Reactions to the Death of a Sibling." *American Journal of Orthopsychiatry* 34(4):741–52.

Caplow, Theodore. 1968. *Two against One: Coalitions in Triads*. Englewood Cliffs, N.J.: Prentice-Hall.

Carandang, Maria; Folkins, Carlyle; Hines, Patricia; and Steward, Margaret. 1979. "The Role of Cognitive Level and Sibling Illness in Childrens' Conceptualizations of Illness." *American Journal of Orthopsychiatry* 49:474–81.

Cicerelli, Victor G. 1972. "The Effect of Sibling Relationship on Concept Learning of Young Children Taught by Child Teachers." *Child Development* 43:282–87.

Cicerelli, Victor G. 1975. "Effects of Mother and Older Siblings on the Problem Solving Behavior of the Younger Child." *Developmental Psychology* 11:749–56.

Cicerelli, Victor G. 1976. "Mother-Child and Sibling-Sibling Interactions on a Problem Solving Task." *Child Development* 46:588–96.

Cicerelli, Victor G. 1977. "Relationship of Siblings to the Elderly Person's Feelings and Concerns." *Journal of Gerontology* 32(3):317–22.

Clarke-Stewart, K. A. 1978. "And Daddy Makes Three: The Father's Impact on Mother and Young Child." *Child Development* 49:466–78.

Cohen, Yehudi. 1978. "The Disappearance of the Incest Taboo." *Human Nature* (July), pp. 72–78.

Coleman, Sandra B. 1978. "Sib-Group Therapy: A Prevention Program for Siblings from Drug-Addicted Families." *International Journal of the Addictions* 13(1):115–27.

Coleman, Sandra. 1979. "Siblings in Session." In Edward and Pauline Kaufman (eds.), *Family Therapy of Drug and Alcohol Abuse*. New York: Gardner Press.

Conley, James J. 1981. "Birth Order and Individual Differences in Emotional Response." Manuscript, Department of Psychology, Wesleyan University.

Connors, Tony. 1968. "My Sister's Papers." *Kon in Springtime*. London: Oxford University Press.

Cooley, C. H. 1922. *Human Nature and the Social Order*. New York: Charles Scribner.

Cumming, Elaine; and Schneider, David. 1961. "Sibling Solidarity: A Property of American Kinship." *American Anthropologist* 63:408–507.

David, Henry P.; and Baldwin, Wendy, P. 1979. "Childbearing and Child Development: Demographic and Psychosocial Trends." *American Psychologist* 34:866–71.

Day, J.; and Kwiatkowska, H. Y. 1979. "The Psychiatric Patient and His 'Well' Sibling: A Comparison through Their Art Productions." *Bulletin of Art Therapy* 1:51–66.

Dicks, Henry V. 1967. *Marital Tensions: Clinical Studies towards a Psychological Theory of Interaction*. New York: Basic Books.

Duberman, Lucille. 1973. "Stepkin Relationships. *Journal of Marriage and the Family* 35(2):283–92.

Eisenstadt, J. Marvin. 1978. "Parental Loss and Genius. *American Psychologist* 33:211–23.

Encyclopaedia Britannica. 1947. "Narcissus."

Engel, George L. 1974. "The Death of a Twin: Mourning and Anniversary Reactions: Fragments of 10 Years of Self-Analysis." *International Journal of Psychoanalysis* 45(1):23–40.

Erikson, Erik. 1959. "Identity and the Life Cycle." In *Psychological Issues*. New York: International Universities Press.

Escalona, Sybil; and Heider, G. 1959. *Prediction and Outcome: A Study of Child Development*. New York: Basic Books.

Essman, Clifford; and Deutch, Francine. 1979. "Siblings as Babysitters: Responses of Adolescents to Younger Siblings in Problem Situations." *Adolescence* 54(Summer):411–20.

Etaugh, Claire. 1980. "Effects of Nonmaternal Care on Children: Research Evidence and Popular Views." *American Psychologist* 35:309–19.

Fagot, B. I. 1978. "The Influence of Sex of Child on Parental Reactions to Toddler Children." *Child Development* 49:459–65.

Fairbairn, W. R. D. 1954. *An Object Relations Theory of Personality*. New York: Basic Books.

Falbo, Toni. 1982. "Only Child in America." In M. Lamb and B. Sutton-Smith (eds.), *Sibling Relationships across the Life Span*. Hillside, N.J.: Lawrence Ehrlbaum.

Farber, Susan. 1981. *Identical Twins Reared Apart*. New York: Basic Books.

Faulkner, William. 1929. *The Sound and the Fury*. New York: Modern Library ed., Random House, 1946.

Featherstone, Helen. 1980. *A Difference in the Family*. New York: Basic Books.

Feinberg, Daniel. 1970. "Preventive Therapy with Siblings of a Dying Child." *Journal of the American Academy of Child Psychiatry* 9(4):644–68.

Ferguson, Eva. D. (University of Pittsburgh). 1958. "The Effect of Sibling Competition and Alliance on Level of Aspiration, Expectation and Performance." *Journal of Abnormal and Social Psychology* 56:213–22.

Festinger, Leon. 1954. "A Theory of Social Comparison Process." *Human Relations* 7:117–40.

Festinger, Leon. 1957. *A Theory of Cognitive Dissonance*. Stanford, Calif.: Stanford University Press.

Finklehor, David. 1979. *Sexually Victimized Children*. New York: Free Press.

Finklehor, David. 1980. "Sex Among Siblings: A Survey on Prevalence, Variety, and Effects." *Archives of Sexual Behavior* 9:171–94.

Fishel, Elizabeth. 1980. *Sisters*. New York: Bantam Books.

Forward, Susan; and Buck, Craig. 1978. *Betrayal of Innocence: Incest and Its Devastation*. New York: Penguin Books.

Fox, J. R. 1962. "Sibling Incest." *British Journal of Sociology* 13(2):128–50.

Fox, Robin J. 1980. *The Red Lamp of Incest*. New York: E. P. Dutton.

Framo, James. 1970. "Symptoms from a Family Transactional Viewpoint." *International Psychiatry Clinics* 7:125–71.

Framo, James. 1972. "Symptoms from a Family Transactional Point of View." In C. Seger and H. S. Kaplan, *Progress in Group and Family Therapy*, pp. 271–308. New York: Brunner/Mazel.

Frances, V.; and Frances A. 1976. "The Incest Taboo and Family Structure." *Family Process* 15:235–44.

Frazer, James G. 1910. *Totemism and Exogamy: A Treatise on Certain Early Forms of Superstition and Society*. 4 vols. London: Macmillan.

Freeman, Douglas S. 1948. *George Washington*. New York: Charles Scribner.

Freud, Anna. 1946. *The Ego and the Mechanisms of Defense*. New York: International Universities Press.

Freud, Anna; and Dann, Sophie. 1951. "An Experiment in Group Upbringing." In Ruth S. Eisler (ed.), *The Psychoanalytic Study of the Child*, vol. VI: New York: International Universities Press.

Freud, Sigmund. 1896. "Further Remarks on the Neuro-Psychoses of Defence." In *The Standard Edition of the Complete Works of Sigmund Freud*, vol. III. James Strachey (trans.). London: Hogarth Press 1953–74.

Freud, Sigmund. 1905. "Fragment of Analysis of a Case of Hysteria." In *Standard Edition*, vol. VII.

Freud, Sigmund. 1909. "Analysis of a Phobia in a Five-Year-Old Boy." In *Standard Edition*, vol. X.

Freud, Sigmund. 1912–13. "Totem and Taboo." In *Standard Edition*, vol. XIII.

Freud, Sigmund. 1918. "From the History of an Infantile Neurosis." In *Sigmund Freud: Collected Papers*, vol. III. New York: Basic Books.

Freud, Sigmund. 1925. "The Resistances to Psychoanalysis." In *Standard Edition*, vol. XVIIII.

Freud, Sigmund. 1930. *Civilization and Its Discontents*. In *Standard Edition*, vol. XXI.

Freud, Sigmund. 1935. *An Autobiographical Study*. James Strachey (trans.). London: Hogarth Press.

Freud, Sigmund. 1937. "Analysis: Terminable and Interminable." In *Standard Edition*, vol. XXIII.

Galton, Frances. 1874. *English Men of Science, Their Nature and Nurture*. London: Macmillan.

BIBLIOGRAPHY

Gallagher, Richard; and Cowen, Emory L. (Temple University). 1976. "Adjustment Problems of Sibling and Non-Sibling Pairs Referred by a School Mental Health Program." *Journal of Consulting and Clinical Psychology* 44(5 [October]): 873.

Garmezy, Norman. 1976. "Vulnerable and Invulnerable Children: Theory, Research and Intervention." Master Lecture on Developmental Psychology, American Psychological Association.

Gebhard, P. H., et al. 1965. *Sex Offenders: An Analysis of Types*. New York: Harper & Row.

Glenn, Jules. 1966. "Opposite Sex Twins." *Journal of the American Psychoanalytic Association* 14:736–59.

Goffman, Erving. 1973. *The Presentation of Self in Everyday Life*. Woodstock, N.Y.: Overlook Press.

Golding, William, *Lord of the Flies*. New York: G. P. Putnam, 1959.

Goodall, Jane. 1967. "Mother Offspring Relationships in Chimpanzees." In D. Morris, (ed.), *Primate Ethology*. Chicago: Aldine Press.

Goode, William. 1970. *World Revolution and Family Patterns*. New York: Free Press.

Grossman, Frances K. 1972. *Brothers and Sisters of Retarded Children: An Exploratory Study*. Syracuse, N.Y.: Syracuse University Press.

Guest, Judith. 1976. *Ordinary People*. New York: Viking Press.

Gunther, John. 1949. *Death, Be Not Proud*. New York: Harper & Row.

Haley, Jay. 1963. *Strategies of Psychotherapy*. New York: Grune & Stratton.

Haley, Jay. 1969. "The Art of Being Schizophrenic." *The Power Tactics of Jesus Christ*. New York: Grossman.

Haley, Jay. 1976. *Problem-Solving Therapy: New Strategies for Effective Family Therapy*. San Francisco: Jossey-Bass.

Haley, Jay. 1979. Family Therapy Conference, New York City, 9 July.

Haley, Jay. 1980. *Leaving Home*. New York: McGraw-Hill.

Hartup, Willard. 1975. "The Origins of Friendship." In M. Lewis and L. A. Rosenblum, *Friendship and Peer Relations*. New York: John Wiley.

Heath, D. H. 1976. "Competent Fathers: Their Personalities and Marriages." *Human Development* 19(1):26–39.

Hegel, G. W. F. 1931. *The Phenomenology of Mind*. New York: Macmillan.

Heider, Fritz. 1958. *The Psychology of Interpersonal Relations*. New York: John Wiley.

Henry, Jules. 1965. *Pathways to Madness*. New York: Random House.

Henry, Jules; and Henry, Zurria. 1942. "Symmetrical Reciprocal Hostility in Sibling Rivalry." *American Journal of Orthopsychiatry* 12:2.

Hilgard, Ernest R. 1944. "Human Motives and the Concept of Self." *American Psychologist* 4:374–82.

Hilgard, Josephine R. 1969. "Depressive and Psychotic States as Anniversaries to Sibling Death in Childhood." *International Psychiatry Clinics*, 6(2):197–211.

Hoffman, Lynn. 1971. "Deviation-Amplifying Processes in Natural Groups." In Jay Haley (ed.), *Changing Families: A Family Therapy Reader*, pp. 285–311. New York: Grune & Stratton.

Hoffman, Lynn. 1976. "'Enmeshment' and the Too Richly Cross Joined System." *Family Process* 14:457–68.

Hofstadter, Richard. 1959. *Social Darwinism in American Thought*. Boston: Beacon Press.

Holinger, Paul C. 1977. "Suicide in Adolescence." *American Journal of Psychiatry* 134(12 [December]):1433–34.

Hoover, C. F.; and Franz, J. D. 1972. "Siblings in the Families of Schizophrenics." *Archives of General Psychiatry* 26:334–42.

Horner, Althea. 1979. *Object Relations and the Developing Ego in Therapy*. New York: Jason Aronson.

Ihinger, Marilyn. 1975. "The Referee Role and Norms of Equity: A Contribution toward a Theory of Sibling Conflict." *Journal of Family and Marriage* 37(3):515–24.

Irish, Donald R. 1964. "Sibling Interaction: A Neglected Aspect in Family Life Research." *Social Forces* 42(3):279–88.

Irving, John. *The Hotel New Hampshire*. New York: E. P. Dutton, 1981.

Jackson, Don. 1970. "The Study of the Family." In N. W. Ackerman, *Family Process*, pp. 111–30. New York: Basic Books.

James, William. 1890. *The Principles of Psychology*, vol. I. New York: Holt.

Johnson, Adelaide; and Szurek, S. A. 1952. "The Genesis of Antisocial Acting Out in Children and Adults." *Psychoanalytic Quarterly* 21:323–43.

Jones, Ernest. 1910. *Hamlet and Oedipus. The Oedipus Complex as an Explanation of Hamlet's Mystery*. Garden City, N.Y.: Doubleday Books, 1949.

Jones, Ernest. 1953. *The Life and Work of Sigmund Freud*, vol. 1. New York: Basic Books.

Joseph, Edward D. 1959. "An Unusual Fantasy in a Twin with an Inquiry into the Nature of Fantasy." *Psychoanalytic Quarterly* 28:189–206.

Joseph, Edward D. 1961. "The Psychology of Twins." *Journal of American Psychoanalytic Association* 9(1):158–66.

Journal of Abnormal Psychology. 1949. "Ambivalence in First Reactions to a Sibling." 44:541–48.

Jung, Carl Gustave. 1953. *The Development of Personality*. New York: Pantheon.

Kahn, Michael D.; and Bank, Stephen. 1981. "In Pursuit of Sisterhood: Adult Siblings as a Resource for Combined Individual and Family Therapy." *Family Process* 20(1):85–95.

Kahn, Robert; and Cannell, Charles F. 1957. *The Dynamics of Interviewing*. New York: John Wiley.

Kahn, Ruth. 1981. "Parents as Teachers: Linguistic and Behavioral Interactions of Middle-Class Mothers and Fathers and Their Normally Developing and Developmentally Delayed Preschoolers During Teaching/Learning Activities." Doctoral Dissertation, University of Connecticut.

Kaiser, Hellmuth. 1955. "The Problem of Responsibility in Psychotherapy." *Psychiatry* 18:205–12.

Karpman, Ben. 1953. "Psychodynamics in Fraternal Twinship Relations." *Psychoanalytic Review* 1:40.

Kaufmann, James M.; Hallahan, Daniel P.; and Ball, Donald. 1975. "Parents' Predictions of Their Children's Perceptions of Family Relations." *Journal of Personality Assessment* 39(3):228–35.

Kendrick, Carol; and Dunn, Judy. 1980. "Caring for a Second Baby: Effects on Interaction between Mother and First Born." *Developmental Psychology* 16(4):303–11.

Keniston, Kenneth; and the Carnegie Council on Children. 1977. *All Our Children: The American Family under Pressure*. New York: Harcourt Brace Jovanovich.

Kernberg, Otto. 1975. *Borderline Conditions and Pathological Narcissism*. New York: Jason Aronson.

Kernberg, Otto. 1980. *Internal World and External Reality: Object Relations Theory Applies*. New York: Jason Aronson.

Kerouac, Jack. 1963. *Visions of Gerard*. New York: Farrar, Straus & Giroux.

Khan, Masud R. 1974. *The Privacy of the Self*. New York: International Universities Press.

Khan, Masud R. 1978. "Secret as Potential Space." In Simon Gralnick and Leonard Barkin (eds.), *Between Reality and Fantasy: Transitional Objects and Phenomena*. New York: Jason Aronson.

Klein, Melanie. 1975. *Envy and Gratitude and Other Works: 1946–1963*. New York: Delacorte.

Klein, Melanie; Heiminn, P.; Isaacs, S.; and Riviere, J. 1952. *Development in Psycho-Analysis*. London: Hogarth.

Koch, Helen L. 1955. "Some Personality Correlates of Sex, Sibling Position, and Sex of Sibling among Five and Six Year Old Children." *Genetic Psychological Monographs* 52:3–50.

Koch, Helen L. 1956. "Sissiness and Tomboyishness in Relation to Sibling Characteristics." *Journal of Genetic Psychology* 88:231–44.

Koch, Helen. 1960. "The Relation of Certain Formal Attributes of Siblings to Attitudes Held Toward Each Other and Toward Their Parents." *Monographs of the Society for Research in Child Development* 25:1–124.

Kohut, Heinz. 1971. *The Analysis of the Self*. New York: International Universities Press.

Kohut, Heinz. 1977. *The Restoration of the Self*. New York: International Universities Press.

BIBLIOGRAPHY

Krell, Robert; and Rabkin, Leslie. 1979. "The Effects of Sibling Death on the Surviving Child: A Family Perspective." *Family Process* 18:471–78.

Kubo, S. 1959. "Researchers and Studies on Incest in Japan." *Hiroshima Journal of Medical Sciences* 8:99–159.

Lamb, Michael E. 1976. "The Role of the Father: An Overview," In M. E. Lamb (ed.), *The Role of the Father in Child Development*. New York: John Wiley.

Lamb, Michael E. 1978. "The Development of Sibling Relationships in Infancy: A Short-Term Longitudinal Study," *Child Development* 49(4):1189–96.

Lamb, Michael; and Sutton-Smith, Brian. 1982. *Sibling Relationships across the Life Span*. Hillside, N.J.: Lawrence Ehrlbaum.

Langs, Robert J. 1977. *The Therapeutic Interaction: A Synthesis*. New York: Jason Aronson.

Lasch, Christopher. 1978. *The Culture of Narcissism: American Life in an Age of Diminishing Expectations*. New York: W. W. Norton.

Lasko, J. K. 1954. "Parent Behavior towards First and Second Children." *Genetic Psychological Monographs* 49:96–137.

Lavigueur, Henry. 1973. "The Use of Siblings as an Adjunct to the Behavioral Treatment of Children in the Home with Parents as Therapists." Doctoral Dissertation, University of Illinois at Urbana-Champaign.

Lederer, William J.; and Jackson, Don D. 1968. *The Mirages of Marriage*. New York: W. W. Norton.

Leitenberg, Harold; Burchard, John D.; Burchard, Sara N.; Fuller, Eloise J.; and Lysaght, Thomas V. 1977. "Using Positive Reinforcement to Suppress Behavior: Some Experimental Comparisons with Sibling Conflict." *Behavior Therapy* 8:168–82.

Leonard, Marjorie R. 1955. "Twins, Myths and Reality." *Child Study* 30:9–13, 38–41.

Leonard, Marjorie R. 1961. "Problems of Identification and Ego Development in Twins." In Ruth S. Eissler (ed.), *The Psychoanalytic Study of the Child*, Vol. XVI, pp. 300–12. Hartford: Yale University Press.

Lesser, Ruth M. 1978. "Sibling Transference and Countertransference." *Journal of the American Academy of Psychoanalysis* 6(1):37–49.

Lester, David C. 1975. *Unusual Sexual Behavior: The Standard Deviations*. Springfield, Ill.: Charles C Thomas.

Levy, David M. 1937. "Sibling Rivalry." *American Orthopsychiatric Association Monograph* 2.

Lewis, Jerry, M.; Beavers, Robert W.; Gossett, John T.; and Phillipps, Virginia A. 1976. *No Single Thread: Psychological Health in Family Systems*. New York: Brunner/Mazel.

Lichtenstein, Heinz. 1977. *The Dilemma of Human Identity*. New York: Jason Aronson.

Lieberman, E. James. 1970. "The Case for Small Families." *New York Times Magazine*, 8 March, pp. 86, 89.

Lifton, Robert J. 1967. *Death in Life: Survivors of Hiroshima*. New York: Random House.

Lindemann, Erich. 1944. "Symptomatology and Management of Acute Grief." *American Journal of Psychiatry* 101:141–48.

Lindzey, Gardner. 1967. "Some Remarks Concerning Incest, the Incest Taboo and Psychoanalytic Theory." *American Psychologist* 22:1051–59.

Lofland, John. 1976. *Doing Social Life*. New York: John Wiley.

Longo, Robert. 1977. *The Therapeutic Interaction: A Synthesis*. New York: Jason Aronson.

Lynch, James. 1979. *The Broken Heart: The Medical Consequences of Loneliness*. New York: Basic Books.

Lynn, David B. 1974. *The Father: His Role in Child Development*. Monterey, Calif.: Brooks Cole.

Lytton, H. 1979. "Disciplinary Encounters between Young Boys and their Mothers: Is There a Contingency System?" *Developmental Psychology* 15(3):256–68.

Lytton, H.; Conway, D.; and Sauve, R. 1977. "The Impact of Twinship on Parent Child Interaction." *Journal of Personality and Social Psychology* 35(2):97–105.

McArdle, Paul E.; and Miller, Sybil C. 1978. "Brothering and Sistering Education." Instructional Program Conducted at West Virginia Wesleyan University.

Machotka, Pavel; Pittman, Frank, S.; and Flomenhaft, Kalman. (Colorado Psychopathic Hospital). 1967. "Incest as a Family Affair." *Family Process* 6(1):98–116.

343

McMahon, Arthur; Schmitt, Phyllis; Patterson, James; and Rothman, Ellen. 1973. "Personality Differences between Inflammatory Bowel Disease Patients and Their Healthy Siblings." *Psychosomatic Medicine* 35(2):91–203.

Mahler, Margaret S.; and Furer, M. 1968. "On Human Symbiosis and the Vicissitudes of Individuation." In *Infantile Psychosis*. New York: International Universities Press.

Mann, Thomas. 1936. *The Blood of the Walsungs: Stories of Three Decades*. H. T. Lowe-Porter (trans.) New York: Alfred A. Knopf.

Mann, Thomas. 1951. *The Holy Sinners*. New York: Alfred A. Knopf.

Marscak, Marianne. 1968. "A Puzzling Episode," *Psychiatry* 31(2):195–98.

Masterman, Beth Jean. 1979. "Siblings during a Family Crisis: A Contextual Study." Honors Thesis, Wesleyan University.

Masters, William H.; and Johnson, Virginia E. 1976. "Incest: The Ultimate Taboo." *Redbook Magazine* 146(6):54–58.

Mead, George Herbert. 1934. *Mind, Self and Society: From the Standpoint of a Social Behaviorist*, C. W. Morris (ed.). Chicago: University of Chicago Press.

Mead, George Herbert. 1956. *The Social Psychology of George Herbert Mead*. Chicago: University of Chicago Press.

Meiselman, Karin C. 1978. *Incest: A Psychological Study of Causes and Effects with Treatment Recommendations*. San Francisco: Jossey-Bass.

Meyendorf, Ruth. 1971. "Infant Depression Due to Separation from Siblings. Syndrome or Depression, Retardation, Starvation and Neurological Symptoms: A Re-Evaluation of the Concept of Maternal Deprivation." *Psychiatrica Clinica* 4:321–35.

Milgram, Joel I.; and Ross, Helgola G. In press. "Effects of Fame in Adult Sibling Relationships." *Journal of Individual Psychology* 38.

Miller, Arthur. 1969. *The Price*. New York: Bantam.

Miller, Daniel R. 1963. "The Study of Social Relationships: Situation, Identity and Social Interaction." In S. Koch (ed.), *Psychology, A Study of a Science*, vol. V, pp. 641–737.

Miller, Daniel R. 1982. "Self, Symptom and Social Control." In T. Sarbin and K. Scheibe (eds.), *Studies in Social Identity*. New York: Praeger.

Milne, A. A. 1927. "Twice Times." *Now We Are Six*. New York: E. P. Dutton.

Minuchin, Salvador. 1974. *Families and Family Therapy*. Cambridge. Harvard University Press.

Minuchin, Salvador; and Fishman, Charles. 1981. *Techniques in Family Therapy*. Cambridge. Harvard University Press.

Minuchin, Salvado; Montalvo, Braulio; Guernez, Bernard; and Schumer, Florence. 1967. *Families of the Slums*. New York: Basic Books.

Minuchin, Salvador; Rosman, Bernice; and Baker, Lester. 1978. *Psychosomatic Families: Anorexia Nervosa in Context*. Cambridge. Harvard University Press.

Mitford, Jessica. 1963. *The American Way of Death*. New York: Simon & Schuster.

Money, J.; and Ehrhardt, A. 1972. *A Man and a Woman, Boy and Girl*. Baltimore: Johns Hopkins University Press.

Moore, S. 1964. "Descent and Symbolic Filiation." *American Anthropologist* 66:1308–21.

Mordock, John G. 1974. "Sibling Sexual Fantasies in Family Therapy: A Case Report." *Journal of Family Counseling* 2(1):60–65.

Napier, Augustus; and Whitaker, Carl. 1978. *The Family Crucible*. New York: Harper & Row.

Nelson, Waldo; Vaughan, Victor; McKay, James, Jr.; and Behrman, Richard. 1979. *Textbook of Pediatrics*, 11th ed. Philadelphia: W. B. Saunders.

Neuman, Gustave. 1966. "Younger Brothers of Schizophrenics," *Psychiatry* 29(2):146–51.

Oberndorf, C. P. 1929. "Psychoanalysis of Siblings." *American Journal of Psychiatry*, pp. 1007–1020.

O'Neill, Eugene. 1956. *Long Day's Journey into Night*. New Haven: Yale University Press.

Orr, Douglas W. 1941. "A Psychoanalytic Study of a Fraternal Twin," *Psychoanalytic Quarterly* 10:284–96.

Ovid. 1958. *Metamorphoses*. Rolfe Humphries (trans.). Bloomington: Indiana University.

BIBLIOGRAPHY

Packard, Vance. 1972. *A Nation of Strangers*. New York: David McKay.

Palazzoli, Mara Selvini; Boscolo, L.; Cecchin, G.; and Prata, C. 1978. *Paradox and Counterparadox*. New York: Jason Aronson.

Panken, S. 1973. *The Joy of Suffering*. New York: Jason Aronson.

Papalia, Diane; and Olds, Sally Wendkos. 1975. *A Child's World: Infancy through Adolescence*. New York: McGraw-Hill.

Parke, R. D. 1979. "Perspectives on Father-Infant Interaction." In J. D. Osofsky (ed.), *Handbook on Infant Development*. New York: John Wiley.

Parrish, David. 1978. "Transitional Objects and Phenomena in a Case of Twinship." In Simon Grolnick and Leonard Barkin (eds.), *Between Reality and Fantasy: Transitional Objects and Phenomena*. New York: Jason Aronson.

Patterson, Gerald. 1975. *A Social Learning Approach to Family Intervention*. vol. I: *Families with Aggressive Children*. Eugene, Ore.: Castalia Publishing.

Patterson, Gerald R. 1980. "Mothers: The Unacknowledged Victims." Monograph of the Society for Research in Child Development, no. 186.

Paul, I. H. 1973. *Letters to Simon*. New York: International Universities Press.

Paul, Norman L.; and Paul, Betty B. 1975. *A Marital Puzzle*. New York: W. W. Norton.

Payne, Robert. 1973. *The Life and Death of Adolf Hitler*. New York: Praeger.

Peters, J. J. 1976. "Children Who Are Victims of Sexual Assault and the Psychology of Offenders." *American Journal of Psychotherapy* 30:398–421.

Pincus, Lily; and Dare, Christopher. 1978. *Secrets in the Family*. New York: Pantheon.

Pines, Maya. 1979. "Superkids." *Psychology Today* (January) pp. 53–64.

Pollock, George H. 1978. "On Siblings, Childhood Sibling Loss and Creativity." *Annual of Psychoanalysis* 6:443–81.

Pomerance, Richard N. 1973. "Sibling Loss in Young Women: A Retrospective Study." *Dissertation Abstracts International* 34(4B [October]):1757.

Potash, Herbert; and Brunell, Lillian. 1973. "Folie à Deux: Some Further Considerations." Proceedings of the 81st Annual Convention of the American Psychological Association, pp. 507–8.

Rabiner, E. L.; Reiser, M. F.; Barr, H. L.; and Gralnick, A. 1971. "Therapists' Attitudes and Patients' Clinical Status: A Study of 100 Psychotherapy Pairs." *Archives of General Psychiatry* 25:505–29.

Rand, E. R. 1963. *Ovid and His Influence*. New York: Cooper Square.

Ransom, Jane W.; Schlesinger, Stephen; and Derdeyn, Andre. 1979. "A Stepfamily in Formation." *American Journal of Orthopsychiatry* 49:36–43.

Reeves, Mary. 1982. "Four Families of Divorce: Case Studies of Sibling and Peer Relationships." Doctoral Dissertation, University of Pennsylvania.

Resick, Patricia A.; Forehand, Rex; and McWharter, Alice Q. 1976. "The Effect of Parental Treatment with One Child on an Untreated Sibling." *Behavior Therapy* (7):544–48.

Rieff, Philip. 1963. "On Narcissism: An Introduction." In P. Rieff (ed.), *General Psychological Theory*, pp. 56–82. New York: Collier Books.

Riegel, Klaus, F. 1979. *Foundations of Dialectical Psychology*. New York: Academic Press.

Rilke, Rainer Maria. 1954. "On Love and Other Difficulties." In Rainer M. Rilke, *Rilke on Love and Other Difficulties: Translations and Considerations of Rainer Maria Rilke*, John L. Mood (trans.) New York: W. W. Norton, 1975.

Roazen, Paul. 1975. *Freud and His Followers*. New York: Alfred A. Knopf.

Roberts, William O. 1982. *The Lost Rite*. New York: Pilgrim Press.

Rodgers, Richard; and Hart, Lorenz. 1953. "My Boy Bill." *Carousel*. Westminster, Md.: Modern Library.

Roe, Ann. 1953. *The Making of a Scientist*. New York: Dodd, Mead.

Rogers, Carl R. 1951. *Client-Centered Therapy*. Boston: Houghton-Mifflin.

Rosenbaum, Milton. 1963. "Psychological Effects on the Child Raised by an Older Sibling." *American Journal of Orthopsychiatry* 33:515–20.

Rosenberg, Elinor B. 1980. "Therapy with Siblings in Reorganizing Families." *International Journal of Family Therapy* 2(3):139–50.

Rosenblatt, Howard. 1980. "So Suzie Wants to Become a Counselor." *Personnel and Guidance Journal* 58(10):654–56.

Rosenblatt, Paul; and Skoogberg, Elizabeth. 1974. "Birth Order in Cross Cultural Perspective." *Developmental Psychology* 10(1):48–54.

Rosenham, David. 1973. "On Being Sane in Insane Places." *Science* 179:250–57.

Rosenthal, David. 1971. *"The Genetics of Psychopathology."* New York: McGraw-Hill.

Ross, Helgola; and Milgram, Joel I. 1982. "Important Variables in Adult Sibling Relationships." In Michael Lamb and Brian Sutton-Smith (eds.), *Sibling Relationships: Their Nature and Significance Across the Life Span* pp. 223–247. Hillsdale, N.J.: Ehrlbaum Associates.

Rossner, Judith. 1975. *Looking for Mr. Goodbar.* New York: Simon & Schuster.

Royce, Josiah. 1916. *The Philosophy of Loyalty.* New York: Folcroft.

Rubin, Zick. 1980. *Children's Friendships.* Cambridge: Harvard University Press.

Sabalis, Robert F.; Frances, Allan; Appenzeller, Susan N.; and Moseley, Willie B. 1974. "The Three Sisters: Transsexual Male Siblings." *American Journal of Psychiatry* 131(8 [August]):907–9.

Sahler, Olle Jane Z. 1978. *The Child and Death.* St. Louis, Mo.: C.V. Mosby.

Salinger, J. D. 1945. *The Catcher in the Rye.* New York: Random House.

Samuels, Laurel; and Chase, Laura. 1979. "The Well Siblings of Schizophrenics." *American Journal of Family Therapy* 7(2):24–35.

Sanford, Nevitt. 1955. "The Dynamics of Identification." *Psychological Review* 62(March):106–18.

Santiago, Luciano, P. R. 1973. *The Children of Oedipus: Brother-Sister Incest in Psychiatry, Literature, History and Mythology.* Roslyn Heights, N.Y.: Libra.

Sarbin, T.; and Scheibe, K. (eds.) 1982. *Studies in Social Identity.* New York: Praeger.

Sarrel, Lorna J.; and Sarrel, Philip M. 1979. *Sexual Unfolding: Sexual Development and Sex Therapies in Late Adolescence.* Boston: Little, Brown.

Satir, Virginia. 1972. *Peoplemaking.* Palo Alto, Calif.: Science and Behavior Books.

Scarf, Maggie. 1980. "The Promiscuous Woman." *Psychology Today* (July) pp. 78–87.

Schaar, John H. 1968. "Loyalty." In *International Encyclopedia of the Social Sciences*, vol. IX, pp. 484–86. New York: Macmillan and Free Press.

Schachter, Frances F; Gilutz, Gabi; Shore, Ellen; and Adler, Michelle. 1978. "Sibling Deidentification Judged by Mothers; Cross Validation and Developmental Studies." *Child Development* 49:543–46.

Schachter, Frances F.; Shore, Ellen; Feldman-Rotman, Susan; Marquis, Ruth; and Campbell, Susan. 1976. "Sibling Deidentification." *Developmental Psychology* 12(5):418–27.

Schachter, Stanley. 1951. "Deviation, Rejection and Communication." *Journal of Abnormal and Social Psychology* 46:190–207.

Schachter, Stanley. 1963. "Birth Order, Eminence, and Higher Education." *American Sociological Review* 28:757–67.

Schatzman, Morton. 1973. Soul Murder. New York: Random House.

Scheibe, Karl E. 1979, *Mirrors, Masks, Lies and Secrets: The Limits of Human Predictability.* New York: Praeger.

Schooler, Carmi. 1972. "Birth Order Effects: Not Here, Not Now." *Psychological Bulletin* 78(3):161–75.

Searles, Harold F. 1959. "The Effort to Drive the Other Person Crazy—An Element in the Aetiology and Psychotherapy of Schizophrenia." *British Journal of Medical Psychology* 32:1–18.

Sears, Robert; Maccoby, Eleanor; and Levin, H. 1957. *Patterns of Childrearing.* Evanston, Ill.: Row, Peterson.

Seligman, Martin. 1975. *Helplessness.* San Francisco: W. H. Freeman.

Sewall, M.; and Smalley, R. 1930. "Two Studies in Sibling Rivalry." *Studies in Social Work* vol. I, pp. 6–40.

Shafi, M.; Salguero, C.; and Finch, S. 1975. "Psychopathology and Treatment of Anorexia Nervosa in Latency Age Siblings: Anorexia à Deux." *Journal of the American Academy of Child Psychiatry* 14(11):617–32.

Sharan, Shlomo. 1966. "Family Interaction with Schizophrenics and Their Siblings." *Journal of Abnormal Psychology* 71:345–53.

Shneidman, Edwin. 1973. *The Deaths of Man.* New York: Quadrangle/New York Times.

BIBLIOGRAPHY

Shopper, Moisy. 1974. "Twinning Reaction in Non-Twin Siblings." *Journal of the American Academy of Child Psychiatry* 13(2):300–318.

Shor, Joel; and Sanville, Jean. 1978. *Illusion in Loving: A Psychoanalytic Approach to the Evaluation of Intimacy and Autonomy.* Los Angeles: Double Helix.

Simon, William; and Gagnon, John H. 1967. *Sexual Deviance.* New York: Harper & Row.

Slater, Eliot. 1953. *Psychotic and Neurotic Illness in Twins.* Medical Research Council, Special Report no. 278. London: Her Majesty's Stationery Office.

Slipp, Samuel. 1973. "The Symbiotic Survival Pattern: A Relational Theory of Schizophrenia." *Family Process* 12:377–98.

Snyder, W. U. 1961. *The Psychotherapy Relationship.* New York: Macmillan.

Speck, Ross; and Attneave, Carolyn. 1973. *Family Networks.* New York: Pantheon.

Spitz, Renee. 1965. *The First Year of Life.* New York: International Universities Press.

Stein, Robert M. 1973. "The Incest Wound." *Spring,* pp. 133–41.

Stein, Robert M. 1974. *Incest and Human Love: The Betrayal of the Soul in Psychotherapy.* New York: Third Press.

Steinmetz, Suzanne K. 1976. "Intra-Familial Patterns of Conflict Resolution: Husband/Wife; Parent/Child; Sibling/Sibling." *Dissertation Abstracts International* 36(8A[February]):5586–87.

Stierlin, Helm. 1974. *Separating Parents and Adolescents.* New York: Quadrangle.

Sullivan, Harry Stack. 1948. "The Meaning of Anxiety in Psychiatry and in Life." *Psychiatry* 11:1–13.

Sullivan, Harry Stack. 1953. *The Interpersonal Theory of Psychiatry.* H. S. Derry and M. L. Gamel (eds.). New York: W. W. Norton.

Sullivan, Harry Stack. 1954. *The Psychiatric Interview.* New York: W. W. Norton.

Suomi, Stephen; and Harlow, Harry. 1975. "The Role of Reason of Peer Relationships in Rhesus Monkeys." In M. Lewis and L. A. Rosenblum, *Friendship and Peer Relations,* chap. 6, pp. 153–85. New York: John Wiley.

Sutton-Smith, Brian. 1977. Commentary on T. S. Weisner and R. Gallimore's "My Brother's Keeper." In *Current Anthropology* 18:169–90.

Sutton-Smith, Brian; and Rosenberg, Benjamin G. 1968. "Sibling Consensus on Power Tactics." *Journal of Genetic Psychology* 112:63–72.

Sutton-Smith, Brian; and Rosenberg, Benjamin G. 1970. *The Sibling.* New York: Holt Rinehart & Winston.

Sutton-Smith, Brian; Rosenberg, Benjamin G.; and Landy, F. 1968. "The Interaction of Father Absence and Sibling Presence on Cognitive Abilities." *Child Development* 39:1213–21.

Szalita, Alberta B. 1968. "Reanalysis." *Contemporary Psychoanalysis* 4:83–102.

Szasz, Thomas. 1963. *Law, Liberty and Psychiatry.* New York: Macmillan.

Szybist, Carol. 1978. "Thoughts of a Mother." In Jane Z. Olle (ed.), *The Child and Death.* pp. 283–88.

Taylor, M. K.; and Kogan, K. L. 1973. "Effects of the Birth of a Sibling on Mother-Child Interaction." *Child Psychiatry and Human Development* 4:53–58.

Thomas, A.; Chess, S.; and Birch, H. G. 1968. *Temperament and Behavior Disorders in Children.* New York: New York University Press.

Toman, Walter. 1969. *Family Constellation.* New York: Springer.

Toman, Walter. 1971. "The Duplication Theorem of Social Relationships as Tested in the General Population." *Psychological Review* 78:380–90.

Toman, Walter. 1976. *Family Constellation: Its Effects on Personality and Social Behavior,* 3rd ed. New York: Springer.

Tooley, Kay. 1977. "The Young Child as Victim of Sibling Attack." *Social Casework* 58:25–28.

Townsend, P. 1957. *The Family Life of Old People.* Glencoe, Ill.: Free Press.

Toynbee, Arnold; et al. (eds.) 1969. *Man's Concern with Death.* New York: McGraw-Hill.

Vogel, E. F.; and Bell, N. W. 1960. "The Emotionally Disturbed Child as the Family Scapegoat." In N. W. Bell and E. F. Vogel (eds.), *The Family,* pp. 382–97. New York: Free Press.

Wagner, Richard. 1870. "The Ring of the Nibelung-Die Walküre." In The Earl of Harewood (ed.), *Kobbe's Complete Opera Book*, pp. 245–63. New York, London: G. P. Putnam.

Wallerstein, Judith S.; and Kelly, Joan B. 1980. *Surviving the Breakup*. New York: Basic Books.

Watzlawick, Paul; Weakland, John J.; and Fisch, Richard. 1974. *Principles of Problem Formation and Problem Resolution*. New York: W. W. Norton.

Waxler, Nancy E.; and Mishler, Elliot. 1971. "Parental Interaction with Schizophrenic Children and Well Siblings: Experimental Test of Some Etiological Theories." *Archives of General Psychiatry* 25:223–31.

Weinberg, S. Kirson. 1955. *Incest Behavior*. Secaucus, N. J.: Citadel Press.

Whitaker, Carl A.; and Malone, Thomas P. 1953. *The Roots of Psychotherapy*. New York: Blakiston.

White, Robert W. 1959. "Motivation Reconsidered: The Concept of Competence." *Psychological Review*, 66:297–333.

White, Robert W. 1976. "Family as a Social System: Brothers and Sisters." *The Enterprise of Living: Growth and Organization in Personality*, chap. 5, pp. 87–118. New York: Holt, Rinehart & Winston.

Wikler, Lynn. 1980. "Folie à Famille: A Family Therapist's Perspective." *Family Process* 19:257–68.

Winnicott, Donald W. 1951. "Transitional Objects and Transitional Phenomena." In *Through Paediatries to Psychoanalysis*. New York: Basic Books, 1958.

Winnicott, Donald W. 1965. *The Maturational Processes and the Facilitating Environment*. New York: International Universities Press.

Winnicott, Donald W. 1971. *Playing and Reality*. New York: Basic Books.

Wynne, L. D. 1968. "The Study of Intrafamilial Alignments and Splits in Exploratory Family Therapy." In N. W. Ackerman, F. Beatman, and S. N. Sherman (eds.), *Exploring the Base for Family Therapy*, pp. 95–115. New York: Family Service Association of America.

Yamamoto, K. 1979. "Children's Ratings of the Stressfulness of Experiences." *Developmental Psychology* 15:581–82.

Zajonc, Robert. 1975. "Dumber by the Dozen." *Psychology Today* 8:37–44.

Zajonc, R.; and Markus, Gregory. 1975. "Birth Order and Intellectual Development." *Psychological Review* 82:74–88.

Zuk, Gerald H. 1971. *Family Therapy: A Triadic-Based Approach*. New York: Behavioral Publications.

INDEX

Abramovitch, Ronah, 198

Abrams, Jules C., 139

abusive parents: reciprocal loyalty in response to, 118; rescuing sibling from, 269

abusive siblings: conflict-amplifying parents of, 204–5; incest with, 181

academic achievement, 220–21

acceptance, loyal, 96–99

access: 9–15, 18–19; assessment of, in psychotherapy, 307; formal, decrease in, 10–11; interdependence and, 11–15; *see also* high-access siblings

accident proneness, 285

achievement, rivalry and, 219–21

Ackerman, Nathan, 321

acting out by survivor-siblings, 285

Adam (case history), 215–17

Adams, Bert, 7

Adler, Alfred, 5*n*, 6, 214

Adler, William, 73

adolescence, 49–83; attraction and repulsion in, 62, 63; birth of sibling in, 207; caretaking siblings in, 126–29; death of sibling in, 278, 282, 283, 286–90, 294; disturbed siblings in, 234, 241–42, 246–47, 251–52, 265; dyadic relationship in, 51; dynamic independent relationships in, 100–101; enmeshment in, 58–59; fear of mental illness in, 254; freedom and separateness of, 10; hostile dependent relationships in, 104; impact of change in, 64–68; incest during, 168, 179, 189–90; parental conflict and, 218–19; perceptions of sameness and difference in, 68–72; persona in, 61–62; promiscuity during, 194; psychotherapy in, 298, 313, 315–16, 319, 321; reciprocal loyalty in, 114–16;

"rites of passage" of, 177*n*; rivalry in, 219–24; sexuality in, 143, 144, 147–53, 164–65, 167; social comparison in, 52; subidentities in, 61; survivor-siblings in, 277; twinning in, 86; twins in, 42–46

adoption, 8; jealousy in response to, 207–12

adulthood: caretaking siblings in, 135–38; core identity in, 60; death of sibling in, 283–86, 294; de-identification in, 110; disturbed siblings in, 234, 238–41, 243–46, 262; frozen misunderstandings in, 75–82, 318–19, 336; hostile dependent relationships in, 104; idealization in, 92–93; identification in, 70–72; impact of early childhood attachment in, 33–37; incest in, 168–69; merging in, 88–92; mutually dependent relationships in, 96–99; polarized rejection in, 106–9; psychotherapy in, 314–15, 317–18, 323–34; reciprocal loyalty in, 117–21; restitutional efforts in, 226; rivalry in, 219–24; satisfaction derived from aggression in, 227–29; twinning in, 87–88

Aeolus, myth of, 158

affinity of siblings, 50; in dynamic independent relationships, 99; partial identification and, 94; sameness and, 69, 72

age spacing: access and, 10, 12; fusion and, 24; loyalty and, 125; sharing developmental events and, 26–27

aggression, 197–205; of caretaking siblings, 134–37, 139; toward disturbed siblings, 259–61, 266; in incest, 178–85; mechanisms for containment of, 224–26; parental management of,

Finch, S., 250
Finklehor, David, 167, 170, 171n
Fisch, Richard, 65
Fishman, Charles, 301
Flomenhaft, Kalman, 171
Falbo, Toni, 128n
folie à deux, 86, 250; psychotherapy for, 309
forgiveness, rituals of, 318–19
Forward, Susan, 167–69
Foundation for the Study of the Holocaust, 129n
Fox, Robin J., 169, 170
Framo, James, 47n, 51, 256–57
Frances, Allan, 169n
Frances, Vera, 169n
Frank (case history), 220–21
Franz, J. D., 259
fratricide, 123
Freeman, Douglas S., 92
Freud, Anna, 121, 200
Freud, Sigmund, 119, 155, 158, 160–65, 197, 206, 212–15, 299, 300
Fromm-Reichmann, Frieda, 299
frozen images, 73–74; in polarized rejection, 105
frozen misunderstandings, 74–75, 336; psychotherapy and, 318–19, 326
fusion, 24–25; close identification in, 86–88; delusion of, love as, 191; with disturbed sibling, 246; mourning based on, 283–85; of orphans of Terezin, 121; parental death and, 151; psychotherapy and, 309, 316, 321; sibling love in, 159; in transitional relationship, 33; of twins, 40, 42–46

Gagnon, John H., 144
Gallagher, Richard, 253
Galton, Francis, 205
Garmezy, Norman, 128
Gebhard, P. H., 170
Gelinas, Denise, 171, 193n
gender: entitlement and, 212–15; *see also* opposite-sex siblings; same-sex siblings

Geneen (case history), 100–101
general systems theory, 6
genetic aspects of mental illness, 253
geographic mobility, 13
geographic separation, containment of aggression through, 224
Gilroy, Frank, 217
Glenn, Jules, 40
Goffman, Erving, 61, 226, 233n
Golding, William, 202
Goodall, Jane, 199
Goode, William, 11
grief, parental influence on, 272–78
Grossman, Frances K., 96, 234, 254
group therapy, 298; resistance in, 306; transference and countertransference in, 303
Guest, Judith, 275
guilt: in abusive sibling, 106; in bereavement, 274, 275, 281, 285–86, 293, 294; of care-receiving siblings, 139, 140; about incest, 178, 186, 188–89; reciprocal loyalty and, 116; residual, 77; resistance and, 305; sexual, 169; about success at expense of sibling, 226; survivor, 264–68
Gunther, John, 274

Haley, Jay, 66, 233n, 300, 301
half-siblings, 14
Hallahan, Daniel P., 203
Hammerstein, Oscar, 22
Hampstead Nursery (England), 121–22, 124n
handicapped siblings, 215–17
Hansel and Gretel, 112
Harlow, Harry, 199
Harris, Judy (case history), 293–94
Hartup, Willard, 122
hatred, 198; *see also* aggression; conflict
haunted siblings, 274–76
Hebrews, ancient, 157–58
Hegel, G. W. F., 102
Heider, Fritz, 59
Heider, G., 23

INDEX